access to history

Democracy and Dictatorship in Germany 1919–63

Geoff Layton

HODDER
EDUCATION
AN HACHETTE UK COMPANY

Acknowledgements

I have been very fortunate with the help of various friends who have given advice and encouragement in the preparation of this text. In particular: Barbara Klass, Chris Moreton, Chris Shingles and Paddy Raybould. I would like to thank them all.

Geoff Layton

Study guide authors: Martin Jones and Sheila Randall

The Publishers would like to thank the following for permission to reproduce copyright material:
AKG-images, pages 14, 111, 193, 214; © Archivo Iconografico, S.A./Corbis, page 104; © Austrian Archives/Corbis, pages 68, 75, 97, 113, 150; Bauhaus-Archiv, page 81; © Bettman/Corbis, pages 4, 9, 69, 116, 128, 168, 169, 172, 176, 239, 289, 356; BPK Berlin, page 243; BPK Berlin/Hildegard Dreyer, page 283; BPK Berlin/Kunstbibliothek, Staatliche Museen zu Berlin Photo: Knud Petersen, pages 183, 324; BPK/Staatliche Museen zu Berlin – Preußischer Kulturbesitz, Nationalgalerie. Photo: Jörg P. Anders, page 80; © Corbis, pages 11, 185, 198, 229, 244, 251; Peter Dittrich/Haus der Geschichte der Bundesrepublik Deutschland, page 330; Erich Lessing Archive/AKG-images, page 79; Getty Images, pages 54, 90, 201; Haus der Geschichte der Bundesrepublik Deutschland, pages 279, 293, 352, 354, 363; Hulton-Deutsch Collection/Corbis, pages 138, 184, 250; Imperial War Museum, page 132; Mary Evans Picture Library, page 170; Mary Evans/Weimar Archive, pages 39, 224; © Michael Nicholson/Corbis, page 234; Josef Partykiewicz/Haus der Geschichte der Bundesrepublik Deutschland, page 357; Klaus Pielert (Künstler)/Haus der Geschichte Bonn, page 382; Private Collection/Archives Charmet/The Bridgeman Art Library, page 307; Süddeutsche Zeitung Photo, page 91; Süddeutsche Zeitung Photo/Scherl, pages 104, 139; Time & Life Pictures/Getty Images, pages 268; Yad Vashem Art Museum, Jerusalem/Mrs Simenhoff, S. Africa, page 228.

The Publishers would like to acknowledge use of the following extracts:
University of North Carolina Press for an extract from *The Nazi Voter: The Social Foundations of Fascism in Germany 1919–1933* by Thomas Childers, 1986.

Every effort has been made to trace all copyright holders, but if any have been inadvertently overlooked the Publishers will be pleased to make the necessary arrangements at the first opportunity.

Hachette UK's policy is to use papers that are natural, renewable and recyclable products and made from wood grown in sustainable forests. The logging and manufacturing processes are expected to conform to the environmental regulations of the country of origin.

Orders: please contact Bookpoint Ltd, 130 Milton Park, Abingdon, Oxon OX14 4SB. Telephone: (44) 01235 827720. Fax: (44) 01235 400454. Lines are open 9.00–5.00, Monday to Saturday, with a 24-hour message answering service. Visit our website at www.hoddereducation.co.uk

© Geoff Layton 2009
First published in 2009 by
Hodder Education,
an Hachette UK Company
338 Euston Road
London NW1 3BH

Impression number   5 4
Year   2013 2012

Cover photo shows a cartoon 'Day of German Unity', by Manfred Oesterle, courtesy of Haus der Geschichte, Bonn
Typeset in 10/12pt Baskerville and produced by Gray Publishing, Tunbridge Wells, Kent
Printed in Great Britain by the MPG Books Group, Bodmin

A catalogue record for this title is available from the British Library.

ISBN: 978 0340 965 825

Contents

Dedication

Keith Randell (1943–2002)

The *Access to History* series was conceived and developed by Keith, who created a series to 'cater for students as they are, not as we might wish them to be'. He leaves a living legacy of a series that for over 20 years has provided a trusted, stimulating and well-loved accompaniment to post-16 study. Our aim with these new editions is to continue to offer students the best possible support for their studies.

1

The German Revolution 1918–19

POINTS TO CONSIDER

The purpose of this chapter is to consider the events that occurred in Germany during the final days of the First World War and the challenges faced by the new democratic Germany during its first months. These were dramatic, but difficult times for German politicians and the German people. The main areas are:

- The collapse of Imperial Germany and the abdication of Kaiser Wilhelm II
- The German Revolution: the establishment of the democratic republic and the failure of the Spartacist revolt
- The establishment of the National Constituent Assembly

Key dates

1918	September	Ludendorff conceded that Germany was defeated
	October 3	Prince Max of Baden appointed chancellor
	November 2	Grand Fleet mutiny at Kiel
	November 8	Bavaria proclaimed a socialist republic
	November 9	Kaiser fled to Holland
		Ebert appointed chancellor
		Germany proclaimed a republic
	November 11	Armistice signed at Compiègne
1919	January 1	German Communist Party founded
	January 5	Start of Spartacist uprising in Berlin
	February 6	National Constituent Assembly met at Weimar

1 | The Collapse of Imperial Germany

Key question
Why did Germany lose the First World War?

When war broke out in 1914 it was assumed in Germany, as well as in all the Great Powers, that the conflict would not last very long. However, by late September 1918, after four years of bloody war, Germany faced military defeat. The reasons for its eventual collapse go right back to the early days of August 1914, but the pressures had developed over the years that followed. The main factors can be identified as follows:

- Germany's failure to achieve rapid victory in the summer of 1914. The German High Command's strategy was built upon the notion of a quick victory in order to avoid a long drawn-out conflict with the Allies. By the autumn of 1914 the **Schlieffen plan** had failed to gain a rapid victory.
- Stalemate. Germany was forced to fight the war on two fronts – the east and the west. The balance of military power resulted in a war of stalemate that put immense pressures on **Imperial Germany**. The situation was made particularly difficult for Germany by the Allies' naval blockade, which seriously limited the import of all supplies. And, although the German policy of **unrestricted submarine warfare** at first seriously threatened Britain, it did not decisively weaken her.
- Strengths of the Allies. Britain and France were major colonial powers and could call upon their overseas empires for manpower, resources and supplies. Furthermore, from April 1917, the Allies were strengthened by America's entry into the war, which resulted in the mobilisation of two million men.
- Limitations of German war economy. Imperial Germany was totally unprepared for the economic costs of a prolonged war. It made great efforts to mobilise the war effort and arms production was dramatically increased. However, the economy was seriously dislocated, which wrecked the government's finances and increased social tension.

A chance for Germany to escape from the military defeat came when Russia surrendered in March 1918. This immediately enabled Germany to launch a last major offensive on the Western Front. Unfortunately, it was unable to maintain the momentum and, by August, German troops were being forced to retreat. At the same time its own allies, Austria, Turkey and Bulgaria, were collapsing.

The socio-economic effects of the First World War

In 1914, the vast majority of Germans supported the war and there were no signs of the country's morale and unity breaking down until the winter months of early 1917. Then, the accumulation of shortages, high prices and the black market, as well as the bleak military situation, began to affect the public mood. Social discontent thereafter grew markedly because of:

- Food and fuel shortages. The exceptionally cold winter of 1916–17 contributed to severe food and fuel shortages in the cities. It was nicknamed the 'turnip winter' because the failure of the potato crop forced the German people to rely heavily on turnips, which were normally for animal fodder.
- Civilian deaths. The number of civilian deaths from starvation and hypothermia increased from 121,000 in 1916 to 293,000 in 1918.
- Infant mortality. The number of child deaths increased by over 50 per cent in the course of the war years.

Key terms

Schlieffen plan
Its purpose was to avoid a two-front war by winning victory on the Western Front before dealing with the threat from Russia. It aimed to defeat France within six weeks by a massive German offensive in northern France and Belgium.

Imperial Germany
The title given to Germany from its unification in 1871 until 1918. Also referred to as the Second Reich (Empire).

Unrestricted submarine warfare
Germany's policy of attacking all military and civilian shipping in order to sink supplies going to Britain.

Key question
How did the war affect the living and working conditions of the German people?

A cartoon drawn in 1918 by the German artist Raemaeker. It underlines the serious situation faced by **Kaiser** Wilhelm II, who is held by two ominous figures – war and starvation.

- The influenza epidemic. In 1918 Europe was hit by the 'Spanish flu', which killed between 20 and 40 million people – a figure higher than the casualties of the First World War. It has been cited as the most devastating epidemic recorded, probably because people's resistance to disease was lowered by the decline in living conditions.
- Inflation. Workers were forced to work even longer hours, but wages fell below the inflation rate. Average prices doubled in Germany between 1914 and 1918, whereas wages rose by only 50–75 per cent.
- Casualties. About two million Germans were killed, with a further six million wounded, many suffering disability. The emotional trauma for all these soldiers and their families was not so easy to put into statistics.

Social discontent, therefore, grew markedly in the final two years of the war. Considerable anger was expressed against the so-called 'sharks' of industry, who had made vast profits from the war.

Resentment grew in the minds of many within the middle class because they felt that their social status had been lowered as their income declined. Above all, opposition began to grow against the political leaders, who had urged total war. Faced with the worsening situation on the domestic front and the likelihood of defeat on the Western Front, the military leaders, Generals Ludendorff and Hindenburg (below and page 69), recognised the seriousness of Germany's position, and decided to seek peace with the Allies.

Profile: Erich Ludendorff 1865–1937

1865	– Born in Kruszewnia in the Polish Prussian province of Posen
1882	– Joined the Prussian army
1894	– Joined the General Staff and worked closely with Schlieffen
1914	– Appointed Chief-of-Staff to Hindenburg on the Eastern Front
1916	– Transferred to Western Front. Promoted to the post of Quartermaster General – virtual military dictator, 1916–18
1917	– Responsible for the dismissal of Chancellor Bethmann-Hollweg (1909–17)
1918	– Masterminded German final offensive
	– Proposed the theory of the 'stab in the back' (see page 5)
	– Fled to Sweden
1919	– Returned to Germany
1920	– Took part in Kapp *putsch* (see pages 39–40)
1923	– Collaborated with Hitler and was involved in Munich *putsch* (see pages 41–3)
1937	– Died in Tutzing, Bavaria

Ludendorff was a soldier of considerable ability, energy and enthusiasm. In the campaign in Belgium he showed considerable initiative and was sent, as Chief-of-Staff, to serve with Hindenburg on the Eastern Front. Here he played an important part in the major victories over the Russians. In 1916, the two men were posted to the Western Front and during the years that followed they were able to assume supreme command of the German war effort. By the end of the war, Ludendorff was effectively the wartime dictator of Germany and, when it was clear that Germany had lost the war, he tried to direct the control of the constitutional reform in October 1918. After the war, he dabbled in extreme right-wing politics and became associated with the activities of Hitler's Nazi Party whose racial views he shared. Later, he became disenchanted with Hitler and in his latter years became a pacifist.

Key term

Putsch
The German word for an uprising (though often the French phrase, *coup d'état*, is used). Normally, a *putsch* means the attempt by a small group to overthrow the government.

The October reform

Once Ludendorff came to appreciate that an Allied invasion of Germany would lead to destructive internal disturbances, he pushed for political change. Ever since Imperial Germany had been created in 1871, it had been an **autocracy**. Now Ludendorff wanted to change Germany into a **constitutional monarchy** by the Kaiser's handing over political power to a civilian government. In other words, he aimed to establish a more democratic government, while maintaining the German monarchy.

Ludendorff's political turnaround had two aims. First, he wanted to secure for Germany the best possible peace terms from the Allies – it was believed that the Allied leaders would be more sympathetic to a democratic regime in Berlin. Secondly, he hoped the change would prevent the outbreak of political revolutionary disturbances.

However, Ludendorff had a third and a more cynical ulterior motive. He saw the need to shift the responsibility for Germany's defeat away from the military leadership and the conservative forces, which had dominated Imperial Germany, e.g. landowners and the army. Instead, he intended to put the responsibility and blame for the defeat on the new leadership. Here lay the origins of the **'stab in the back' myth**, which was later to play such a vital part in the history of the Weimar Republic. It was a theme soon taken up by sympathisers of the political right wing (see page 36).

It was against this background that on 3 October 1918 Prince Max of Baden, a moderate conservative, was appointed chancellor. He had democratic views and also a well-established international reputation because of his work with the Red Cross. In the following month a series of constitutional reforms came into effect, which turned Germany into a parliamentary democracy:

- Wilhelm II gave up his powers over the army and the navy to the *Reichstag*.
- The chancellor and his government were made accountable to the *Reichstag*, instead of to the Kaiser.
- At the same time, armistice negotiations with the Allies were opened.

What pushed Germany, in such a short space of time, from political reform towards revolution was the widespread realisation that the war was lost. The shock of defeat, after years of hardship and optimistic propaganda, hardened popular opinion. By early November it was apparent that the creation of a constitutional monarchy would not defuse what had become a revolutionary situation.

Key question
Why did Ludendorff support constitutional reform?

Key terms

Autocracy
A system where one person (usually a hereditary sovereign) has absolute rule.

Constitutional monarchy
Where the monarch has limited power within the lines of a constitution.

'Stab in the back' myth
The distorted view that the army had not really lost the First World War and that unpatriotic groups, such as socialists and Jews, had undermined it. The myth severely weakened the Weimar democracy from the start.

Reichstag
The German parliament. Although created in 1871, it had very limited powers. Real power lay with the Emperor.

Key dates

Ludendorff conceded that Germany was defeated: September 1918

Prince Max of Baden appointed chancellor: 3 October 1918

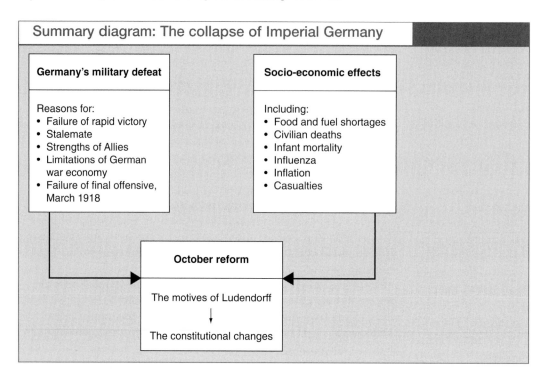

Summary diagram: The collapse of Imperial Germany

Germany's military defeat

Reasons for:
- Failure of rapid victory
- Stalemate
- Strengths of Allies
- Limitations of German war economy
- Failure of final offensive, March 1918

Socio-economic effects

Including:
- Food and fuel shortages
- Civilian deaths
- Infant mortality
- Influenza
- Inflation
- Casualties

October reform

The motives of Ludendorff

↓

The constitutional changes

2 | The German Revolution

On 29 October, a mutiny began to spread among some sailors who refused to obey orders at Wilhelmshaven, near Kiel. Prince Max's government quickly lost control of the political situation and by 2 November sailors gained control of other major ports, such as Kiel and Hamburg. These take-overs had been prompted by a real fear amongst the sailors that their officers were planning a suicide attack on the British fleet, in order to restore the honour of the German navy. The news of the Kiel mutiny fanned the flames of discontent to other ports, Bremen and Lübeck, and soon throughout Germany. By 6 November, numerous workers' and soldiers' councils, similar to the **soviets** that had been set up by the **Bolsheviks** in Russia, were established in the major cities of Berlin, Cologne and Stuttgart. In Bavaria, the last member of the House of Wittelsbach, King Louis III, was deposed and the socialist Kurt Eisner proclaimed Bavaria an independent democratic socialist republic.

By the end of the first week of November it was clear that the October reforms had failed to impress the German people. The popular discontent was turning into a more fundamental revolutionary movement whose demands were for an immediate peace and the abdication of Kaiser Wilhelm II. The disturbances were prompted by:

- The realisation by troops and sailors that the war was lost and nothing was to be gained by carrying on.

Key question
How and why did the October reform fail?

Key dates

Grand Fleet mutiny at Kiel: 2 November 1918

Bavaria proclaimed a socialist republic: 8 November 1918

Key terms

Soviet
A Russian word meaning an elected council. Soviets developed during the Russian Revolution in 1917. In Germany many councils were set up in 1918, which had the support of the more radical and revolutionary left-wing working class.

Bolsheviks
Followers of Bolshevism – Russian communism.

- The sense of national shock when the news came of Germany's military defeat – propaganda and censorship had really delayed the reality for too long.
- The increasing anger and bitterness over socio-economic conditions.

Key term

Coalition government
Usually formed when a party does not have an overall majority in parliament; it then combines with more parties and shares government positions.

Prince Max would certainly have liked to preserve the monarchy, and possibly even Wilhelm II himself, but the Emperor's delusions that he could carry on without making any more political changes placed the chancellor in a difficult position. In the end, Prince Max became so worried by the revolutionary situation in Berlin that on 9 November he announced that the Kaiser would renounce the throne and that a **coalition** left-wing **government** would be formed by Friedrich Ebert. It was in this chaotic situation that Philipp Scheidemann, one of the provisional government's leaders, appeared on the balcony of the *Reichstag* building and proclaimed Germany a republic. (Actually, an hour later Germany was also declared a 'soviet republic' – a statement crucial for the shaping of the next few months of the German Revolution.) It was only at this point in the evening of 9 November that the Kaiser, who was in Belgium, accepted the advice of leading generals. In that way, the Kaiser did not formally abdicate, he simply walked away and went into exile voluntarily in Holland.

Key date

Kaiser fled to Holland
Ebert appointed chancellor
Germany proclaimed a republic:
9 November 1918

The left-wing movement

A genuinely revolutionary situation existed in Germany in early November 1918. However, the revolutionary wave that swept Germany was not a united force. In fact, the left-wing movement behind it consisted of three main strands (Table 1.1).

Key question
In what ways was the left-wing movement divided?

Key terms

Socialist republic
A system of government without a monarchy that aims to introduce social changes for collective benefit.

Soviet republic
A system of government without a monarchy that aims to introduce a communist state organised by the workers' councils and opposed to private ownership.

Table 1.1: The German left-wing movement

	Moderate socialists	Radical socialists	Revolutionary socialists
Party names	SPD (German Social Democratic Party)	USPD (German Independent Social Democratic Party)	Spartacists (Spartacus League)
Aim	To establish a **socialist republic** by the creation of parliamentary democracy	To create a socialist republic governed by workers' and soldiers' councils in conjunction with a parliament	To create a **soviet republic** based on the rule of the workers' and soldiers' councils
Leaders	Friedrich Ebert Philipp Scheidemann	Karl Kautsky Hugo Haase	Rosa Luxemburg Karl Liebknecht

The SPD (German Social Democratic Party)

The SPD represented moderate socialist aims and was led by Friedrich Ebert and Philipp Scheidemann. It dated from 1875. In the election of 1912 it had become the largest party in the *Reichstag* with a membership of over one million. Its fundamental aim was to create a socialist republic, but being wholly committed to parliamentary democracy, it totally rejected anything that might have been likened to Soviet-style communism.

The Spartacists

On the extreme left stood the Spartacus League (otherwise known as the Spartacists), led by Karl Liebknecht and the Polish-born Rosa Luxemburg, one of the few women to be prominent in German political history (see profile, page 9).

The Spartacists had been formed in 1905 as a minor faction of the SPD. By 1918 it had a national membership of about 5000. From 1914, they had opposed the war and they were deeply influenced by Lenin and Bolshevism. They had come to believe that Germany should follow the same path as Communist Russia. The fundamental aim of the Spartacists was to create a soviet republic based on the rule of the **proletariat** through workers' and soldiers' councils.

> **Key term**
>
> **Proletariat**
> The industrial working class who, in Marxist theory, would ultimately take power in the state.

The USPD (Independent German Social Democratic Party)

The USPD had been formed in 1917 as a breakaway group from the SPD. It was led by Hugo Haase and Karl Kautsky. Although the USPD was a minority of the assembly in the *Reichstag* it had a substantial following of 300,000 members.

The USPD demanded radical social and economic change as well as political reforms. However, as a political movement, it was far from united and internal divisions and squabbles seriously curtailed its influence. The main disagreement was between those who sympathised with the creation of a parliamentary democracy and those who advocated a much more revolutionary democracy based on the workers' councils.

Ebert's coalition government

Because of the different aims and methods of the socialist movement, there was a lack of unity in Ebert's coalition government. Moreover, it should also be remembered that German society was in a chaotic state of near collapse, so the leading political figures at the time had little room to manoeuvre when they had to make hasty and difficult decisions.

On 9 November 1918 Ebert created a provisional coalition government:

> **Key question**
> What were the main problems faced by Ebert?

- 'Provisional' in the sense that it was short term until a national election was held to vote for a National Constituent Assembly (parliament).
- 'Coalition' in the sense that it was a combination of parties, the SPD and the USPD.

Key profile: Rosa Luxemburg ('Red Rosa') 1871–1919

1870	– Born in Poland of Jewish origins. Badly disabled and walked with a limp, endured continual pain
1905	– Took part in the revolutionary troubles in Russia
	– Joined with Karl Liebknecht in Germany to establish the revolutionary group that founded the Spartacist League
1914–18	– Imprisoned for the duration of the war
	– Campaigned secretly for a revolutionary end to the war
1917	– Welcomed the Bolshevik revolution in Russia (but soon came to criticise Lenin's repressive methods)
1918	– Freed from prison
1919	– Supported the creation of KPD (German Communist Party) from the Spartacist League
	– Opposed the Spartacus uprising in January 1919
	– Murdered in police custody in Berlin

After her death, Luxemburg was described as 'arguably one of the finest political theorists of the twentieth century' who famously said, 'Freedom is always for the person who thinks differently'. In 1905, she was one of the founders of the Spartacist League and continued to champion the cause of armed revolution that would sweep the capitalist system away. Ironically, she spoke against the uprising in January 1919 (see page 13) because she felt that Germany was not ready for communism. Although she died a committed revolutionary, she had a humane and optimistic view of communism at odds with the brutality of the Bolsheviks in Russia.

Ebert himself was a moderate and was frightened that the political situation in Germany could easily run out of control. In Table 1.2, the nature of Ebert's major problems can be seen.

Ebert's main worry was that the extreme left would gain the upper hand. He recognised the growing number of workers' councils and feared that they might threaten his policy of gradual change. He was determined to maintain law and order to prevent the country collapsing into civil war. He also feared that the return of millions of troops after the Armistice agreement, which was eventually signed on 11 November, would create enormous social and political problems (see Table 1.2). These were the main concerns in the minds of Ebert and the SPD leadership in the months that followed and were the main reasons why they made agreements with the army and industrialists.

Key date

Armistice signed between Germany and the Allies at Compiègne in northern France: 11 November 1918

Ebert-Groener agreement

On 10 November, the day after the declaration of the Republic, General Wilhelm Groener, Ludendorff's successor, telephoned Chancellor Ebert. Their conversation was very significant. The

Table 1.2: Ebert's main problems

Socio-economic	Left-wing opposition	Right-wing opposition	Military
1. Inflation Wages were falling behind prices, which was increasing social discontent	**1. Strikes** From the autumn of 1918 the number of strikes and lock-outs increased markedly	**1. Freikorps** A growing number of right-wing, nationalist soldiers were forming paramilitary units	**1. Demobilisation** About 1.5 million soldiers had to be returned home to Germany
2. Shortages From the winter of 1916–17 fuel and food shortages were causing real hardship in the cities	**2. German communists** Inspired by the events of 1917–18 in Russia, communists aimed to bring about a revolution in Germany	**2. The army** The army was generally conservative, but also deeply embittered by the military defeat	**2. Allied blockade** The Allies maintained the naval blockade even after the Armistice. Social distress was not relieved until June 1919
3. Flu epidemic The 'Spanish flu' killed thousands. It was the most serious flu epidemic of the twentieth century	**3. Workers' and soldiers' councils** Hundred of councils were created and many wanted changes to the army and industries	**3. Nationalists** Nationalist-conservatives were deeply against the abdication of the Kaiser and did not support the creation of a democratic republic	**3. Peace terms** The Armistice was when they agreed to stop fighting, but there was great public concern about the actual effects of the peace treaty

Supreme Army Command agreed to support the new government and to use troops to maintain the stability and security of the new republic. In return, Ebert promised to oppose the spread of revolutionary socialism and to preserve the authority of the army officers. The deal has become known simply as the Ebert-Groener agreement.

Stinnes-Legien agreement

A few days later, on 15 November, Karl Legien, leader of the trade unions, and Hugo Stinnes, leader of the industrial employers, held another significant discussion. The Stinnes-Legien agreement was, in effect, a deal where the trade unions made a commitment not to interfere with private ownership and the free market, in return for workers' committees, an eight-hour working day and full legal recognition. Ebert's provisional government endorsed this because the German trade unions were a powerful movement and traditionally closely tied with the SPD.

So, on one level, the agreement to bring about some key, long-desired reforms was a real success. However, these two

Key profile: Friedrich Ebert 1871–1925

1871	– Born in Heidelberg of humble background
1885–8	– Trained as a saddler
1889	– Became a trade union organiser and SPD member
1912	– Elected as a member of the *Reichstag*
1916	– Chosen as leader of the Party
1918	– 9 November – became chancellor of the provisional government when Imperial Germany collapsed
	– 10 November – Ebert-Groener agreement (see pages 9–10)
1919	– 11 February – chosen as the country's first president, a position he held until his death
1925	– Died at the age of 54 of a ruptured appendix

Ebert rose from a humble background as a saddler to become the first president of Germany. His character and achievements significantly shaped the development of Weimar democracy.

The political activist

During his apprenticeship he became quickly involved in trade union work and the socialist movement. His written and spoken skills were soon recognised by the SPD leadership and he advanced through the party covering a range of full-time political jobs such as journalist and secretary. He entered the *Reichstag* in 1912 and just a year later he became chairman of the SPD as he was seen capable of conciliating the developing differences in the Party.

Leader of the SPD

The First World War divided the SPD fundamentally. Ebert worked really hard to keep it together and in 1916 he was chosen as leader. However, it proved impossible to overcome the differences and a year later the Party split and the USPD was created.

The German Revolution

When Germany collapsed in autumn 1918, Ebert wanted a democratic parliamentary government with a constitutional monarchy – along English lines – but when events got out of hand in November 1918, the monarchy collapsed and he accepted the chancellorship. It was a major success to manage to hold the first truly democratic German elections, which led to the National Constituent Assembly and the creation of the Weimar Constitution. However, Ebert has been criticised for endorsing the use of the army, the *Freikorps* (see page 37) and other conservative forces to brutally suppress the more radical elements of the left.

President

He was chosen to be the country's first president by the National Constituent Assembly in February 1919, a position he held until his death. He oversaw the years of crisis and applied the emergency decrees of Article 48 (see page 21) with success. However, he became the focus of scurrilous criticism from the extreme right – which almost certainly contributed to his early death. He was a man of great integrity and decency and, despite the critics, he was a patriot and served his office with distinction and correctness.

Key term

Freikorps
Means 'free corps' who acted as paramilitaries. They were right-wing, nationalist soldiers who were only too willing to use force to suppress communist activity.

agreements have been severely criticised over the years, particularly by the left wing. Critics have accused Ebert of having supported compromises with the forces of conservatism. The army was not reformed at all and it was not really committed to democracy. Employers resented the concessions and were unsympathetic to the Weimar system. Nevertheless, there is a counter-argument that Ebert and the SPD leadership were motivated by the simple desire to guarantee stability and a peaceful transition.

Left-wing divisions

By the last days of 1918 it was clear that the SPD had become distanced from its political 'allies' on the left and their conflicting aims resulted in fundamental differences over strategy and policies.

Key question
Why did the left-wing movement split?

USPD

In late December 1918, the USPD members of Ebert's government resigned over the shooting of some Spartacists by soldiers. However, the split had really emerged over the USPD's desire to introduce fundamental social and economic changes that the SPD did not want to adopt.

Aim
To create a socialist republic governed by workers' and soldiers' councils in conjunction with a parliament.

Strategy
To introduce radical social and economic changes.

Policies
To reform the army fundamentally.
To nationalise key industries.
To introduce welfare benefits.

SPD

The SPD government became increasingly isolated. It moved further to the political right and grew dependent on the civil service and the army to maintain effective government.

Aim
To establish a socialist republic by the creation of parliamentary democracy.

Strategy
To make arrangements for a democratic *Reichstag* election leading to a National Constituent Assembly.
To introduce moderate changes, but to prevent the spread of communist revolution.

Policies
To maintain law and order by running the country with the existing legal and police systems.
To retain the army.
To introduce welfare benefits.

Spartacists

On 1 January 1919, the Spartacists formally founded the *Kommunistische Partei Deutschlands*, the KPD – German Communist Party. It refused to participate in the parliamentary elections, preferring instead to place its faith in the workers' councils, as expressed in the Spartacist manifesto:

Key date
German Communist Party founded: 1 January 1919

The question today is not democracy or dictatorship. The question that history has put on the agenda reads: bourgeois democracy or socialist democracy? For the dictatorship of the proletariat is democracy in the socialist sense of the word. Dictatorship of the proletariat does not mean bombs, *putsches*, riots and anarchy, as the agents of capitalist profits deliberately and falsely claim. Rather, it means using all instruments of political power to achieve socialism, to expropriate [dispossess of property] the capitalist class, through and in accordance with the will of the revolutionary majority of the proletariat.

Aim
To create a soviet republic based on the rule of the workers' and soldiers' councils.

Strategy
To oppose the creation of a National Constituent Assembly and to take power by strikes, demonstrations and revolts leading to fundamental social and economic changes.

Policies
To replace the army by local militias of workers.
To carry out extensive nationalisation of industries and land.
To introduce welfare benefits.

The Spartacist revolt

Key question
Why did the Spartacist revolt fail?

Key date
Start of Spartacist uprising in Berlin: 5 January 1919

In January 1919 the Spartacists decided that the time was ripe to launch an armed rising in Berlin with the aim of overthrowing the provisional government and creating a soviet republic.

On 5 January, they occupied public buildings, called for a general strike and formed a revolutionary committee. They denounced Ebert's provisional government and the coming elections. However, they had little chance of success. There were three days of savage street fighting and over 100 were killed. The Spartacist *coup* was easily defeated and afterwards, most notoriously, Liebknecht and Luxemburg were brutally murdered whilst in police custody.

The events of January 1919 showed that the Spartacists were strong on policies, but detached from political realities. They had no real strategy and their 'revolutionaries' were mainly just workers with rifles. By contrast, the government had not only the backing of the army's troops, but also 5000 'irregular' military-style groups, *Freikorps*.

This event created a very troubled atmosphere for the next few months. The elections for the National Constituent Assembly duly took place in February 1919 (see page 17), although the continuation of strikes and street disorders in Berlin meant that, for reasons of security, the Assembly's first meeting was switched to the town of **Weimar**. More serious disturbances in Bavaria in April resulted in a short-lived soviet-type republic being established there. The *Freikorps* brought the disturbances under control though, in each case, at the cost of several hundred lives. The infant republic had survived the traumas of its birth.

Prost Noskel — — das Proletariat ist entwaffnet!

'Cheers Noske! The Young Revolution is Dead!' A cartoon drawn in 1919 by the German Georg Grosz. Grosz was a communist artist and his images can be stark and disturbing. In this cartoon he satirises the savagery of the *Freikorps*.

Key term

Weimar Republic
Took its name from the first meeting of the National Constituent Assembly in Weimar. The Assembly had moved there because there were still many disturbances in Berlin. Weimar was chosen because it was a town with a great historical and cultural tradition.

Summary diagram: The German Revolution

The birth of the Republic

Mutiny and revolts

↓

Abdication of the Kaiser

↓

Why did October reform fail?

The left-wing movement

- SPD
- USPD
- Spartacists

Ebert's leadership

- The coalition government
- Ebert-Groener and Stinnes-Legien agreements

Early problems

- Socio-economic factors
- Left-wing opposition
- Right-wing opposition
- Military consequences

The Spartacist uprising
Why did it fail?

Key question
Was the election a success for democracy?

Key date
National Constituent Assembly met at Weimar: 6 February 1919

3 | The National Constituent Assembly

Despite the disturbances across Germany, in the months after the collapse of Imperial Germany, the new republic was still able to hold its first elections for a National Constituent Assembly on 19 January 1919. Most political parties took the opportunity to retitle themselves, but new names did not disguise the fact that there was considerable continuity in the structure of the party system (see Table 1.3, page 16).

The election results (see Figure 1.1, page 17) quickly led to the creation of the National Constituent Assembly on 6 February. In many respects the results represented a major success for the forces of parliamentary democracy:

- The high turnout of 83 per cent in the election suggested faith in the idea of democracy.
- 76.1 per cent of the electorate voted for pro-democratic parties.
- The solid vote for the three main democratic parties, the SPD, the DDP and the ZP, made it straightforward to form a coalition government, which became known as the 'Weimar Coalition'.

Table 1.3: The major political parties in the Weimar Republic

BVP Bayerische Volkspartei (Bavarian People's Party)	Leader: Heinrich Held	The BVP was a regional party formed from elements of the ZP in 1919 in order to uphold Bavaria's local interests. It was conservative, but generally supported the Republic.
DDP Deutsche Demokratische Partei (German Democratic Party)	Leaders: Walther Rathenau and Hugo Preuss	Formed from the National Liberals party in the old *Reichstag*, it attracted support from the professional middle classes, especially the intellectuals and some of the businessmen. The party supported the democratic republic and was committed to constitutional reform.
DNVP Deutschnationale Volkspartei (German National People's Party)	Leaders: Karl Helfferich and Alfred Hugenberg (see page 68)	The DNVP was a right-wing party formed from the old conservative parties and some of the racist, anti-Semitic groups, such as the Pan-German League. It was monarchist and anti-republican. Generally, it was closely tied to the interests of heavy industry and agriculture, including landowners and small farmers.
DVP Deutsche Volkspartei (German People's Party)	Leader: Gustav Stresemann (see pages 75–6)	A new party founded by Gustav Stresemann, who was a conservative and monarchist and at first suspicious of the Weimar Republic and voted against the new constitution (see page 21). From 1921, under Stresemann's influence, the DVP became a strong supporter of parliamentary democracy. It attracted support from the protestant middle and upper classes.
KPD Kommunistische Partei Deutschlands (German Communist Party)	Leader: Ernst Thälmann	The KPD was formed in January 1919 by the extreme left wing, e.g. Spartacists. It was anti-republican in the sense that it opposed Weimar-style democracy and supported a revolutionary overthrow of society. Most of its supporters were from the working class and strengthened by the defection of many USPD members in 1920.
NSDAP Nationalsozialistische Partei Deutschlands (National Socialist German Workers' Party – Nazi Party)	Leader: Adolf Hitler (see pages 128–9)	Extreme right-wing party formed in 1919. It was anti-republican, anti-Semitic and strongly nationalist. Until 1930 it remained a fringe party with support from the lower middle classes.
SPD Sozialdemokratische Partei Deutschlands (German Social Democratic Party)	Leaders: Friedrich Ebert (see page 11) and Philipp Scheidemann	The moderate wing of the socialist movement, it was very much the party of the working class and the trade unions. It strongly supported parliamentary democracy and was opposed to the revolutionary demands of the more left-wing socialists.
USPD Unabhängige Sozialdemokratische Partei Deutschlands (Independent German Social Democratic Party)	Leaders: Karl Kautsky and Hugo Haase	The USPD broke away from the SPD in April 1917. It included many of the more radical elements of German socialism and, therefore, sought social and political change. About half its members joined the KPD during 1919–20 whilst by 1922 most of the others had returned to the ranks of the SPD.
ZP Zentrumspartei (Centre Party)	Leaders: Matthias Erzberger and Heinrich Brüning (see page 113)	The ZP had been created in the nineteenth century to defend the interests of the Roman Catholic Church. It continued to be the major political voice of Catholicism and enjoyed a broad range of supporters from aristocratic landowners to Christian trade unionists. Most of the ZP was committed to the Republic. From the late 1920s it became more sympathetic to the right wing.

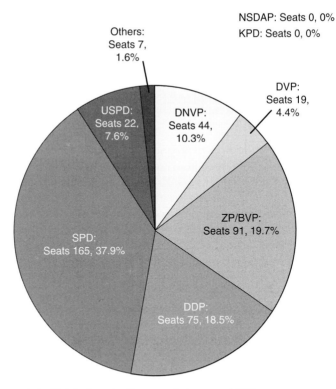

Figure 1.1: *Reichstag* election result January 1919
Turnout 83 per cent
Total number of seats 423

However, it should be borne in mind that:

- Although the DNVP gained only 10.3 per cent, it had backing from important conservative supporters, e.g. the landowners, the army officers, industrialists.
- The DVP and its leader, Stresemann, did not support the Weimar Republic in 1919 because they wanted Germany to have a constitutional monarchy.

What kind of revolution?

Key question
How fundamental were the changes brought about by the German Revolution?

By May 1919 a degree of stability had returned to Germany. The revolution had run its course and the Weimar Republic had been established. However, serious doubts remain about the nature and real extent of these revolutionary changes.

Undoubtedly, there existed the possibility of revolution in Germany as the war came to an end. The effects of war and the shock of defeat shook the faith of large numbers of the people in the old order. Imperial Germany could not survive, so Wilhelm II and the other princes were deposed and parliamentary democracy was introduced. These were important changes.

However, in the end, the German Revolution did not go much further than the October reforms and was strictly limited in scope. Society was left almost untouched by these events, for there was no attempt to reform the key institutions.

- The civil service, judiciary and army all remained essentially intact.
- Similarly, the power and influence of Germany's industrial and commercial leaders remained unchanged.
- There were no changes in the structure of big business and land ownership.

Certainly, plans for the improvement of working conditions and the beginnings of a welfare state were outlined by the government, but the SPD leadership hoped that all the changes would follow in the wake of constitutional reform. With hindsight, it seems that more thoroughgoing social and economic changes might well have been a better basis on which to establish democracy. As it was, the divisions on the left played into the hands of the conservative forces. As one historian, M. Hughes, has claim, 'it is more accurate to talk of a potential revolution which ran away into the sand rather than the genuine article'. Indeed, during the first half of 1919 the increasing reliance of the moderate left on the conservative forces of Imperial Germany became a major factor in German politics. These conservative forces were soon to put into doubt the very survival of Weimar democracy.

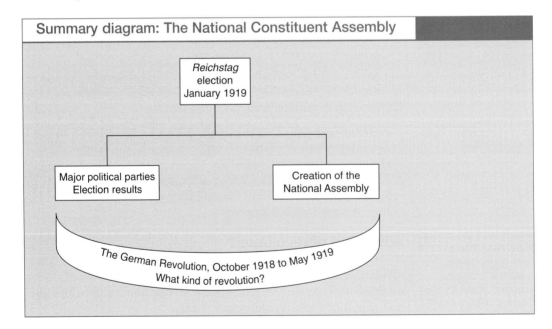

Summary diagram: The National Constituent Assembly

Reichstag election January 1919

Major political parties Election results

Creation of the National Assembly

The German Revolution, October 1918 to May 1919 What kind of revolution?

Study Guide: AS Question

In the style of OCR A

Assess the reasons why the Second Reich collapsed.   (50 marks)

Exam tips

This question asks you to evaluate reasons. 'Assess' does not mean look at each reason in isolation. Important events usually happen when several factors combine to create a new dynamic, so explain also how each reason influenced others, and was itself affected by some factors. Do not sit on the fence either. Work out which you think was the most important in bringing down the Reich, and explain why to justify your claim.

Do not divert yourself to examine why Germany lost the war; that is not what the question wants, although the impact of military collapse in 1918 is one reason you need to assess. The Kaiser's regime was tainted by failure, but it wasn't just military. Germany suffered badly in 1917–18 (inflation, starvation, epidemics) and the Reich was blamed. Does that mean the Kaiser himself was doomed or does it mean the monarchy would be abolished? They are not the same thing and examining why both happened (rather than just the first) takes you to the heart of this question. Move next to examine the October reform. What were Ludendorff's motives? Why did Prince Max's constitutional reforms fail? The answers to those questions will explain why setting up a constitutional monarchy would not solve the crisis. At that point you are now looking at the final reason: why reform was overtaken by revolution.

You have linked events into a sequence of reasons. But one fundamental question remains. Were these problems building since 1917 sufficient to explain everything, or was something further needed: very immediate factors in October/November 1918 that tipped an already unstable Germany into abolishing the Reich?

2 Weimar's Political Crisis

POINTS TO CONSIDER

In the summer of 1919 two crucial documents were drawn up that influenced the history of the Weimar Republic: the Weimar Constitution that was agreed by the German *Reichstag*, and the Treaty of Versailles which was imposed by the Allies. The importance of each document is examined in three ways:

- The key terms of the documents
- The issues of controversy
- Their significance in the history of Weimar Germany

Although the forces of democracy had successfully established the Weimar Republic, Germany remained in turmoil in the years 1919–23. This chapter concentrates on the extent of Weimar's political problems and the range of political threats it faced. It examines:

- The threats from the extreme left and the extreme right
- Uprisings of the extreme right
- Elections and governments – 'a republic without republicans'

The country also faced fundamental economic problems and these will be the focus of the next chapter.

Key dates

1919	February 6	National Assembly first meeting at Weimar
	June 28	Treaty of Versailles signed
	July 31	Weimar Constitution adopted by the National Constituent Assembly
	August 11	Weimar Constitution signed by President Ebert
1920	March	Kapp *putsch*
1921	August 26	Murder of Erzberger
1922	June 24	Murder of Rathenau
1923	Summer	The 'German October' in Saxony
	November	Munich Beer Hall *putsch*

1 | The Weimar Constitution

The key terms of the Constitution

Key question
What were the
significant terms of the
Weimar Constitution?

Back in November 1918, Ebert invited the liberal lawyer Hugo Preuss to draw up a new **constitution** for Germany and a draft was outlined by the time the National Assembly was established in February 1919. Preuss worked closely with a constitutional committee of 28 members over the next six months, though their discussions were deeply overshadowed by the dispute about the Treaty of Versailles (see pages 26–33).

The proposals for the new constitution were influenced by the long-established democratic ideas of Britain and the USA. Nevertheless, Germany's particular circumstances and traditions were not ignored as, for example, in the introduction of **proportional representation** and the creation of a **federal structure**. Eventually, on 31 July 1919, the *Reichstag* voted strongly in favour of the constitution (for: 262; against: 75) and on 11 August the president ratified it. The main features of the constitution are outlined below and in Figure 2.1 on page 22.

Key dates

National Assembly
first meeting at
Weimar: 6 February
1919

The Weimar
Constitution was
adopted by the
National Assembly:
31 July 1919

Weimar Constitution
signed by President
Ebert: 11 August
1919

Definition

Germany was declared a 'democratic state', although it retained the title of 'Reich' (empire). It was a republic (all monarchies were ended). It had a federal structure with 17 *Länder* (regional states), e.g. Prussia, Bavaria, Saxony.

President

The people elected the president every seven years. He enjoyed considerable powers, such as:

- The right to dissolve the *Reichstag*.
- The appointment of the chancellor. (Although the president was not obliged, he tended to choose the chancellor as the leader of the largest party in the *Reichstag*. In order to form a workable coalition government, it was necessary to negotiate with the leaders of other political parties.)
- The Supreme Commander of the Armed Forces.
- The capacity to rule by decree at a time of national emergency (Article 48) and to oversee the *Reichstag*.

But this created a very complex relationship between the powers of the president and the *Reichstag*/chancellor.

Parliament

There were two houses in the German parliament:

- The *Reichstag* was the main representative assembly and law-making body of the parliament. It consisted of deputies elected every four years on the basis of a system of proportional representation. The PR system allocated members to parliament from the official list of political party candidates. They were distributed on the basis of one member for every 60,000 votes in an electoral district.

Key terms

Constitution
The principles and
rules that govern a
state. The Weimar
Constitution is a
good example.
(Britain is often
described as having
an unwritten
constitution. It is
not drawn up in *one*
document, but built
on statutes,
conventions and
case law.)

**Proportional
representation**
A system that
allocates
parliamentary seats
in proportion to the
total number of
votes.

Federal structure
Where power and
responsibilities are
shared between
central and regional
governments, for
example, the USA.

- The *Reichsrat* was the less important house in the parliament. It was made up of representatives from all of the 17 state regional governments (*Länder*), which all held local responsibilities such as education, police, etc. But the *Reichsrat* could only initiate or delay proposals, and the *Reichstag* could always overrule it.

Bill of Rights

The constitution also drew up a range of individual rights. It outlined broad freedoms, for example:

- personal liberty
- the right to free speech
- censorship was forbidden
- equality before the law of all Germans
- religious freedom and conscience (and no State Church was allowed).

In addition to this, the Bill of Rights provided a range of social rights, for example:

- welfare provision, e.g. for housing, the disabled, orphans
- protection of labour.

Article 48
Gave the Weimar president the power in an emergency to rule by decree and to override the constitutional rights of the people.

Key term

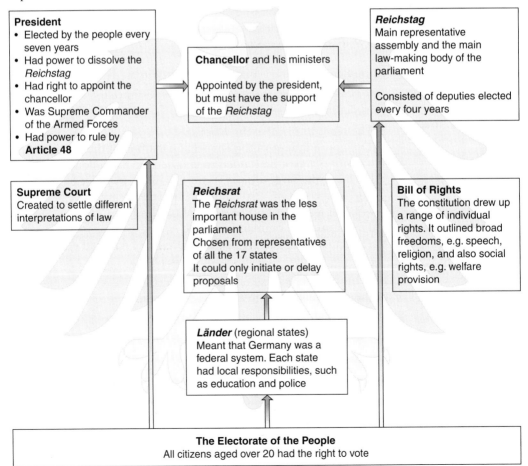

President
- Elected by the people every seven years
- Had power to dissolve the *Reichstag*
- Had right to appoint the chancellor
- Was Supreme Commander of the Armed Forces
- Had power to rule by **Article 48**

Chancellor and his ministers

Appointed by the president, but must have the support of the *Reichstag*

Reichstag
Main representative assembly and the main law-making body of the parliament

Consisted of deputies elected every four years

Supreme Court
Created to settle different interpretations of law

Reichsrat
The *Reichsrat* was the less important house in the parliament
Chosen from representatives of all the 17 states
It could only initiate or delay proposals

Bill of Rights
The constitution drew up a range of individual rights. It outlined broad freedoms, e.g. speech, religion, and also social rights, e.g. welfare provision

Länder (regional states)
Meant that Germany was a federal system. Each state had local responsibilities, such as education and police

The Electorate of the People
All citizens aged over 20 had the right to vote

Figure 2.1: The Weimar Constitution.

Supreme Court

In order to settle different interpretations of law, a Supreme Court was created.

Key question
What were the arguments for and against the terms of Weimar Constitution?

The issues of controversy

Since the Weimar Republic lasted only 14 crisis-ridden years, it is hardly surprising that its written constitution has been the focus of considerable attention. Some historians have gone so far as to argue that the real causes of the collapse of the Republic and the success of Hitler and National Socialists can be found in its clauses. Such claims are based on three aspects of the constitution. These are:

- The introduction of proportional representation.
- The relationship between the president and the *Reichstag* and, in particular, the emergency powers available to the president under Article 48.
- The fact that the traditional institutions of Imperial Germany were allowed to continue.

Proportional representation

The introduction of proportional representation became the focus of criticism after 1945 because, it was argued, it had encouraged the formation of many new, small splinter parties, e.g. the Nazis. This made it more difficult to form and maintain governments.

In Weimar Germany it was virtually impossible for one party to form a majority government, and so coalitions were required – sometimes of three and even four parties. Furthermore, it was argued that all the negotiations and compromises involved in forming governments contributed to the political instability of Weimar. It is for these reasons that many critics of Weimar felt that a voting political system based upon two major parties, like in Britain (or the USA), which favoured the so-called **'first past the post'** model, would have created more political stability.

However, it is difficult to see how an alternative voting system, without proportional representation, could have made for a more effective parliamentary democracy in early twentieth century Germany. The main problem was the difficulty of creating coalitions amongst the main parties, which had been well established in the nineteenth century. The parties were meant to reflect the different political, religious and geographical views and so a system of PR was the only fair way. By comparison, the existence of all the splinter parties was a relatively minor issue.

There is also the view that, after the economic and political crisis of 1929–33 (see pages 102–5), proportional representation encouraged the emergence of political extremism. However, it now seems clear that the changes in the way people voted and the way they changed their allegiance from one party to another were just too volatile to be kept in check. It may also have been the case that a 'first past the post' system would have actually helped the rise of Nazism and communism.

Key term

'First past the post' An electoral system that simply requires the winner to gain one vote more than the second placed candidate. It is also referred to as the plurality system and does not require 50 per cent plus one votes. In a national election it tends to give the most successful party disproportionately more seats than its total vote merits.

The relationship between the president and the *Reichstag*

The relationship created between the *Reichstag* and the president in the Weimar Constitution was meant to have a fair system of checks and balances, but this was very complex.

It was intended to lessen the fears that an unrestricted parliament would become too powerful. Fear of an over-powerful parliament was strong on the right wing, and within liberal circles. It therefore aimed to create a presidency that could provide leadership 'above the parties' and limit the powers of the *Reichstag* (see page 21 and Figure 2.1 on page 22). The president's powers were seen as amounting to those of an *Ersatzkaiser*, a substitute emperor. When the power of the president is compared with the authority of the *Reichstag*, it seems that the attempt to prevent too much power being placed in the hands of one institution resulted in massive power being granted to another. As a result, there was uncertainty in constitutional matters from the start.

The framers of the constitution struggled to keep a balance of power between the president and the *Reichstag*. Was the ultimate source of authority in the democratic republic vested in the representative assembly of the people – the *Reichstag* – or in the popularly elected head of state – the president?

Matters were made more difficult by the powers conferred upon the president by Article 48. This Article provided the head of state with the authority to suspend civil rights in an emergency and restore law and order by the issue of presidential decrees. The intention was to create the means by which government could continue to function in a crisis. However, the effect was to create what the historian Gordon Craig referred to as 'a constitutional anomaly'. Such fears, which were actively expressed by some deputies in the constitutional debate of 1919, later assumed a particular importance during the crisis that brought

Table 2.1: Weimar *Reichstag* election results for 1919–32

	1919	1920	1924	1924	1928	1930	1932	1932
Total on register (in millions)	36.8	35.9	38.4	39.0	41.2	43.0	44.2	44.4
Size of poll (%)	83.0	79.2	74.4	78.8	75.6	82.0	84.1	80.6
Total No. of seats in *Reichstag*	423	459	472	493	491	577	608	584
NSDAP	–	–	32	14	12	107	230	196
DNVP	44	71	95	103	73	41	37	52
DVP	19	65	45	51	45	30	7	11
ZP/BVP	91	85	81	88	78	87	97	90
DDP	75	39	28	32	25	20	4	2
SPD	165	102	100	131	153	143	133	121
USPD	22	84						
KPD	–	4	62	45	54	77	89	100
Others	7	9	29	29	51	72	11	12

Hitler to power in 1933. However, it should be remembered that in the crisis of 1923 the presidential powers were used as intended and to very good effect.

The continuity of traditional institutions

Although the Weimar Constitution introduced a wide range of democratic rights and civil liberties, it made no provision to reform the old traditional institutions of Imperial Germany, such as:

- The civil service was well educated and professional, but tended to conform to the old-fashioned conservative values of Imperial Germany.
- The judiciary continued to enjoy its traditional independence under the Weimar Constitution, but the hearts of many judges did not lie with the Weimar Republic. Bluntly, they were biased and tended to favour the extreme right and condemn the extreme left. Only 28 out of 354 right-wing assassins were found guilty and punished, but 10 of the 22 left-wing assassins were sentenced to death.
- The army enjoyed great status and many of the generals were socially linked with the Prussian landowners. It sought to maintain its influence after 1918 and was generally not sympathetic to democratic Germany. It was the only real authority that had military capacity.
- Universities were very proud of their traditional status and generally more sympathetic to the old political ideas and rules.

In Weimar's difficult early years effective use was made of the established professional skills and educated institutions of the state. However, the result was that powerful conservative forces were able to exert great influence in the daily life of the Weimar Republic. This was at odds with the left wing's wishes to extend civil rights and to create a modern, democratic society. So, whilst the spirit of the Weimar Constitution was democratic and progressive, many of the institutions remained dedicated to the values of Imperial Germany.

Key question
Was the Weimar Constitution fatally flawed?

The significance of the Weimar Constitution

With hindsight, it is easy to highlight those parts of the Weimar Constitution that contributed to the ultimate collapse of the Republic. However, it should be remembered that the new constitution was a great improvement upon the previous undemocratic constitution of Imperial Germany and a very large majority voted in favour of it. Indeed, Weimar was initially seen as 'the most advanced democracy in the world'. What the Constitution could not control were the conditions and circumstances in which it had to operate. And the Weimar Republic had other more serious problems than just the Constitution, such as the Treaty of Versailles and its socio-economic problems. As Theodor Heuss, the first president of the German Federal Republic in 1949, said: 'Germany never conquered democracy for herself. Democracy came to Germany … in the wake of defeat.'

Therefore, it seems unrealistic to imagine that any piece of paper could have resolved all Germany's problems after 1918. The Weimar Constitution had weaknesses, but it was not fatally flawed – there were many more serious and fundamental problems within the Weimar Republic.

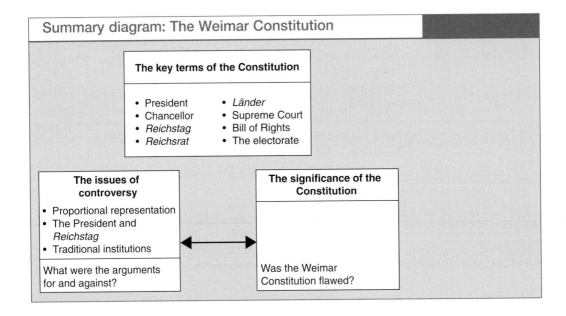

Summary diagram: The Weimar Constitution

The key terms of the Constitution

- President
- Chancellor
- *Reichstag*
- *Reichsrat*
- *Länder*
- Supreme Court
- Bill of Rights
- The electorate

The issues of controversy

- Proportional representation
- The President and *Reichstag*
- Traditional institutions

What were the arguments for and against?

The significance of the Constitution

Was the Weimar Constitution flawed?

2 | The Treaty of Versailles

Key question
In what ways did the Allies differ over war aims?

For most Germans the Paris peace settlement of 1919 was a far more controversial issue than the new constitution. It had been generally assumed among German public opinion that the treaty would result in a fair peace. This was partly because defeat had never really been expected, even as late as the summer of 1918, and partly because it was generally assumed that President Wilson's Fourteen Points would lay the basis of the terms.

The German government signed the Treaty of Versailles: 28 June 1919

Key date

However, it soon became clear that the peace treaty would not be open for discussion with Germany's representatives. When the draft terms were presented in May 1919 there was national shock and outrage in Germany. In desperation, the first Weimar government led by Scheidemann resigned. The Allies were not prepared to negotiate, which obliged an embittered *Reichstag* finally to accept the Treaty of Versailles by 237 votes to 138 in June. This was because Germany simply did not have the military capacity to resist. And so, on 28 June 1919, the German representatives, led by Hermann Müller, signed the treaty in the Hall of Mirrors at Versailles near Paris.

The Treaty of Versailles was a compromise, but only in the sense that it was a compromise *between* the Allied powers. So the really decisive negotiations were between the so-called 'Big Three':

Key terms

Self-determination
The right of people of the same nation to decide their own form of government. In effect, it is the principle of each nation ruling itself. Wilson believed that the application of self-determination was integral to the Peace Settlement and it would lead to long-term peace.

League of Nations
The international body initiated by President Wilson to encourage disarmament and to prevent war.

Buffer state
The general idea of separating two rival countries by leaving a space between them. Clemenceau believed that the long-established Franco-German military aggression could be brought to an end by establishing an independent Rhineland state (though this was not implemented because Wilson saw it as against the principle of self-determination).

- Woodrow Wilson, President of the USA
- Georges Clemenceau, Prime Minister of France
- David Lloyd George, Prime Minister of Great Britain.

Woodrow Wilson

He has traditionally been portrayed as an idealist, as he had a strong religious framework. Initially, he had been an academic, but he was drawn into politics when he had campaigned against corruption. At first he had opposed American entry into the war. Once he declared war against Germany in April 1917 he drew up the Fourteen Points in the hope of creating a more just world. His main aims were:

- to bring about international disarmament
- to apply the principle of **self-determination**
- to create a **League of Nations** in order to maintain international peace.

Georges Clemenceau

He was an uncompromising French nationalist. He had been in his country twice when Germany had invaded and he was deeply influenced by the devastation from the war in northern France. He was motivated by revenge and he was determined to gain financial compensation and to satisfy France's security concerns. His main aims were:

- to annex the Rhineland and to create a '**buffer state**'
- to impose the major disarmament of Germany
- to impose heavy reparations in order to weaken Germany
- to get recompense from the damage of the war in order to finance rebuilding.

David Lloyd George

He may be seen as a pragmatist. He was keen to uphold British national interests and initially he played on the idea of revenge. However, he recognised that there would have to be compromise. In particular, he saw the need to restrain Clemenceau's revenge. His main aims were:

- to guarantee British military security – especially, to secure naval supremacy
- to keep communism at bay
- to limit French demands because he feared that excessively weakening Germany would have serious economic consequences for the European economy.

Key question
What were the significant terms of the Treaty of Versailles?

The terms of the Treaty of Versailles

The key terms of the Treaty of Versailles can be listed under the following headings: territorial arrangements, war guilt, reparations, disarmament and maintaining peace.

a) Territorial arrangements
- Eupen-Malmedy. Subject to **plebiscite**, the districts of Eupen and Malmedy to be handed over to Belgium.
- Alsace-Lorraine. Germany to return these provinces to France.
- North Schleswig. Subject to plebiscite, Germany to hand over the North Schleswig.
- West Prussia and Posen. Germany to surrender West Prussia and Posen, thus separating East Prussia from the main part of Germany (creating 'the Polish Corridor').
- Upper Silesia. A plebiscite was to be held in the province of Upper Silesia and as a result it was divided between Poland and Germany.
- Danzig. The German city and port of Danzig (Gdansk in Polish) was made an international 'free city' under the control of the League of Nations.
- Memel. The German port of Memel was also made an international 'free city' under the League.
- Austria. The reunification (*Anschluss*) of Germany with Austria was forbidden.
- Kiel Canal and rivers. All major rivers to be open for all nations and to be run by an international commission.
- Saar area (see 'Reparations' below).
- Rhineland (see 'Disarmament' below).
- Germany's colonies. All German colonies were distributed as '**mandates**', under control of countries supervised by the League, for example Britain took responsibility for German East Africa.

b) War guilt
Germany was forced to sign the War Guilt clause (Article 231) accepting blame for causing the war and therefore responsibility for all losses and damage:

> Germany accepts the responsibility of Germany and her allies for causing all the loss and damage to which the Allied governments and their peoples have been subjected as a result of the war.

c) Reparations
- Reparations sum to be fixed later by the IARC (Inter-Allied Reparations Commission). In 1921 the sum was fixed at £6600 million.
- Germany to make substantial payments in kind, e.g. coal.
- The Saar to be under the control of the League until 1935, when there was to be a plebiscite. Until then all coal production was to be given to France.

d) Disarmament
- Germany to abolish conscription and to reduce its army to 100,000. No tanks or big guns were allowed.
- Rhineland was to be demilitarised from the French frontier to a line 32 miles east of the Rhine. (The Rhineland remained part of Germany.)

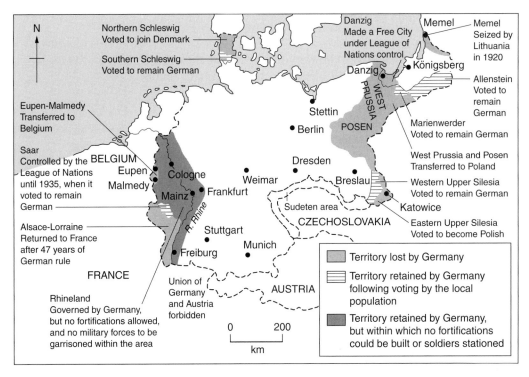

Figure 2.2: The terms of the Treaty of Versailles 1919.

- Germany allowed no military aircraft.
- German navy limited to:
  - six battleships, six cruisers, 12 destroyers, 12 torpedo boats
  - no submarines were allowed.

  (The German fleet surrendered to Britain in 1918, but sank its own ships at Scapa Flow on 28 June 1919.)

e) Maintaining peace

The Treaty also set out the Covenant of the League of Nations, which included the aims and organisation of the League. Germany had to accept the League, but it was initially not allowed to join.

Table 2.2: German losses resulting from the Treaty of Versailles

Type of loss	Percentage of loss
Territory	13 per cent
Population	12 per cent (6.5 million)
Agricultural production	15 per cent
Iron-ore	48 per cent
Coal	15 per cent

The 'Diktat'

Key question
Why did the Germans view the Treaty as unfair?

No other political issue produced such total agreement within Weimar Germany as the rejection and condemnation of the Treaty of Versailles. The Treaty's terms were seen as unfair and were simply described as a '*Diktat*'. Germany's main complaints were as follows:

- The Treaty was considered to be very different from President Wilson's Fourteen Points. Most obviously, many Germans found it impossible to understand how and why the guiding principle of self-determination was *not* applied in a number of cases. They viewed the following areas as 'German', but excluded from the new German state and placed under foreign rule:
  Austria
  Danzig
  Posen and West Prussia
  Memel
  Upper Silesia
  Sudetenland
  Saar.
  Similarly, the loss of Germany's colonies was not in line with the fifth of Wilson's Fourteen Points, which had called for 'an impartial adjustment of all colonial claims'. Instead, they were passed on to the care of the Allies as mandates.
- Germany found it impossible to accept the War Guilt clause (Article 231), which was the Allies' justification for demanding the payment of reparations. Most Germans argued that Germany could not be held solely responsible for the outbreak of the war. They were convinced that the war of 1914 had been fought for defensive reasons because their country had been threatened by 'encirclement' from the Allies in 1914.
- Germans considered the Allied demand for extensive reparations as totally unreasonable. Worryingly, the actual size of the reparations payment was not stated in the Treaty of Versailles – it was left to be decided at a later date by the IARC. From a German viewpoint this amounted to their being forced to sign a 'blank cheque'.
- The imposition of the disarmament clauses was seen as grossly unfair as Britain and France remained highly armed and made no future commitments to disarm. It seemed as if Germany had been **unilaterally disarmed**, whereas Wilson had spoken in favour of universal disarmament.
- Germany's treatment by the Allies was viewed as undignified and unworthy of a great power. For example, Germany was excluded from the League of Nations but, as part of the Treaty, was forced to accept the rules of its Covenant. This simply hardened the views of those Germans who saw the League as a tool of the Allies rather than as a genuine international organisation.

Altogether, the treaty was seen as a *Diktat*. The Allies maintained a military blockade on Germany until the Treaty was signed. This had significant human consequences such as increasing food shortages. Furthermore, the Allies threatened to take further military action if Germany did not co-operate.

Key terms

Diktat
A dictated peace. The Germans felt that the Treaty of Versailles was imposed without negotiation.

Unilateral disarmament
The disarmament of one party. Wilson pushed for general (universal) disarmament after the war, but France and Britain were more suspicious. As a result only Germany had to disarm.

A cartoon drawn in July 1919 from the German newspaper *Kladderatsch*. It portrays Georges Clemenceau (the French Prime Minister) as a vampire sucking the blood and life from the innocent German maiden.

Versailles: a more balanced view

Key question
To what extent was the Treaty of Versailles motivated by anti-German feeling?

In the years 1919–45, most Germans regarded the Treaty of Versailles as a *Diktat*. In Britain, too, there developed a growing sympathy for Germany's position. However, this was not the case in France, where the Treaty was generally condemned as being too lenient. It was only after the Second World War that a more balanced view of the Treaty of Versailles emerged in Europe. As a result, recent historians have tended to look upon the peacemakers of 1919 in a more sympathetic light. Earlier German criticisms of the Treaty are no longer as readily accepted as they once were.

Of course, at the Paris peace conferences Allied statesmen were motivated by their own national self-interests, and the representatives of France and Britain were keen to achieve these at the expense of Germany. However, it is now recognised that it was the situation created by the war that shaped the terms of the Treaty and not just anti-German feeling. The aims and objectives of the various Allies differed and achieving agreement was made more difficult by the complicated circumstances of the time. It should be remembered that the Paris peace settlement was not solely concerned with Germany, so Austria-Hungary, Bulgaria and Turkey were forced to sign separate treaties. In addition, numerous other problems had to be dealt with. For example, Britain had national interests to look after in the Middle East as a result of the collapse of the Turkish Empire. At the same time the Allies were concerned by the threat of Soviet Russia and were motivated by a common desire to contain the Bolshevik menace.

In the end, the Treaty of Versailles was a compromise. It was not based on Wilson's Fourteen Points as most Germans thought it would be, but equally it was not nearly so severe as certain sections of Allied opinion had demanded. It should be borne in mind that:

- Clemenceau, the French representative, was forced to give way over most of his country's more extreme demands, such as the creation of an independent Rhineland and the **annexation** of the Saar.
- The application of self-determination was not nearly so unfair as many Germans believed:
  - Alsace-Lorraine would have voted to return to France anyway, as it had been French before 1871.
  - Plebiscites were held in Schleswig, Silesia and parts of Prussia to decide their future.
  - Danzig's status under the League was the result of Woodrow Wilson's promise to provide 'Poland with access to the sea'.
  - The eastern frontier provinces of Posen and West Prussia were rather more mixed in ethnic make-up than Germans were prepared to admit (in these provinces Germans predominated in the towns, whereas the Poles did so in the countryside – which made it very difficult to draw a clear frontier line).
  - Austria and Sudetenland had never been part of Germany before 1918, anyway.
- Germany was not physically occupied during the war and, as a result, the real damage was suffered on foreign soil, e.g. France and Belgium.
- In comparison the Treaty of Versailles appeared relatively moderate to the severity of the terms imposed by the Germans on the Russians at the Treaty of Brest-Litovsk in 1918, which annexed large areas of Poland and the Baltic states.

> **Key term**
>
> **Annexation**
> Taking over of another country against its will.

The significance of the Treaty of Versailles

The historical significance of the Treaty of Versailles goes well beyond the debate over its fairness. It raises the important issue of its impact upon the Weimar Republic and whether it acted as a serious handicap to the establishment of long-term political stability in Germany.

> **Key question**
> Did the Treaty of Versailles fundamentally weaken Weimar Germany?

The economic consequences of reparations were undoubtedly a genuine concern. The English economist, Keynes, feared in 1919 that the reparations would fundamentally weaken the economy of Germany with consequences for the whole of Europe. However, Germany's economic potential was still considerable. It had potentially by far the strongest economy in Europe and still had extensive industry and resources. As will be seen later (pages 48–51), the Republic's economic problems cannot be blamed on the burden of reparations alone. And it should also be remembered that by 1932 Germany actually received more in loans under the Dawes Plan (see pages 72–3) than it paid in reparations.

It is not really possible to maintain that the Treaty had weakened Germany politically. In some respects, Germany in

1919 was in a stronger position than in 1914. The great empires of Russia, Austria-Hungary and Turkey had gone, creating a power vacuum in central and eastern Europe that could not be filled at least in the short term by a weak and isolated Soviet Russia or by any other state. In such a situation, cautious diplomacy might have led to the establishment of German power and influence at the heart of Europe.

However, on another level, the Treaty might be considered more to blame because, in the minds of many Germans, it was regarded as the real cause of the country's problems and they really believed that it was totally unfair. In the war German public opinion had been strongly shaped by nationalist propaganda and then deeply shocked by the defeat. Both the Armistice and Versailles were closely linked to the 'stab in the back' myth that the German Army had not really lost the First World War in 1918 (see page 5). It may have been a myth, but it was a very powerful one.

As a result, although the war had been pursued by Imperial Germany, it was the new democracy of Weimar that was forced to take the responsibility and the blame for the First World War. Therefore, Weimar democracy was deeply weakened by Versailles, which fuelled the propaganda of the Republic's opponents over the years. Even for sympathetic democrats like Hugo Preuss, Versailles only served to disillusion many into thinking that the gains of the revolution were being undone: '… the German Republic was born out of its terrible defeat … The criminal madness of the Versailles *Diktat* was a shameless blow in the face to such hopes based on international law and political common sense'. In this way the Treaty of Versailles contributed to the internal political and economic difficulties that evolved in Germany after 1919.

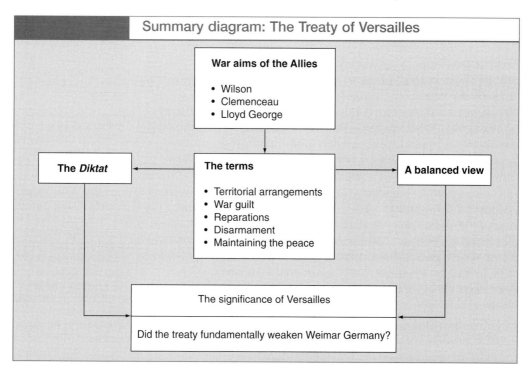

Summary diagram: The Treaty of Versailles

War aims of the Allies

- Wilson
- Clemenceau
- Lloyd George

The Diktat ← **The terms** → **A balanced view**

- Territorial arrangements
- War guilt
- Reparations
- Disarmament
- Maintaining the peace

The significance of Versailles

Did the treaty fundamentally weaken Weimar Germany?

3 | The Threat from the Extreme Left

Key question
How serious was the opposition of the extreme left to the Weimar Republic?

After the German revolution of 1918–19 the left-wing movement (see pages 6–14) at first remained in a state of confusion:

- The moderate socialists of the SPD were committed to parliamentary democracy.
- The communists (the KPD) pressed for a workers' revolution.
- The USPD stood for the creation of a radical socialist society, but within a democratic framework.

This situation became clearer when, in 1920, the USPD disbanded and its members joined either the KPD or the SPD. So, from that time there were two left-wing alternative parties, but with fundamental differences.

The KPD believed that the establishment of parliamentary democracy fell a long way short of its real aims. It wanted the revolution to proceed on **Marxist** lines with the creation of a one-party communist state and the major restructuring of Germany both socially and economically. As a result of the 1917 Russian Revolution, many German communists were encouraged by the political unrest to believe that international revolution would spread throughout Europe.

The KPD's opposition to the Republic was nothing less than a complete rejection of the Weimar system. It was not prepared to be part of the democratic opposition or to work within the parliamentary system to bring about desired changes. The differences between the moderate and extreme left were so basic that there was no chance of political co-operation between them, let alone a coming together into one socialist movement. The extreme left was totally committed to a very different vision of German politics and society, whereas the moderate left was one of the pillars of Weimar democracy.

Key terms

Marxism
The political ideology of Karl Marx. His two major books, *Communist Manifesto* and *Capital*, outline his beliefs that the working classes will overthrow the industrial classes by revolution and create a classless society.

Red Threat
A 'Red' was a loose term used to describe anyone sympathetic to the left and it originated from the Bolshevik use of the red flag in Russia.

KPD opposition

The KPD was indeed a reasonable political force in the years 1919–23. It enjoyed the support of 10–15 per cent of the electorate and there were continuous revolutionary disturbances – protests, strikes and uprisings (see Table 2.3, page 35). However, all these actions by the extreme left gave the impression that Germany was really facing a Bolshevik-inspired '**Red Threat**'. Consequently, as a result of right-wing propaganda, many Germans began to have exaggerated fears about the possibility of impending revolution.

Looking back, it is clear that the extreme left posed much less of a threat to Weimar than was believed at the time. So, despite all the disturbances, the revolutionary left was never really likely to be able to seize political power. The main reasons lie in a combination of their own weaknesses and the effective resistance of the Weimar governments:

- Bad co-ordination. Even during the chaos and uncertainty of 1923, the activities of the extreme left proved incapable of mounting a unified attack on Weimar democracy.

Key date

The revolutionary uprising in Germany in 1923 is often referred to as the German October, but it is a confusing term. Mass protests started before this, in the summer of 1923, though the uprising did not actually come to a head until October 1923 (which was also emotionally associated with the Bolshevik Revolution in Russia in October 1917)

- Poor leadership. The repression it suffered at the hands of the *Freikorps* removed some of its ablest and most spirited leaders, e.g. Liebknecht and Luxemburg (see page 9). The later leadership suffered from internal divisions and disagreements on tactics.
- Concessions. The Weimar governments played on the differences within the extreme left by making concessions which split it, e.g. over the Kapp *putsch* in March 1920 (see pages 39–40).
- Repression. The authorities systematically repressed the rebels with considerable brutality.

In the end, the extreme left was just not powerful enough to lead a revolution against the Weimar Republic.

Table 2.3: Major communist uprisings 1919–23

Date	Place	Action	Response
January 1919	Berlin	Spartacist uprising to seize power	Crushed by German army and *Freikorps*
March 1919	Bavaria	Creation of soviet republic	Crushed by the *Freikorps*
March 1920	Ruhr	Formation of the Ruhr Army by 50,000 workers to oppose the Kapp *putsch* (pages 39–41)	Crushed by German Army and *Freikorps*
March 1921	Merseburg and Halle	'March Operation'. Uprising of strikes organised by KPD	Put down by police
Summer 1923	Saxony	'German October' A wave of strikes and the creation of an SPD/KPD state government	Overthrown by German army

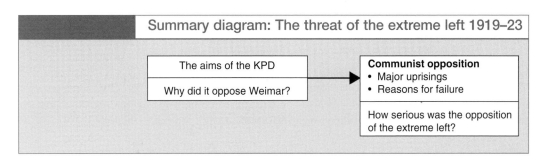

Summary diagram: The threat of the extreme left 1919–23

The aims of the KPD
Why did it oppose Weimar?

Communist opposition
- Major uprisings
- Reasons for failure

How serious was the opposition of the extreme left?

Key question
What did the extreme right stand for?

4 | The Threat from the Extreme Right

Opposition from the extreme right was very different both in its form and in its extent to that of the extreme left. On the right wing there was a very mixed collection of opponents to the Republic and their resistance found expression in different ways.

The extreme right in theory

In contrast to Marxist socialism, the extreme right did not really have an alternative organised ideology. It was simply drawn together by a growing belief in the following:

- **Anti-democracy**: it was united by its rejection of the Weimar system and its principles. It aimed to destroy the democratic constitution because it was seen as weak, which it believed had contributed to Germany's problems.
- **Anti-Marxism**: even more despised than democracy was the fear of communism. It was seen as a real threat to traditional values and the ownership of property and wealth – and when Russian communism was established, it reinforced the idea that communism was anti-German.
- **Authoritarianism**: the extreme right favoured the restoration of some authoritarian, dictatorial regime – though in the early 1920s there was no real consensus on what kind of strong government and leadership would be established.
- **Nationalism**: nationalism was at the core of the extreme right, but Germany's national pride had been deeply hurt by the events of 1918–19. Not surprisingly, from the time of the Treaty of Versailles, this conservative-nationalist response reinforced the ideas of the 'stab in the back' myth and the '**November criminals**'. The war, it was argued, had been lost not because of any military defeat suffered by the army, but as a result of the betrayal by unpatriotic forces within Germany. These were said to include pacifists, socialists, democrats and Jews. Right-wing politicians found a whole range of scapegoats to take the blame for German acceptance of the Armistice.

Worse still, these 'November criminals' had been prepared to overthrow the monarchy and establish a republic. Then, to add insult to injury, they had accepted the 'shameful peace' of Versailles. The extreme right accepted such interpretations, distorted as they were. They not only served to remove any responsibility from Imperial Germany, but also acted as a powerful stick with which to beat the new leaders of Weimar Germany.

Organisations of the extreme right

The extreme right appeared in various forms. It included a number of political parties and was also the driving force behind the activities of various paramilitary organisations.

DNVP

The DNVP (German National People's Party) was a coalition of nationalist-minded old imperial conservative parties and included such groups as the Fatherland Party and the Pan-German League. From the very start, it contained extremist and racist elements. Although it was still the party of landowners and industrialists, it had a broad appeal amongst some of the middle classes. It was by

Key terms

Anti-Marxism
Opposition to the ideology of Karl Marx.

Authoritarianism
A broad term meaning government by strong non-democratic leadership.

Nationalism
Grew from the national spirit to unify Germany in the nineteenth century. Supported a strong policy to embrace all German-speakers in eastern Europe.

November criminals
Those who signed the November Armistice and a term of abuse to vilify all those who supported the democratic republic.

Key question
How did the extreme right manifest itself in different ways?

far the largest party in the *Reichstag* on the extreme right and was able to poll 15.1 per cent in the 1920 election.

Racist nationalism

The emergence of racist nationalism, or *völkisch* nationalism, was clearly apparent before 1914, but the effects of the war and its aftermath increased its attraction for many on the right. By the early 1920s there were probably about 70 relatively small splinter nationalist parties, which were also racist and anti-Semitic, e.g. the Nazi Party.

Bavaria became a particular haven for such groups, since the regional state government was sufficiently **reactionary** to tolerate them. One such group was the German Workers' Party, originally founded by Anton Drexler. Adolf Hitler joined the party in 1919 and within two years had become its leader. However, during the years 1919–24, regional and policy differences divided such groups and attempts to unify the nationalist right ended in failure. When, in 1923, Hitler and the Nazis attempted to organise an uprising with the Munich Beer Hall *putsch*, it ended in fiasco (see pages 41–3). It was not until the mid-1920s, when Hitler began to bring the different groups together under the leadership of the NSDAP, that a powerful political force was created.

Freikorps

The *Freikorps* that flourished in the post-war environment attracted the more brutal and ugly elements of German militarism. As a result of the demobilisation of the armed forces there were nearly 200 **paramilitary units** around Germany by 1919.

The *Freikorps* became a law unto themselves and they were employed by the government in a crucial role to suppress the threats from the extreme left. However, as the *Freikorps* was anti-republican and committed to the restoration of authoritarian rule, they had no respect for the Weimar governments. Their bloody actions became known as the '**White Terror**' and showed they were quite prepared to use acts of violence and murder to intimidate others.

Consul Organisation

From 1920 the Weimar governments tried to control the actions of the *Freikorps*, but a new threat emerged from the right wing in the form of political assassination. In the years 1919–22 there were 376 political murders – 22 by the left and 354 by the right. The most notorious terrorist gang was known as the 'Consul Organisation' because it was responsible for the assassination of a number of key republican politicians:

- Matthias Erzberger, Finance Minister 1919–21. Murdered because he was a Catholic and a member of the ZP and had signed the Armistice.

Key terms

Reactionary
Opposing change and supporting a return to traditional ways.

Paramilitary units
Informal non-legal military squads.

White Terror
The 'Whites' were seen as the opponents (in contrast to the Reds). The 'White Terror' refers to the suppression of the soviet republic in Bavaria in March 1919.

Key date

The murder of Matthias Erzberger: 26 August 1921

A cartoon drawn in 1919 by the German artist Grosz. He caricatures the stereotyped right-wing officer. The title, *The White General*, relates to the 'White Terror' in opposition to the Reds of the left-wing movement.

- Walther Rathenau, Foreign Minister, 1921–2 (who drew up the Rapallo treaty with USSR). Murdered because he was Jewish and was committed to democracy.
- Karl Gareis, leader of the USPD. Murdered on 9 June 1921 because he was a committed socialist.

> **Key date**
>
> The murder of Walter Rathenau: 24 June 1922

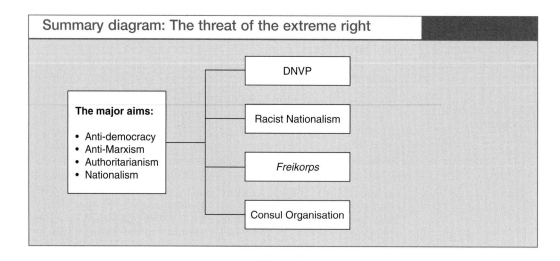

Summary diagram: The threat of the extreme right

The major aims:

- Anti-democracy
- Anti-Marxism
- Authoritarianism
- Nationalism

- DNVP
- Racist Nationalism
- *Freikorps*
- Consul Organisation

Key question
How significant was the Kapp *putsch*?

Key date

The Kapp *putsch*:
March 1920

5 | Extreme Right Uprisings

The Kapp *putsch*

The *Freikorps* played a central role in the first attempt by the extreme right wing to seize power from the constitutional government. This was because by early 1920 there was considerable unease within the ranks of the *Freikorps* at the demands to reduce the size of the German army according to the terms of the Versailles Treaty.

When it was proposed to disband two brigades of the army, the Ehrhardt Marine Brigade and the Baltikum that were stationed in the Berlin area, Wolfgang Kapp (see profile below) and General Lüttwitz decided to exploit the situation. They encouraged 12,000 troops to march on Berlin and seize the main buildings of the capital virtually unopposed, where they installed a new government.

Significantly, the German army did not provide any resistance to this *putsch*. In spite of requests from Ebert and the Chancellor to put down the rebellious forces, the army was not prepared to become involved with either side. Although it did not join those involved in the *putsch*, it failed to support the legitimate government. General von Seeckt, the senior officer in the Defence Ministry, spoke for many colleagues when he declared:

> Troops do not fire on troops. So, you perhaps intend, Herr Minister, that a battle be fought before the Brandenburger Tor between troops that have fought side by side against a common enemy? When *Reichswehr* fires on *Reichswehr* all comradeship within the officers' corps will have vanished.

Profile: Wolfgang Kapp 1868–1922

1868	– Born in New York
1870	– Returned to Germany with his family
1886–1920	– Qualified as a doctor of law and then appointed as a Prussian civil servant in various posts
1917	– Helped to found the right-wing German Fatherland Party
1918	– Elected to the *Reichstag*
	– Opposed the abdication of Wilhelm II and remained committed to the restoration of the monarchy
1920	– Collaborated with Ehrhardt and Lüttwitz to launch the *putsch*. Briefly appointed chancellor by the leaders of the *putsch*. Fled to Sweden
1922	– Returned to Germany but died whilst awaiting trial

Really, only a few points stand out about Kapp. He has been described as 'a neurotic with delusions' or simply a 'crank' who represented the extreme nationalist-conservative views. He did not play any major part in politics of Imperial Germany until the war, when he was one of the founders of the German Fatherland Party. After the war he campaigned for the restoration of Kaiser Wilhelm, but his *putsch* was a fiasco. Interestingly, some of the men involved in his *putsch* had swastika symbols on their helmets.

The army's decision to put its own interests before its obligation to defend the government forced the latter to flee the capital and move to Stuttgart. However, the *putsch* collapsed. Before leaving Berlin, the SPD members of the government had called for a general strike, which soon paralysed the capital and quickly spread to the rest of the country. After four days, it was clear that Kapp and his government exerted no real authority and they fled the city.

The aftermath of the Kapp *putsch*

At first sight the collapse of the Kapp *putsch* could be viewed as a major success for the Weimar Republic. In the six days of crisis, it had retained the backing of the people of Berlin and had effectively withstood a major threat from the extreme right. However, what is significant is that the Kapp *putsch* had taken place at all. In this sense, the Kapp *putsch* highlights clearly the weakness of the Weimar Republic. The army's behaviour at the time of the *putsch* was typical of its right-wing attitudes and its lack of sympathy for the Republic. During the months after the *coup*, the government failed to confront this problem.

The army leadership had revealed its unreliability. Yet, amazingly, at the end of that very month Seeckt was appointed Chief of the Army Command (1920–6). He was appointed because he enjoyed the confidence of his fellow officers and ignored the fact that his support for the Republic was at best lukewarm. Under Seeckt's influence, the organisation of the army was remodelled and its status redefined:

- He imposed very strict military discipline and recruited new troops, increasingly at the expense of the *Freikorps*.
- However, he was determined to uphold the independence of the army. He believed it held a privileged position that placed it beyond direct government control. For example, he turned a blind eye to the Versailles disarmament clauses in order to increase the size of the army with more modern weapons.

Many within its ranks believed that the army served some higher purpose to the nation as a whole. It had the right to intervene as it saw fit without regard to its obligations to the Republic. All this suggests that the aftermath of the Kapp *putsch*, the Ebert-Groener Pact (see pages 9–10) and the Constitution's failure to reform the structures of army had made it a '**state within a state**'.

The judiciary also continued with the old political values that had not changed since imperial times. It enjoyed the advantage of maintaining its independence from the Weimar Constitution, but it questioned the legal rights of the new republic and reached some dubious and obviously biased decisions. Those involved in the *putsch* of 1920 never felt the full rigour of the law:

- Kapp died awaiting trial.
- Lüttwitz was granted early retirement.
- Only one of the 705 prosecuted was actually found guilty and sentenced to five years' imprisonment.

State within a state A situation where the authority and government of the state are threatened by a rival power base.

Key term

Over the years 1919–22 it was clear that the judges were biased and their hearts did not lie with the Weimar Republic:

- Out of the 354 right-wing assassins only 28 were found guilty and punished (but no-one was executed).
- Of the 22 left-wing assassins 10 were sentenced to death.

The Munich Beer Hall *putsch*

Key question
Who were the plotters and why did they fail?

Key date

The Munich Beer Hall *putsch*:
8–9 November 1923

Although the Munich Beer Hall *putsch* was one of the threats faced by the young republic in the year 1923, the event is also a crucial part of the rise of Hitler and the Nazis. So the details of the events also relate to Chapter 5 on pages 90–2.

In the short term it should be noted that the government of the State of Bavaria was under the control of the ultra-conservative Gustav von Kahr, who blamed most of Germany's problems on the national government in Berlin. Like Hitler, he wished to destroy the republican regime, although his long-term aim was the creation of an independent Bavaria. By October 1923 General von Lossow, the Army's commander in Bavaria, had fallen under von Kahr's spell and had even begun to disobey orders from the Defence Minister from Berlin. And so it was both of these ultra-conservatives who plotted with Hitler and the Nazis to 'March on Berlin'.

A cartoon of 1924 derides the judiciary after the trial of Hitler and Ludendorff. The judge simply says 'High treason? Rubbish! The worst we can charge them with is breaking by-laws about entertaining in public.'

Table 2.4: The plotters in the Munich Beer Hall *putsch*

Name	Position	Background/attitude	Involvement
Erich von Ludendorff	Retired general	Took part in Kapp *putsch*. Opposed to democracy (see also pages 39–41)	Collaborated with Hitler and supported the *putsch* on 8–9 November
Gustav von Kahr	Leader of the Bavarian state government	Deeply anti-democratic and sympathetic to many of the right-wing extremists. Committed to the restoration of the monarchy in an independent Bavaria	Planned with Hitler and Lossow to seize power, but became wary. Forced to co-operate with his rally on 8 November, though did not support the *putsch* on 9 November
Otto von Lossow	Commander of the Bavarian section of the German army	Despised Weimar democracy and supported authoritarian rule. Very conservative	Planned with Hitler and Kahr to seize power, but became wary. Forced to co-operate in the rally on 8 November, though did not support the *putsch* on 9 November
Adolf Hitler	Leader of the Nazi Party	Extremist: anti-Semitic, anti-democratic and anti-communist. Backed by the Nazi SA	Planned and wholly committed to seize power. Forced the hands of Kahr and Lossow and carried on with the *putsch* on 9 November
Hans von Seeckt	General. Chief of the Army Command, 1920–6	Unsympathetic to democracy and keen to preserve the interests of the army, but suspicious of Hitler and the Nazis (see page 43)	Initially ambiguous attitude in early November. But in the crisis he used his powers to command the armed forces to resist the *putsch*

By the first week of November 1923, Kahr and Lossow, fearing failure, decided to abandon the plan. However, Hitler was not so cautious and preferred to press on rather than lose the opportunity. On 8 November Hitler, together with his Nazi supporters, stormed into and took control of a large rally, which von Kahr was addressing in one of Munich's beer halls, and declared a 'national revolution'. Under pressure, Kahr and Lossow co-operated and agreed to proceed with the uprising, but in reality they had lost their nerve when Seeckt used his powers to command the armed forces to resist the *putsch*. So when, on the next day, the Nazis attempted to take Munich they had insufficient support and the Bavarian police easily crushed the *putsch*. Fourteen Nazis were killed and Hitler himself was arrested on a charge of treason.

Key question
How significant was the Munich Beer Hall *putsch*?

The aftermath of the Munich Beer Hall *putsch*

On one level the inglorious result of the Nazi *putsch* was encouraging for Weimar democracy. It withstood a dangerous threat in what was a difficult year. Most significantly, Seeckt and the army did not throw in their lot with the Nazis – which upset Hitler so much that he described him as a 'lackey of the Weimar Republic'. However, once again it was the dealings of the judiciary that raised so much concern:

- Hitler was sentenced to a mere five years (the minimum stipulation for treason). His imprisonment at Landsberg provided quite reasonable conditions and he was released after less than 10 months.
- Ludendorff was acquitted on the grounds that although he had been present at the time of the *putsch*, he was there 'by accident'!

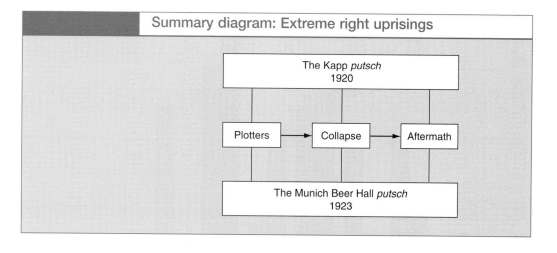

Summary diagram: Extreme right uprisings

6 | Weimar Democracy: A Republic Without Republicans

Key question
What was the greatest threat to Weimar democracy?

The optimism of the first election of the Republic (see pages 17–18) gave way to concerns in the election of June 1920. The results can be seen in Figure 2.3 and they raise several key points:

- The combined support for the three main democratic parties declined dramatically:
  - 1919: 76.1 per cent
  - 1920: 48.0 per cent
  (The figures do not include the DVP under the leadership of Stresemann which voted against the Weimar Constitution at first, but became committed to the Republic from 1921.)
- The performance for each of the pro-democratic parties was as follows:
  - the SPD declined sharply from 37.9 to 21.7 per cent
  - the DDP declined catastrophically from 18.5 to 8.3 per cent
  - the ZP dropped down slightly from 19.75 to 18.0 per cent.
- The support for the extreme left and right increased, especially the DNVP:
  - the DNVP increased from 10.3 to 15.1 per cent
  - the KPD/USPD increased from 7.6 to 20.0 per cent.

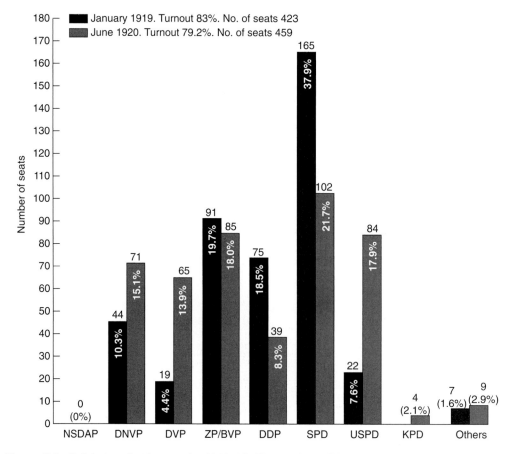

Figure 2.3: *Reichstag* election results 1919–20. (See major political parties on page 16.)

Weimar governments

The Weimar Republic not only faced overt opposition from both the extremes but also its democratic supporters struggled with the practical problem of creating and maintaining workable government coalitions. In the four years 1919–23 Weimar had six governments – the longest of which lasted just 18 months (see Table 2.5).

Table 2.5: Governments of the Weimar Republic 1919–23

Period in office	Chancellor	Make-up of the coalition
1919	Philipp Scheidemann	SPD, ZP, DDP
1919–20	Gustav Bauer	SPD, ZP, DDP
1920	Hermann Müller	SPD, Centre, DDP
1920–1	Konstantin Fehrenbach	ZP, DDP, DVP
1921–2	Joseph Wirth	SPD, DDP, ZP
1922–3	Wilhelm Cuno	ZP, DDP, DVP

Conclusion

The success of the democratic parties in the *Reichstag* elections of January 1919 at first disguised some of Weimar's fundamental problems in its political structure. But opposition to the Republic ranged from indifference to brutal violence and, as early as 1920, democratic support for Weimar began to switch to the extremes. This is shown by the results of the first election after the Treaty of Versailles.

The extent of the opposition from the extreme right to democracy was not always appreciated. Instead, President Ebert and the Weimar governments overestimated the threat from the extreme left and they came to rely on the forces of reaction for justice and law and order. This was partly because the conservative forces successfully exploited the image of the left as a powerful threat. So, in many respects, it was the persistence of the old attitudes in the major traditional national institutions that represented the greatest long-term threat to the Republic. The violent forces of counter-revolution, as shown by the *putsches* of Kapp and Hitler, were too weak and disorganised to seize power in the early years. But the danger of the extreme right was actually insidious; it was the real growing threat to Weimar democracy.

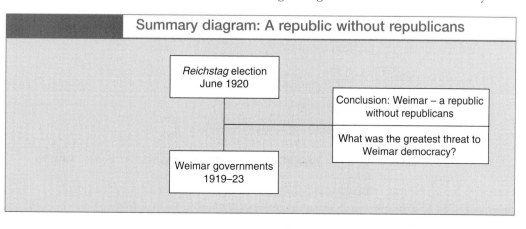

Summary diagram: A republic without republicans

Reichstag election
June 1920

Conclusion: Weimar – a republic without republicans

What was the greatest threat to Weimar democracy?

Weimar governments
1919–23

Study Guide: AS Question

In the style of OCR A

How flawed was the Weimar Constitution? Explain your
answer. (50 marks)

Exam tips

The cross-references are intended to take you straight to the material that will help you to answer the question.

The question gives you a very focused problem to consider and you will need to assess the various areas of potential weakness: the use of proportional representation (PR); the role of the president; and the continuation of traditional institutions. Try hard not to think about this only in terms of 1933. The Third Reich was not inevitable. Was the PR system wrong for Germany in the 1920s? Look at both sides and use your knowledge to judge the matter. Did it make stable government very difficult? Did it encourage extremist parties? Do not overlook the communists and others on the left; this is about much more than the impact of PR on the political right. To answer these questions you will need to look at material in other chapters: the 'golden years' of 1924–9 (Chapter 4, pages 60–84) as well as the troubled years of 1929–32 (Chapter 6, pages 101–21). The same constitution underpinned the politics and the elections of both (Table 2.1, page 24).

Next you need to examine the powers of the president. The case here might be stronger: was the political balance of power between the president and the *Reichstag* badly drawn? Article 48 needs a special focus in your answer. To do that you could compare how the president acted in two periods of crisis: 1923–4 (Chapters 2 and 3, pages 20–45 and 47–58) and 1933 (Chapters 6 and 7). Does that show us that the real problem was how an individual president used those powers, i.e. Ebert acted properly as the president of a democracy whereas Hindenburg did not?

Finally, the third area to think about is the constitution's failure to reform institutions. Weimar needed a civil service, a judiciary and an army, but none had strong loyalties to the republic. Did the continuation of powerful conservative forces undermine the republic and democracy? Your conclusion needs to pull together the conclusions in each part to take an overview. In that, do not overlook the context in which Weimar was born. Was the fundamental flaw of post-1918 Germany a people divided about what they wanted?

3 The Great Inflation

Key dates

1921	May	IARC (Inter-Allied Reparations Commission) fixed reparations at £6600 million (132 billion gold marks)
1923	January	Franco-Belgian occupation of the Ruhr Passive resistance proclaimed
	Jan–Nov	Period of hyper-inflation
	August	Stresemann made chancellor of Germany
	Aug–Nov	Stresemann's 100 days
	December	Introduction of the *Rentenmark*
1924	April	Dawes Plan proposed and accepted

1 | The Economic Background

In the 20 years before the First World War the German economy grew immensely. By 1914 it had become arguably the most powerful economy on the continent and it was in a position to compete with Britain's supremacy. These strengths were based upon:

- extensive natural resources, e.g. coal, iron-ore
- an advanced and well-developed industrial base, e.g. engineering, chemicals, electrics
- a well-educated population, with special technical skills
- an advanced banking system.

However, the result of four years of **total war** seriously dislocated the German economy. So, although the economy still had many natural strengths and great potential, by 1919 it faced fundamental economic problems. The most notable of these were:

- The loss of resources from such territories as the Saar, Alsace-Lorraine and Silesia which, for example, resulted in a 16 per cent decline in coal production, 13 per cent decline in arable agricultural land and 48 per cent loss of iron-ore.
- The cost of paying reparations (set at £6600 million in 1921).
- The growing increase in prices. Between 1914 and 1918 the real value of the mark fell, dropping from 4.2 to 8.9 against the US dollar, while the prices of basic goods increased nearly four-fold.
- The increase in national debt to 144,000 million marks by 1919 compared with 5000 million marks in 1914.

Significantly, Germany had always depended on its ability to export to achieve economic growth. However, between 1914 and 1918 world trade had collapsed and even after 1919 it remained very sluggish.

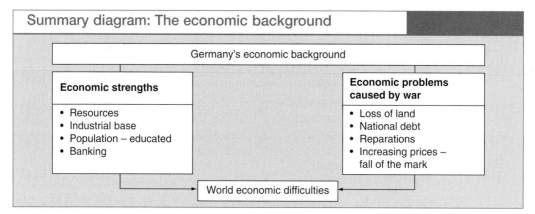

Summary diagram: The economic background

2 | The Causes of the German Inflation

Germany's growing economic problems came to a head in 1923 when prices soared and money values spiralled down. This is often referred to as **hyper-inflation**. However, the crises of that year blinded many to the fact that prices had been rising since the early months of the war. Many Germans glibly assumed it was a result of the Treaty of Versailles and particularly the reparations. Still more unthinking explanations simply blamed it on the financial greed and corruption of the Jews.

However, with hindsight it is clear that the fundamental cause of the inflation was the huge increase in the amount of paper money in circulation, resulting from the government's printing more and more notes to pay off the interest on its massive debts. The causes of the Great Inflation can be divided into three phases:

- long term – the military demands of the First World War (1914–18) led to an enormous increase in financial costs
- medium term – the costs of introducing social reforms and welfare and the pressure to satisfy the demands for reparation payments from 1921
- short term – the French occupation of the Ruhr in 1923 resulted in crisis and the government of Cuno encouraged a policy of '**passive resistance**'.

Key question
Why did Germany suffer hyper-inflation?

Key terms

Hyper-inflation
Hyper-inflation is unusual. In Germany in 1923, it meant that prices spiralled out of control because the government increased the amount of money being printed. As a result, it displaced the whole economy.

Passive resistance
Refusal to work with occupying forces.

Key terms

War bonds
In order to raise more money to pay for the war, Imperial Germany encouraged people to invest into government funds in the belief they were helping to finance the war and their savings would be secure.

Balanced budget
A financial programme in which a government does not spend more than it raises in revenue.

Long term

Not surprisingly, Germany had made no financial provision for a long drawn-out war. However, despite the increasing cost of the war, the Kaiser's government had decided, for political reasons, against increases in taxation. Instead, it had borrowed massive sums by selling '**war bonds**' to the public. When this proved insufficient from 1916, it simply allowed the national debt to grow bigger and bigger.

The result of Imperial Germany's financial policies was that by the end of 1918 only 16 per cent of war expenditure had been raised from taxation – 84 per cent had been borrowed.

Another factor was that the war years had seen almost full employment. This was because the economy had concentrated on the supply of military weapons. But, since production was necessarily military based, it did not satisfy the requirements of the civilian consumers. Consequently, the high demand for, and the shortage of consumer goods began to push prices up.

Victory would doubtless have allowed Imperial Germany to settle its debts by claiming reparations from the Allies, but defeat meant the reverse. The Weimar Republic had to cope with the massive costs of war. By 1919, Germany's finances were described by Volker Berghahn as 'an unholy mess'.

Medium term

The government of the Weimar Republic (like any government with a large deficit) could control inflation only by narrowing the gap between the government's income and expenditure through:

- increasing taxation in order to raises its income
- cutting government spending in order to reduce its expenditure.

However, in view of Germany's domestic situation neither of these options was particularly attractive, as both would alienate the people and cause political and social difficulties, such as increased unemployment and industrial decline.

Consequently, from 1919 the Weimar government guided by Erzberger, the Finance Minister (see page 37), extensively increased taxation on profits, wealth and income. However, it decided not to go so far as aiming to **balance the budget**. It decided to adopt a policy of deficit financing in the belief that it would:

- maintain the demand for goods and, thereby, create work
- overcome the problems of demobilising millions of returning troops
- cover the cost of public spending on an extensive welfare state, e.g. health insurance, housing and benefits for the disabled and orphans
- reduce the real value of the national debt.

Deficit financing means planning to increase the nation's debt by reducing taxation in order to give the people more money to spend and so increase the demand for goods and thereby create work. The government believed that this would enable Germany to overcome the problems of demobilisation – a booming economy would ensure there were plenty of jobs for the returning soldiers and sailors – and also reduce the real value of the national debt. Unfortunately, an essential part of this policy was to allow inflation to continue.

The reparations issue should be seen as only a contributory factor to the inflation. It was certainly not the primary cause. Nevertheless, the sum drawn up by the Reparations Commission added to the economic burden facing the Weimar government because the reparation payments had to be in **hard currency**, like dollars and gold (not inflated German marks). In order to pay their reparations, the Weimar governments proceeded to print larger quantities of marks and sell them to obtain the stronger currencies of other countries. This was not a solution. It was merely a short-term measure that had serious consequences. The mark went into sharp decline and inflation climbed even higher (see Table 3.1).

Table 3.1: The Great Inflation: exchange rate and wholesale prices

The Great Inflation	Exchange rate of German marks against the dollar	Wholesale price index. The index is created from a scale of prices starting with 1 for 1914
1914 July	4.2	1
1919 January	8.9	2
1920 January	14.0	4
1920 July	39.5	N/A
1921 January	64.9	14
1921 July	76.7	N/A
1922 January	191.8	37
1922 July	493.2	100
1923 January	17,792	2,785
1923 July	353,412	74,787
1923 September	98,860,000	23,949,000
1923 November	200,000,000,000	750,000,000,000

Short term

Germany had already been allowed to postpone several instalments of her reparations payments in early 1922, but an attempt to resolve the crisis on an international level by calling the Genoa Economic Conference was ill fated. When, in July 1922, the German government made another request for a 'holiday' from making reparations payments, the final stage of the country's inflationary crisis set in.

The French government, at this time led by Raymond Poincaré, suspected German intentions and was determined to secure what was seen as France's rightful claims. Therefore, when in December 1922 the Reparations Commission declared Germany to be in default, Poincaré ordered French and Belgian troops to occupy the Ruhr, the industrial heartland of Germany. In the next few months the inflationary spiral ran out of control – hyper-inflation.

Key dates

'Passive resistance' in Ruhr against French and Belgian soldiers: 13 January 1923

Period of hyper-inflation: January–November 1923

The government, led by Wilhelm Cuno, embarked on a policy of 'passive resistance' and in a way the invasion did help to unite the German people. It urged the workers to go on strike and refuse to co-operate with the French authorities, although it also promised to carry on paying their wages. At the same time, the government was unable to collect taxes from the Ruhr area and the French prevented the delivery of coal to the rest of Germany, thus forcing the necessary stocks of fuel to be imported.

In this situation, the government's finances collapsed and the mark fell to worthless levels. By autumn 1923, it cost more to print a bank note than the note was worth and the *Reichsbank* was forced to use newspaper presses to produce sufficient money. The German currency ceased to have any real value and the German people had to resort to barter (see Table 3.2).

Table 3.2: Prices in the Great Inflation (in German marks)

Items for sale in	1913	Summer 1923	November 1923
1 kg of bread	0.29	1,200	428,000,000,000
1 egg	0.08	5,000	80,000,000,000
1 kg of butter	2.70	26,000	6,000,000,000,000
1 kg of beef	1.75	18,800	5,600,000,000,000
1 pair of shoes	12.00	1,000,000	32,000,000,000,000

Conclusion

The fundamental cause of the German Inflation is to be found in the mismanagement of Germany's finances from 1914 onwards. Certainly, the inflationary spiral did not increase at an even rate and there were short periods, as in the spring of 1920 and the winter of 1920–1, when it did actually slacken. However, at no time was there willingness by the various German governments to bring spending and borrowing back within reasonable limits.

Until the end of 1918 the cost of waging war was the excuse, but in the immediate post-war period the high levels of debt were allowed to continue. It has been argued by some that the inflation remained quite modest in the years 1914–22 and perhaps acceptable in view of all the various difficulties facing the new government. However, the payment of reparations from 1921 simply added to an already desperate situation and the government found it more convenient to print money than to tackle the basic problems facing the economy.

By the end of 1922 hyper-inflation had set in. Cuno's government made no effort to deal with the situation. Indeed, it could be said that Cuno deliberately exacerbated the economic crisis and played on the nationalist fervour brought by the popular decision to encourage 'passive resistance'. It was only in August 1923 when the German economy was on the verge of complete collapse that a new coalition government was formed under Gustav Stresemann. He found the will to introduce an economic policy, which was aimed at controlling the amount of money in circulation.

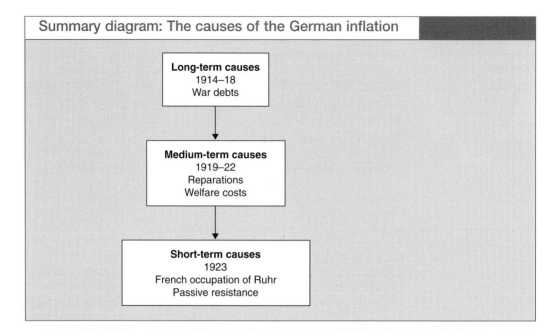

Summary diagram: The causes of the German inflation

Long-term causes
1914–18
War debts

Medium-term causes
1919–22
Reparations
Welfare costs

Short-term causes
1923
French occupation of Ruhr
Passive resistance

3 | The Consequences of the Great Inflation

It has been claimed that the worst consequence of the inflation was the damage done to the German middle class. Stresemann himself said as much in 1927. Later on in the 1930s it was generally assumed that the reason a large proportion of the middle class voted for the Nazis was because of their economic sufferings in 1923. In the light of recent historical research, such assumptions have come to be questioned and a much more complex interpretation has emerged about the impact of the inflation on the whole of society.

The key to understanding who gained and who lost during the period of the hyper-inflation lies in considering each individual's savings and their amount of debt. However, it was not always clearly linked to class differences. So what did this mean in practice?

The real winners were those sections of the community who were able to pay off their debts, mortgages and loans with inflated and worthless money. This obviously worked to the advantage of such groups as businessmen and homeowners, which included members of the middle class. Those who recognised the situation for what it was exploited it by making massive gains from buying up property from those financially desperate. Some businessmen profited from the situation by borrowing cheaply and investing in new industrial enterprises. Amongst these, one of the most notorious examples was Hugo Stinnes who, by the end of 1923, controlled 20 per cent of German industry.

At the other extreme, were those who depended on their savings. Any German who had money invested in bank accounts with interest rates found their real value had eroded. Most famously, millions who had bought and invested in war bonds now could not get their money back. The bonds were worth

Key question
Why did some Germans lose and some win?

nothing. Those living on fixed incomes, such as pensioners, found themselves in a similar plight. Their savings quickly lost value, since any increase was wiped out by inflation (see Table 3.3).

Table 3.3: Financial winners and losers

Financial winners and losers	Explanation of gains or losses
Mortgage holders	Borrowed money was easily paid off in valueless money
Savers	Money invested was eroded
Exporters	Sales to foreign countries was attractive because of the rate of exchange
Those on fixed incomes	Income declined in real terms dramatically
Recipients of welfare	Depended on charity or state. Payments fell behind the inflation rate
Long-term renters/landlords	Income was fixed in the long term and so it declined in real terms
The German State	Large parts of the government debt were paid off in valueless money (but not reparations)

Key question
Who were the winners and the losers?

The human consequences

The material impact of the hyper-inflation has recently been the subject of considerable historical research in Germany and, as a result, our understanding of this period has been greatly increased and many previous conclusions have been revised. However, you should remember that the following discussion of the effects of the hyper-inflation on whole classes deals with broad categories, e.g. region and age, rather than individual examples. Two people from the same social class could be affected in very different ways depending on their individual circumstances.

Peasants

In the countryside the peasants coped reasonably well as food remained in demand. They depended less on money for the provision of the necessities of life because they were more self-sufficient.

Mittelstand

Shopkeepers and craftsmen also seem to have done reasonably good business, especially if they were prepared to exploit the demands of the market.

Industrial workers

Workers' real wages and standard of living improved until 1922. It was in the chaos of 1923 that, when the trade unions were unable to negotiate wage settlements for their members, wages could not keep pace with the rate of inflation and a very real decline took place. However, as they had fewer savings, they lost proportionally less than those living on saved income. Unemployment did go up to 4.1 per cent in 1923, but it was still at a relatively low level.

Key term

Mittelstand
Can be translated as 'the middle class', but in German society it tends to represent the lower middle classes, e.g. shopkeepers, craft workers and clerks. Traditionally independent and self-reliant but increasingly felt squeezed out between the power and influence of big business and industrial labour.

Children playing with blocks of worthless banknotes in 1923.

Civil servants

The fate of public employees is probably the most difficult to analyse. Their income fell sharply in the years 1914–20, but they made real gains in 1921–2. They suffered again in the chaos of 1923 because they depended on fixed salaries, which fell in value before the end of each month. They tended to gain – if they were buying a property on a mortgage – but many had been attracted to buy the war bonds and so lost out.

Retired

The old generally suffered badly because they depended on fixed pensions and savings.

Businessmen

Generally, they did well because they bought up property with worthless money and they paid off mortgages. They also benefited if they made sales to foreign countries, as the rate of exchange was very attractive.

Key question
In what other ways
did the Great Inflation
affect people's lives?

Other social effects

By merely listing the financial statistics of the Great Inflation, there is a danger of overlooking the very real human dimension. As early as February 1923 the health minister delivered a speech to the *Reichstag*:

> … It is understandable that under such unhygienic circumstances, health levels are deteriorating ever more seriously. While the figures for the Reich as a whole are not yet available, we do have a preliminary mortality rate for towns with 100,000 or more inhabitants. After having fallen in 1920–1, it has climbed again for the year 1921–2, rising from 12.6 to 13.4 per thousand inhabitants … thus, oedema [an unpleasant medical condition which occurs when water accumulates in parts of the body] is reappearing, this so-called war dropsy, which is a consequence of a bad and overly watery diet. There are increases in stomach disorders and food poisoning, which are the result of eating spoiled foods. There are complaints of the appearance of scurvy, which is a consequence of an unbalanced and improper diet. From various parts of the Reich, reports are coming in about an increase in suicides … More and more often one finds 'old age' and 'weakness' listed in the official records as the cause of death; these are equivalent to death through hunger.

Even more telling than the health minister's description about Germany's declining health were the possible effects on behaviour, as people began to resort to desperate solutions:

- a decline in law and order
- an increase in crime
- a decline in 'morality', for example, more prostitution
- a growth in suicides
- an increase in prejudice and a tendency to find scapegoats, e.g. Jews.

It has often been suggested that such social problems contributed to people's lack of faith in the republican system. The connection is difficult to prove, as it is not easy to assess the importance of morality and religious codes in past societies. However, it would be foolish to dismiss out of hand their effects upon German society and its traditional set of values. At the very least, the loss of some old values led to increased tensions. Even more significantly, when another crisis developed at the end of the decade, the people's confidence in the ability of Weimar to maintain social stability was eventually lost. In that sense the inflation of 1923 was not the reason for the Weimar Republic's decline, but it caused psychological damage that continued to affect the Republic in future years.

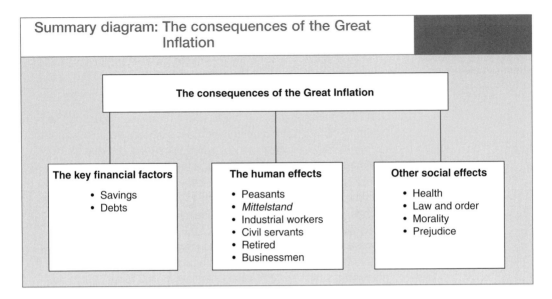

Summary diagram: The consequences of the Great Inflation

The consequences of the Great Inflation

The key financial factors
- Savings
- Debts

The human effects
- Peasants
- *Mittelstand*
- Industrial workers
- Civil servants
- Retired
- Businessmen

Other social effects
- Health
- Law and order
- Morality
- Prejudice

4 | Stresemann's 100 Days

In the summer of 1923 the problems facing the Weimar Republic came to a head and it seemed close to collapse:

- the German currency had collapsed and hyper-inflation had set in
- French and Belgian troops were occupying the Ruhr
- the German government had no clear policy on the occupation, except for 'passive resistance'
- there were various left-wing political disturbances across the country – in Saxony the creation of an SPD/KPD regional state government resulted in an attempted communist uprising (pages 34–5)
- the ultra-conservative state government in Bavaria was defying the national government. This finally resulted in the Munich Beer Hall *putsch* (see pages 41–3).

Yet, only a few months later a semblance of calm and normality returned. The Weimar Republic's remarkable survival illustrates the telling comment of the historian Peukert that even 1923 shows 'there are no entirely hopeless situations in history'.

Stresemann's achievements

It is important to recognise that, during the summer of 1923, things had just been allowed to slide under the chancellor, Cuno. Nevertheless, the appointment of Gustav Stresemann as chancellor in August 1923 resulted in the emergence of a politician who was actually prepared to take difficult political decisions. Stresemann led a broad coalition of DVP, DDP, ZP and SPD and aimed to resolve Germany's economic plight and also tackle the problem of her weakness internationally.

Key question
How did the Weimar Republic survive the crisis of 1923?

Key dates

Stresemann appointed chancellor: 12 August 1923

Stresemann's 100 days of leadership: August–November 1923

Within a few weeks Stresemann made a series of crucial initiatives:

- First, in September, he called off the 'passive resistance' in the Ruhr and promised to resume the payment of reparations. He needed to conciliate the French in order to evoke some sympathy for Germany's economic and international position.
- Under the guidance of Finance Minister, Hans Luther, the government's expenditure was sharply cut in order to reduce the deficit. Over 700,000 public employees were sacked.
- He appointed the leading financial expert Hjalmar Schacht to oversee the introduction of a new German currency. In December 1923 the trillions of old German marks were replaced and a new stable currency, the *Rentenmark*, was established.
- He evoked some sympathy from the Allies for Germany by the 'miracle of the *Rentenmark*' and his conciliatory policy. He therefore asked the Allies to hold an international conference to consider Germany's economic plight and, as a result, the Dawes Committee was established. Its report, the Dawes Plan, was published in April 1924. It did not reduce the overall reparations bill, but for the first five years it fixed the payments in accordance with Germany's ability to pay (see pages 72–3).
- The extremists of the left and the right were defeated (pages 35 and 41–3).

Key dates

Introduction of the *Rentenmark*: December 1923

Dawes Plan proposed and accepted: April 1924

The survival of Weimar

Although Stresemann's resolute action in tackling the problems might help to explain why the years of crisis came to an end, on its own it does not help us to understand why the Weimar Republic was able to come through. The Republic's survival in 1923 was in marked contrast to its collapse 10 years later when challenged by the Nazis.

Why, then, did the Republic not collapse during the crisis-ridden months before Stresemann's emergence on the political scene? This is a difficult question to answer, though the following factors provide clues:

- Popular anger was directed more towards the French and the Allies than towards the Weimar Republic itself.
- Despite the effects of inflation, workers did not suffer to the same extent as they did during the mass unemployment of the 1930s.
- Similarly, employers tended to show less hostility to the Republic in its early years than they did in the early 1930s at the start of the depression.
- Some businessmen did very well out of the inflation, which made them tolerant of the Republic.

If these suggestions about public attitudes towards the Republic are correct, then it seems that, although there was distress and disillusionment in 1923, hostility to the Weimar Republic had not yet reached unbearable levels – as it was to do 10 years later.

Moreover, in 1923 there was no obvious political alternative to Weimar. The extreme left had not really recovered from its divisions and suppression in the years 1918–21 and, in its isolated position, it did not enjoy enough support to overthrow Weimar.

The extreme right, too, was not yet strong enough. It was similarly divided and had no clear plans. The failure of the Kapp *putsch* served as a clear warning of the dangers of taking hasty action and was possibly the reason why the army made no move in 1923.

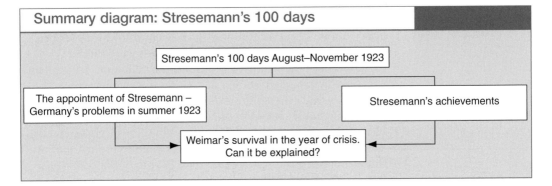

Summary diagram: Stresemann's 100 days

Study Guide: AS Question

In the style of OCR A

'Reparations were the **main** cause of the hyper-inflation of 1923.' How far do you agree with this view? Explain your answer.

(50 marks)

Exam tips

The question asks you to assess the relative importance of a series of causal factors. That means you must establish a clear rank order of importance between the factors you examine. One cause is given in the question. You must, therefore, examine the importance of reparations seriously, even if you are going to reject it in favour of a cause that you believe to have been more important. You might divide your answer into three separate sections: the long, the medium and the short term. Alternatively, you might decide from the start your rank order and examine the relative significance of individual factors throughout your essay. However you structure your answer, point out instances where different factors linked together, influencing each other.

Reparations put a massive burden on Germany, especially since they had to be paid in hard currency. How could such sums be gathered, especially in so impoverished a country? Payments depended on a healthy economy, but international trade was sluggish. Reparations brought about the occupation of the Ruhr. Reparations guaranteed Germany's ruin – or did they? Germany was allowed to postpone payments. Might the real problem with reparations have been not the reparations themselves but the government's decision to deal with them by printing banknotes, which undermined the value of the mark and caused further inflation? What of other possible causes? Make clear the very weak economic position of Germany after the war. That base affected everything. Equally, be clear that inflation had been rising since 1915. Examine the implications of deficit financing for a state already crippled by massive debts. Consider also the significance of the passive resistance to the occupation of the Ruhr – you must be able to explain not just why there was hyper-inflation, but why it happened in 1923. Or, had it already started in 1922? Answering that will help prioritise causes and settle your answer. In your final conclusion, do not just state that 'x' was the main cause. Justify your claim with evidence.

---

4 Weimar: The Years of Stability 1924–9

POINTS TO CONSIDER
It is generally held that after the turmoil of the early 1920s, the years 1924–9 were a time of recovery and stability in German history. Indeed, it is quite common to refer to the period as the 'golden twenties'. The purpose of this chapter is to consider the accuracy of this picture by examining the following themes:

• The extent of Germany's economic recovery
• The political stability of the Weimar Republic
• The achievements of Gustav Stresemann
• The developments in German foreign policy
• The development of Weimar culture

Key dates

1922		Treaty of Rapallo
1923–9		Stresemann as Foreign Minister
1924	April	Dawes Plan
1925		Hindenburg elected president
	October	Locarno Conference
1928	May	Müller's Grand Coalition
		Hugenberg leader of DNVP
	August	Kellogg-Briand Pact
1929		Young Plan
	October	Death of Stresemann
	October	Wall Street Crash

1 | The Economic Recovery

It is often claimed that after the hyper-inflation, the introduction of the new currency – the *Rentenmark* – and the measures brought about by the Dawes Plan ushered in five years of economic growth and affluence. Certainly the period stands out between the economic chaos of 1922–3 and the **Great Depression** of 1929–33. So, for many Germans looking back from the end of the 1920s, it seemed as if Germany had made a remarkable recovery.

The strengths of the German economy

In spite of the loss of resources as a result of the Treaty of Versailles, heavy industry was able to recover reasonably quickly and, by 1928, production levels reached those of 1913. This was

Key term

Great Depression
The severe economic crisis of 1929–33 that was marked by mass unemployment, falling prices and a lack of spending.

Key question
What were the strengths of the German economy?

the result of the use of more efficient methods of production, particularly in coal-mining and steel manufacture, and also because of increased investment. Foreign bankers were particularly attracted by Germany's high interest rates.

At the same time, German industry had the advantage of being able to lower costs because of the growing number of **cartels**, which had better purchasing power than smaller industries. For example, *IG Farben*, the chemicals giant, became the largest manufacturing enterprise in Europe, whilst *Vereinigte Stahlwerke* combined the coal, iron and steel interests of Germany's great industrial companies and grew to control nearly half of all production.

Between 1925 and 1929, German exports rose by 40 per cent. Such economic progress brought social benefits as well. Hourly wage rates rose every year from 1924 to 1930 and by as much as 5–10 per cent in 1927 and 1928.

The benefits of social welfare

There were striking improvements in the provision of social welfare. The principles of a welfare state were written into the new Weimar Constitution and in the early 1920s generous pensions and sickness benefits were introduced. In 1927, a compulsory unemployment insurance covering 17 million workers was created, which was the largest scheme of its kind in the world. In addition, state subsidies were provided for the construction of local amenities such as parks, schools, sports facilities and especially council housing. All these developments, alongside the more obvious signs of wealth, such as the increasing number of cars and the growth of the cinema industry, supported the view that the Weimar Republic's economy was enjoying boom conditions. However, it should be borne in mind that the social costs had economic implications.

The weaknesses in the German economy

From the statistics for 1924–9 it is easy to get an impression of the 'golden twenties'. However, the actual rate of German recovery was unclear:

- There was economic growth, but it was uneven, and in 1926 production actually declined. In overseas trade, the value of **imports** always exceeded that of **exports**.
- Unemployment never fell below 1.3 million in this period. And even before the effects of America's financial crisis began to be felt (see pages 102–3), the number of unemployed workers averaged 1.9 million in 1929.
- In agriculture, grain production was still only three-quarters of its 1913 figure and farmers, many of whom were in debt, faced falling incomes. By the late 1920s, income per head in agriculture was 44 per cent below the national average.

Fundamental economic problems

The economic indicators listed above suggest that the German economy had fundamental problems in this period and it is

---

Key terms

Cartel
An arrangement between businesses to control the market by exercising a joint monopoly.

Imports
Goods purchased from foreign countries.

Exports
Goods sold to foreign countries.

Key question
Was the Weimar economy fundamentally weak?

therefore important to appreciate the broader view by looking at the following points.

- World economic conditions did not favour Germany. Traditionally, Germany had relied on its ability to export to achieve economic growth, but world trade did not return to pre-war levels. German exports were hindered by protective **tariffs** in many parts of the world. By the Treaty of Versailles, they were also handicapped by the loss of valuable resources in territories, such as Alsace-Lorraine and Silesia (see page 28). German agriculture also found itself in difficulties because of world economic conditions. The fall in world prices from the mid-1920s placed a great strain on farmers, who made up one-third of the German population. Support in the form of government financial aid and tariffs could only partially help to reduce the problems. Most significantly, this decline in income reduced the spending power of a large section of the population and this led to a fall in demand within the economy as a whole.
- The changing balance of the population. From the mid-1920s, there were more school leavers because of the high pre-war birth rate. The available workforce increased from 32.4 million in 1925 to 33.4 million in 1931. This meant that, even without a recession, there was always likely to be an increase in unemployment in Germany.
- Savings and investment discouraged. Savers had lost a great deal of money in the Great Inflation and, after 1924, there was less enthusiasm to invest money again. As a result, the German economy came to rely on investors from abroad, for example the USA, who were attracted by the prospect of higher interest rates than those in their own countries. Germany's economic well-being became ever more dependent on foreign investment.
- Government finances raised concern. Although the government succeeded in balancing the budget in 1924, from 1925 it continually ran into debt. It continued to spend increasing sums of money and by 1928 public expenditure had reached 26 per cent of **GNP**, which was double the pre-war figure. The government found it difficult to encourage domestic savings and was forced to rely more and more on international loans. Such a situation did not provide the basis for solid future economic growth.

Conclusion

It has been suggested that the problems faced by the German economy before the world **depression** of 1929 were disguised by the flood of foreign capital and exacerbated by the development of an extensive social welfare system. The German economy could be seen to be in a poor state because:

- The foreign loans made it liable to suffer from any problems that arose in the world economy.
- The investment was too low to encourage growth.

Key terms

Tariffs
Taxes levied by an importing nation on foreign goods coming in, and paid by the importers.

GNP
Gross national product is the total value of all goods and services in a nation's economy (including income derived from assets abroad).

Depression
An economic downturn marked by mass unemployment, falling prices and a lack of spending. The world depression lasted from 1929 to 1933. In the USA it was called the Great Depression.

Key question
Was the Weimar economy a fundamentally sick economy?

- The cost of the welfare state could only be met by the government taking on increasing debts.
- The agricultural sector faced serious problems from mid-1920s and various sectors of the German economy had actually started to slow down from 1927.

Whether this amounts to the view of Weimar Germany as 'an abnormal, in fact a sick economy' (Borchardt) remains controversial, and it is hard to assess what might have happened without a world economic crisis. However, it is interesting that Stresemann wrote in 1928, 'Germany is dancing on a volcano. If the short-term credits are called in, a large section of our economy would collapse.' So, on balance, the evidence suggests that by 1929 the Weimar Republic was facing serious difficulties and was already heading for a major economic downturn of its own making.

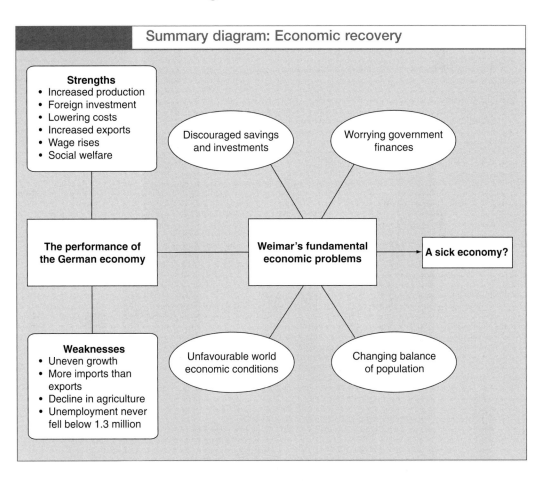

Summary diagram: Economic recovery

Strengths
- Increased production
- Foreign investment
- Lowering costs
- Increased exports
- Wage rises
- Social welfare

Discouraged savings and investments

Worrying government finances

The performance of the German economy

Weimar's fundamental economic problems

A sick economy?

Weaknesses
- Uneven growth
- More imports than exports
- Decline in agriculture
- Unemployment never fell below 1.3 million

Unfavourable world economic conditions

Changing balance of population

2 | Political Stability

The election results during the middle years of the Weimar Republic gave grounds for cautious optimism about its survival (see Figure 4.1). The extremist parties of both left and right lost ground and altogether they polled less than 30 per cent of the votes cast. The DNVP peaked in December 1924 with 103 seats (20.5 per cent of the vote) and fell back to 73 (14.2 per cent) in May 1928. The Nazis lost ground in both elections and were

Key question
Did the general election results of 1924–8 reflect optimism about the Weimar Republic among German voters?

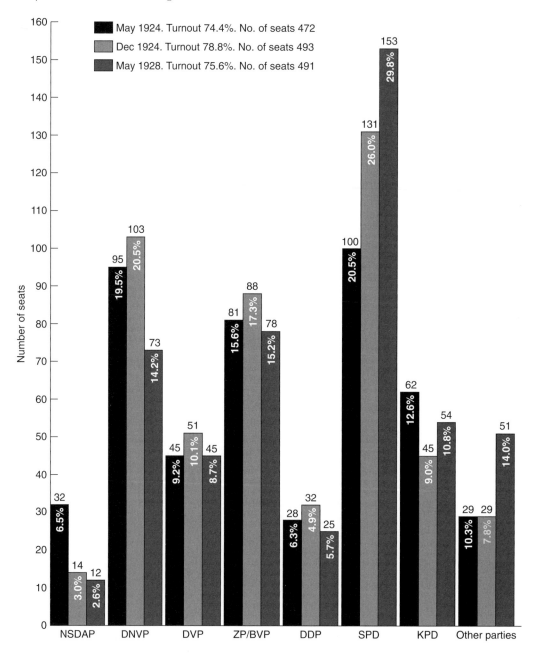

Figure 4.1: Weimar *Reichstag* election results 1924 and 1928. (See major political parties on page 16.)

Key date

Müller's 'Grand Coalition' formed: May 1928

reduced to only 12 seats (2.6 per cent) by 1928. The KPD, although recovering slightly by 1928 with 54 seats (10.6 per cent), remained below their performance of May 1924 and well below the combined votes gained by the KPD and USPD in June 1920 (see page 51).

In comparison, the parties sympathetic to the Republic maintained their share of the vote and the SPD made substantial gains, winning 153 seats (29.8 per cent) in 1928. As a result, following the 1928 election, a 'Grand Coalition' of the SPD, DDP, DVP and Centre was formed under Hermann Müller, the leader of the SPD. It enjoyed the support of over 60 per cent of the *Reichstag* and it seemed as if democracy was at last beginning to emerge in Weimar politics.

Key question

Why did the political parties find it so difficult to co-operate?

Coalition politics

The election of 1928 must not be regarded as typical in Weimar history, and it should not hide the continuing basic weaknesses of the German parliamentary system. These included not only the problems created by proportional representation (see page 23), but also the ongoing difficulty of creating and maintaining coalitions from the various parties. In such a situation each party tended to put its own self-interests before those of the government.

The parties tended to reflect their traditional interests; in particular, religion and class. So attempts to widen their appeal made little progress. As a result, the differences between the main parties meant that opportunities to form workable coalitions were very limited.

- There was never any possibility of a coalition including both the SPD and the DNVP because the former believed in parliamentary democracy whereas the latter fundamentally rejected the Weimar political system.
- The Communists, KPD, remained totally isolated.
- A right–centre coalition of Centre, DVP and DNVP created a situation in which the parties tended to agree on domestic issues, but disagree on foreign affairs.
- On the other hand, a broad coalition of SPD, DDP, DVP and Centre meant that these parties agreed on foreign policy, but differed on domestic issues.
- A minority government of the political centre, including the DDP, DVP and Centre, could only exist by seeking support from either the left or right. It was impossible to create a coalition with a parliamentary majority that could also consistently agree on both domestic and foreign policy.

In this situation, there was very little chance of democratic government being able to establish any lasting political stability. Of the seven governments between 1923 and 1930 (see Table 4.1), only two had majorities and the longest survived for just 21 months. In fact, the only reason governments lasted as long as they did was that the opposition parties were also unable or unwilling to unite. More often than not, it was conflicts within the parties that formed the coalition governments that led them to collapse.

Table 4.1: Governments of the Weimar Republic, 1923–30

Period in office	Chancellor	Make-up of the coalition
1923–4	Wilhelm Marx	Centre, DDP, DVP
1924–5	Wilhelm Marx	Centre, DDP, DVP
1925	Hans Luther	Centre, DVP, DNVP
1926	Hans Luther	Centre, DDP, DVP
1926	Wilhelm Marx	Centre, DDP, DVP
1927–8	Wilhelm Marx	Centre, DDP, DNVP
1928–30	Hermann Müller	SPD, DDP, Centre, DVP

The responsibility of the parties

The attitude of the Weimar Republic's political parties towards parliamentary government was irresponsible. This may well have been a legacy from the imperial years. In that time the parties had expressed their own narrow interests in the knowledge that it was the Kaiser who ultimately decided policy. However, in the 1920s, parliamentary democracy needed the political parties to show a more responsible attitude towards government. The evidence suggests that no such attitude existed, even in the most stable period of the Republic's history.

The SPD

Until 1932 the SPD remained the largest party in the *Reichstag*. However, although firm in its support of the Republic, the Party was divided between its desire to uphold the interests of the working class and its commitment to democracy. Some members, and especially those connected with the trade unions, feared that joining coalitions with other parties would lead to a weakening of their principles. Others, the more moderate, wanted to participate in government in order to influence it. At the same time, the Party was hindered by the old argument between those committed to a more extreme left-wing socialist programme and those who favoured moderate, gradual reform.

As a result, during the middle years of the Republic the SPD did not join any of the fragile government coalitions. This obviously weakened the power base of those democratic coalitions from 1924 to 1928. The SPD remained the strongest party during those years: although it was committed to democracy, it was not prepared to take on the responsibility of government until 1928.

Key question
In what ways was the SPD divided?

The Centre Party

It therefore fell to the Centre Party to provide real political leadership in Weimar politics. The ZP electoral support was solid and the Party participated in all the coalition governments from 1919 to 1932 by taking ministerial posts. However, its support did not increase because its appeal was restricted to traditional Catholic areas. Further, its social and economic policies which aimed at bridging the gaps between the classes led to internal quarrels.

Key question
What were the limitations of the Centre Party?

In the early years, such differences had been put to one side under the strong left-wing leadership of Matthias Erzberger and Josef Wirth. However, during the 1920s, the Party moved decisively to the right and the divisions within the Party widened. In 1928, the leadership eventually passed to Ludwig Kaas and Heinrich Brüning, who appealed more to the conservative partners of the coalition than to the liberal or social democratic elements. This was a worrying sign both for the future of the Centre Party and for Germany herself.

The liberal parties

Key question
What were the weaknesses of the German liberal parties?

The position of the German liberals was not a really strong one. The DDP and DVP joined in all the coalition governments of this period and in Gustav Stresemann, the leader of the DVP, they possessed the Republic's only really capable statesman. However, this hid some worrying trends. Their share of the vote, though constant in the mid-1920s, had nearly halved since 1919–20, when it had been between 22 and 23 per cent.

The reasons for the liberals' eventual collapse after 1930 were already established beforehand. This decline was largely a result of the divisions within both parties. The DDP lacked clear leadership and its membership was involved in internal bickering over policy. The DVP was also divided and, despite Stresemann's efforts to bring unity to the Party, this remained a source of conflict. It is not really surprising that moves to bring about some kind of united liberal party came to nothing. As a result, German liberalism failed to gain popular support; and after 1929 its position declined dramatically.

The DNVP

Key question
How did the DNVP change over time?

One promising feature of German party politics came unexpectedly from the conservative DNVP. Since 1919, the DNVP had been totally opposed to the Republic and it had refused to take part in government. In electoral terms, it had enjoyed considerable success, and in December 1924, gained 103 seats (20.5 per cent). However, as the Republic began to recover after the 1923 crisis (see pages 56–8), it became increasingly clear that the DNVP's hopes of restoring a more right-wing government were diminishing. The continuous opposition policy meant that the Party had no real power and achieved nothing. Some influential groups within the DNVP realised that if they were to have any influence on government policy, then the Party had to be prepared to participate in government. As a result, in 1925 and 1927, the DNVP joined government coalitions. This more sympathetic attitude towards the Weimar Republic was an encouraging development.

However, that more conciliatory policy was not popular with all groups within the Party. When, in the 1928 election, the DNVP vote fell by a quarter, the more extreme right wing asserted its influence. Significantly, it elected Alfred Hugenberg, an extreme nationalist, as the new leader (see profile, page 68). Hugenberg was Germany's greatest media tycoon: he owned 150 newspapers,

Key date
Hugenberg leader of DNVP: October 1928

a publishing house, and had interests in the film industry. He utterly rejected the idea of a republic based on parliamentary democracy. He now used all his resources to promote his political message. The DNVP reverted to a programme of total opposition to the Republic and refused to be involved in government. A year later, his party was working closely with the Nazis against the Young Plan (see pages 76 and 106).

President Hindenburg

A presidential election was due in 1925. It was assumed that President Friedrich Ebert would be re-elected. So his unexpected death in February 1925 created political problems. There was no clear successor in the first round of the election and so a second round was held. It did result in the choice of Hindenburg as president, but the figures clearly underlined the divisions in German society (see Table 4.2).

Key question
Was the appointment of Hindenburg as president a good or a bad sign for Weimar democracy?

Hindenburg elected president: 1925

Key date

Table 4.2: Presidential election, second round, 26 April 1925

Candidate (party)	Votes (millions)	Percentage
Paul von Hindenburg (DNVP)	14.6	48
Wilhelm Marx (ZP)	13.7	45
Ernst Thälmann (KPD)	1.9	6

Profile: Alfred Hugenberg 1865–1951

1865	– Born in Hanover
1894	– Founder of Pan-German League
1920	– *Reichstag* DNVP deputy
1927	– Leader of UFA, Germany's largest film company
1928	– Leader of DNVP until 1933
1929	– Campaigned against the Young Plan
1931	– Joined the Harzburg Front against Brüning (see page 112)
1933	– Member of Hitler's coalition, but replaced in June
1945	– Survived (his fortune intact) and was not prosecuted by the Allies
1951	– Death

Hugenburg was a civil servant, banker, industrialist and 'press baron' who was strongly against the Weimar Republic from the outset. He played a crucial role in forming the DNVP in 1919 from various established conservative-nationalist parties and he became a member of the *Reichstag* in 1920. Most significantly, he used his massive fortune to finance the DNVP and several other campaigns against reparations and the Treaties of Versailles and Locarno. Once he became leader of the Party he began to fund Hitler and the Nazis and in 1931–3 his political and financial power were instrumental in Hitler's rise to power. However, although he remained a member of the *Reichstag*, he lost his political power and influence when Hitler established the Nazi dictatorship from mid-1933.

Profile: Paul von Hindenburg 1847–1934

1847	– Born in Posen, East Prussia
1859	– Joined the Prussian army
1870	– Fought in the Franco-Prussian war
1911	– Retired with the rank of General
1914	– Recalled at start of First World War
	– Won the victory of the Battle of Tannenberg on Eastern Front
1916	– Promoted to Field Marshal and war supremo
1918	– Accepted the defeat of Germany and retired again
1925	– Elected president of Germany
1930–2	– Appointed Brüning, Papen and Schleicher as chancellors, who ruled by presidential decree
1932	– Re-elected president
1933	– Persuaded to appoint Hitler as chancellor
1934	– Death. Granted a national funeral

Background and military career

Hindenburg was born into a Prussian noble family that could trace its military tradition back over many centuries. Described as 'steady rather than exceptional', he was regularly promoted.

In 1914, he was recalled from retirement. His management of the campaign against the Russians on the Eastern Front earned him distinction. However, Hindenburg, who was distinguished in appearance and 'looked the part', did not have great military skills and was outshone by his chief-of-staff, Ludendorff.

After 1916, his partnership with Ludendorff was less successful against the British and French on the Western Front. During the years 1917 and 1918, the two men were effectively the military dictators of Germany.

Appointment as president of Weimar Republic

After the war, Hindenburg briefly retired but in 1925 he was elected president of Germany, a position he held until 1934. He was not a democrat and looked forward to the return of the monarchy and in many respects he only accepted the post reluctantly. Nevertheless, he took up the responsibility of his office and performed his duties correctly.

Rise of Hitler

From 1930 Hindenburg's political significance increased when Weimar faced growing political and economic crisis. As president, he was responsible for the appointment of all the chancellors from 1930–4, though he became a crucial player in the political intrigue of the competing forces. Given his authority, he must be held ultimately responsible for the events that ended with the appointment of Hitler, but he was very old and easily influenced by Papen and Schleicher. He had no respect for Hitler, but he did not have the will and determination to make a stand against Nazism.

The appointment of President Hindenburg has remained controversial. On the one hand, on Hindenburg's coming to power there was no immediate swing to the right. The new president proved totally loyal to the constitution and carried out his presidential duties with correctness. Those nationalists who had hoped that his election might lead to the restoration of the monarchy, or the creation of a military-type regime, were disappointed. Indeed, it has been argued that Hindenburg as president acted as a true substitute kaiser or *Ersatzkaiser* (so although Wilhelm II had abdicated and Germany had lost its monarchy, Hindenburg was seen by monarchists as, in effect, fulfilling the role of sovereign). In that sense, the status of Hindenburg as president at last gave Weimar some respectability in conservative circles.

On the other hand, it is difficult to ignore the pitfalls resulting from the appointment of an old man. In his heart, Hindenburg had no real sympathy for the Republic or its values. Those around him were mainly made up of anti-republican figures, many of them from the military. He preferred to include the DNVP in government and, if possible, to exclude the SPD. From the start, Hindenburg's view was that the government should move towards the right, although it was really only after 1929 that the serious implications of his outlook became fully apparent for Weimar democracy. As the historian A.J. Nicholls put it: 'he refused to betray the republic, but he did not rally the people to its banner'.

The limitations of the political system

During this period the parliamentary and party political system in Germany failed to make any real progress. It just coped as best it could. Government carried out its work but with only limited success. There was no *putsch* from left or right and the anti-republican extremists were contained. Law and order were restored and the activities of the various paramilitary groups were limited.

However, these were only minor and very negative successes and, despite the good intentions of certain individuals and groups, there were no signs of any real strengthening of the political structure. Stable government had not been established. This is not surprising when it is noted that one coalition government collapsed in 1926 over a minor issue about the use of the national flag and the old imperial flag. Another government fell over the creation of religious schools.

Even more significant for the future was the growing contempt and cynicism shown by the people towards party politics. This was particularly connected with the negotiating and bargaining involved in the creation of most coalitions. The turn-out of the elections declined in the mid-1920s compared to 1919 and 1920. There was also an increasing growth of small fringe parties. The apparent stability of these years was really a deception, a mirage. It misled some people into believing that a genuine basis for lasting stable government had been achieved. It had not.

Key term

Ersatzkaiser
Means 'substitute emperor'. After Marshal Hindenburg was elected president, he provided the *ersatzkaiser* figure required by the respectable right wing – he was a conservative, a nationalist and a military hero.

Key question
Was Weimar's political recovery a 'false stability'?

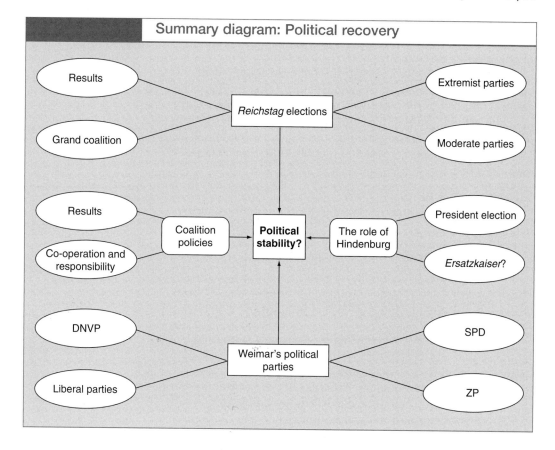

Summary diagram: Political recovery

3 | Gustav Stresemann's Achievements

Key question
How did
Stresemann's career
change and develop?

Before 1921–2, there was little to suggest that Stresemann was to become the mainstay of Weimar democracy. In the years before 1914 his nationalism found expression in his support of the Kaiser's *Weltpolitik* and from the start of the First World War, Stresemann was an ardent supporter of the *Siegfriede*. He campaigned for 'unrestricted submarine warfare' and opposed supporters of peace in 1917 (page 2).

By 1918 his support for the military regime and the Treaty of Brest-Litovsk had earned him the title of 'Ludendorff's young man' (see pages 4–5). And when the war came to an end in defeat, Stresemann was deliberately excluded from the newly created DDP and, so, was left no real option but to form his own party, the DVP. At first, his party was hostile to the revolution of 1918 and the Republic and campaigned for the restoration of the monarchy.

Key terms

Weltpolitik
'World policy' – the imperial policy of Kaiser Wilhem II to make Germany a great power by overseas expansion.

Siegfriede
'A peace through victory' – referring to Germany fighting the First World War to victory and making major land gains.

Turning point
Indeed, it was only after the failed Kapp *putsch* and the murders of Erzberger and Rathenau (pages 39–41) that Stresemann led his party into adopting a more sympathetic approach towards the Weimar Republic. His sudden change of heart has provided plenty of evidence for those critics who have regarded his support of the Weimar Republic as sham. This charge is not entirely fair.

Despite the conservatism of his early years, Stresemann's subsequent career shows that he was a committed supporter of constitutional government.

Stresemann's ideal was a constitutional monarchy. But that was not to be. By 1922 he had become convinced that the Republic and its constitution provided Germany with its only chance of preventing the dictatorship of either left or right. This was his realistic assessment of the situation and why he was referred to as a *Vernunftrepublikaner*, a rational republican, rather than a convinced one.

Stresemann's aims

Key question
What were Stresemann's aims and objectives?

From the time he became responsible for foreign affairs at the height of the 1923 crisis, Stresemann's foreign policy was shaped by his deep understanding of the domestic and international situations. He recognised, unlike many nationalists, that Germany had been militarily defeated and not simply 'stabbed in the back'. He also rejected the solutions of those hardliners who failed to understand the circumstances that had brought Germany to its knees in 1923.

Stresemann's main aims were to free Germany from the limitations of Versailles and to restore his country to the status of a great power, the equal of Britain and France. Offensive action was ruled out by Stresemann and so his only choice therefore was diplomacy. As he himself once remarked, he was backed up only by the power of German cultural traditions and the German economy. So, at first, he worked towards his main aims in the 1920s by pursuing the following objectives:

Vernunftrepublikaner 'A rational republican' – used in the 1920s to define those people who really wanted Germany to have a constitutional monarchy but who, out of necessity, came to support the democratic Weimar Republic.

Key term

- To recognise that France did rightly have security concerns and that France also controlled the balance of power on the continent. He regarded Franco-German friendship as essential to solving outstanding problems.
- To play on Germany's vital importance to world trade in order to earn the goodwill and co-operation of Britain and the USA. The sympathy of the USA was also vital so as to attract American investment into the German economy.
- To maintain the Rapallo-based friendship with the USSR. He rejected out of hand those 'hardliners' who desired an alliance with Soviet Russia and described them as the 'maddest of foreign policy makers'. Stresemann's strategy was in the tradition of Wirth's fulfilment.
- To encourage co-operation and peace, particularly with the Western powers. This was in the best interests of Germany to make it the leading power in Europe once again.

Stresemann and foreign affairs 1923–9

The Dawes Plan

Key question
What were the strengths and weaknesses of the Dawes Plan?

The starting point of Stresemann's foreign policy was the issue of reparations. As chancellor, he had called off 'passive resistance' and agreed to resume the payment of reparations. The result of this was the US-backed Dawes Plan (see Figure 4.2 on page 73), which has

Key date

The US-backed Dawes Plan was accepted by the German government: April 1924

THE DAWES PLAN 1924

The reorganisation of German currency
- One new *Rentenmark* was to be worth one billion of the old marks.
- The setting up of a German national bank, the *Reichsbank*, under Allied supervision.

An international loan of 800 million gold marks to aid German economic recovery
- The loan was to be financed mainly by the USA.

New arrangements for the payment of reparations
- Payment to be made annually at a fixed scale over a longer period.

Figure 4.2: The Dawes Plan.

been described as 'a victory for financial realism'. Despite opposition from the right wing it was accepted in April 1924.

Although the Dawes Plan left the actual sum to be paid unchanged, the monthly instalments over the first five years were calculated according to Germany's capacity to pay. Furthermore, it provided for a large loan to Germany to aid economic recovery. For Stresemann, its advantages were many:

- For the first time since the First World War, Germany's economic problems received international recognition.
- Germany gained credit for the cash-starved German economy by means of the loan and subsequent investments.
- It resulted in a French promise to evacuate the Ruhr during 1925.

In the short term, the Dawes Plan was a success. The German economy was not weakened, since it received twice as much capital from abroad as it paid out in reparations. The mere fact that reparations were being paid regularly contributed to the improved relations between France and Germany during these years. However, the whole system was dangerously dependent on the continuation of American loans, as can be seen in Figure 4.3. In attempting to break out of the crisis of 1923, Stresemann had linked Germany's fortunes to powerful external forces, which had dramatic effects after 1929.

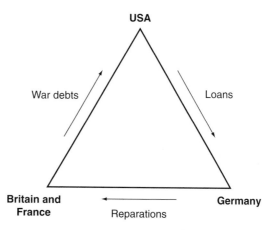

Figure 4.3: The reparations triangle in the 1920s.

The Locarno Pact

The ending of the occupation of the Ruhr and the introduction of the Dawes Plan showed that the Great Powers were prepared to take Germany's interests seriously. However, Stresemann continued to fear that Anglo-French friendship could lead to a military **alliance**. In order to counter this concern, Stresemann proposed an international security pact for Germany's western frontiers. Although France was at first hesitant, Britain and the USA both backed the idea. This formed the basis for the Locarno Pact.

In October 1925 a series of treaties was signed which became known as the Locarno Pact. The main points were:

- A **mutual guarantee agreement** accepted the Franco-German and Belgian-German borders. These terms were guaranteed by Britain and Italy. All five countries renounced the use of force, except in self-defence.
- The **demilitarisation** of the Rhineland was recognised as permanent.
- The **arbitration treaties** between Germany, Poland and Czechoslovakia agreed to settle future disputes peacefully – but the existing frontiers were not accepted as final.

To see the territories affected by the Treaty of Locarno, refer to the map on page 29.

The Locarno treaties represented an important diplomatic development. Germany was freed from its isolation by the Allies and was again treated as an equal partner. Stresemann had achieved a great deal at Locarno at very little cost.

He had confirmed the existing frontiers in the west, since Germany was in no position to change the situation. In so doing he had also limited France's freedom of action since the occupation of the Ruhr or the possible annexation of the Rhineland was no longer possible. Moreover, by establishing the beginnings of a solid basis for Franco-German understanding, Stresemann had lessened France's need to find allies in eastern Europe. The Poles viewed the treaties as a major setback, since Stresemann had deliberately refused to confirm the frontiers in the east.

Further diplomatic progress

Stresemann hoped that further advances would follow Locarno, such as the restoration of full German rule over the Saar and the Rhineland, a reduction in reparations, and a revision of the eastern frontier. However, although there was further diplomatic progress in the years 1926–30 it remained limited:

- Germany had originally been excluded from the League of Nations (see page 29) but, in 1926, she was invited to join the League and was immediately recognised as a permanent member of the Council of the League.
- Two years later in 1928 Germany signed the Kellogg-Briand Pact, a declaration that outlawed 'war as an instrument of

Key question
Why were the Locarno treaties so significant?

Key date

Locarno Pact: the conference was held in October 1925 and the treaties were signed in December

Key terms

Alliance
An agreement where members promise to support the other(s), if one or more of them is attacked.

Mutual guarantee agreement
An agreement between states on a particular issue, but not an alliance.

Demilitarisation
The removal of military personnel, weaponry or forts. The Rhineland demilitarised zone was outlined by the Treaty of Versailles (pages 27–9).

Arbitration treaty
An agreement to accept the decision by a third party to settle a conflict.

Profile: Gustav Stresemann 1878–1929

1878	– Born in Berlin, the son of a publican and brewer
1900	– Graduated from Berlin University in Political Economy and went into business
1907	– Elected the youngest member of *Reichstag*
1914–18	– Unconditional nationalist and supporter of the war. Worked politically closely with Hindenburg and Ludendorff
1919	– Formed the DVP and became its leader, 1919–29. Initially opposed the creation of the Weimar Republic
1921	– Decided to work with the Weimar Republic and became a *Vernunftrepublikaner*, a republican by reason
1923	– Chancellor of Germany
1923–9	– Foreign Minister in all governments; major successes:
	1924 – Dawes Plan
	1925 – Locarno Pact
	1926 – Treaty of Berlin
	– Germany entry into League of Nations
	1928 – Kellogg-Briand Pact
	1929 – Young Plan
1926	– Awarded the Nobel Peace Prize
1929	– Death at the age of 51

Political background 1878–1918

Stresemann was born in Berlin, the son of a publican, and successfully entered university to study economics. He went into business and quickly earnt a reputation as a skilled trade negotiator, which laid the basis for his political outlook. His wife was the daughter of a leading Jewish family with strong social and business contacts.

Stresemann joined the old National Liberals and was elected in 1907 to the *Reichstag* at the age of just 29. He was a committed monarchist and nationalist and in the years before 1914 he supported the Kaiser's *Weltpolitik*. In the war, Stresemann was an ardent supporter of the *Siegfriede* and more expansionist policies with the result that he was forced to leave his old party.

His turning-point 1919–22

Stresemann was appalled by the defeat of Germany in the First World War and the Treaty of Versailles. In his heart, he remained a monarchist and hoped to create a constitutional monarchy. So, in the years 1919–21, he formed the DVP and opposed the Weimar Republic. However, by 1921 he came to recognise the political reality and finally committed himself and his party to the Republic.

Chancellor 1923

In the year of crisis Stresemann was made chancellor, and it is generally recognised by historians that it marked the climax of his career. All the problems were confronted: the occupation of the Ruhr, the hyper-inflation and the opposition from left and right wing extremists. So, although his term in office lasted for just three months it laid the basis for the recovery 1924–9.

Foreign Minister 1923–9

Stresemann was Foreign Minister in all the Weimar governments and was the 'main architect of republican foreign policy' (Kolb). Most significantly, he showed a strength of character and a realism which allowed him to negotiate with the Allies. Stresemann achieved a great deal in securing Germany's international position. Nevertheless, it should be remembered that that he failed to generate real domestic support for Weimar. So, it is questionable whether he could have saved the Weimar Republic from Nazism.

national policy'. Although of no real practical effect it showed that Germany was working with 68 nations.
- In 1929 the Allies agreed to evacuate the Rhineland earlier than intended, in return for a final settlement of the reparations issue. The result was the Young Plan, which further revised the scheme of payments. Germany now agreed to continue to pay reparations until 1988, although the total sum was reduced to £1850 million, only one-quarter of the figure demanded in 1921 (see page 28).

Key dates

Treaty of Rapallo: 1922

Stresemann as Foreign Minister: 1923–9

Kellogg-Briand Pact: August 1928

Young Plan: 1929

The Treaty of Berlin

Although Stresemann viewed friendship with the West as his priority, he was not prepared to drop the **Rapallo treaty**. He was still determined to stay on good terms with the USSR. As a result, the two countries signed the Treaty of Berlin in April 1926 in order to continue the basis of a good Russo-German relationship. This was not double-dealing by Stresemann, but was simply a recognition that Germany's defence needs in the heart of Europe meant that she had to have understanding with both the East and the West. The treaty with the Soviet Union therefore reduced strategic fears on Germany's Eastern Front and placed even more pressure on Poland to give way to German demands for frontier changes. It also opened up the possibility of a large commercial market and increased military co-operation.

Key question
How was Stresemann able to reach agreements with both the USSR and the West?

Key term

Rapallo treaty
This was not an alliance, but a treaty of friendship between Germany and the USSR.

Assessment of Stresemann

In 1926 Stresemann was awarded the Nobel Peace Prize (along with his British and French counterparts Aristide Briand and Austen Chamberlain). Only three years later, at the early age of 51, he died suddenly of a heart attack. However, Stresemann has always been the focus of debate. He has been regarded by some as a fanatical nationalist and by others as a 'great European' working for international reconciliation. He has been praised for his staunch support of parliamentary government, but condemned for pretending to be a democrat. He has also been portrayed as an idealist on the one hand and an opportunist on the other.

Key question
Did Stresemann fail or succeed?

Key date

Death of Gustav Stresemann in the same month as the Wall Street Crash: October 1929

Stresemann achieved a great deal in a short time to change both Germany's domestic and international positions. Moreover, the improvement had been achieved by peaceful methods. When one also considers the dire situation he inherited in 1923 with forces, both internal and external, stacked against him, it is perhaps not surprising that his policy has been described as 'astonishingly successful' (Kolb) and he has been referred to as 'Weimar's greatest statesman' (Wright).

However, it should be borne in mind that the circumstances in the years 1924–9 were working strongly in Stresemann's favour. Also, in terms of foreign policy, he failed to achieve his aims to revise Versailles fundamentally. By 1929 it seems that these limited changes had come to a dead end – and there was no hint of any revision of the Polish frontier.

Also, Stresemann's policies failed to generate real domestic support for Weimar. The right wing was always totally against 'fulfilment' and, although a minority, they became increasingly loud and influential, so by the time of Stresemann's death, the nationalist opposition was already mobilising itself against the Young Plan (see pages 75 and 106). Even more significantly, it seems that the silent majority had not really been won over by Stresemann's policy of conciliation. Consequently, by 1929 his policy had not had time to establish itself and generate sufficient support to survive the difficult circumstances of the 1930s.

'He looks to the right, he looks to the left – he will save me.' A German cartoon drawn in 1923 portrays Stresemann as the guardian angel of the young Republic. However, it is worth noting that the little boy is the German Michael – a stereotype for the naïve German.

Summary diagram: Gustav Stresemann and Weimar foreign policy

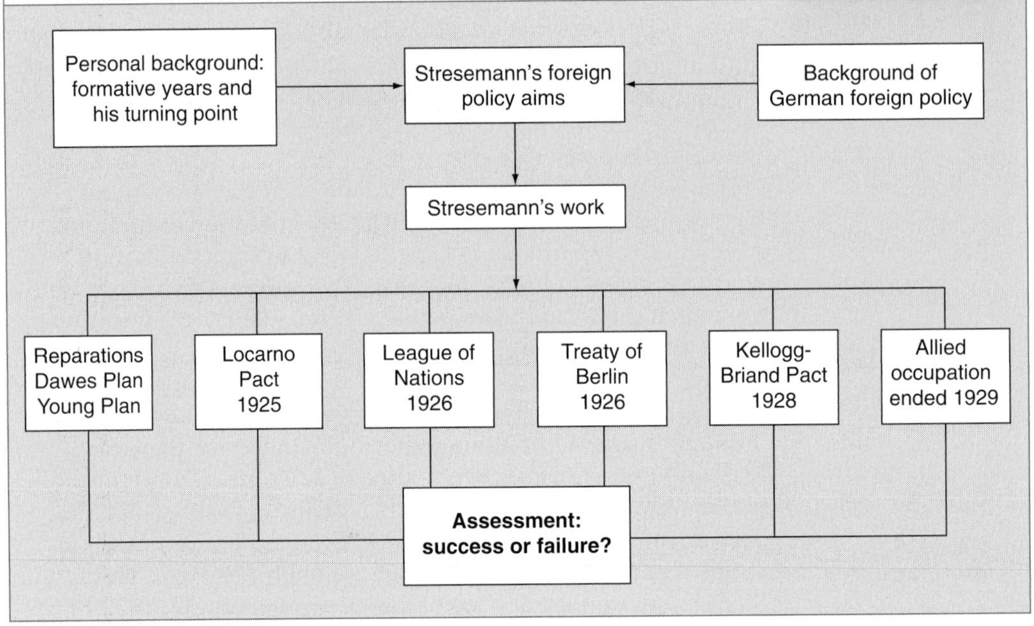

Personal background: formative years and his turning point
Stresemann's foreign policy aims
Background of German foreign policy
Stresemann's work
Reparations Dawes Plan Young Plan
Locarno Pact 1925
League of Nations 1926
Treaty of Berlin 1926
Kellogg-Briand Pact 1928
Allied occupation ended 1929
Assessment: success or failure?

4 | Weimar Culture

Key question
Why were the 1920s a culturally rich period?

The Weimar years witnessed a radical cultural reaction to the turmoil that followed the war and defeat. Whereas the Germany of the Second Reich had been conservative, authoritarian and conformist, in contrast, the Weimar Republic was a liberal society that upheld **toleration** and reduced censorship. These factors contributed to the label of the 'golden years', as described by William Shirer, the European correspondent of the American newspaper, the *Chicago Tribune*:

> A wonderful ferment was working in Germany. Life seemed more free, more modern, more exciting than in any place I had ever seen. Nowhere else did the arts or the intellectual life seem so lively … In contemporary writing, painting, architecture, in music and drama, there were new currents and fine talents.

More broadly, the period was also one of dramatic changes in communication and the media, for this decade saw the emergence of film, radio and the car.

Key terms

Toleration Acceptance of alternative political, religious and cultural views.

New functionalism A form of art that developed in post-war Germany which tried to express reality with a more objective view of the world.

The new cultural ferment

Key question
What was *Neue Sachlichkeit* and how did it express itself?

The term generally used to reflect the cultural developments in Weimar Germany was *Neue Sachlichkeit*. It can be translated as 'new practicality' or '**new functionalism**', which means essentially a desire to show reality and objectivity. These words are best explained by looking at some of the major examples of different art forms.

Art

Artists in favour of the 'new objectivity' broke away from the traditional nostalgia of the nineteenth century. They wanted to understand ordinary people in everyday life – and by their art they aimed to comment on the state of society. This approach was epitomised by Georg Grosz and Otto Dix whose paintings and caricatures had strong political and social messages.

Architecture and design

One of the most striking artistic developments in Weimar Germany was the Bauhaus school led by the architect Walter Gropius, which was established in 1919 in the town of Weimar itself. The Bauhaus movement was a new style that influenced all aspects of design. Its approach was functional and it emphasised the close relationship between art and technology, which is underlined by its motto 'Art and Technology – a new unity'.

Literature

It is impossible to categorise the rich range of writing which emerged in Weimar Germany. Not all writers were **expressionists** influenced by the *Neue Sachlichkeit*. For example, the celebrated Thomas Mann, who won the Nobel Prize for literature, was not part of that movement. In fact, the big sellers were the authors who wrote traditional nostalgic literature – such as Hans Grimm. In the more *avant garde* style were the works of Arnold Zweig and Peter Lampel, who explored a range of social issues growing out of the distress and misery of working people in the big cities. Two particular books to be remembered are: the pacifist *All Quiet on the Western Front*, published in 1928 by Erich Maria von Remarque, an ex-soldier critical of the First World War; and *Berlin Alexanderplatz* written by Alfred Döblin, which examined the life of a worker in Weimar society.

Key terms

Expressionism
An art form which suggests that the artist transforms reality to express a personal outlook.

Avant garde
A general term suggesting new ideas and styles in art.

A painting from 1927 by the German artist Otto Dix. Dix's war service deeply influenced his experiences and this piece underlines the contrast between the good-life of the affluent and the seedier side of the poor and disabled.

Pillars of Society: a painting from 1926 by the German artist Georg
Grosz. Grosz was wounded in the war and in 1918 he joined the KPD.
The title is an ironic comment on the dominant social forces in Germany,
as he mocks the image of the soldier, the priest, the banker.

The *Weißenhofsiedlung* was built on the Killesberg in Stuttgart in 1927. It is one of the best examples of the 'new architecture' in Germany and formed part of the exhibition *Die Wohnung* ('The flat') organised by the German *Werkbund*.

Theatre

In drama, *Neue Sachlichkeit* developed into what was called *Zeittheater* (theatre of the time) that introduced new dramatic methods often with an explicit left-wing sympathies – and were most evident in the plays of Bertolt Brecht and Erwin Piscator. They used innovative techniques such as banners, slogans, film and slides, and adopted controversial methods to portray characters' behaviour in their everyday lives.

Mass culture

Key question
In what ways did Weimar culture reach out to ordinary people?

The 1920s were a time of dramatic changes that saw the emergence of a modern mass culture. Germany was no exception. It saw the development of mass communication methods and international influences, especially from USA, such as jazz music and consumerism.

Film

During the 1920s, the German film industry became the most advanced in Europe. German film-makers were well respected for their high-quality work; most notable of the films of the time were:

- *Metropolis* (1926) by Fritz Lang
- *Fridericus Rex* (*King Frederick the Great*) (1922)
- *Blue Angel* (1930), with the young actress Marlene Dietrich.

However, although the German film market was very much dominated by the organisation, UFA, run by Alfred Hugenberg (see page 68), from the mid-1920s American 'movies' quickly made an exceptional impact. The popular appeal of the comedy of Charlie Chaplin shows that Weimar culture was part an international mass culture and was not exclusively German.

Radio

Radio also emerged very rapidly as another mass medium. The German Radio Company was established in 1923 and by 1932, despite the depression, one in four Germans owned a radio.

Cabaret

Berlin had a vibrant nightlife. Cabaret clubs opened up with a permissiveness that mocked the conventions of the old Germany: satirical comedy, jazz music, and women dancers (and even wrestlers) with varying degrees of nudity.

The conflict of cultures

There were some respected conservative intellectuals, like Arthur Möller and Oswald Spengler, who condemned democratic and industrial society. Moreover, many of the writers in the 1920s opposed pacifism and proudly glorified the sacrifices of the First World War. Berlin was definitely not typical of all Germany, but it left a very powerful impression – both positive and negative. Some could enjoy and appreciate the cultural experimentation, but most Germans were horrified by what they saw as the decline in established moral and cultural standards. It has also been suggested that Weimar culture never established a genuinely tolerant attitude. The *avant garde* and the conservatives were clearly at odds with each other. More significantly, both sides took advantage of the freedoms and permissiveness of Weimar liberalism to criticise it, while not being genuinely tolerant or sympathetic towards each other. Weimar society was become increasingly **polarised** before the onset of the political and economic crisis in 1929.

> **Key question**
> Who reacted against *Neue Sachlichkeit* and why?

> **Polarisation**
> The division of society into distinctly opposite views (the comparison is to the north and south poles).
>
> Key term

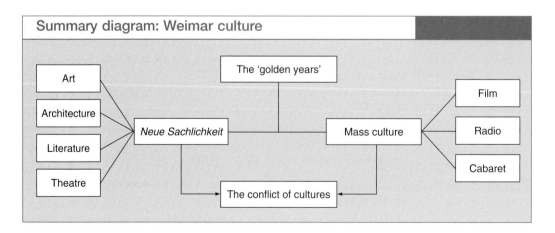

Summary diagram: Weimar culture

- Art
- Architecture
- Literature
- Theatre

→ *Neue Sachlichkeit* →

The 'golden years'

→ Mass culture ←

- Film
- Radio
- Cabaret

The conflict of cultures

Key question
Were the years
1924–9 deceptively
stable?

5 | Weimar 1924–9: An Overview

The years 1924–9 marked the high point of the Weimar Republic.
By comparison with the periods before and after, these years do
appear stable. The real increase in prosperity experienced
by many, and the cultural vitality of the period, gave support
to the view that these years were indeed the 'golden years'.
However, historians have generally tended to question this
stability because it was in fact limited in scope. This is the reason
why the historian Peukert describes these years as a 'deceptive
stability'.

An unstable economy

Germany's economic recovery was built on unstable foundations
that created a false idea of prosperity. Problems persisted in the
economy and they were temporarily hidden only by an increasing
reliance on credit from abroad. In this way Germany's economy
became tied up with powerful external forces over which it had no
control. Hindsight now allows historians to see that, in the late
1920s, any disruption to the world's trade or finance markets was
bound to have a particularly damaging effect on the uncertain
German economy.

A divided society

German society was still divided by deep class differences
as well as by regional and religious differences that prevented
the development of national agreement and harmony.
The war and the years of crisis that followed had left
bitterness, fear and resentment between employers and their
workers. Following the introduction of the state scheme for
settling disputes in 1924, its procedure was used
as a matter of course, whereas the intention had been that it
would be the exception, not the rule. As a result, there was
arbitration in some 76,000 industrial disputes between 1924
and 1932.

In 1928, workers were locked out from their place of work in
the Ruhr ironworks when the employers refused to accept the
arbitration award. It was the most serious industrial confrontation
of the Weimar period. A compromise solution was achieved, but it
showed the extent of the bitterness of industrial relations even
before the start of the world depression.

Political division

Tension was also evident in the political sphere where the
parliamentary system had failed to build on the changes of 1918.
The original ideals of the Constitution had not been developed
and there was little sign that the system had produced a
stable and mature system. In particular, the main democratic
parties had still not recognised the necessity of working together
in a spirit of compromise. It was not so much the weaknesses of
the Constitution, but the failure to establish a shared political
outlook that led to its instability.

Foreign affairs

Even the successes of Stresemann in the field of foreign affairs were offset by the fact that significant numbers of his fellow countrymen rejected his policy out of hand and pressed for a more hardline approach.

In reality, the middle years of the Weimar Republic were stable only in comparison with the periods before and after. Weimar's condition suggested that the fundamental problems inherited from war and the years of crisis had not been resolved. They persisted, so that when the crisis set in during 1929–30 the Weimar Republic did not prove strong enough to withstand the storm.

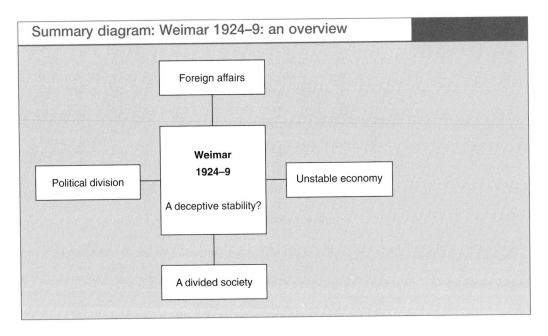

Summary diagram: Weimar 1924–9: an overview

Study Guide: AS Question

In the style of OCR A

Assess the reasons why Weimar Germany was stable during the years 1924–8. (50 marks)

Exam tips

This question asks you to evaluate reasons. 'Assess' does not mean look at each reason in isolation. Events happen because of the combined influence of factors, so explain also how each one influenced another. Work out which you think was most important to stability, and justify your choice with evidence.

Your answer needs to consider the reasons for two different (but related) elements: political stability and economic stability. Each helped underpin the other so one was itself a reason for the other. The underlying answer is probably the relative economic recovery of Germany so you might start there, considering the impact of the *Rentenmark* and the Dawes/Young Plans. Industry developed and exports rose, earning the country and individual workers much-needed money. In turn, that allowed Weimar governments to introduce strong welfare programmes. People felt well-off and secure, especially after 1918–23. That more relaxed atmosphere encouraged a calmer politics (and thus lower turnouts at elections). Binding everything together was Stresemann whose realistic policies have come to symbolise these 'golden years'.

You might question the question, asking how stable things really were. Significant economic weaknesses remained. Costs and debts were rising. Unemployment was serious. Did 'stability' depend on short-term credit and foreign money? Most governments did not have majorities in the *Reichstag* and were coalitions of limited stability. Most parties were badly divided, and the pro-democracy parties (DDP, DVP, SPD) failed to give a strong lead. In your final conclusion, you might add a new element to your essay by questioning how 'genuine' Stresemann was.

5 The Early Years of the Nazis 1919–29

POINTS TO CONSIDER
In the 1920s Hitler and the Nazi Party enjoyed a rather
chequered history and they did not made any real political
impact until the onset of the Great Depression. However,
Nazism did take root. The purpose of this chapter is to
examine the role of the Nazis in 1920s' Germany through
the following themes:

- The personal background of Adolf Hitler and the creation
  of the Nazi Party
- The Munich Beer Hall *putsch*
- Nazi ideas
- Mixed fortunes of Nazism in the 1920s

Key dates

1919		Creation of German Workers' Party (DAP) by Anton Drexler
1920	February	Party name changed to NSDAP (National Socialist German Workers' Party)
		25-Points party programme drawn up by Drexler and Hitler
1923	November 8–9	Beer Hall *putsch* in Munich
1924		Hitler in Landsberg prison
		Mein Kampf written
1925	February	NSDAP refounded in Munich
1926	February	Bamberg conference: Hitler's leadership of the Party re-established
1928	May	*Reichstag* election result
1929–33		The Great Depression

1 | Adolf Hitler and the Creation of the Nazi Party

Hitler's early years

There was little in the background of Adolf Hitler (1889–1945) to
suggest that he would become a powerful political figure. Hitler
was born at Braunau-am-Inn in 1889 in what was then the Austro-
Hungarian Empire. He failed to impress at school, and after the
death of his parents he moved to Vienna in 1907. There he

Key question
How did Hitler
become involved in
politics?

Key terms

Anti-Semitism
The hatred of Jews. It became the most significant part of Nazi racist thinking. For Hitler, the 'master-race' was the pure Aryan (the people of northern Europe) and the Germans represented the highest caste. The lowest race for Hitler was the Jews.

Volk
Often translated as 'people', although it tends to suggest a nation with the same ethnic and cultural identities and with a collective sense of belonging.

applied unsuccessfully for a place as a student at the Academy of Fine Arts. For the next six years he led an aimless and unhappy existence in the poorer districts of the city. It was not until he joined the Bavarian Regiment on the outbreak of war in 1914 that he found a real purpose in life. He served bravely throughout the war and was awarded the Iron Cross First Class.

When the war ended he was in hospital recovering from a British gas attack. By the time he had returned to Bavaria in early 1919 he had already framed in his mind the core of what was to become National Socialism:

- fervent German nationalism
- support of authoritarianism and opposition to democracy and socialism
- a racially inspired view of society which exhibited itself most obviously in a rabid **anti-Semitism** and a veneration of the German *Volk* as the master race.

Such a mixture of ideas in a man whose personal life was much of a mystery – he had no close family and few real friends – has excited some historians to resort to psychological analysis leading to extraordinary speculation. Did his anti-Semitism originate from contracting syphilis from a Jewish prostitute? Could his authoritarian attitude be explained by his upbringing at the hands of an old and repressive father? Such psychological diagnoses – and there are many – may interest the student, but the supporting evidence for such explanations is at best flimsy. As a result, the conclusions reached are highly speculative and do not really help to explain the key question of how and why Hitler became such an influential political force.

Key question
How significant was the NSDAP by 1922?

Key date
Creation of the German Workers' Party (DAP) by Anton Drexler: 1919

Key term
Anti-capitalism
Rejects the economic system based upon private property and profit. Early Nazi ideas laid stress upon preventing the exploitation of workers and suggesting social reforms.

The creation and emergence of the Nazi Party

It was because of his committed right-wing attitudes that Hitler was employed in the politically charged atmosphere of 1919 as a kind of spy by the political department of the Bavarian section of the German Army. One of his investigations brought him into contact with the DAP (*Deutsche Arbeiterpartei* – German Workers' Party) which was not a movement of the revolutionary left, as Hitler had assumed on hearing its name, but one committed to nationalism, anti-Semitism and **anti-capitalism**. Hitler joined the tiny party and immediately became a member of its committee. His energy, oratory and propaganda skills soon made an impact on the small group and it was Hitler who, with the Party's founder, Anton Drexler, drew up the Party's 25-points programme in February 1920 (see Figure 5.1). At the same time, it was agreed to change the Party's name to the NSDAP, the National Socialist German Workers' Party. (For analysis of Nazi ideology, see pages 92–5.)

By mid-1921 it was clear Hitler was the driving-force behind the Party. Although he still held only the post of propaganda chief, it was his powerful speeches that had impressed local audiences and had helped to increase party membership to 3300. He had encouraged the creation of the armed squads to protect

1. We demand the union of all Germans in a Greater Germany on the basis of the right of national self-determination.

2. We demand equality of rights for the German People in its dealings with other nations, and the revocation of the peace treaties of Versailles and Saint Germain.

3. We demand land and territory (colonies) to feed our people and to settle our surplus population.

4. Only members of the *Volk* (nation) may be citizens of the State. Only those of German blood, whatever their creed may be members of the nation. Accordingly no Jew may be a member of the nation.

7. We demand that the State shall make it its primary duty to provide a livelihood for its citizens. If it should prove impossible to feed the entire population, non-citizens must be deported from the Reich.

10. It must be the first duty of every citizen to perform physical or mental work. The activities of the individual must not clash with the general interest, but must proceed within the framework of the community and be for the general good.

14. We demand profit sharing in large industrial enterprises.

15. We demand the extensive development of insurance for old age.

18. We demand the ruthless prosecution of those whose activities are injurious to the common interest. Common criminals, usurers, profiteers must be punished with death, whatever their creed or race.

22. We demand the abolition of the mercenary army and the formation of a people's army.

23. We demand legal warfare on deliberate political mendacity and its dissemination in the press.

25. We demand the creation of a strong central power of the Reich.

Key dates

Name of the DAP party changed to NSDAP (National Socialist German Workers' Party): February 1920

Party's programme of 25 points drawn up by Drexler and Hitler: February 1920

Figure 5.1: Extracts from the 25 points of the programme of the German Workers' Party.

Party meetings and to intimidate the opposition, especially the communists. It was his development of early propaganda techniques – the Nazi salute, the swastika, the uniform – that had done so much to give the Party a clear and easily recognisable identity.

Alarmed by Hitler's increasing domination of the Party, Drexler and some other members of the committee tried to limit his influence. However, it was here, for the first time, that Hitler showed his political ability to manoeuvre and to gamble. He was by far the most influential speaker and the Party knew it, so, shrewdly, he offered to resign. In the ensuing power struggle he was quickly able to mobilise support at two meetings in July 1921. He was invited back in glory. Embarrassed, Drexler resigned and Hitler became chairman and Führer (leader) of the Party.

Having gained supreme control over the Party in Munich, Hitler aimed to subordinate all the other right-wing groups under his Party's leadership and certainly, in the years 1921–3, the Party was strengthened by a number of significant developments:

Key term

SA
Sturm Abteilung became known in English as the Stormtroopers. They were also referred to as the Brownshirts after the colour of the uniform. They supported the radical socialist aspects of Nazism.

- The armed squads were organised and set up as the **SA** in 1921 as a paramilitary unit led by Ernst Röhm (see page 150). It was now used to organise planned thuggery and violence. Most notoriously, the conflict in the town of Coburg degenerated into a pitched battle between the communists and the SA, but it showed how politically vital it was to win to control of the streets.
- The Party established its first newspaper in 1921, the *Völkischer Beobachter* (the *People's Observer*).
- In 1922 Hitler won the backing of Julius Streicher, who previously had run a rival right-wing party in northern Bavaria. Streicher also published his own newspaper, *Der Stürmer*, which was overtly anti-Semitic with a range of seedy articles devoted to sex and violence.
- Hitler was also fortunate to win the support of the influential Hermann Göring, who joined the Party in 1922 (see page 172). He was born into a Bavarian landowning family, while his wife was a leading Swedish aristocratic. They made many very helpful social contacts in Munich, which gave Hitler and Nazism respectability.

By 1923, the Party had a membership of about 20,000. Hitler certainly enjoyed an impressive personal reputation and, as a result, Nazism successfully established an influential role on the extreme right in Bavaria. However, despite Nazi efforts, it still proved difficult to control all the radical right-wing political groups, which remained independent organisations across Germany. The Nazi Party was still very much a fringe party, limited to the region of Bavaria.

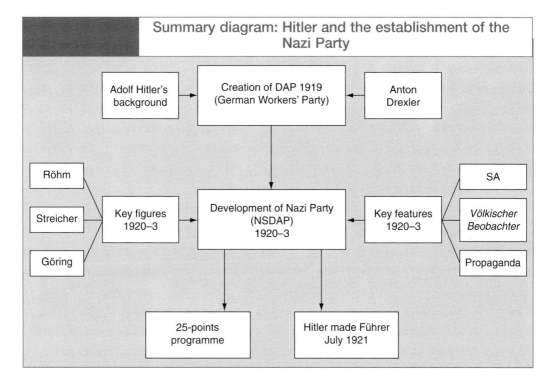

Summary diagram: Hitler and the establishment of the Nazi Party

2 | The Beer Hall *Putsch* 1923

The successful take-over of power by Mussolini in Italy in October 1922, combined with the developing internal crisis in Germany, convinced Hitler that the opportunity to seize power had arrived. Indeed, a leading Nazi introduced Hitler at one of his speeches in Munich by saying: 'Germany's Mussolini is called Adolf Hitler'. However, the Nazis were far too weak on their own to stage any kind of political take-over and Hitler himself was still seen merely as a 'drummer' who could stir up the masses for the national movement. It was the need for allies which led Hitler into negotiations with Kahr and the Bavarian State Government and the Bavarian section of the German army under Lossow (see pages 41–2).

It was with these two men that Hitler plotted to 'March on Berlin' (in the style of Mussolini's *coup* which, only the previous year, had become known as the 'March on Rome'). They aimed to mobilise all the military forces from Bavaria – including sections of the German army, the police, the SA and other paramilitaries – and then, by closing in on Berlin, to seize national power. With hindsight, Hitler's plan was unrealistic and doomed because:

- he grossly over-estimated the level of public support for a *putsch* – despite the problems faced by Weimar's democratic government in 1923
- he showed a lack of real planning
- he relied too heavily on the promise of support of Ludendorff
- most significantly, at the eleventh hour, Kahr and Lossow, fearing failure, decided to hold back.

Key question
How did Hitler manage to turn the failure of the Munich Beer Hall *putsch* to his advantage?

Key date
The Beer Hall *putsch* in Munich:
8–9 November 1923

A photograph of the main leaders of the Beer Hall *putsch* posing before the trial in February 1924. Frick (A), Ludendorff (B), Hitler (C), and Röhm (D) can be identified by the letters.

Hitler was not so cautious and preferred to press on rather than lose the opportunity. On 8 November, when Kahr was addressing a large audience in one of Munich's beer halls, Hitler and the Nazis took control of the meeting, declared a 'national revolution' and forced Kahr and Lossow to support it. The next day Hitler, Göring, Streicher, Röhm, Himmler (and Ludendorff) marched into the city of Munich with 2000 SA men, but they had no real military backing, and the attempted take-over of Munich was easily crushed by the Bavarian police. Fourteen Nazis were killed and Hitler himself was arrested on a charge of treason.

The consequences

In many respects the *putsch* was a farce. Hitler and the *putschists* were arrested and charged with treason and the NSADP itself was banned. However, Hitler gained significant political advantages from the episode:

- He turned his trial into a great propaganda success both for himself and for the Nazi cause. He played on all his rhetorical

'Hitler's entry into Berlin.' A cartoon published by the *Simplicissimus* magazine in April 1924 just after Hitler's trial. It mocks Hitler's march on Berlin and shows Ebert in chains.

skills and evoked admiration for his patriotism. For the first time he made himself a national figure.

- He won the respect of many other right-wing nationalists for having had the courage to act.
- The leniency of his sentence – five years, the minimum stipulated by the Weimar Constitution and actually reduced to 10 months – seemed like an act of encouragement on the part of the judiciary.
- He used his months in prison to write and to reassess his political strategy (see below), including dictating *Mein Kampf*.

Hitler imprisoned in Landsberg prison; *Mein Kampf* written: 1924

Mein Kampf
'My struggle'. The book written by Hitler in 1924, which expresses his political ideas.

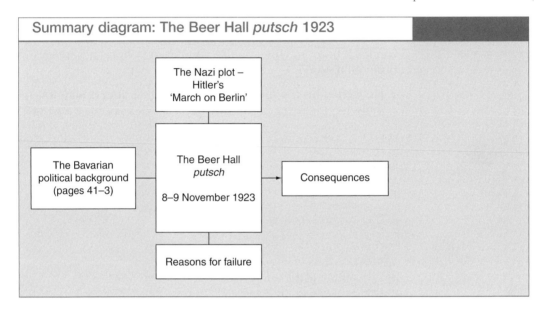

Summary diagram: The Beer Hall *putsch* 1923

3 | Nazi Ideas

Nazism always emphasised the importance of action over thought. However, whilst in Landsberg prison, Hitler dictated the first part of *Mein Kampf* which, in the following years, became the bible of National Socialism. Together with the 25-points programme of 1920, it provides the basic framework of Hitler's ideology and of Nazism itself.

Racism

Hitler's ideas were built upon his concept of race. He believed that humanity consisted of a hierarchy of races and that life was no more than 'the survival of the fittest'. He argued that **social Darwinism** necessitated a struggle between races, just as animals fought for food and territory in the wild. Furthermore, he considered it vital to maintain racial purity, so that the blood of the weak would not undermine the strong.

It was a crude philosophy, which appears even more simplistic when Hitler's analysis of the races is considered. The *Herrenvolk*

What were the main elements of Nazi thinking?

Social Darwinism
A philosophy that portrayed the world as a 'struggle' between people, races and nations. Hitler viewed war as the highest form of 'struggle' and was deeply influenced by the theory of evolution based upon natural selection.

Key terms

Aryan
Broadly refers to all the peoples of the Indo-European family. However, the term was more specifically defined by the Nazis as the non-Jewish people of northern Europe.

Führerprinzip
'The leadership principle'. Hitler upheld the idea of a one-party state, built on an all-powerful leader.

(master-race) was the **Aryan** race and was exemplified by the Germans. It was the task of the Aryan to remain pure and to dominate the inferior races. In the following extract from *Mein Kampf* Hitler writes:

> The adulteration of the blood and racial deterioration conditioned thereby are the only causes that account for the decline of ancient civilisations; for it is never by war that nations are ruined, but by the loss of their powers of resistance, which are exclusively a characteristic of pure racial blood. In this world everything that is not of sound stock is like chaff. Every historical event in the world is nothing more nor less than a manifestation of the instinct of racial self-preservation, whether for weal or woe [for better or for worse].

(See also the 25-points programme, page 88: points 4 and 7.)

Anti-democracy

In Hitler's opinion there was no realistic alternative to strong dictatorial government. Ever since his years in Vienna he had viewed parliamentary democracy as weak and ineffective. It went against the German historical traditions of militarism and the power of the state. Furthermore, it encouraged the development of an even greater evil, communism.

More specifically, Hitler saw Weimar democracy as a betrayal. In his eyes, it was the democratic and socialist politicians of 1918, 'the November criminals', who had stabbed the German army in the back, by accepting the armistice and establishing the Republic (page 5). Since then Germany had lurched from crisis to crisis.

In place of democracy Hitler wanted an all-embracing one-party state that would be run on the *Führerprinzip*, which rejected representative government and liberal values. Thus, the masses in society were to be controlled for the common good, but an individual leader was to be chosen in order to rouse the nation into action, and to take the necessary decisions. (See also the 25-points programme, page 88: point 25.)

Nationalism

A crucial element in Nazi thinking was an aggressive nationalism, which developed out of the particular circumstances of Germany's recent history. The armistice of 1918 and the subsequent Treaty of Versailles had to be overturned, and the lost territories had to be restored to Germany (see pages 26–9). But Hitler's nationalism called for more than a mere restoration of the 1914 frontiers. It meant the creation of an empire (*Reich*) to include all those members of the German *Volk* who lived beyond the frontiers of the Kaiser's Germany: the Austrian Germans; the Germans in the Sudetenland; the German communities along the Baltic coast; all were to be included within the borderlands of Germany.

Yet, Hitler's nationalist aims did not end there. He dreamed of a Greater Germany, a superpower, capable of competing with the British Empire and the United States. Such an objective could be achieved only by territorial expansion on a grand scale. This was the basis of Hitler's demand for **Lebensraum** for Germany. Only by the conquest of Poland, the Ukraine and Russia could Germany obtain the raw materials, cheap labour and food supplies so necessary for continental supremacy. The creation of his 'New Order' in eastern Europe also held one other great attraction: namely, the destruction of the USSR, the centre of world communism.

In *Mein Kampf* Hitler wrote:

> The German people must be assured the territorial area which is necessary for it to exist on earth ... People of the same blood should be in the same Reich. The German people will have no right to engage in a colonial policy until they shall have brought all their children together in one state. When the territory of the Reich embraces all the Germans and finds itself unable to assure them a livelihood, only then can the moral right arise, from the need of the people, to acquire foreign territory ... Germany will either become a World Power or will not continue to exist at all. ... The future goal of our foreign policy ought to be an Eastern policy, which will have in view the acquisition of such territory as is necessary for our German people.

(See also the 25-points programme, page 88: points 1, 2 and 3.)

The socialist aspect of Nazism

A number of points in the 1920 programme demanded socialist reforms and, for a long time, there existed a faction within the Party that emphasised the anti-capitalist aspect of Nazism, for example:

- profit-sharing in large industrial enterprises
- the extensive development of insurance for old age
- the nationalisation of all businesses.

Hitler accepted these points in the early years because he recognised their popular appeal but he himself never showed any real commitment to such ideas. As a result they were the cause of important differences within the Party and were not really dropped until Hitler had fully established his dominant position by 1934. (See also the 25-points programme, page 88: points 10, 14 and 15.)

What Hitler and Goebbels later began to promote was the concept of the **Volksgemeinschaft** (people's community). This remained the vaguest element of the Nazi ideology, and is therefore difficult to define precisely. First, it was intended to overcome the old differences of class, religion and politics. But secondly, it aimed to bring about a new collective national identity by encouraging people to work together for the benefit of the nation and by promoting 'German values'. Such a system could of course only benefit those who racially belonged to the German *Volk* and who willingly accepted the loss of individual freedoms in an authoritarian system.

Key terms

Lebensraum
'Living space'. Hitler's aim to create an empire by establishing German supremacy over the eastern lands in Europe.

Volksgemeinschaft
'A people's community'. Nazism stressed the development of a harmonious, socially unified and racially pure community.

Key question
Was Nazism an
original German
ideology?

The ideology of National Socialism

Early historians and biographers of Hitler simply saw him as a cynical opportunist motivated by the pursuit of power. Others have now generally come to view him as a committed political leader influenced by certain key ideas that he used to lay the basis of a consistent Nazi programme.

However, to describe Hitler's thinking, or Nazism, as an ideology is really to flatter it. An 'ideology' suggests a coherent thought-through system or theory of ideas, as found, for example, in Marxism. Nazism lacked coherence and was intellectually superficial and simplistic. It was not genuinely a rational system of thought. It was merely a collection of ideas which grew out of the age of enlightenment and the spirit of German romanticism. It was not in any positive sense original – every aspect of Hitler's thinking was to be found in the nationalist and racist writings of the nineteenth century:

- His nationalism was an outgrowth of the fervour generated in the years leading up to Germany's unification of 1871.
- His idea of an all-German *Reich* was a simple repetition of the demands for the 'Greater Germany' made by those German nationalists who criticised the limits of the 1871 unification.
- Even the imperialism of *Lebensraum* had already found expression in the programme of 'Germanisation' supported by those writers who saw the German race as somehow superior.
- The growing veneration for the *Volk* had gone hand-in-hand with the development of racist ideas, and in particular of anti-Semitism.

Thus, even before Hitler and other leading Nazis were born, the core of what would become Nazism was already current in political circles. It was to be found in the cheap and vulgar pamphlets sold to the masses in the large cities; in the political programme of respectable pressure groups, such as the **Pan-German League**; within the corridors of Germany's great universities; and in the creative works of certain cultural figures, such as the composer Richard Wagner.

However, despite these links, one must avoid labelling Nazi ideology as the logical result of German intellectual thinking. It is all too easy to emphasise those elements that prove the linkage theory, whilst ignoring the host of other evidence that points to entirely different views, e.g. the strong socialist tradition in Germany. Moreover, it is well to remember that a number of countries, but especially Britain and France, also witnessed the propagation of very similar ideas at this time. In that sense nationalism and racism were an outgrowth of nineteenth-century European history. Nazi ideology may not have been original, but it should not therefore be assumed that it was an inevitable result of Germany's past.

Key term

Pan-German League
A movement founded at the end of the nineteenth century campaigning for the uniting of all Germans into one country.

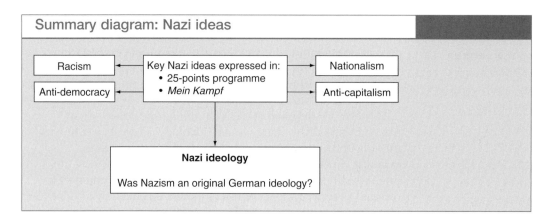

Summary diagram: Nazi ideas

4 | Nazi Fortunes in the 1920s

Key question
In what ways was the Nazi Party revitalised?

When Hitler left prison in December 1924 the future for Nazism looked bleak. The Party was in disarray; its leading members were split into factions and the membership was in decline. More significantly, the atmosphere of crisis that had prevailed in the early years of the Republic had given way to a period of political and economic calm (see pages 60–70). Nevertheless, the Party was officially refounded on 27 February 1925 and at the same time Hitler wrote a lengthy editorial for the *Völkischer Beobachter* with the heading 'A new beginning'.

Key dates

NSDAP refounded in Munich: 27 February 1925

Bamberg conference: Hitler established his leadership of the Party: 14 February 1926

Strategy and leadership

In Landsberg prison Hitler, reflecting on the failure of the 1923 *putsch*, became convinced of two vital points:

- He must establish his own absolute control over the Party.
- An armed *coup* was no longer an appropriate tactic and the only sure way to succeed was to work within the Weimar Constitution and to gain power by legal means. Such a policy of legality would necessitate the creation of a party structure geared to gaining success in the elections. As Hitler himself said in prison in 1924:

> … we shall have to hold our noses and enter the *Reichstag* against the Catholic and Marxist deputies. If out-voting them takes longer than our shooting them, at least the result will be guaranteed by their own Constitution. Any lawful process is slow.

However, the Party remained deeply divided in a number of ways:

- Not everyone agreed with the new policy of legality.
- Traditional regional hostilities continued to exist, particularly between the Party's power base in Bavaria and the branches in northern Germany.
- Most importantly, policy differences had got worse between the nationalist and anti-capitalist wings of the Party (see page 94).

For over a year Hitler struggled with this internal friction. The problem was highlighted by the power and influence of Gregor Strasser and also his brother Otto. Gregor Strasser joined the NSDAP in 1920 and stood loyally next to Hitler in the Munich *putsch*, but he epitomised the opposing standpoint within the Party. He favoured the more socialist anti-capitalist policies for the workers and he was in effect the leader of the movement in northern Germany.

Eventually, in February 1926, the differences within the Party came to a head at a special party conference in Bamberg. On the one hand it was a significant victory for Hitler, as he mobilised sufficient support to re-establish his supremacy. The Nazi Party was to be run according to the *Führerprinzip* and there was to be no place for disagreements. On the other hand, the Party declared that the original 25 points of the programme with its socialist elements remained unchangeable. So, although Hitler had cleverly outmanoeuvred his greatest threat and he had re-established a degree of unity within the Party, there were still significant rivalries and differences.

Profile: Gregor Strasser 1892–1934

1892		– Born in Bavaria
1914–18		– Served in the First World War
1920		– Joined the NASDP and supported the anti-capitalist 'left-wing' socialist faction
1923	November	– Took part in the Munich *putsch*
1926	February	– Defeated by Hitler over the Party's leadership at the Bamberg Conference, but he continued to criticise Hitler's policies
1926–32		– Responsible for building the mass movement of the Party in the 1920s
		– Led the NSDAP in northern Germany
1932	December	– Offered the post of vice-chancellor by Schleicher (see page 137). Differences with Hitler came to a head in a major row and he was expelled from the Party
1934	June	– Murdered in the SA purge (see page 152)

Because Gregor Strasser was murdered in 1934 and because he played no role in the government of the Third Reich, it is easy to ignore his significance in the rise of Nazism. Yet, until the day he resigned from the Party, Strasser was, in effect, second to Hitler. He was always a supporter of the anti-capitalist 'left-wing' socialist faction, which became increasingly disillusioned when Hitler courted big business. Like Hitler, an inspiring political speaker, he also showed the administrative skills to develop a mass movement for the Party. (He also worked closely with his brother until Otto left the Party in 1930.)

The creation of the Party structure

The most significant development in the years before the Great Depression lay in the reorganisation of the Party structure. The whole of Germany was divided into regions (*Gaue*), which reflected the electoral geography of Weimar's system of proportional representation. The control of each region was placed in the hands of a **Gauleiter**, who then had the responsibility of creating district (*Kreis*) and branch (*Ort*) groups. In this way a vertical Party structure was created throughout Germany, which did not detract from Hitler's own position of authority as leader.

Perhaps the most renowned of the *Gauleiters* was the holder of the Berlin post, Joseph Goebbels. Goebbels had originally been a sympathiser of Gregor Strasser's socialist ideas, but from 1926 he gave his support to Hitler. He was then rewarded by being given the responsibility for winning over the capital, a traditionally left-wing stronghold of the SPD. He showed a real interest in propaganda and created the newspaper, *Der Angriff* (*The Attack*), but was not appointed chief of party propaganda until 1930 (see pages 244–5).

The Nazis also founded a number of new associated Nazi organisations that were geared to appeal to the specific interests of particular groups of Germans. Among these were:

- The Hitler Youth
- The Nazi Teachers' Association
- Union of Nazi Lawyers
- The Order of German Women.

Gregor Strasser was mainly responsible for building up an efficient Party structure and this was reflected in its increasing membership during these years (see Table 5.1).

Table 5.1: NSDAP membership

Year	Membership numbers
1925	27,000
1926	49,000
1927	72,000
1928	108,000

One other significant initiative in these years was the creation of the **SS**. It was set up in 1925 as an élite body of black-shirted guards, sworn to absolute obedience to the Führer. In 1929 it had only 200 members. At first, it was just Hitler's personal bodyguard though, when it was placed under the control of Himmler later that year, it soon developed its own identity.

Key terms

Gauleiter
Means 'leader of a regional area'. The Nazi Party was organised into 35 regions from 1926.

SS
Schutz Staffel (protection squad); became known as the Blackshirts, named after the uniform.

Key question
How strong was the Nazi Party by the end of the 1920s?

The *Reichstag* election of May 1928

By 1928 it can be seen clearly that the Party had made progress and was really an effective political machine, most obviously because:

- the structure was effectively organised
- the membership had increased four-fold since 1925
- Hitler's leadership was authoritative and secure (despite the ongoing challenge from the Strasser faction).

As a result, the Nazi Party had also successfully taken over many of the other right-wing racist groups in Germany.

Such advances, however, could not compensate for Nazi disappointment after the *Reichstag* election in May 1928. When the votes were counted, the Party had won only 2.6 per cent of the vote and a mere 12 seats (see page 64). It seemed as if Hitler's policy of legality had failed to bring political success, whereas in the favourable socio-economic circumstances Weimar democracy had managed to stabilise its political position. So, Nazism may have taken root, but there was no real sign that it could flourish in Germany.

If this evidence confirmed the belief of many that Hitler was nothing more than an eccentric without the personal leadership to establish a really broad national appeal, there was just one telling sign. In the election, the Party made significant gains in the northern part of Germany amongst the rural and middle and lower middle classes of areas such as Schleswig-Holstein.

This trend was reflected in the regional state elections of 1929, which suggested that the fall in agricultural prices was beginning to cause discontent – demonstrations and protests were giving way to bankruptcies and violence. Most significantly, in the province of Thuringia, in central Germany, the Nazi Party trebled its vote and broke the 10 per cent barrier for the first time, recording 11.3 per cent. Such figures suggested that the Nazis could exploit the increasingly difficult economic times of the Great Depression.

Key dates

Reichstag election result, very disappointing Nazi performance: May 1928

Great Depression: 1929–33

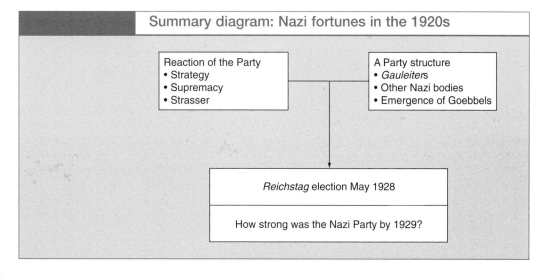

Summary diagram: Nazi fortunes in the 1920s

Reaction of the Party
- Strategy
- Supremacy
- Strasser

A Party structure
- *Gauleiters*
- Other Nazi bodies
- Emergence of Goebbels

Reichstag election May 1928

How strong was the Nazi Party by 1929?

Study Guide: AS Question

In the style of OCR A

'A little group of no consequence.' How far do you agree with this view of the Nazi Party in 1928? Explain your answer.　　(50 marks)

Exam tips

The cross-references are intended to take you straight to the material that will help you to answer the question.

The question asks you to evaluate the historical validity of a statement. Your answer must therefore keep its focus firmly on the three elements of the quotation: little; unimportant; 1928. To help you, look also at Table 4.1 (page 64) as well as material in that chapter. Do not divert yourself into discussing the *Putsch* of 1923, and only discuss ideas/ideology if you make it relevant to the Nazi's position in 1928.

　You may be tempted to see the statement as 'obviously' correct and so not explain carefully with solid evidence why you agree. The Party did very badly in the 1928 election (worse than in either 1924 vote). It was badly divided on key policy issues (not settled at Bamberg in 1926), split by regional rivalries and had been sliding in popularity for some time (Hitler had been convicted of treason). Now look again at the picture. Party organisation was transformed from 1925 while party unity was significantly improved (key inputs of Strasser and Goebbels, as well as Hitler). Party membership may have remained tiny, but it more than doubled from 1926 to 1928 (and quadrupled from 1925) by taking over the supporters and members of most far-right groups. In 1928, the Nazis were still of no consequence, but that position was rapidly changed – compare Table 4.1 (page 64) with Table 6.3 (page 117).

6 The Decline of Weimar and the Rise of Nazism 1929–32

POINTS TO CONSIDER

Weimar already faced pressures before 1929, but the Wall Street Crash, in the very same month as the death of Gustav Stresemann, ushered in the Great Depression that precipitated a political and economic crisis in Germany. This chapter focuses on the collapse of the Weimar Republic and the emergence of the Nazis, which, although closely linked, raises two questions. The first one is why did the Weimar Republic collapse? This is the subject of this chapter. Its main themes are:

- The effects of the world economic crisis on Germany
- The breakdown of parliamentary government
- The advent of presidential government under Brüning, 1930–2
- The appointment of Papen as chancellor
- The death of the Weimar Republic

The next chapter of this book will concentrate on how and why the Nazis established a brutal dictatorship.

Key dates

1929	October	Wall Street Crash
1930	March	Resignation of Müller's government. Brüning appointed chancellor. Young Plan approved by the *Reichstag*
	September	*Reichstag* election: Nazis emerged as second largest party in the *Reichstag*
	December	Brüning's economic measures imposed by presidential decree
1931	July	Five leading German banks failed
	October	Formation of Harzburg Front
1932	January	Unemployment peaked at 6.1 million
	April	Re-election of Hindenburg as president of Germany
	May	Brüning resigned. Papen appointed chancellor
	July	*Reichstag* election: Nazis emerged as largest party in the *Reichstag*

1 | The Impact of the World Economic Crisis on Germany

Key question
Did the Wall Street Crash cause the economic crisis in Germany?

There is no dispute amongst historians that the world economic crisis, which is known as the Great Depression, was an event of major significance. Its effects were felt throughout the world; although not in the Soviet Union.

The Wall Street Crash: October 1929

Key date

Germany undoubtedly felt it in a particularly savage way. It suffered the consequences of the Wall Street Crash – the collapse of share prices on the New York Stock Exchange in October 1929 – more than any other country. Almost immediately the American loans and investment dried up and this was quickly followed by demands for the repayment of those short-term loans. At the same time, the crisis caused a further decline in the price of food and raw materials as the industrialised nations reduced their imports. As demand for exports collapsed, so world trade slumped. In this situation, German industry could no longer pay its way. Without overseas loans and with its export trade falling, prices and wages fell and the number of bankruptcies increased.

Table 6.1: Economic effects of the world economic crisis on Germany

Economic effects	Key features
Trade Slump in world trade. Demand for German exports fell rapidly, e.g. steel, machinery and chemicals	Exports value fell by 55 per cent 1929 = £630m 1932 = £280m
Employment Workers laid off – mass unemployment	Number of registered unemployed (annual averages) 1929 = 1.8m 1932 = 5.6m
Industry Industrial production declined sharply	Production: (1928 = 100) 1929 = 100 1932 = 58 50,000 businesses collapsed
Agriculture Wages and incomes fell sharply. Many farms sold off	Agricultural prices (1913 = 100) 1927 = 138 1932 = 77
Finance Banking sector dislocated by loss of confidence	Five major banks collapsed in 1931 50,000 businesses bankrupted

However, it is all too easy to put Germany's economic crisis down to the Wall Street Crash. It should be borne in mind that there were fundamental weaknesses in the German economy *before* the Wall Street Crash:

- The balance of trade was in the red, i.e. in debt.
- The number of unemployed averaged 1.9 million in 1929, even before the Wall Street Crash.

- Many farmers were already in debt and had been facing falling incomes since 1927.
- German government finances from 1925 were continually run in deficit.

So, although the Wall Street Crash contributed to Germany's economic problems, it is *probable* that the Germany economy faced a chance of a serious depression without it. This suggests that the world economic crisis should really be seen as simply the final push that brought the Weimar economy crashing down. In that sense, it could be said that the Wall Street Crash was merely the occasion, not the cause of Germany's economic crisis.

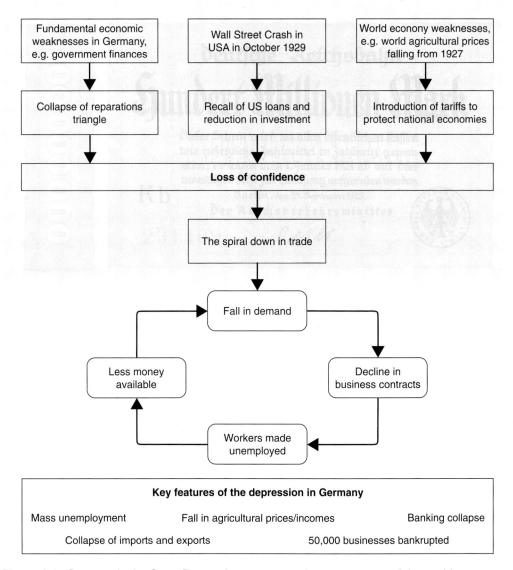

Figure 6.1: Germany in the Great Depression: causes and consequences of the world economic crisis.

A camp for the unemployed and homeless in Berlin. Because there were so many poor people, large camps of tents were set up. These camps gave the impression of orderliness: numbered tents in neat rows with names, like streets.

The human effects of the Great Depression

During the winter of 1929–30, unemployment rose above two million and only 12 months after the Crash, it had reached three million. By January 1932 it stood at 6.1 million, which did not substantially fall until the spring of 1933. On their own, such figures can provide only a limited understanding of the effects of the depression of this magnitude. Unemployment figures, for example, do not take into account those who did not register. Nor do they record the extent of part-time working throughout German industry.

Above all, statistics fail to convey the extent of the human suffering that was the consequence of this disaster because the depression in Germany affected virtually everyone; few families escaped its effects.

Many manual industrial workers, both skilled and unskilled, faced the prospect of long-term unemployment. For their wives, there was the impossible task of trying to feed families and keep homes warm on the money provided by limited social security benefits.

However, such problems were not to be limited to the working class. This depression dragged down the middle classes. From the small shopkeepers to the well-qualified professionals in law and medicine, people struggled to survive in a world where there was little demand for their goods and services. For such people, the decline in their economic position and the onset of poverty were made more difficult by the loss of pride and respectability.

The situation in the countryside was no better than in the towns. As world demand fell further, the agricultural depression deepened, leading to widespread rural poverty. For some tenant farmers there was even the ultimate humiliation of being evicted

Key question
How did the economic crisis affect the German people's lives?

Key date
Unemployment peaked at 6.1 million: January 1932

from their homes, which had often been in their families for generations.

In the more prosperous times we live in today, it is difficult to appreciate the scale of the suffering that struck German people in the early 1930s. The city of Cologne could not pay the interest on its debts, banks closed their doors and, in Berlin, large crowds of unemployed youngsters were kept occupied with open-air games of chess and cards. To many ordinary respectable Germans it seemed as if society itself was breaking down uncontrollably. It is not surprising that many people lost faith in the Weimar Republic, which seemed to offer no end to the misery, and began to see salvation in the solutions offered by political extremists. This was why the economic crisis in Germany quickly degenerated into a more obvious political crisis.

The political implications

Key question
Why did the economic crisis turn into a political one?

The impact of the depression in Germany was certainly more severe than in either Britain or France, but it was on a par with the American experience. In Germany, one in three workers was unemployed in 1933 and by 1932 industrial production had fallen by 42 per cent of its 1929 level. In the USA, the comparable figures were one in four and 46 per cent.

However, in Germany the economic crisis quickly became a political crisis, simply because there was a lack of confidence that weakened the Republic's position in its hour of need. Britain, France and the USA were all well-established democracies and did not face the possibility of a wholesale collapse of their political systems.

Taken together these two points suggest that the Great Depression hastened the end of the Weimar Republic, but only because its economy was already in serious trouble, and the democratic basis of its government was not sufficiently well established.

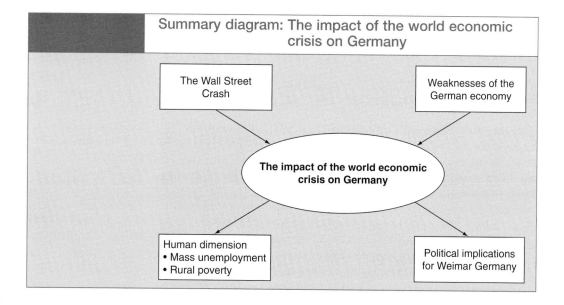

Summary diagram: The impact of the world economic crisis on Germany

2 | Parliamentary Government's Breakdown

In 1929 the German government was in the hands of Hermann Müller's Grand Coalition, which had been formed after the general election of May 1928 (see pages 64–8). Yet, at the very time when unity and firm government were required to tackle the economic crisis, the Weimar Republic was being torn apart by the re-emergence of the emotive issue of reparations.

The Dawes Plan (1924) successfully overcame the reparations crisis of the early 1920s by rescheduling payments based on Germany's capacity to pay but, from the outset, it was seen as a temporary measure until Germany regained its economic strength (see pages 72–3). In early 1929 the IARC (Inter-Allied Reparations Commission) formed a committee of international financiers under the chairmanship of the American banker Owen Young. Its report in June 1929 suggested a new scheme of payments. Germany was to continue paying reparations until 1988 but the final sum was reduced to £1850 million (only one-quarter of the figure demanded in 1921). So, after some negotiation by Stresemann with the Allies, the German government accepted the Young Plan shortly before Stresemann's death.

However, in right-wing circles in Germany, Stresemann's diplomatic achievement was seen as yet another betrayal of national interests to the Allies. In the view of the right wing, any payment of reparations was based upon the 'lie' of Germany's war guilt (Article 231 of the Treaty of Versailles) and the new scheme had, therefore, to be opposed. A national committee, led by the new leader of the Nationalists, Alfred Hugenberg, was formed to fight the Young Plan (see page 76). Hugenberg was also Germany's greatest media tycoon. He owned 150 newspapers and a publishing house, as well as UFA, a world-famous film organisation. He now used all his resources to promote his message. Moreover, he generated support from a wide variety of right-wing nationalist factions:

- DNVP
- *Stahlhelm* (the largest ex-servicemen's organisation) led by Franz Seldte
- Pan-German League
- some leading industrialists, e.g. Fritz Thyssen
- Hitler and the Nazi Party.

Together this '**National Opposition**' drafted a *Law against the Enslavement of the German People*, which denounced any payment of reparations and demanded the punishment of any minister agreeing to such a treaty. The proposal gained enough signatures for it to be made the issue of a national referendum in December 1929. In the end the National Opposition won only 5.8 million votes, a long way short of the 21 million required by the constitution for success.

However, the campaign of the National Opposition had stirred nationalist emotions, focusing opposition on the democratic government at a vital time. It had also brought together many

Key question
How and why did the Young Plan increase political exposure for the Nazis?

Key date

Young Plan approved by *Reichstag*: March 1930

Key term

National Opposition
A title given to various political forces that united to campaign against Weimar. It included the DNVP, the Nazis, the Pan-German League and the *Stahlhelm* – an organisation of ex-soldiers. The 'National Opposition' was forged out of the Young Plan in 1929 to oppose all reparations payments.

right-wing opponents of the Republic. For Hitler, the campaign showed clear-cut benefits:

- The Party membership grew to 130,000 by end of 1929.
- Nazism really gained a national standing for the first time.
- The main Party rally at Nuremberg had been a great propaganda success on a much more grandiose scale than any before.
- Hitler made influential political contacts on the extreme right wing.
- The opportunity of having access to Hugenberg's media empire.

The collapse of Müller's Grand Coalition

Key question
Why could the Grand Coalition not agree?

Müller's coalition government successfully withstood the attack from the 'National Opposition'. However, it was not so successful in dealing with its own internal divisions. Müller, a Social Democrat, struggled to hold the coalition together but, not surprisingly, it was an issue of finance which finally brought down the government in March 1930.

Key dates

Resignation of Müller's government: March 1930

Brüning appointed chancellor: March 1930

The sharp increase in unemployment had created a large deficit in the new national insurance scheme, and the four major parties in the coalition could not agree on how to tackle it. The SPD, as the political supporters of the trade unions, wanted to increase the contributions and to maintain the levels of welfare payments. The DVP, on the other hand, had strong ties with big business and insisted on reducing benefits. Müller could no longer maintain a majority and he had no option but to tender the resignation of his government.

The appointment of Heinrich Brüning

Key question
How was parliamentary government weakened by the leadership of Heinrich Brüning?

President Hindenburg granted the post of chancellor to Heinrich Brüning. At first sight, this appeared an obvious choice, since he was the parliamentary leader of the ZP, the second largest party in the *Reichstag*. However, with hindsight, it seems that Brüning's appointment marked a crucial step towards the end of true parliamentary government. This was for two reasons.

First, because he was manoeuvred into office by a select circle of political intriguers, who surrounded the ageing President Hindenburg:

- Otto Meissner, the president's State Secretary
- Oskar von Hindenburg, the president's son
- Major General Kurt von Schleicher, a leading general who had held a series of government and military posts.

All three were conservative-nationalists and had no real faith in the democratic process. Instead, they looked to the president and the emergency powers of Article 48 of the constitution (see pages 21 and 24) as a means of creating a more authoritarian government. In Brüning, they saw a respectable, conservative figure, who could offer firm leadership.

Secondly, Brüning's response to the growing economic crisis led to a political constitutional crisis. His economic policy was to propose cuts in government expenditure, so as to achieve a balanced budget and prevent the risk of reviving inflation. However, the budget was rejected in the *Reichstag* by 256 votes to

193 in July 1930. When, despite this, Brüning put the proposals into effect by means of an emergency decree, signed by the president according to Article 48, the *Reichstag* challenged the decree's legality and voted for its withdrawal. Deadlock had been reached. Brüning, therefore, asked Hindenburg to dissolve the *Reichstag* and to call an election for September 1930.

Nazi breakthrough

Brüning had hoped that in the developing crisis the people would be encouraged to support the parties of the centre-right from which a coalition could be formed. However, the election results proved him wrong and the real beneficiary was the Nazi Party, which increased its vote from 810,000 to a staggering 6,409,600 (see Figure 6.2).

Key question
Why was the 1930 *Reichstag* election so significant?

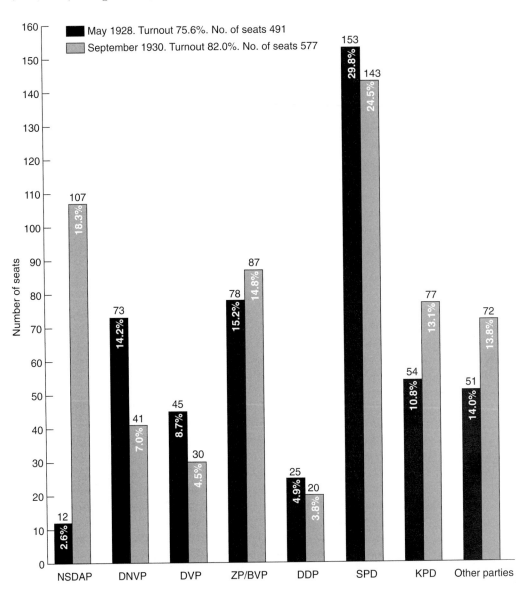

Figure 6.2: *Reichstag* election results for 1928 and 1930. (See major political parties on page 16.)

Key date

Reichstag election – Nazis emerged as second largest party in *Reichstag:* September 1930

The key features about the performance of the political parties are as follows:

- Nazis: With 107 seats and 18.3 per cent, the NSDAP became the second largest political party in Germany.
- Nationalists: The vote of the DNVP was halved from 14.2 per cent to 7 per cent, largely benefiting the Nazis.
- Middle-class democratic parties: The DDP and the DVP lost 20 seats between them.
- Left-wing parties: The vote of the SPD declined from 29.8 per cent to 24.5 per cent, though in contrast the vote of the KPD increased from 10.8 per cent to 13.1 per cent.

Because the result of the 1928 *Reichstag* election had been so disappointing, not even Hitler could have expected the dramatic gains of 1930. Nevertheless, there are several key factors to explain the Nazi breakthrough:

- Since 1928 the Nazi leaders had deliberately directed their propaganda at rural and middle-class/lower middle-class audiences. Nazi gains were at the expense of the DNVP, DVP and DDP.
- Nazi success cannot just be explained by these 'protest votes'. Nearly half of the Nazi seats were won by the Party's attracting 'new' voters:
  - The electorate had grown by 1.8 million since the previous election because a new generation of voters had been added to the roll.
  - The turn-out had increased from 75.6 per cent to 82 per cent.

It would seem that the Nazis had not only picked up a fair proportion of these young first-time voters, but also persuaded many people who had not previously participated in elections to support their cause.

The implications of the 1930 *Reichstag* election were profound. It meant that the left and right extremes had made extensive gains against the pro-democratic parties. This now made it very difficult for proper democratic parliamentary government to function.

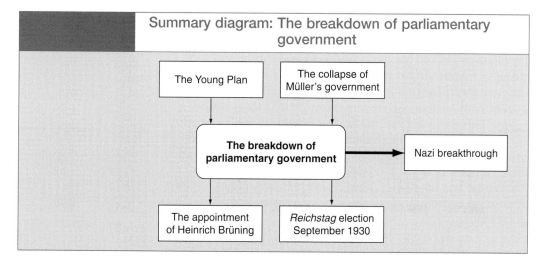

Summary diagram: The breakdown of parliamentary government

3 | Brüning: Presidential Government

Key question
Was Brüning simply a victim of the circumstances?

Brüning's political position after the election was undoubtedly very difficult. His plan of reinforcing his parliamentary support from the centre–right had not succeeded. Instead, he faced the committed opposition of the more powerful extremes of left and right. However, he was not dismissed as chancellor. Brüning still enjoyed the support of Hindenburg and the SPD decided to 'tolerate' his cabinet. So, although the SPD did not join the government, given the threat now facing the Republic from the extremists it was not prepared to defeat the emergency decrees by the use of Article 48.

In this way, true parliamentary democracy gave way to 'presidential government' with some backing from the *Reichstag*. From 1930–2 Brüning remained as chancellor and he governed Germany by the use of Article 48 through President Hindenburg. He was almost a semi-dictator, as can be seen from his growing use of presidential decrees (see Table 6.2).

Table 6.2: Presidential government, 1930–2

	1930	1931	1932
Presidential decree laws (Article 48)	5	44	66
Reichstag laws	98	34	5
Sitting days of the *Reichstag*	94	42	13

Initially, many historians were sympathetic to Brüning and saw him as a sincere statesman struggling in the face of enormous difficulties to save democracy. They believed that his decision to use Article 48 was an understandable reaction to the failure of party government in the crisis. Others, however, saw him as a reactionary, opposed to democracy, who used his position to introduce emergency powers that paved the way to destroying the Republic and to building the road towards Hitler's dictatorship.

Surprisingly, original defenders of Brüning were forced to give way after the publication of his *Memoirs, 1918–34* following his death in 1970. This shows beyond any doubt that Brüning was an ultra-conservative and monarchist, who had little sympathy for the democratic Republic. His aims in government were decisively to weaken the *Reichstag* and to re-establish an authoritarian constitution that would ignore the power and influence of the left. To these ends, he was prepared to use the emergency powers of the presidency and to look for backing from the conservative vested interests. Therefore, it is now generally accepted that Brüning's appointment did mark a decisive move away from parliamentary government.

Das tote Parlament

The Dead Parliament. A cartoon/photomontage published by the German communist John Heartfield in October 1930. It shows an empty *Reichstag* with the number 48 superimposed on it, reflecting Brüning's use of the emergency decrees. The caption below the picture reads: 'The dead parliament. It's what's left from 1848! That's what the parliament looks like which is going to open on 13 October.'

DAS BLIEB VOM JAHRE 1848 ÜBRIG!

So sieht der Reichstag aus, der am 13. Oktober eröffnet wird.

Key question
Was Brüning economically incompetent?

Economic policy

Brüning's economic policy was at least consistent. Throughout his two years in office his major aims were imposed by presidential decree:

- To balance the budget.
- To prevent the chance of restarting inflation.
- To get rid of the burden of German reparations.

And so, his policy's main measures were:

- To cut spending drastically.
- To raise taxes.

This clearly lowered demand and it led to a worsening of the slump. Most obviously, there was a large increase in the number of unemployed and a serious decline in the welfare state provision. Soon he was mocked with the title 'the Hunger Chancellor'.

Many historians have condemned Brüning's economic regime of sticking to his policy of reducing expenditure, for seriously worsening the situation and making possible the rise of the Nazis. He was criticised particularly for his failure to introduce economic measures in the summer of 1931, such as work creation schemes in the construction industry and the reduction of agricultural subsidies. These might just have been enough to lessen the worst effects of the depression during 1932.

However, it could be argued that Brüning had no real alternatives to his economic policy. This was because the German economy had *entered* the depression with such severe weaknesses from the 1920s (see pages 61–2) that economic failure was unavoidable. On these grounds, therefore, it could be argued that no Chancellor would have been in a position to expand the economy and Brüning was at the mercy of other forces.

Key dates

Brüning's economic measures imposed by presidential decree: December 1930

Five leading German banks failed: July 1931

Formation of Harzburg Front: October 1931

Brüning's fall from power

In the spring of 1932, Hindenburg's first seven-year term of office as President came to an end. Brüning committed himself to securing the old man's re-election and after frenetic campaigning Hindenburg was re-elected on the second ballot. He gained 19.3 million votes (53 per cent) compared with Hitler's 13.4 million (36.8 per cent). However, it was a negative victory. Hindenburg had only been chosen because he was the only alternative between Hitler and the KPD candidate, Ernst Thälmann. Also, Hitler had doubled the Nazi vote, despite losing, and had projected an even more powerful personal image. Moreover, Hindenburg showed no real gratitude to Brüning and, at the end of May 1932, the president forced his chancellor to resign by refusing to sign any more emergency decrees. Why was this?

Key question
Why did Hindenburg force Brüning to resign?

Banking crisis

The collapse of the major bank, the Danat, and several others in June 1931, revived fears of financial crisis. By the end of the year unemployment was approaching five million people and there were demonstrations in the streets. Moreover, in October 1931 the 'National Opposition' (see pages 106–7) was reborn as the Harzburg Front. It brought together again a range of right-wing political, military and economic forces who demanded the resignation of Brüning and a new *Reichstag* election. The Front arranged a massive rally to denounce Brüning, but in the winter 1931–2 the chancellor still enjoyed the support of Hindenburg.

Land reform

The fundamental cause of Brüning's fall from grace with Hindenburg was his aim to issue an emergency decree to turn some *Junker* estates in east Prussia into 600,000 allotments for

Profile: Heinrich Brüning 1885–1970

1885		– Born into a Catholic trading family
1904–11		– Attended the universities of Munich and Strasbourg and awarded a doctorate in economics
1915–18		– Volunteered to fight in the First World War and gained a commission in the Machine Gun Corps
1918		– Won the Iron Cross First Class
1920		– Entered politics after the war and joined the ZP
1924–33		– Elected to the *Reichstag* and rapidly rose up the ranks of the ZP
1929		– Chosen as leader of the ZP
1930	March	– Appointed chancellor by Hindenburg
	July	– Tried to pass the budget with a presidential decree, but rejected by *Reichstag*. This resulted in the *Reichstag* election of September 1930
1931	July	– Hoover Moratorium on reparations
1932	April	– Proposed the land reform of the Prussian estates
	May	– Dismissed by Hindenburg
1934		– Fled to Holland and then emigrated to America. Lectured at Harvard University
1947		– Returned to Germany and lectured at Cologne University
1970		– Died

The significance of Brüning's career is almost completely concentrated into the two years of his chancellorship, 1930–2. He was very much on the right wing of the ZP so, when he became the leader of the Party, his anti-socialism made it impossible for him to work with the left-wing parties. In his heart, he remained a monarchist and he hoped to amend the Weimar Constitution to make it a more authoritarian system. However, he was opposed to the Nazis – his real mistake was that he underestimated the extent of their threat.

His policies and decisions have been heavily criticised on various fronts:

- He called for the *Reichstag* election in September 1930 and misread the political consequences.
- He remained committed to the economic programme of balancing the budget, which resulted in enormous economic and political pressures.
- He relied on Hindenburg for the use of emergency decrees – and he failed to recognise his over-dependence on the president.

In his defence, it may be claimed that he was a man of integrity and a victim of exceptional circumstances. His historic reputation is perhaps overshadowed by the later development of the Nazi dictatorship.

unemployed workers. Landowners saw this as a threat to their property interests and dubbed it 'agrarian bolshevism'.

Intrigue

Brüning's unpopularity over the above spurred on the group of right wingers, led by Kurt von Schleicher. He managed to persuade Hindenburg to force the chancellor's resignation at the end of May 1932 and to create a right-wing government.

One might be tempted to view Brüning as an innocent sacrifice who was removed by Hindenburg without consultation with the *Reichstag*. However, it should be borne in mind that he had only survived as chancellor because he enjoyed the personal backing of the president. Brüning had agreed with the creation of presidential government based on the powers granted by Article 48 of the constitution, but he was not astute enough to recognise the precarious nature of his own position. He depended solely on retaining the confidence of the president. This makes it harder to sympathise with him when he became the victim of the intrigue of the presidential court.

Assessment of Brüning

Brüning was an honest, hard-working and honourable man who failed. He was not really a committed democrat, but neither was he sympathetic to Nazism, and it is very important to remember that last point. In many respects, Brüning was making good progress towards his aims, when he was dismissed:

- He succeeded in ending the payment of reparations.
- He sympathised with the reduction of the democratic powers of the *Reichstag*.

However:

- He was not clever enough to appreciate how dangerous and unstable the economic crisis had become in Germany by 1932.
- Neither did he realise how insecure was his own position. For as long as Brüning retained the confidence of Hindenburg, presidential government protected his position.

With no real hope of improvement in the economic crisis, it is not surprising that large sections of the population looked to the Nazis to save the situation. Brüning would have nothing to do with Hitler and the Nazis and he continued to uphold the **rule of law**. Sadly, presidential rule had accustomed Germany again to rule by decree. In this way democracy was undermined and the way was cleared for more extreme political parties to assume power. In the end, it is hard to escape the conclusion that Brüning's chancellorship was a dismal failure, and, in view of the Nazi tyranny that was soon to come, a tragic one.

Key dates

Re-election of Hindenburg as president of Germany: April 1932

Brüning resigned. Papen appointed chancellor: May 1932

Key question
Was Brüning a failure?

Key term

Rule of law
Governing a country according to its laws.

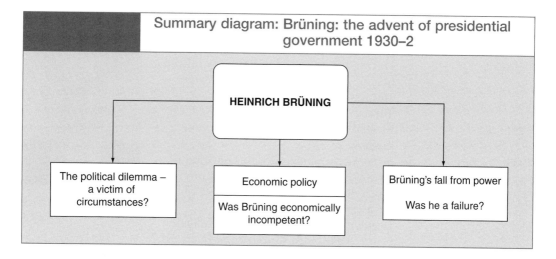

Key question
What was Papen's
political aim?

4 | From Brüning to Papen

Schleicher had recommended the new chancellor, Franz von
Papen, to Hindenburg. As an aristocrat, Papen had good
connections with high society; as a Catholic he was a member of
the Centre Party, although his political views mirrored those of
the Nationalists. His outlook quickly formed the basis for a close
friendship with Hindenburg.

Papen was also politically ambitious, but his understanding and
experience of politics was limited (he did not even hold a seat in
the *Reichstag*). If many greeted the choice of Papen with disbelief, it
was the man's very lack of ability which appealed to Schleicher, who
saw the opportunity to influence events more directly through him.

The new cabinet was called a non-party government of
'national concentration', though it was soon nicknamed the
'Cabinet of Barons'. It was a presidential government dominated
by aristocratic landowners and industrialists – and many were not
even members of the *Reichstag*. In order to strengthen the
government, Papen and Schleicher wanted to secure political
support from the Nazis – though Hitler only agreed not to
oppose the new government in return for two concessions:

- The dissolution of the *Reichstag* and the calling of fresh elections.
- The ending of a government ban on the SA and SS, which had
  been introduced in the wake of violence during the presidential
  campaign.

In this way, Papen and Schleicher hoped that this agreement with
the Nazis would result in the creation of a right-wing
authoritarian government with a measure of popular support in
the form of the Nazis. The *Reichstag* was therefore dissolved and
an election was arranged to take place on 31 July 1932.

Key question
Why was the
Reichstag election of
July 1932 so
politically significant?

Reichstag election: July 1932

The election campaign was brutal, as street violence once again
took hold in the large cities. In the month of July alone 86
people died as a result of political fights.

Profile: Franz von Papen 1879–1969

1879		– Born into a Catholic aristocratic family
1913–18		– Having been trained as a cavalry officer, he embarked on his diplomatic career and served in the USA, Mexico and Turkey
1921		– Elected to the Prussian regional state as a member of ZP
1932	May	– Appointed as chancellor by Hindenburg to head the so-called 'Cabinet of Barons', which did not include any member of the *Reichstag*
		– Decided to call for the *Reichstag* election of July 1932, with serious consequences
	July	– Removed the state regional government of Prussia and appointed himself as Reich Commissioner of Prussia
	September	– Personally defeated by a massive vote of 'no confidence' in the *Reichstag* (512 votes to 42)
	November	– Dismissed by Hindenburg but schemed to replace Schleicher and to recover his power
1933	January	– Appointed as vice-chancellor in Hitler's Nazi–Nationalist coalition
1934	July	– Resigned after the Night of Long Knives
1934–44		– German ambassador in Austria and Turkey
1946		– Charged with war crimes in the Nuremberg trials, but found not guilty
1969		– Lived privately until his death

There have been few political careers that were so short and so disastrous as that of Franz von Papen. He had limited political experience and was out of his depth. His advance was mainly due to his connections with the aristocracy, the Catholic Church and big business (his wife was the daughter of a very rich industrialist).

He was always a monarchist and a nationalist (although he remained nominally a member of ZP). When he became chancellor, he aspired to undo the Weimar Constitution and so he was quite happy to rule by presidential decrees and to denounce the state government of Prussia. Despite his failings, he pursued his personal ambitions and was quickly outmanoeuvred by Hitler in the early months of 1933.

Yet, such bloodshed provided Schleicher and Papen with the excuse to abolish the most powerful regional state government in Germany, Prussia. This government of Prussia had long been a coalition of the SPD and the ZP and had been the focus of right-wing resentment since 1919. So, on 20 July 1932, it was simply removed by Papen who declared a state of emergency and appointed himself as Reich Commissioner of Prussia. This was of immense significance:

- It was an arbitrary and unconstitutional act.
- It replaced a parliamentary system with a presidential authoritarian government.

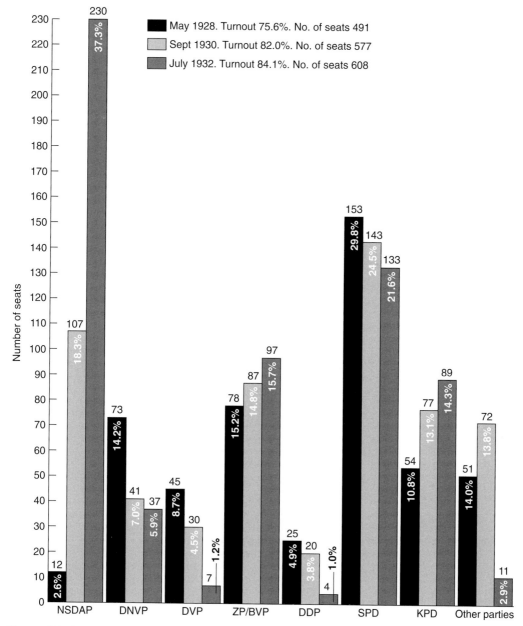

Legend:
- May 1928. Turnout 75.6%. No. of seats 491
- Sept 1930. Turnout 82.0%. No. of seats 577
- July 1932. Turnout 84.1%. No. of seats 608

Figure 6.3: *Reichstag* election results 1928–32. (See major political parties on page 16.)

- Democrats – especially the SPD and the trade unions – gave in without any real opposition. Their passive response shows how far the forces of democracy had lost the initiative.

Many on the right wing congratulated Papen on the Prussian *coup*. However, it did not win him any additional electoral support. When the election results came in, it was again the Nazis who had cause to celebrate. They had polled 13.7 million votes and had won 230 seats. Hitler was the leader of by far the largest party in Germany and constitutionally he had every right to form a government.

It is worth bearing in mind the following key features about the performance of the political parties:

- Nazis: With 230 seats and 37.3 per cent the NSDAP became the largest political party in Germany.
- Nationalists: The vote of the DNVP fell further to 5.9 per cent.
- Middle-class democratic parties: The DDP and the DVP collapsed disastrously. They polled only 2.2 per cent of the vote and gained just 11 seats between them.
- Left-wing parties: The vote of the SPD declined further to 21.6 per cent, though in contrast the vote of the KPD increased to 14.3 per cent.

Nazis emerged as the largest party in the *Reichstag* election: July 1932

Key date

In electoral terms the gains of the Nazis could be explained by:

- the collapse of the DDP and DVP vote
- the decline of the DNVP
- a small percentage of disgruntled workers changing from SPD to NSDAP
- the support for the 'other parties' falling from 13.8 per cent to 2.9 per cent, which suggests their loyalty transferred to the Nazis

Table 6.3: Germany's governments 1928–33

Chancellors	Dates in office	Type of government
Hermann Müller (SPD)	May 1928– March 1930	Parliamentary government. A coalition cabinet of SPD, ZP, DDP, DVP
Heinrich Brüning (ZP)	March 1930– May 1932	Presidential government dependent on emergency decrees. A coalition cabinet from political centre and right
Franz von Papen (ZP, but very right wing)	May 1932– December 1932	Presidential government dependent on emergency decrees. Many non-party cabinet members
General Kurt von Schleicher (Non-party)	December 1932– January 1933	Presidential government dependent on emergency decrees. Many non-party cabinet members
Adolf Hitler (NSDAP)	1933–45	Coalition cabinet of NSDAP and DNVP, but gave way to Nazi dictatorship

- the turnout increasing to 84 per cent which indicated the same trend as September 1930 that the Party was attracting even more 'new voters'.

Two further points worth remembering about the *Reichstag* election of July 1932 are:

- Only 39.5 per cent voted for the pro-democratic parties.
- Added together, the percentage of votes for the KPD and NSDAP combined to 51.6 per cent.

These two political facts are telling indeed. The German people had voted to reject democracy.

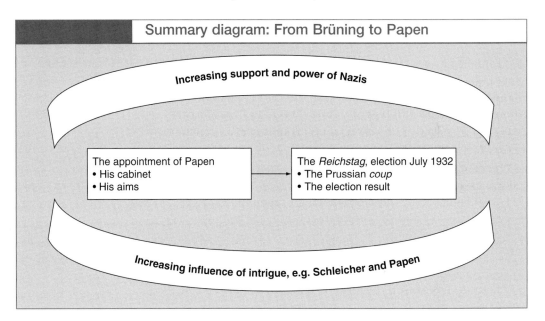

Summary diagram: From Brüning to Papen

Increasing support and power of Nazis

The appointment of Papen
- His cabinet
- His aims

The *Reichstag*, election July 1932
- The Prussian *coup*
- The election result

Increasing influence of intrigue, e.g. Schleicher and Papen

5 | The Death of the Weimar Republic

Key question
Why did Weimar democracy fail?

It is now clear that Weimar democracy was really dead before the establishment of the Nazi dictatorship in early 1933 (see pages 140–4). The problem for the historian is trying to determine when the Weimar Republic expired and why.

Three major themes stand out as fundamental weaknesses of the Weimar Republic.

(i) The hostility of Germany's vested interests

From the very start, the Weimar Republic faced the hostility of Germany's established élites. Following military defeat and the threat of revolution, this opposition was at first limited. However, the fact that so many key figures in German society and business rejected the idea of a democratic republic was a major problem for Weimar. They worked against the interests of Weimar and hoped for a return to the pre-war situation. This was a powerful handicap to the successful development of the Republic in the 1920s and, in the 1930s, it was to become a decisive factor in its final collapse.

(ii) Ongoing economic problems

The Republic was also troubled by an almost continuous economic crisis that affected all levels of society. It inherited the enormous costs of the First World War followed by the burden of post-war reconstruction, Allied reparations and the heavy expense of the new welfare benefits. So, even though the inflation crisis of 1923 was overcome, problems in the economy were disguised and remained unresolved. These were to have dramatic consequences with the onset of the world economic crisis in 1929.

(iii) Limited base of popular support

Weimar democracy never enjoyed widespread political support. There was never total acceptance of, and confidence in, its system and its values. From the Republic's birth its narrow base of popular support was caught between the extremes of left and right. But, as time went by, Weimar's claims to be the legitimate government became increasingly open to question. Sadly, Weimar democracy was associated with defeat and the humiliation of the Treaty of Versailles and reparations. Its reputation was further damaged by the crisis of 1922–3. Significantly, even the mainstays of the Weimar Republic had weaknesses:

- The main parties of German liberalism, DDP and DVP, were losing support from 1924.
- The ZP and DNVP were both moving to the political right.
- Even the loyalty and the commitment of the SPD to democracy has to be balanced against its failure to join the coalitions in the mid-1920s and its conflict with its left-wing partner, the KPD.

In short, a sizeable proportion of the German population never had faith in the existing constitutional arrangements and, as the years passed, more were looking for change.

These unrelenting pressures meant that Weimar democracy went through a number of phases:

- The difficult circumstances of its birth in 1918–19 left it handicapped. It was in many respects, therefore, a major achievement that it survived the problems of the period 1919–23.
- The years of relative stability from 1924 to 1929, however, amounted to only a short breathing space and did not result in any strengthening of the Weimar system. On the eve of the world economic crisis it seemed that Weimar's long-term chances of survival were already far from good.
- In the end, the impact of the world depression, 1929–33, intensified the pressures that brought about Weimar's final crisis.

In the view of some historians, Weimar had been a gamble with no chance of success. For others, the Republic continued to offer the hope of democratic survival right until mid-1932, when the Nazis became the largest party in the July *Reichstag* election. However, the manner of Brüning's appointment and his decision to rule by emergency decree created a particular system of presidential government. This fundamentally undermined the Weimar system and was soon followed by the electoral breakthrough of the Nazis. From this time, democracy's chance of surviving was very slim indeed. Democracy lived on with ever increasing weakness before it reached its demise in July 1932. However, in truth, democratic rule in Weimar Germany was terminal from the summer of 1930.

Summary diagram: The death of the Weimar Republic

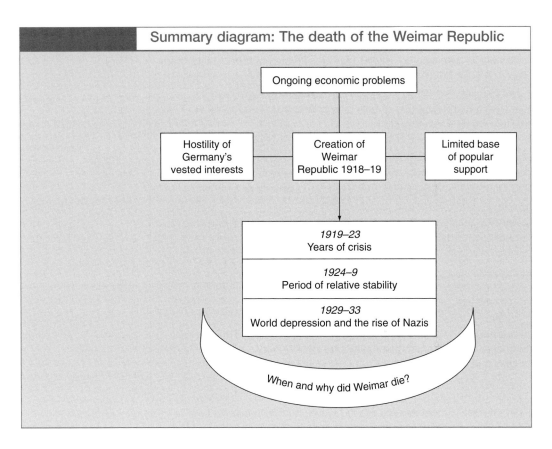

Study Guide: AS Question

In the style of OCR A

Assess the reasons why the governments of 1930–2 failed.

(50 marks)

Exam tips

The question focuses on the governments of Brüning and von Papen when Germany was suffering first the aftermath of the Wall Street Crash and then the first waves of the Depression. The command 'Assess …' tells you not just to list causal reasons but to weigh them up and work out the relative importance of those various factors so you can say that 'x' or 'x' and 'y' were more important than the others in causing failure. In turn, this question is therefore about the failure of the Weimar system.

One place to start would be with political contrasts in 1930–2. Both chancellors were appointed, not elected. Both ruled by emergency presidential decree. Both governments were thus fundamental attacks on Weimar itself. Brüning was an able politician whereas von Papen was weak, but neither believed in democracy or the republic. You might argue, therefore, that they failed because, in a national crisis, both governments undermined the republic from within. You will need, however, to look more widely to answer this question fully. Under these two governments, unemployment tripled, exports more than halved, banks collapsed. The cost in human suffering was even greater. Could any government survive such an assault? Loss of confidence was massive, and Weimar had not established itself deeply so riding the storm was bound to be difficult. Another core reason was that Brüning faced particular difficulties in 1930: deadlock with the *Reichstag* over his controversial budget and then because of the success of extremist parties in the election that followed the budget crisis. Building directly from there, the next reason would be that parliamentary government had collapsed. Brüning survived as long as he had the president's support. That was true of von Papen too. Your conclusions must make clear cases for your choices about rank order. Your core choice is between the weight of economic collapse and the anti-democratic nature of both governments.

7

The Nazi Road to Dictatorship 1932–4

POINTS TO CONSIDER

Although Weimar democracy was, in effect, dead by the summer of 1932, it should not be assumed that Hitler's appointment was inevitable. The purpose of this chapter is to consider two questions that are inextricably linked: 'Why did Hitler and the Nazis become so politically powerful?' and 'Why was Weimar Germany replaced by a Nazi dictatorship?' The main points are:

- The creation of a Nazi mass movement: who voted for the Nazis and why?
- Nazi political methods: propaganda and violence
- Political intrigue: the appointment of Hitler as chancellor
- The establishment of the Nazi dictatorship, January–March 1933
- Co-ordination
- The Night of the Long Knives

Key dates

1932	May	Brüning dismissed as chancellor and replaced by Papen
	July	*Reichstag* election: Nazis won 230 seats (37.3 per cent)
	September	*Reichstag* passed a massive vote of 'no confidence' in Papen's government (512 votes to 42)
	November	*Reichstag* election: Nazi vote dropped to 33.1 per cent, winning 196 seats
	December	Papen dismissed as chancellor and replaced by Schleicher
1933	January 30	Schleicher dismissed and Hitler appointed as chancellor
	February 27	*Reichstag* fire: communists blamed
	March 5	Final *Reichstag* elections according to Weimar Constitution
	March 21	The 'Day of Potsdam'
	March 23	Enabling Act passed
	July 14	All political opposition to NSDAP declared illegal

1934	June 30	Night of the Long Knives: destruction of the SA by the SS
	August 2	Death of Hindenburg: Hitler combined the offices of chancellor and president. Oath of loyalty taken by the army

1 | The Creation of a Nazi Mass Movement

Key question
Who voted for the Nazis?

The point is often made that Hitler and the Nazis never gained an overall majority in *Reichstag* elections. However, such an occurrence was unlikely because of the number of political parties in Weimar Germany and the operation of the proportional representation system. Considering this, Nazi electoral achievements by July 1932 were very impressive. The 13,745,000 voters who had supported them represented 37.3 per cent of the electorate, thus making Hitler's party the largest in the *Reichstag*. Only one other party on one other occasion had polled more: the SPD in the revolutionary atmosphere of January 1919. Nazism had become a mass movement with which millions identified and, as such, it laid the foundations for Hitler's coming to power in January 1933. Who were these Nazi voters and why were they attracted to the Nazi cause?

Nazis won 230 seats out of 608 (37.3 per cent) in *Reichstag* election: July 1932

Key date

The results of the elections 1928–32 show the changing balance of the political parties (see pages 108 and 115–19), although really these figures on their own are limited in what they show us about the nature of Nazi support. However, the graph and table in Figure 7.1 reveal a number of significant points about the kind of people who actually voted for the Nazis.

From this it seems fairly clear that the Nazis made extensive gains from those parties with a middle-class and/or a Protestant identity. However, it is also apparent that the Catholic parties, the Communist Party and, to a large extent, the Social Democrats were able to withstand the Nazi advances.

Geography and denomination

These political trends are reflected in the geographical base of Nazi support, which was generally higher in the north and east of the country and lower in the south and west. Right across the North German Plain, from East Prussia to Schleswig-Holstein, the Nazis gained their best results and this seems to reflect the significance of two important factors – religion and the degree of urbanisation.

In those areas where Catholicism predominated (see Figure 7.2) the Nazi breakthrough was less marked, whereas the more Protestant regions were more likely to vote Nazi. Likewise, the Nazis fared less well in the large industrial cities, but gained greater support in the more rural communities and in residential suburbs.

The Nazi vote was at its lowest in the Catholic cities of the west, such as Cologne and Düsseldorf. It was at its highest in the

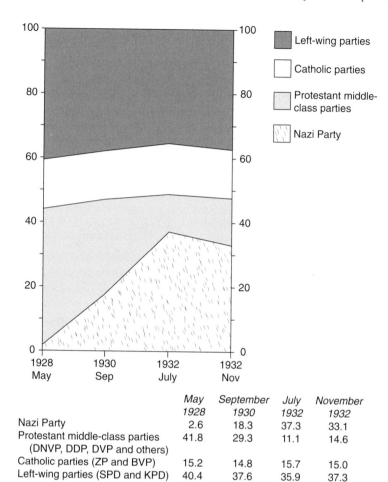

Figure 7.1:
Percentage of vote gained by each major political grouping in the four *Reichstag* elections 1928–32.

	May 1928	September 1930	July 1932	November 1932
Nazi Party	2.6	18.3	37.3	33.1
Protestant middle-class parties (DNVP, DDP, DVP and others)	41.8	29.3	11.1	14.6
Catholic parties (ZP and BVP)	15.2	14.8	15.7	15.0
Left-wing parties (SPD and KPD)	40.4	37.6	35.9	37.3

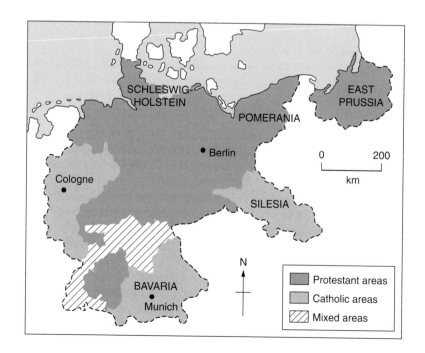

Figure 7.2:
Electoral split by religion

Protestant countryside of the north and north-east, such as Schleswig-Holstein and Pomerania. Ironically, therefore, Bavaria, a strongly Catholic region, and the birthplace of Nazism, had one of the lowest Nazi votes in Germany. Such a picture does not of course take into account the exceptions created by local circumstances. For instance, parts of the province of Silesia, although mainly Catholic and urbanised, still recorded a very high Nazi vote. This was probably the result of nationalist passions generated in a border province, which had lost half its land to Poland.

Class

Nazi voters also reflected the rural/urban division in terms of their social groupings. It seems that the Nazis tended to win a higher proportion of support from:

- the peasants and farmers
- the '*Mittelstand*' (the lower middle classes, e.g. artisans, craftsmen and shopkeepers)
- the established middle classes, e.g. teachers, **white-collar workers**, public employees.

White-collar workers
Workers not involved in manual labour.

Key term

This tendency is shown in the figures of the Nazi Party's membership lists, which can be seen in Figure 7.3.

From this it is clear that a significantly higher proportion of the middle-class subsections tended to join the Nazi Party than the other classes, i.e. government officials/employees, self-employed, white-collar workers. However, it is worth bearing in mind two other points. First, although the working class did join the Nazi Party in smaller proportions, it was still the largest section in the NSDAP. Secondly, although the peasants tended to vote for the Nazis, the figures show they did not join the NSDAP in the same proportion.

The appeal of Nazism

It is clear that more of the Protestants and the middle classes voted for Nazism in proportion to their percentage in German society. The real question is why were those with a loyalty to Catholicism or socialism not so readily drawn to voting for the Nazis?

Key question
Why were the Protestants, the middle classes and the young more attracted to Nazism?

- First, both of them represented well-established ideologies in their own right and both opposed Nazism on an intellectual level.
- Secondly, the organisational strength of each movement provided an effective counter to Nazi propaganda. For socialism, there was the trade union structure. For Catholicism, there was the Church hierarchy, extending right down to the local parish priest.
- Thirdly, both movements had suffered under the Imperial German regime. As so often happens, persecution strengthened commitment. It was, therefore, much harder for the Nazis to break down the established loyalties of working-class and

Figure 7.3: Nazi Party members in 1932.

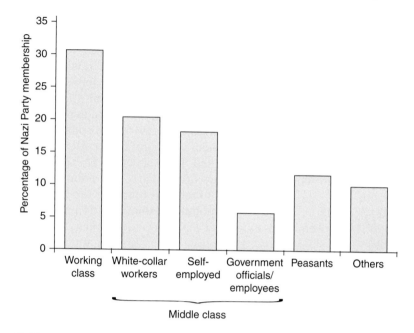

Table 7.1: German society as a whole in 1933 (%)

Working class	Middle class			Peasants	Others
	White-collar workers	Self-employed	Government officials/ employees		
46.3	12.4	9.6	4.8	20.7	6.2

Key term

Associationism Having a strong identity or affiliation with a particular group.

Catholic communities and their traditional '**associationism**', or identity, remained strong. In contrast, the Protestants, the farmers and the middle classes had no such loyalties. They were therefore more likely to accept the Nazi message.

The 'politics of anxiety'

What was common among many Nazi voters was their lack of faith in, and identity with, the Weimar system. They believed that their traditional role and status in society was under threat. For many of the middle classes (see Figure 7.3 above) the crisis of 1929–33 was merely the climax of a series of disasters since 1918. Hitler was therefore able to exploit what is termed 'the politics of anxiety', as expressed by the historian T. Childers in his book *The Nazi Voter*:

> [By 1930] the NSDAP had become a unique phenomenon in German electoral politics, a catch-all party of protest, whose constituents, while drawn primarily from the middle class electorate were united above all by a profound contempt for the existing political and economic system.

In this way Hitler seemed able to offer to many Germans an escape from overwhelming crisis and a return to former days.

Profile: Adolf Hitler 1889–1945

1889	April	– Born at Braunau-am-Inn, Austria
1905		– Left school with no real qualifications
1907–13		– Lived as a dropout in Vienna
1914		– Joined the German army
1918	August	– Awarded the Iron Cross, first class
	October	– Gassed and stayed in hospital at the time of Germany's surrender
1919	September	– Joined the DAP led by Drexler
1920	February	– Drew up the Party's 25 points programme with Drexler. The Party was renamed the NSDAP
1921	July	– Appointed leader of the Party
1923	November 8–9	– Beer Hall *putsch* at Munich
1924		– Found guilty of treason and sentenced to five years, reduced to nine months. Wrote *Mein Kampf*
1925	February 27	– NSDAP refounded at Munich
1925–33		– Committed the Party to a legality policy
		– Restructured the Party
1930	September	– Nazi breakthrough in the *Reichstag* election: 107 seats won
1932	July	– Nazis elected the largest party in the *Reichstag* election
	August	– Requested the post of chancellor, but rejected by Hindenburg
1933	January 30	– Appointed chancellor of coalition government by Hindenburg
	March 23	– Given dictatorial powers by the Enabling Act
1934	June 30	– Ordered the purge of the SA, known as the Night of the Long Knives
	August 2	– Combined the posts of chancellor and president on the death of Hindenburg. Thereafter, referred to as *Der Führer*
1935		– Declaration of military conscription
1936	March	– Remilitarisation of the Rhineland
1937	November	– Hossbach Conference
1938	February	– Blomberg–Fritsch crisis. Purge of army generals and other leading conservatives
1938	March	– *Anschluss* with Austria
	September	– Czech crisis resulting in the take-over of Sudetenland
1939	September 1	– Ordered the invasion of Poland (resulting in the declaration of war by Britain and France on 3 September)
1941	June 22	– Ordered the invasion of the USSR
	December 11	– Declared war on the USA after Japan attacked Pearl Harbor
1944	July 20	– Stauffenberg Bomb Plot
1945	April 30	– Committed suicide in the ruins of Berlin

Background

Hitler's upbringing has provoked much psychological analysis, and the character that has emerged has been seen as repressed, lonely and moody. It also seems that much of Hitler's outlook on life was shaped by his unhappy years in Vienna (1907–13) when he failed to become an art student. It was here, too, that the real core of his political ideas was firmly established: anti-Semitism, German nationalism, anti-democracy and anti-

Marxism. Hitler himself found a real purpose in the First World War. His belief in German nationalism and the camaraderie of the troops combined to give him direction. However, the shock of hearing of Germany's surrender in November 1918 confirmed all his prejudices.

The early years of the Nazi Party

Hitler in 1919 was drawn to the DAP, which was just one of many ultra-right-wing racist parties in post-war Germany. His dynamic speeches and his commitment quickly resulted in his becoming the NSDAP's leader by 1921 and it was he who prompted many of the Party's early features, which gave it such a dynamic identity. Nevertheless, despite all the noise and trouble he caused, Hitler was still only the leader of a fringe political party in Bavaria. So when Germany hit the problems of 1923, Hitler grossly overestimated the potential of the *putsch* in November 1923 and it ended in disaster.

Hitler used the next few months to good effect. He exploited his trial by turning himself into a hero of the right-wing nationalists and in prison he wrote *Mein Kampf*. He also reassessed his long-term strategy to one based on legality. The following years were relatively stable and economically prosperous years for Weimar, and the election results for Hitler and the Nazi Party in 1928 were very disappointing. Nevertheless, he managed to restore his leadership and restructure the Party and its organisation.

The road to power 1929–33

The Great Depression created the environment in which Hitler could exploit his political skills. His charisma, his speeches and his advanced use of propaganda, directed by his disciple Goebbels, were the key features of his political success. Nevertheless, although he emerged by 1932 as the leader of the largest party and the most serious opponent to Weimar democracy, he was only invited to be chancellor in January 1933 when he joined a coalition with other nationalists and conservatives.

Dictator 1933–45

Hitler established his dictatorship with immense speed. He was given unlimited powers by the Enabling Act, which provided the legal basis for the suppression of political opposition, and he destroyed the dissident faction in his own Party on the Night of the Long Knives. After the death of Hindenburg, he styled himself *Führer* of Germany.

Hitler was portrayed as the all-powerful dictator, but there has been considerable debate about the image and reality of his direction of daily affairs (see page 236) Nevertheless, it is fair to conclude that Hitler leadership directed German events:

- by upholding the creation of a one-party state maintained by the brutal SS-Police system, which was totally loyal to him (see pages 237–42)
- by supporting the gradualist racial policy that culminated in the genocide (see pages 222–31)
- by pursuing an expansionist foreign policy to establish a 'greater Germany' by means of *Lebensraum* (see pages 253–8).

Below the surface Hitler's regime was chaotic; but the cult of the *Führer* was upheld by Goebbels's propaganda machine as well as by the diplomatic and military successes from 1935–41. However, the winter of 1942–3 marked the 'turn of the tide' and Hitler increasingly deluded himself and refused to consider surrender. It was only when the Red Army closed in on the ruins of Berlin that the spell of the *Führer*'s power was finally broken – by his own suicide in the bunker on 30 April 1945.

The young

Another clearly identifiable group of Nazi supporters was the youth of Germany. The Depression hit at the moment when youngsters from the pre-war baby-boom came of age and, however good their qualifications were, many had little chance of finding work. In a study of Nazi Party membership, 41.3 per cent of those who joined before 1933 had been born between 1904 and 1913 – despite this age group representing only 25.3 per cent of the total population. Equally striking, of the youngsters aged 20–30 who became members of political parties, 61 per cent joined the Nazis. Thus, it was the young who filled the ranks of the SA – often unemployed, disillusioned with traditional politics and without hope for the future. They saw Nazism as a movement for change – not a search for respectability. Equally, the SA activities gave them something to do. All ages were prepared to vote for the Nazis, but the younger members of society were actually more likely to become involved by joining the Party.

Nazism: the people's party

However, the previous analysis should not obscure the fact that the Nazis still boasted a broader cross-section of supporters than any other political party. Unlike most of the other parties, the Nazis were not limited by regional, religious or class ties. So, by 1932 it is fair to say that the NSDAP had become Germany's first genuine *Volkspartei* or broad-based people's party. This point was made in a recent study of voting habits that suggests the Nazis became a mass party only by making inroads into the working-class vote. Hitler therefore succeeded in appealing to *all* sections of German society – it is simply that those from Protestant, rural and middle-class backgrounds supported in much greater numbers.

Key question
Why has Nazism been described as a 'people's party'?

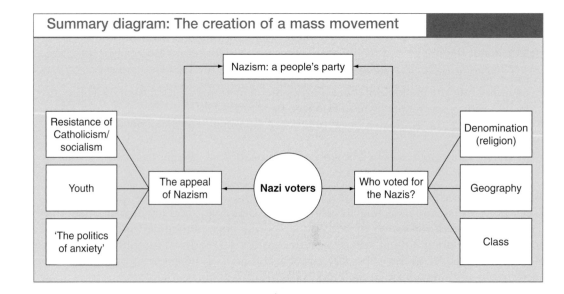

Summary diagram: The creation of a mass movement

2 | Nazi Political Methods

It would be wrong to assume that voters for the Nazi Party were simply won over by the appeal of a radical political ideology at a time of economic crisis. There were still various fringe parties on the extreme right, which publicised similar messages. What made the Nazis stand out for the voters was their revolutionary political style. Or, to use present-day jargon, it was the presentation and packaging of the Party and its programme.

Propaganda

Key question
What were the main aims of Nazi propaganda?

From his earliest days in politics Hitler had shown an uncanny, but cynical awareness of the power of propaganda. In 1924 in *Mein Kampf* he had written:

> The receptive powers of the masses are very restricted, and their understanding is feeble. On the other hand, they quickly forget. Such being the case, all-effective propaganda must be confined to a few bare essentials and those must be expressed as far as possible in stereotyped formulas. These slogans should be persistently repeated until the very last individual has come to grasp the idea that has been put forward.

Such thinking was to remain the basis of Nazi propaganda, and there can be little doubt that its implementation in the years 1929–33 played a vital part in Nazi success.

The whole process of Nazi propaganda was highly organised. From April 1930 Joseph Goebbels was promoted and put in complete charge of the Party's propaganda machine, which reached right down to branch level. In this way, information and instructions could be sent out from Party headquarters and adapted to local circumstances. It also allowed the Party to target its money and efforts in the key electoral districts. Finally, it encouraged feedback from the grass roots, so that particularly effective ideas could be put into practice elsewhere.

Canvassing

Key question
In what ways did Goebbels develop propaganda?

Posters and leaflets had always played an important role in Nazi electioneering, but Goebbels was able to initiate a new approach. He practised mass politics on a grand scale. The electorate was deluged with material that had a range of propaganda techniques and an increasingly sophisticated application. He showed a subtlety and an understanding of psychology, which we now associate with advertising agencies.

Yet, Goebbels also correctly recognised the need to direct propaganda according to people's social and economic interests. Specific leaflets were produced for different social groups, and Nazi speakers paid particular attention to the worries and concerns of the individual clubs and societies they addressed. In this way, the Nazi propaganda message was tailored to fit a whole range of people. For example:

'Our Last Hope.' Nazi poster of the 1932 presidential election. Note the image of despair portrayed and the range of Germans – class, age and sex.

- To appeal to farmers and peasants by offering special benefits to offset the collapse of agricultural prices.
- To appeal to the unemployed and the industrial workers by aiming to overcome the depression and offering 'Bread' and 'Work'.
- To appeal to the *Mittelstand*, for example, by limiting the control of large department stores.
- To appease the industrialists by playing down the fear of nationalisation and the state control of the economy.

Technology

Modern technology was also exploited. Loudspeakers, radio, film and records were all used. Expensive cars and aeroplanes were hired, not only for the practical purpose of transporting Hitler quickly to as many places as possible, but also to project a statesman-like image. In 1932, three major speaking programmes were organised for Hitler called 'Flight over Germany'. At a local level the political message was projected by the Party arranging social events and entertainments – sports, concerts and fairs.

Mass suggestion

However, it was in the organisation of the mass rallies that the Nazis showed their mastery of propaganda. The intention was to create an atmosphere so emotional that all members of the crowd would succumb to the collective will. This is the idea of '**mass suggestion**' and every kind of device was used to heighten the effect: uniforms, torches, music, salutes, flags, songs and anthems, and speeches from leading personalities. Many people have since described how they were converted as a result of such meetings.

Key term

Mass suggestion
A psychological term suggesting that large groups of people can be unified simply by the atmosphere of the occasion. Hitler and Goebbels used their speeches and large rallies to particularly good effect.

Scapegoats and unifying themes

In order to project itself as a mass people's party, Nazism tried to embrace and bring together many of the disparate elements in Germany. This was partly achieved by Goebbels who showed an astute ability to play on social and psychological factors in Nazi propaganda. Three key unifying themes dominated Nazi propaganda:

- The *Führer* cult. Hitler was portrayed as a messiah-type figure, who could offer strong authoritarian leadership and a vision for Nazi Germany's future.
- The *Volksgemeinschaft* (national community). To appeal to the people for the development of a unifying idea, regardless of class.
- German nationalism. To play on German nationalism and to exploit the discontent since the First World War. To make Germany great again.

Through these themes, Nazi propaganda successfully portrayed itself as both revolutionary and reactionary. The Party aimed to destroy the Republic, while at the same time promising a return to a glorious bygone age.

In addition, Nazism cynically played on the idea of 'scapegoats'. It focused on several identifiable groups, which were denounced and blamed for Germany's suffering:

- The 'November criminals'. The politicians responsible for the Armistice and the creation of the Republic became representative of all aspects associated with Weimar democracy.
- Communists. By playing on the fears of communism – the KPD was a sizeable party of 13–17 per cent in 1930–2 – and the increasing threat of Communist USSR.
- Jews. It was easy to exploit the long-established history of anti-Semitism in Europe as a whole, and in Germany in particular.

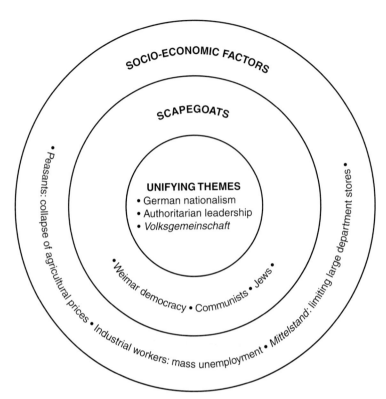

Figure 7.4: Nazi propaganda.

Violence

There was one other strand to the political style of this Nazi revolution: the systematic encouragement and use of violence. Weimar politics had been a bloody affair from the start, but the growth of the SA and SS unleashed an unprecedented wave of violence, persecution and intimidation.

The growth of unemployment resulted in a phenomenal expansion of the SA, led by Röhm, in 1921–3 and 1930–4. Understandably, many people joined as members of the SA out of desperation, for food and accommodation, although much of it was just thuggery. The SA mainly was responsible for the violence against the opposition, especially the communists. All this helped to destabilise the already difficult situation in Germany and, in the wake of the presidential election (see page 112), the SA was actually banned for three months. However, it was restored by the new chancellor, Papen, in June 1932. So, during the campaign of July 1932, there were 461 political riots in Prussia alone: battles between communists and Nazis on 10 July left 10 people dead; a week later, 19 died after the Nazis marched through a working-class suburb of Hamburg.

Such violent activities were encouraged by the Nazi leadership, as control of the streets was seen as essential to the expansion of Nazi power. The ballot box of democracy remained merely a means to an end, and, therefore, other non-democratic tactics were considered legitimate in the quest for power. The Nazis

Key question
Did SA violence advance the rise of Nazism?

poured scorn on rational discussion and fair play. For them the end did justify the means. For their democratic opponents, there was the dilemma of how to resist those who exploited the freedoms of a democratic society merely to undermine it.

The Stennes' revolt

Despite the Nazi violence, Hitler became increasingly keen to maintain the policy of legality. He felt it was important to keep discipline, so he could maintain the image of a Party that could offer firm and ordered government. The SA had generally supported the radical socialist aspects of Nazism, and yet Hitler was concerned increasingly with appealing to the middle-class conservative Nazi voters. The most serious disagreement between the SA and the Party leadership has become known as the Stennes' revolt in February 1931.

Walther Stennes, the leader of the Berlin SA, rebelled against the orders of Hitler and Goebbels to act legally and to limit the violence. Hitler defeated the revolt with a small purge, but it underlined the fact that the relationship between the Party leadership and the SA was at times very difficult. These differences were not really resolved until the infamous **Night of the Long Knives** in 1934 (see pages 148–53).

Key term

Night of the Long Knives
A crucial turning point when Hitler arranged for the SS to purge the SA leadership and murder about 200 victims, including Ernst Röhm, Gregor Strasser and Kurt von Schleicher.

Summary diagram: Nazi political methods

Canvassing — Technology — SA
The role of Goebbels — **Propaganda** ⬌ **Violence** — The role of Röhm
Mass suggestion — Scapegoats and unifying themes — Stennes' revolt

Key question
Why did Papen fail to prevent Hitler's coming to power?

3 | Political Intrigue, July 1932 to January 1933

The political strength of the Nazi Party following the July 1932 *Reichstag* elections was beyond doubt (see pages 115–19). However, there still remained the problem for Hitler of how to translate this popular following into real power. He was determined to take nothing less than the post of chancellor for himself. This was unacceptable to both Schleicher and Papen, who were keen to have Nazis in the cabinet, but only in positions of limited power. Therefore, the meeting between Hitler, Papen and Hindenburg on 13 August ended in deadlock.

Papen's failure

As long as Papen retained the sympathy of Hindenburg, Hitler's ambitions would remain frustrated. Indeed, a leading modern historian, Jeremy Noakes, describes the period from August to December 1932 as 'the months of crisis' for the Nazis, since 'it appeared the policy of legality had led to a cul-de-sac'. Party morale declined and some of the wilder SA members again became increasingly restless.

On the other hand, Papen was humiliated when on 12 September the *Reichstag* passed a massive vote of 'no confidence' in Papen's government (512 votes to 42). Consequently, he dissolved the new *Reichstag* and called for yet another election. In some respects

Key dates

Reichstag passed a massive vote of 'no confidence' in Papen's government (512 votes to 42): September 1932

Nazi vote dropped to 33.1 per cent and won 196 seats in the *Reichstag* election: November 1932

'A Breakdown: A Pleasing Phenomenon!' Cartoon by Oskar Garvens mocking the German people in 1932 for showing no interest in the competing political parties.

Papen's reading of the situation was sound. The Nazis were short of money, their morale was low and the electorate was growing tired of repeated elections. These factors undoubtedly contributed to the fall in the Nazi vote on 6 November to 11.7 million (33.1 per cent), which gave them 196 seats. However, Papen's tactics had not achieved their desired end, since the fundamental problem of overcoming the lack of majority *Reichstag* support for his cabinet remained. Hitler stood firm: he would not join the government except as chancellor.

In his frustration, Papen began to consider a drastic alternative: the dissolution of the *Reichstag*, the declaration of martial law and the establishment of a presidential dictatorship. However, such a plan was completely opposed by Schleicher, who found Papen's growing political desperation and his friendship with President Hindenburg additional causes for concern. Schleicher still believed that the popular support for the Nazis could not be ignored, and that Papen's plan would give rise to civil commotion and perhaps civil war. When he informed Hindenburg of the army's lack of confidence in Papen, the President was forced, unwillingly, to demand the resignation of his friendly chancellor.

Key date

Papen dismissed as chancellor and replaced by Schleicher: December 1932

Key question
Why did Schleicher fail to prevent Hitler's coming to power?

Schleicher's failure

Schleicher at last came out into the open. Over the previous two years he had been happy to play his role behind the scenes, but he now decided to become the dominant player, when he gained the favour of Hindenburg and was appointed chancellor on 2 December. Schleicher's aims, rather ambitiously, were to achieve political stability and restore national confidence by creating a more broadly based government. He had a two-pronged strategy:

- First, to gain some support from elements of the political left, especially the trade unions, by suggesting a programme of public works.
- Secondly, to split the Nazis and attract the more socialist wing of the Nazi Party, under Gregor Strasser, by offering him the position of vice-chancellor.

With these objectives Schleicher, therefore, intended to project himself as the chancellor of national reconciliation. However, his political manoeuvres came to nothing.

First, the trade unions remained deeply suspicious of his motives and, encouraged by their political masters from the SPD, they broke off negotiations. Moreover, the idea of public works alienated some of the landowners and businessmen. Second, although Schleicher's strategy to offer Strasser the post of vice-chancellor was a very clever one, in the end it did not work. Strasser himself responded positively to Schleicher's overtures and he was keen to accept the post, but the fundamental differences between Hitler and Strasser led to a massive row. Hitler retained the loyalty of the Party's leadership and Strasser was left isolated and promptly forced to resign from the Party.

Profile: Kurt von Schleicher 1882–1934

1882		– Born in Brandenburg, Prussia
1900–18		– Professional soldier and became an officer in Hindenburg's regiment
1919–32		– Worked in the German civil service in the Defence Ministry
1932	June	– Appointed defence minister in Papen's presidential government
	December	– Chancellor of Germany, until his forced resignation on 28 January 1933
1933	January	– Dismissed by Hindenburg
1934	June	– Murdered in the Night of the Long Knives

Schleicher was a shadowy figure and yet, he still had an important influence in the years 1930–3. He really preferred to exert political power behind the scenes and he did not take any high-ranking post until he became defence minister in June 1932. Nevertheless, he was undoubtedly the 'fixer', who set up the appointments of Brüning and Papen before, through Hindenburg, he finally contrived his own chancellorship. As a general, his primary aim was to preserve the interests and values of the German army, but in the end he was unable to control the intrigue – and a year later he lost his own life.

Nevertheless, the incident had been a major blow to Party morale and tensions remained high in the last few weeks of 1932, as the prospect of achieving power seemed to drift away.

Key question
Why did President Hindenburg eventually appoint Hitler as chancellor?

Hitler's success

Hitler's fortunes did not begin to take a more favourable turn until the first week of 1933. Papen had never forgiven Schleicher for dropping him. Papen was determined to regain political office and he recognised he could only achieve this by convincing Hindenburg that he could muster majority support in the *Reichstag*. Consequently, secret contacts were made with Nazi leaders, which culminated in a meeting on 4 January 1933 between Papen and Hitler. Here it was agreed in essence that Hitler should head a Nazi–Nationalist coalition government with Papen as vice-chancellor.

Back-stage intrigue to unseat Schleicher now took over. Papen looked for support for his plan from major landowners, leaders of industry and the army. It was only now that the conservative establishment thought that they had identified an escape from the threat of communism and the dangerous intrigues of Schleicher. But, above all, Papen had to convince the president himself. Hindenburg, undoubtedly encouraged by his son, Oskar, and his state secretary, Meissner, eventually gave in. Schleicher

Key date

Schleicher dismissed
and Hitler appointed
as chancellor:
30 January 1933

had failed in his attempt to bring stability. In fact, he had only succeeded in frightening the powerful vested interests with his ambitious plans. Hindenburg, therefore, heeded the advice of Papen to make Hitler chancellor of a coalition government, secure in the knowledge that those traditional conservatives and Nationalists would control the Nazis. On 28 January 1933, Hindenburg withdrew his support for Schleicher as chancellor.

It was only in this situation that Hindenburg finally agreed, on the suggestion of Papen, to appoint Hitler as chancellor in the mistaken belief Hitler could be controlled and used in the interests of the conservative establishment. Papen believed that Hitler would be a chancellor in chains and so two days later, on 30 January 1933, Hindenburg agreed to sanction the creation of a Nazi–Nationalist coalition.

Nazi parade celebrating Hitler's appointment as chancellor near the Brandenburg Gate during the evening of 30 January 1933.

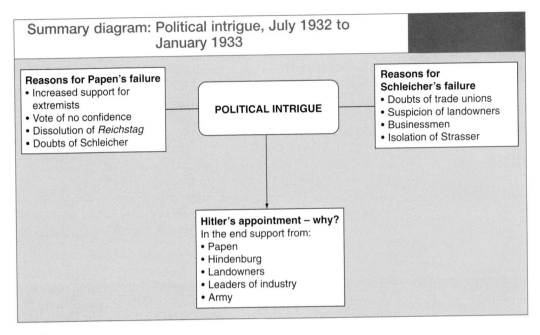

4 | The Nazi 'Legal Revolution', January–March 1933

Although Hitler had been appointed chancellor, his power was by no means absolute. Hindenburg had not been prepared to support Hitler's appointment until he had been satisfied that the chancellor's power would remain limited. Such was Papen's confidence about Hitler's restricted room for manoeuvre that he boasted to a friend, 'In two months we'll have pushed Hitler into a corner so hard that he'll be squeaking.'

The limitations of Hitler as chancellor

At first sight, the confidence of the conservatives seemed to be justified, since Hitler's position was weak in purely constitutional terms:

- There were only two other Nazis in the cabinet of 12: Wilhelm Frick as minister of the interior, and Hermann Göring as a minister without portfolio (a minister with no specific responsibility) (see profile, page 172). There were, therefore, nine other non-Nazi members of the cabinet, all from conservative-nationalist backgrounds, such as the army, industry and landowners.
- Hitler's coalition government did not have a majority in the *Reichstag*, suggesting that it would be difficult for the Nazis to introduce any dramatic legislation.
- The chancellor's post, as the previous 12 months had clearly shown, was dependent on the whim of President Hindenburg, and he openly resented Hitler. Hindenburg had made Hitler chancellor but he could as easily sack him.

Hitler was very much aware of the potential power of the army and the trade unions. He could not alienate these forces, which

Key question
What were the political constraints on Hitler?

could break his government. The army could arrange a military *coup* or the trade unions could organise a general strike, as they had done in 1920 (see pages 39–40).

Key question
What were Hitler's main political strengths?

Hitler's strengths

Within two months, the above weaknesses were shown not to be real limitations when Hitler became a dictator. Moreover, power was to be achieved by carrying on with the policy of legality which the Party had pursued since 1925. Hitler already possessed several key strengths when he became chancellor:

- He was the leader of the largest political party in Germany, which was why the policy of ignoring him had not worked. During 1932 it had only led to the ineffectual governments of Papen and Schleicher. Therefore, political realism forced the conservatives to work with him. They probably needed him more than he needed them. The alternative to Hitler was civil war or a communist *coup* – or so it seemed to many people at the time.
- More importantly, the Nazi Party had now gained access to the resources of the state. For example, Göring (see page 172) not only had a place in the cabinet but was also minister of the interior in Prussia, with responsibility for the police. It was a responsibility that he used blatantly to harass opponents, while ignoring Nazi crimes. Goebbels (see pages 244–5), likewise, exploited the propaganda opportunities on behalf of the Nazis. 'The struggle is a light one now,' he confided in his diary, '... since we are able to employ all the means of the state. Radio and press are at our disposal.'
- Above all, however, Hitler was a masterly political tactician. He was determined to achieve absolute power for himself whereas Papen was really politically naïve. It soon became clear that 'Papen's political puppet' was too clever to be strung along by a motley collection of ageing conservatives.

Key question
How did Hitler create a dictatorship in two months?

The *Reichstag* election, 5 March 1933

Hitler lost no time in removing his strings. Within 24 hours of his appointment as chancellor, new *Reichstag* elections had been called. He felt new elections would not only increase the Nazi vote, but also enhance his own status.

The campaign for the final *Reichstag* elections held according to the Weimar Constitution had few of the characteristics expected of a democracy: violence and terror dominated with meetings of the socialists and communists being regularly broken up by the Nazis. In Prussia, Göring used his authority to enrol an extra 50,000 into the police; nearly all were members of the SA and SS. Altogether 69 people died during the five-week campaign.

The Nazis also used the atmosphere of hate and fear to great effect in their election propaganda. Hitler set the tone in his 'Appeal to the German People' of 31 January 1933. He blamed the prevailing poor economic conditions on democratic government and the terrorist activities of the communists. He

'Not the most comfortable seat.' A US cartoon drawn soon after Hitler's appointment as chancellor. What does it suggest about Hitler's political position at that time?

cultivated the idea of the government as a 'national uprising' determined to restore Germany's pride and unity. In this way he played on the deepest desires of many Germans, but never committed himself to the details of a political and economic programme.

Another key difference in this election campaign was the improved Nazi financial situation. At a meeting on 20 February with 20 leading industrialists, Hitler was promised three million *Reichsmarks*. With such financial backing and Goebbels' exploitation of the media, the Nazis were confident of securing a parliamentary majority.

The *Reichstag* fire

As the campaign moved towards its climax, one further bizarre episode strengthened the Nazi hand. On 27 February the *Reichstag* building was set on fire, and a young Dutch communist, van der Lubbe, was arrested in incriminating circumstances. At the time, it was believed by many that the incident was a Nazi plot to support the claims of a communist *coup*, and thereby to justify Nazi repression. However, to this day the episode has defied satisfactory explanation. A major investigation in 1962 concluded that van der Lubbe had acted alone; a further 18 years later the West Berlin authorities posthumously acquitted him; whereas the recent biography of Hitler by Ian Kershaw remains convinced that van der Lubbe acted on his own in a series of three attempted arsons within a few weeks. So, it is probable that the true explanation will never be known. The real significance of the *Reichstag* fire is the cynical way it was exploited by the Nazis to their advantage.

On the next day, 28 February, Frick drew up, and Hindenburg signed, the 'Decree for the Protection of People and State'. In a few short clauses most civil and political liberties were suspended and the power of central government was strengthened. The justification for the decree was the threat posed by the communists. Following this, in the final week of the election campaign, hundreds of anti-Nazis were arrested, and the violence reached new heights.

Key dates

The Nazis blame the communists for the *Reichstag* fire: 27 February 1933

Final elections according to the Weimar Constitution: 5 March 1933

Election result

In this atmosphere of fear, Germany went to the polls on 5 March. The election had a very high turnout of 88 per cent – a figure this high suggests the influence and intimidation of the SA, corruption by officials and an increased government control of the radio.

Somewhat surprisingly, the Nazis increased their vote from 33.1 per cent to only 43.9 per cent, thereby securing 288 seats. Hitler could claim a majority in the new *Reichstag* only with the help of the 52 seats won by the Nationalists. It was not only disappointing; it was also a political blow, since any change in the existing Weimar Constitution required a two-thirds majority in the *Reichstag*.

The Enabling Act, March 1933

Despite this constitutional hurdle, Hitler decided to propose to the new *Reichstag* an Enabling Act that would effectively do away with parliamentary procedure and legislation and which would instead transfer full powers to the chancellor and his government for four years. In this way the dictatorship would be grounded in legality. However, the successful passage of the Act depended on gaining the support or abstention of some of the other major political parties in order to get a two-thirds majority.

A further problem was that the momentum built up within the lower ranks of the Nazi Party was proving increasingly difficult for Hitler to contain in the regional areas. Members were impatiently taking the law into their own hands and this gave the impression of a '**revolution from below**'. It threatened to destroy Hitler's image of legality, and antagonise the conservative vested interests and his DNVP coalition partners. Such was his concern that a grandiose act of reassurance was arranged. On 21 March, at Potsdam Garrison Church, Goebbels orchestrated the ceremony to celebrate the opening of the *Reichstag*. In the presence of Hindenburg, the Crown Prince (the son of Kaiser Wilhelm II), and many of the army's leading generals, Hitler symbolically aligned National Socialism with the forces of the old Germany.

Two days later the new *Reichstag* met in the Kroll Opera House to consider the Enabling Act, and on this occasion the Nazis revealed a very different image. The communists (those not already in prison) were refused admittance, while the deputies in attendance faced a barrage of intimidation from the ranks of the SA who surrounded the building.

However, the Nazis still required a two-thirds majority to pass the Act and, on the assumption that the Social Democrats would vote against, they needed the backing of the Centre Party. Hitler thus promised in his speech of 23 March to respect the rights of the Catholic Church and to uphold religious and moral values. These were false promises, which the ZP deputies deceived themselves into believing. In the end only the Social Democrats voted against, and the Enabling Act was passed by 444 to 94 votes.

Germany had succumbed to what Karl Bracher, a leading German scholar, has called 'legal revolution'. Within the space of a few weeks Hitler had legally dismantled the Weimar Constitution. The way was now open for him to create a one-party totalitarian dictatorship.

Key term

Revolution from below
The radical elements in the Party, e.g. the SA, that wanted to direct the Nazi revolution from a more local level rather than from the leadership in Berlin.

Key dates

Day of Potsdam ceremony: 21 March 1933

Enabling Act passed: 23 March 1933

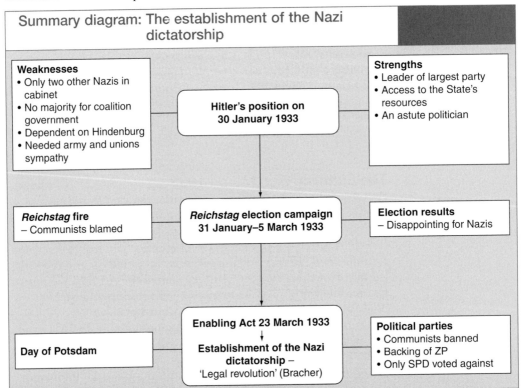

Summary diagram: The establishment of the Nazi dictatorship

Weaknesses
- Only two other Nazis in cabinet
- No majority for coalition government
- Dependent on Hindenburg
- Needed army and unions sympathy

Hitler's position on 30 January 1933

Strengths
- Leader of largest party
- Access to the State's resources
- An astute politician

Reichstag **fire**
– Communists blamed

Reichstag **election campaign 31 January–5 March 1933**

Election results
– Disappointing for Nazis

Day of Potsdam

Enabling Act 23 March 1933
↓
Establishment of the Nazi dictatorship –
'Legal revolution' (Bracher)

Political parties
- Communists banned
- Backing of ZP
- Only SPD voted against

Key question
What was
Gleichschaltung?

5 | Co-ordination: *Gleichschaltung*

The Enabling Act was the constitutional foundation stone of the Third Reich. In purely legal terms the Weimar Constitution was not dissolved until 1945, but in practice the Enabling Act provided the basis for the dictatorship which evolved from 1933. In that legal way, the intolerance and violence used by the Nazis to gain power could now be used as tools of government by the dictatorship of Hitler and the Party.

Key term

Gleichschaltung
'Bringing into line'
or 'co-ordination'.

The degeneration of Weimar's democracy into the Nazi state system is usually referred to as *Gleichschaltung* or co-ordination. In practice, it applied to the Nazifying of German society and structures and refers specifically to the establishment of the dictatorship, 1933–4. To some extent it was generated by the power and freedom exploited by the SA at the local level – in effect a 'revolution from below'. But it was also directed by the Nazi leadership from the political centre in Berlin – a 'revolution from above'. Together, these two political forces attempted to 'co-ordinate' as many aspects of German life as possible along Nazi lines, although differences over the exact long-term goals of National Socialism laid the basis for future conflict within the Party (see pages 148–53).

In practice, co-ordination has been viewed rather neatly as the 'merging' of German society with Party associations and institutions in an attempt to Nazify the life of Germany. At first many of these Nazi creations had to live alongside existing bodies, but over the years they gradually replaced them. In this way, much of Germany's cultural, educational and social life became increasingly controlled (see Chapter 9). However, in the spring and summer of 1933 the priority of the Nazi leadership was to secure its political supremacy. So its real focus of attention was the 'co-ordination' of the federal states, the political parties and the independent trade unions – which were at odds with Nazi political aspirations.

Key question
In what ways did
Nazism achieve
co-ordination?

Main features of co-ordination
The federal states

The regions had a very strong tradition in Germany history. Even after the creation of the German Empire in 1871 the previously independent states had carried on as largely self-governing federal states. And in 1919 the Weimar Constitution had agreed on a federal structure with 17 *Länder* (regional states), e.g. Prussia, Bavaria and Saxony (see page 22). Yet, this stood in marked contrast to Nazi desires to create a fully unified country.

Nazi activists had already exploited the climate of February–March 1933 to intimidate opponents and to infiltrate federal governments. Indeed, their 'political success' rapidly degenerated into terror and violence that seemed even beyond the control of Hitler, who called for restraint because he was afraid of losing the support of the conservatives. Consequently, the situation was resolved in three legal stages:

- First, by a law of 31 March 1933, the regional parliaments (*Landtage*) were dissolved and then reformed with acceptable majorities, which allowed the Nazis to dominate regional state governments.
- Secondly, a law of 7 April 1933 created Reich Governors (*Reichstatthalter*) who more often than not were the local party *Gauleiters* with full powers.
- The process of centralisation was finally completed in January 1934 when the regional parliaments were abolished. Federal governments and governors were subordinated to the authorities of the ministry of the interior in the central government.

By early 1934 the federal principle of government was as good as dead. Even the Nazi Reich governors existed simply 'to execute the will of the supreme leadership of the Reich'.

The trade unions

Germany's trade union movement was powerful because of its mass membership and its strong connections with socialism and Catholicism. Back in 1920 it had clearly shown its industrial muscle when it had successfully ended a right-wing *putsch* against the Weimar government by calling a general strike. On the whole, German organised labour was hostile to Nazism and, so, posed a major threat to the stability of the Nazi state.

Yet, by May 1933 it was shown to be a spent force. Admittedly, the depression had already severely weakened it by reducing membership and lessening the will to resist. However, the trade union leaders deceived themselves into believing that they could work with the Nazis and thereby preserve a degree of independence and at least the structure of trade unionism. Their hope was that:

- in the short term, trade unionism would continue to serve its social role to help members
- in the long term, it could provide the framework for development in the post-Nazi era.

However, the labour movement was deceived by the Nazis.

The Nazis surprisingly declared 1 May (the traditional day of celebration for international socialist labour) a national holiday, which gave the impression to the trade unions that perhaps there was some scope for co-operation. This proved to be the briefest of illusions. The following day, trade union premises were occupied by the SA and SS, union funds were confiscated and many of the leaders were arrested and sent to the early concentration camps, such as Dachau.

Independent trade unions were then banned and in their place all German workers' organisations were absorbed into the German Labour Front (*Deutscher Arbeitsfront*, DAF), led by Robert Ley (see page 185). DAF became the largest organisation in Nazi Germany with 22 million members, but it acted more as an instrument of control than as a genuine representative body of workers' interests and concerns (see page 182). Also, it lost the most fundamental right to negotiate wages and conditions of work. So, by the end of 1933, the power of the German labour movement had been decisively broken.

Political parties

It was inconceivable that *Gleichschaltung* could allow the existence of other political parties. Nazism openly rejected democracy and any concessions to alternative opinions. Instead, it aspired to establish authoritarian rule within a one-party state. This was not difficult to achieve:

- The Communists had been outlawed since the *Reichstag* fire (see page 143).
- Soon after the destruction of the trade unions the assets of the Social Democrats were seized and they were then officially banned on 22 June.
- Most of the major remaining parties willingly agreed to dissolve themselves in the course of late June 1933 – even the Nationalists (previously coalition partners to the Nazis) obligingly accepted.
- Finally, the Catholic Centre Party decided to give up the struggle and followed suit on 5 July 1933.

Key date
All political opposition to NSDAP declared illegal: 14 July 1933

Thus, there was no opposition to the decree of 14 July that formally proclaimed the Nazi Party as the only legal political party in Germany.

Key question
How advanced was the process of Nazi co-ordination by the end of 1933?

Success of *Gleichschaltung* in 1933

By the end of 1933 the process of *Gleichschaltung* was well advanced in many areas of public life in Germany. However, it was certainly far from complete. In particular, it had failed to make any impression on the role and influence of the churches, the army and big business. Also, the civil service and education had only been partially co-ordinated. This was mainly due to Hitler's determination to shape events through the 'revolution from above' and to avoid antagonising such powerful vested interests. Yet, there were many in the lower ranks of the Party who had contributed to the 'revolution from below' and who now wanted to extend the process of *Gleichschaltung*. It was this internal party conflict which laid the basis for the bloody events of June 1934.

A photograph of Prussian policemen in Berlin in 1933. Although they wore the traditional helmet with the insignia, they are 'brought into line' by carrying Nazi flags and give the Nazi salute.

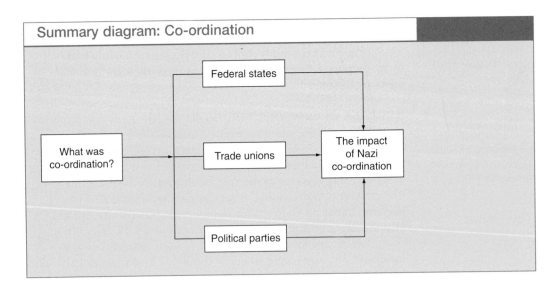

Summary diagram: Co-ordination

```
                              Federal states
                                   |
   What was            Trade unions           The impact
co-ordination?  ---->                 ---->    of Nazi
                                              co-ordination
                              Political parties
```

6 | From Chancellor to *Führer*

Within just six months of coming to power Hitler had indeed managed to turn Germany into a one-party dictatorship. However, in a speech on 6 July 1933 to the Reich Governors, Hitler warned of the dangers posed by a permanent state of revolution. He therefore formally declared an end to the

Key question
What exactly was the political dilemma faced by Hitler in 1933?

revolution and demanded that 'the stream of revolution must be guided into the safe channel of evolution'.

Hitler was caught in a political dilemma. He was increasingly concerned that the behaviour of Party activists was running beyond his control. This was likely to create embarrassment in his relations with the more conservative forces whose support he still depended on, e.g. big business, civil service and, above all, the army. Hitler's speech amounted to a clear-cut demand for the Party to accept the realities of political compromise and also the necessity of change from above.

The position of the SA

However, Hitler's appeal failed to have the desired effect. If anything, it reinforced the fears of many Party members that the Nazi leadership was prepared to dilute the ideology of National Socialism. Such concerns came in particular from within the ranks of the SA giving rise to calls for **'a second revolution'**.

Table 7.2: SA membership 1931–4

	1931	1932	1933	1934
Membership figures	100,000	291,000	425,000	3,000,000

SA membership grew at first because of the large number of unemployed young men, but from 1933 many joined as a way to advance themselves.

The SA represented the radical, left wing of the Nazi Party and to a large extent it reflected a more working-class membership, which in the depression was often young and unemployed. It placed far more emphasis on the socialist elements of the Party programme than Hitler ever did and, therefore, saw no need to hold back simply for the sake of satisfying the élites. It had played a vital role in the years of struggle by winning the political battle on the streets, and many of its members were embittered and frustrated over the limited nature of the Nazi revolution. They were also disappointed by their own lack of personal gain from this acquisition of power.

Such views were epitomised by the leader of the SA, Ernst Röhm, who openly called for a genuine 'National Socialist Revolution'. Röhm was increasingly disillusioned by the politics of his old friend Hitler and he recognised that the developing confrontation would decide the future role of the SA in the Nazi state. In a private interview in early 1934 with a local Party boss, Rauschning, Röhm gave vent to his feelings and his ideas:

Adolf is a swine. He will give us all away. He only associates with the reactionaries now. ... Getting matey with the East Prussian generals. They're his cronies now ... Adolf knows exactly what I want. I've told him often enough. Not a second edition of the old imperial army.

Key term

'A second revolution' Refers to the aims of the SA, led by Ernst Röhm, which wanted social and economic reforms and the creation of a 'people's army' merging the German army and the SA. The aims of 'a second revolution' were more attractive to the 'left-wing socialist Nazis' or 'radical Nazis', who did not sympathise with the conservative forces in Germany.

Profile: Ernst Röhm 1887–1934

1887		– Born in Munich
1914–18		– Served in the First World War and reached the rank of captain
1919		– Joined the *Freikorps*
		– Met Hitler and joined the Nazi Party
1921		– Helped to form the SA and became its leader in the years 1921–3
1923	November	– Participated in the Munich Beer Hall *putsch*
1924		– Initially jailed, but soon released on probation
1925–30		– Left for Bolivia in South America
1930		– Returned to Germany at Hitler's request
1930–4		– SA leader
1933	December	– Invited to join the cabinet
1934	June	– Arrested and then murdered in the Night of the Long Knives

Röhm was always a controversial character. He was an open homosexual, a heavy drinker and enjoyed the blood and violence of war and political street battles. Yet, he was one of Hitler's closest friends in the years 1919–34, which partially explains why Hitler found it so painful to destroy the SA and its leader.

He played a key role in the earliest years, when he introduced Hitler to the Nazi Party in 1919. He formed the SA in 1921, but he left Germany after the Beer Hall *putsch*. Most significantly, in the years 1930–3 Röhm was given the responsibility by Hitler of reorganising the SA and restoring its discipline. By intimidation and street violence Röhm's SA had turned itself into a powerful force by 1931, although conflict between the Party leadership and the SA grew increasingly serious.

After the Nazi consolidation of power, Röhm was committed to pursue 'a second revolution' that reflected the reforms of the 'left-wing socialist Nazis' or 'radical Nazis'. He did not sympathise with the conservative forces in Germany and, above all, aimed to create a 'people's army' by merging the German army and the SA. This fundamental difference culminated in the Night of the Long Knives and his own death.

Röhm, therefore had no desire to see the SA marches and rallies degenerating into a mere propaganda show now that the street-fighting was over. He wanted to amalgamate the army and the SA into a people's militia – of which he would be the commander.

The power struggle between the SA and the army

However, Röhm's plan was anathema to the German army which saw its traditional role and status being directly threatened. Hitler was therefore caught between two powerful, but rival, forces – both of which could create considerable political difficulties for him.

On the one hand, the SA consisted of three million committed Nazis with his oldest political friend leading it. It had fought for Hitler in the 1923 Munich *putsch* and also in the battle of the streets, 1930–3. The SA was also far larger than the army.

On the other hand, the army was the one organisation that could unseat Hitler from his position of power. The officer class was suspicious of Hitler and it had close social ties with many of the powerful interests, e.g. civil service and *Junkers*. Moreover, the army alone possessed the military skills which were vital to the success of his foreign policy aims. Also, however large the SA was, it could never hope to challenge the discipline and professional expertise possessed by the army.

So, political realities dictated that Hitler had to retain the backing of the army but, in the winter of 1933–4, he was still loath to engineer a showdown with his old friend, Röhm. He tried to make concessions to Röhm by bringing him into the cabinet. He also called a meeting in February between the leaders of the army, the SA and the SS in an attempt to reach an agreement about the role of each organisation within the Nazi state. However, the tension did not ease. Röhm and the SA resented Hitler's apparent acceptance of the privileged position of the army. Moreover, the unrestrained actions and ill-discipline of the SA only increased the feelings of dissatisfaction among the generals.

Key term

Junkers
The landowning aristocracy, especially those from eastern Germany.

Key question
When and why did the political conflict come to a head?

The Night of the Long Knives

The developing crisis came to a head in April 1934 when it became apparent that President Hindenburg did not have much longer to live. The implications of his imminent death were profound; for Hitler wanted to assume the presidency without opposition. He certainly did not want a contested election, nor did he have any sympathy for those who wanted the restoration of the monarchy. It seems that Hitler's hand was forced by the need to secure the army's backing for his succession to Hindenburg.

The support of the army had become the key to the survival of Hitler's regime in the short term, while in the long term it offered the means to fulfil his ambitions in the field of foreign affairs. Whatever personal loyalty Hitler felt for Röhm and the SA was finally put to one side. The army desired their elimination and an end to the talk of a 'second revolution' and a 'people's militia'. By agreeing to this, Hitler could gain the favour of the army generals, secure his personal position and remove an increasingly embarrassing millstone from around his neck.

Without primary written evidence it is difficult to establish the exact details of the events in June 1934. However, it seems highly probable that, at a meeting on the battleship *Deutschland* in April 1934, Hitler and the two leading generals, Blomberg and Fritsch, came to an agreed position against Röhm and the SA. Furthermore, influential figures within the Nazi Party, in particular Göring and Himmler, were also manoeuvring behind the scenes. They were aiming for a similar outcome in order to further their own ambitions by removing a powerful rival. Given all that, Hitler probably did not decide to make his crucial move to solve the problem of the SA until mid-June when Vice-Chancellor Papen gave a speech calling for an end to SA excesses and criticised the policy of co-ordination. Not surprisingly, these words caused a real stir and were seen as a clear challenge. Hitler now recognised that he had to satisfy the conservative forces – and that meant he had to destroy the power of the SA immediately.

The purge

On 30 June 1934, the Night of the Long Knives, Hitler eliminated the SA as a political and military force once and for all. Röhm and the main leaders of the SA were shot by members of the SS – although the weapons and transport were actually provided by the army. There was no resistance of any substance. In addition, various old scores were settled: Schleicher, the former chancellor, and Strasser, the leader of the radical socialist wing of the Nazi Party, were both killed. Altogether it is estimated that 200 people were murdered.

From a very different perspective, on 5 July 1934 the *Völkischer Beobachter* (*The People's Observer*), the Nazi newspaper, reported on the Reich cabinet meeting held two days earlier:

> Defence Minister General Blomberg thanked the *Führer* in the name of the cabinet and the army for his determined and courageous action, by which he had saved the German people from civil war.…
>
> The Reich cabinet then approved a law on measures for the self-defence of the state. Its single paragraph reads: 'The measures taken on 30 June and 1 and 2 July to suppress the acts of high treason are legal, being necessary for the self-defence of the state.'

The significance of the Night of Long Knives

It would be difficult to overestimate the significance of the Night of the Long Knives. In one bloody action Hitler overcame the radical left in his own Party, and the conservative right of traditional Germany. By the summer of 1934, the effects of the purge could be seen clearly:

Key question
How significant was the Night of the Long Knives?

- The German army had clearly aligned itself behind the Nazi regime, as was shown by Blomberg's public vote of thanks to Hitler on 1 July. Perhaps, even more surprisingly, German soldiers agreed to take a personal oath of loyalty to Hitler.
- The SA was rendered almost unarmed and it played no significant role in the political development of the Nazi state. Thereafter its major role was to attend propaganda rallies as a showpiece force.
- More ominously for the future, the incident marked the emergence of the SS. German generals had feared the SA, but they failed to recognise the SS as the Party's élite institution of terror.
- Above all, Hitler had secured his own personal political supremacy. His decisions and actions were accepted, so in effect

Key term

Führer
Meaning leader.
Hitler was declared
leader of the Nazi
Party in 1921. In
1934 he became
leader of the
country after the
death of
Hindenburg.

Key dates

Night of the Long
Knives – destruction
of SA by SS: 30 June
1934

Death of Hindenburg:
Hitler combined the
offices of chancellor
and president. Oath
of loyalty taken by
army: 2 August 1934

he had managed to legalise murder. From that moment, it was clear that the Nazi regime was not a traditional authoritarian one, like Imperial Germany 1871–1918; it was a personal dictatorship with frightening power.

Consequently, when Hindenburg died on 2 August, there was no political crisis. Hitler was simply able to merge the offices of chancellor and president, and also to take on the new official title of *Führer*. The Nazi regime had been stabilised and the threat of a 'second revolution' had been completely removed.

A cartoon/photomontage published by the German communist John Heartfield in July 1934. The image is of a Stormtrooper who has been murdered on Hitler's order in the Night of the Long Knives. What is ironic about his Heil Hitler salute?

Summary diagram: From Chancellor to *Führer*

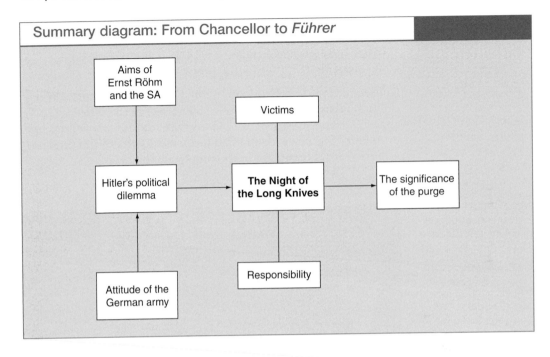

7 | Conclusions: Why was Weimar Germany Replaced by a Nazi Dictatorship?

In 1932 only 43 per cent of the electorate voted in the July *Reichstag* elections for pro-Republican parties. The majority of the German people had voted in a free (and reasonably fair) election to reject democracy, despite the fact that there was no clear alternative. So, Germany did not necessarily have to end up with a Nazi dictatorship. Yet, within just six months Hitler had assumed the mantle of power and by 1934 he was the leader of a brutal dictatorship.

The appointment of Hitler

The depression transformed the Nazis into a mass movement. Admittedly, 63 per cent of Germans never voted for them, but 37 per cent of the electorate did, so the Nazis became by far the strongest party in a multi-party democracy. The depression had led to such profound social and economic hardship that it created an environment of discontent, which was easily exploited by the Nazis' style of political activity. Indeed, it is questionable whether Hitler would have become a national political figure without the severity of that economic downturn. However, his mixture of racist, nationalist and anti-democratic ideas was readily received by a broad spectrum of German people, and especially by the disgruntled middle classes.

Other extreme right-wing groups with similar ideas and conditions did not enjoy similar success. This is partially explained by the impressive manner in which the Nazi message was communicated: the use of modern propaganda techniques, the violent exploitation of scapegoats – especially the Jews and

Key question
Why was Hitler appointed as chancellor?

communists – and the well-organised structure of the Party apparatus. All these factors undoubtedly helped but, in terms of electoral appeal, it is impossible to ignore the powerful impact of Hitler himself as a charismatic leader with a cult following. Furthermore, he exhibited a quite extraordinary political acumen and ruthlessness when he was involved in the detail of political in-fighting.

Nevertheless, the huge popular following of the Nazis, which helped to undermine the continued operation of democracy, was insufficient on its own to give Hitler power. In the final analysis, it was the mutual recognition by Hitler and the representatives of the traditional leaders of the army, the landowners and heavy industry that they needed each other, which led to Hitler's appointment as chancellor of a coalition government on 30 January 1933. Since September 1930 every government had been forced to resort almost continuously to the use of presidential emergency decrees because they had lacked a popular mandate.

In the chaos of 1932 the only other realistic alternative to including the Nazis in the government was some kind of military regime – a presidential dictatorship backed by the army, perhaps. However, that, too, would have faced similar difficulties. Indeed, by failing to satisfy the extreme left and the extreme right, there would have been a very real possibility of civil war. A coalition with Hitler's Nazis, therefore, provided the conservative élites with both mass support and some alluring promises: a vigorous attack on Germany's political left wing and rearmament as a precursor to economic and political expansion abroad. For Hitler, the inclusion of Papen and Hugenberg gave his cabinet an air of conservative respectability.

The establishment of the Nazi dictatorship

Key question
In what ways was Hitler able to consolidate Nazi power between 1933 and 1934?

In the end, Hitler became chancellor because the political forces of the left and centre were too divided and too weak, and because the conservative right wing was prepared to accept him as a partner in government in the mistaken belief that he could be tamed. With hindsight, it can be seen that 30 January 1933 was decisive and Hitler was entrenched in power.

These are the key factors which help to explain the establishment of the dictatorship:

- *Terror.* The Nazis used violence – and increasingly so without legal restriction, e.g. the Night of the Long Knives and the arrest of the communists. Nazi organisations also employed violence at a local level to intimidate opposition.
- *Legality.* The use of law by the Nazis gave a legal justification for the development of the regime, e.g. the Enabling Act, the Emergency Decree of 28 February 1933, the dissolution of the parties.
- *Deception.* Hitler misled powerful groups in order to destroy them, e.g. the trade unions and the SA.
- *Propaganda.* The Nazis successfully cultivated powerful images – especially when Goebbels took on responsibility for the

Propaganda Ministry. Myths were developed about Hitler as a respectable statesman, e.g. the Day of Potsdam (see page 144).

- *Weaknesses of the opposition.* In the early Weimar years, the left had considerable potential power, but it became divided between the Social Democrats and the Communists – and was marred by the economic problems of the depression.
- *Sympathy of the conservative right.* Many of the traditional vested interests, e.g. the army, civil service, were not wholly committed to Weimar and they really sympathised with a more right-wing authoritarian regime. They accepted the Night of the Long Knives.

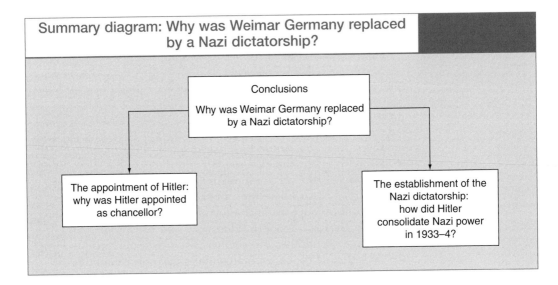

Summary diagram: Why was Weimar Germany replaced by a Nazi dictatorship?

Conclusions

Why was Weimar Germany replaced by a Nazi dictatorship?

The appointment of Hitler: why was Hitler appointed as chancellor?

The establishment of the Nazi dictatorship: how did Hitler consolidate Nazi power in 1933–4?

Study Guide: AS Questions

In the style of OCR A

'The Nazis were the Party of the people.' To what extent do you agree with this assessment of the political appeal in 1932?

(50 marks)

Exam tips

This question is about the people who voted for and supported the Nazi Party at the tipping moment that brought Hitler to power. You need to examine the range of support they received, but 'To what extent … ?' has to be addressed seriously so you must also examine those who did not support the Nazis. Only with all this plotted can you decide how far they were 'the party of the people'.

Who were the 13.7 million who voted Nazi in July 1932? They fall into clearly identifiable groups. Most came from the north and east. Either they tended to be artisans and shopkeepers or white-collar workers living in suburbs or small towns. Or they were rural farmers and peasants. Most were Protestant. Why did they vote Nazi? On the whole, they saw their position as threatened and they had little faith in the Republic. The crises from 1918 had made them deeply fearful and Hitler offered solutions to their anxieties. Support from such groups made the Nazis a mass party in 1930–2, but there were plenty of Germans who did not vote for Hitler. The core groups he failed to win over were Catholics and the left (52 per cent of the vote).

Where does this leave your conclusions? Does it mean the Nazis could not have been 'the party of the people'? By a strict headcount, the answer must be 'yes'. Nearly two-thirds of Germans voted for a party other than the Nazis in July 1932. Decide how to interpret these results and pull together your answer to judge the matter.

In the style of OCR A

Study the four sources on the Nazi road to dictatorship and then answer **both** sub-questions. It is recommended that you spend two-thirds of your time in answering part **(b)**.

(a) Study Sources A and D.
Compare these sources as evidence for reactions to a speech by Hitler.

(30 marks)

(b) Study all the sources.
Use your own knowledge to assess how far the sources support the interpretation that use of the SA and SS was the **main** reason why the Nazi Party took power by the end of March 1933.

(70 marks)

Source A

A Hamburg schoolteacher, married to a former army officer, gives her immediate impression of a Nazi mass rally in 1932.

There was immaculate order and discipline. Hitler, in a simple black coat, looked out over the crowd with their forest of swastika pennants. They gave vent to the jubilation of this moment in a roaring salute. His main theme was 'Out of parties shall grow a nation, the German nation'. His speech was greeted with roaring applause. How many looked up to him with touching faith as their helper, their saviour, their deliverer from unbearable distress. To them he was the rescuer of the Prussian prince, the scholar, the clergyman, the farmer, the worker, the unemployed. He would rescue them from the parties back into the nation.

Source B

Hitler attempts to remove the radical image of the Nazi Party in this speech to the Industry Club in Düsseldorf in January 1932. He had been invited to speak there by Fritz Thyssen, a major Ruhr industrialist and keen Nazi supporter.

How mighty is the force of an ideal! In the Nazi movement today, hundreds of thousands of young men risk their lives to withstand our opponents. Property owners draw back their curtains to witness the nightly fights. But remember that many hundreds of thousands of SA and SS men have to get on their lorries, protect meetings, undertake marches, sacrifice themselves night after night and then come back in the grey dawn to workshop and factory, or, as unemployed, take the pittance of the dole every day. If the whole German nation possessed their idealism, we might restore a sound German economy, a state renewed and armed to strike against foreign oppression and extortion.

Source C

Hitler's propaganda chief Josef Goebbels comments on a meeting on 13 August 1932 where Hitler had failed to persuade von Hindenburg to allow him to form the next government.

The Führer is back in half an hour. So it has ended in failure. Papen is to remain Chancellor and the *Führer* has to be content with the position of Vice-Chancellor! It is out of the question to accept such a proposal. There is no alternative but to refuse. The *Führer* did so immediately.

In the back room, the SA leaders assemble. The *Führer* will give them a fairly full outline of events. Who knows if their units will be able to hold together? Nothing is harder than to tell a troop with victory already in their grasp that their assignment has come to nothing. The idea of the *Führer* as Vice-Chancellor of a bourgeois Cabinet is too ludicrous to be treated seriously. The *Führer* maintains an admirable calm. Well, the fight goes on! In the end our strength and tenacity will make them give in.

Source D

A Bavarian SPD deputy gives his account of the atmosphere during the Reichstag *debate on the Enabling Act in March 1933.*

The wide square in front of the Kroll Opera House was crowded with dark masses of people. Youths with swastikas on their chests blocked our way and called us names like 'Centre pig' and 'Marxist sow'. The building was crawling with armed SA and SS men. When we Social Democrats had taken our seats on the extreme left, SA and SS men lined up at the exits and along the walls behind us in a semicircle with aggressive expressions. Hitler demanded the execution of van der Lubbe and uttered dark threats as to what would happen if the *Reichstag* did not pass the Enabling Act: a Nazi Revolution and bloody anarchy. How could this speaker carry away thousands of people with enthusiasm? His speech made a terrifying impression on us.

Exam tips

The cross-references are intended to take you straight to the material that will help you to answer the questions.

(a) Part **(a)** requires you to examine closely the content of the two sources and compare the way they show people's reactions to a speech by Hitler. Source A suggests Hitler's audience were carried away with enthusiasm and very positive, whereas Source B suggests that he terrified some parts of his audience and their response was negative. The main focus of an effective answer is on comparing and contrasting the content and provenance of the two sources in the light of the question asked and reaching a substantiated judgement.

(b) Part **(b)** requires you to use the content and provenance of all four sources, grouping them by view, and to integrate pertinent factual knowledge into your argument to answer the question. Knowledge should be used to develop, validate or criticise the views in the sources. You should reach a balanced judgement supported by knowledge, source content and provenance.

Consider the following:

- the role of the SA and SS (the key issue in the question) (pages 134–5)
- the creation of a mass movement (page 124–6)
- Hitler's propaganda methods (pages 131–5)
- political intrigue (pages 125–9)
- the *Reichstag* fire and the Enabling Act (pages 141–4).

8 The Nazi Economy

POINTS TO CONSIDER
The purpose of this chapter is to consider Nazi economic
policies and their effects on the performance of the Nazi
economy over the years of the Third Reich. The economy
went through various stages and to appreciate the
significance of these, it is important to consider the
following main themes:

- The economic background to the establishment of the
  Nazi regime
- The economic recovery of Germany 1933–6
- The introduction of the Four-Year Plan 1936–9
- The economy at war 1939–45

Key dates

1933	March	Appointment of Schacht as President of the *Reichsbank*
1934	July	Appointment of Schacht as Minister of Economics
	September	New Plan introduced
1936	October	Four-Year Plan established under Göring
1937	November	Resignation of Schacht as Minister of Economics
1939	December	War Economy decrees
1941	December	Rationalisation Decree issued by Hitler
1942	February	Appointment of Albert Speer as Minister of Armaments
1944	August	Peak of German munitions production

1 | The Economic Background

Key question
Did the Nazis have an economic policy?

In the years before 1933, Hitler had been careful not to become
tied down to the details of an economic policy. Hitler even told
his cabinet in February 1933 to 'avoid all detailed statements
concerning an economic programme of the government'.

However, Hitler was also politically astute enough to realise
that his position depended on bringing Germany out of

depression and so during 1932 the Nazi leadership had begun to consider a number of *possible* approaches to the management of the economy.

- First were the socio-economic aspects of the Nazi Party's original aims, as outlined in the anti-capitalist sentiments of the **25-points programme** of the Nazi Party of 1920 such as:
  - profit sharing in large industrial enterprises
  - the extensive development of insurance for old age
  - the **nationalisation** of all businesses.

  Hitler accepted these points in the early years because he recognised their popular appeal but he himself never showed any real commitment to such ideas. As a result, they created important differences within the Party, as a faction within it still demanded these.
- Secondly, attention was given to the emerging idea of deficit financing. This found its most obvious expression in the theories of the British economist J.M. Keynes and the new President of the USA, F.D. Roosevelt, from 1933. By spending money on public works, deficit financing was intended to create jobs, which would then act as an artificial stimulus to demand within the economy. Indeed, work schemes were actually started in Germany in 1932 by Chancellors Papen and Schleicher.
- Finally, there was the idea of the *Wehrwirtschaft* (defence economy), whereby Germany's peacetime economy was geared to the demands of total war. This was to avoid a repetition of the problems faced during the First World War when a long, drawn-out conflict on two fronts eventually caused economic collapse. Related to this was the policy of **autarky**. This envisaged a scheme for the creation of a large trading area in Europe under the dominating influence of Germany, which could be developed to rival the other great economic powers. It played upon the idea of German power and harked back to the expansionist views of some First World War nationalists (see page 36).

(see page 36).

Key terms

25-Points programme
Hitler drew up the Party's 25-points programme in February 1920 with the Party's founder, Anton Drexler.

Nationalisation
The socialist principle that the ownership of key industries should be transferred to the state.

Autarky
The aim for self-sufficiency in the production of food and raw materials, especially when at war.

Of these three economic approaches, Hitler identified his long-term political and military aims most clearly with the defence economy. However, there were important differences within the Party over economic planning so, despite the consideration given to such policies by the Nazi leaders, no coherent plan had emerged by January 1933. Hitler had no real understanding of economics and to a large extent the implementation of economic policy was initially left to bankers and civil servants.

From the start, then, there was a lack of real direction and elements of all three approaches can be detected in the economic history of the Third Reich. This suggests that economic policy tended to be pragmatic. It evolved out of the demands of the situation rather than being the result of careful planning. As the leading historian A. Schweitzer stated, 'no single unified economic system prevailed throughout the entire period of the Nazi regime'.

Key question
How serious were
Germany's economic
problems in the Great
Depression 1929–33?

Germany's economic condition in 1933

Germany had faced continuing economic problems since the end
of the First World War. However, as can be seen on pages 102–5,
the sheer scale of the world economic depression that began in
1929 meant that Germany undoubtedly suffered in a particularly
savage way:

- *Trade*. Germany depended heavily on its capacity to sell
  manufactured goods. In the slump of global trade, the demand
  for German exports declined rapidly and its sale of
  manufactured goods, e.g. steel, machinery and chemicals,
  collapsed.
- *Industry*. Despite its post-war problems, Germany was an
  industrial power. However, when it began to lose economic
  confidence from 1929, demand fell and businesses cut
  production, or worse, collapsed.
- *Employment*. The most obvious feature of the industrial
  contraction was mass long-term unemployment. The length
  and severity of the economic recession greatly increased the
  number of unemployed, with all the associated social problems.
  In 1932 the figure rose to 5.6 million. If the number of
  unregistered unemployed is added, the total without work was
  about eight million in 1932.
- *Agriculture*. The situation in the countryside was no better than
  in the towns. The agricultural depression deepened, leading to
  widespread rural poverty. As global demand fell, agricultural
  prices, farmers' wages and incomes fell sharply, which forced
  some to sell off their farms.
- *Finance*. Because of war debts, reparations and inflation,
  German banking had faced serious financial problems in the
  years even *before* 1929. The onset of the depression
  undermined the confidence of the financial sector: foreign
  investment disappeared, German share prices collapsed and
  five major banks collapsed in 1931.

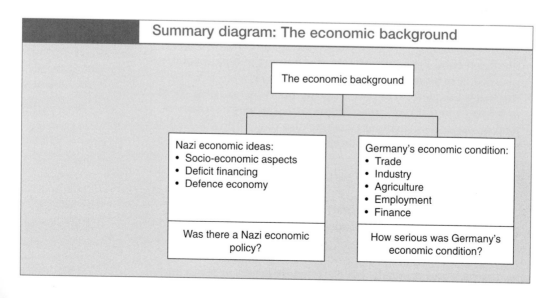

Summary diagram: The economic background

The economic background

Nazi economic ideas:
- Socio-economic aspects
- Deficit financing
- Defence economy

Was there a Nazi economic
policy?

Germany's economic condition:
- Trade
- Industry
- Agriculture
- Employment
- Finance

How serious was Germany's
economic condition?

2 | Economic Recovery 1933–6

Schacht's economic strategy

Key question
How did Schacht's policies stimulate economic recovery?

In the early years Nazi economic policy was under the control of Hjalmar Schacht, President of the *Reichsbank* (1933–9) and Minister of Economics (1934–7). This reflected the need of the Nazi leadership to work with the powerful forces of big business. Schacht was already a respected international financier because of his leading role in the creation of the new currency in the wake of the 1923 hyperinflation.

Appointment of Schacht as President of the *Reichsbank*: March 1933

Key date

It is certainly true that the economic depression reached its low-point in the winter of 1932–3 and that afterwards the trade cycle began to improve. This undoubtedly worked to the political and economic advantage of the Nazis. Nevertheless, there was no single, easy 'quick fix' solution.

The heart of economic recovery lay in the major revival of public investment led, for the most part, by the state itself, which embarked on a large-scale increase in its own spending in an effort to stimulate demand and raise national income. So, under Schacht's guidance and influence, deficit financing was adopted through a range of economic measures.

Banking and the control of capital

Initially, because the German banking system had been so fundamentally weakened, the state increasingly assumed greater responsibility for the control of capital within the economy. It then proceeded to set interest rates at a lower level and to reschedule the large-scale debts of local authorities.

Assistance for farming and small businesses

Particular financial benefits were given to groups such as farmers and small businesses. This not only stimulated economic growth, but also rewarded some of the most sympathetic supporters of the Nazis in the 1930–3 elections. Some of the measures included (see also pages 184–7):

- maintaining tariffs on imported produce in order to protect German farmers
- the Reich Food Estate giving subsidies as part of a nationally planned agricultural system (see pages 186–7)
- the Reich Entailed Farm Law reducing debts by tax concessions and lower interest rates in an attempt to offer more security of land ownership to small farmers (see also pages 186–7)
- giving allowances to encourage the rehiring of domestic servants
- allocating grants for house repairs.

State investment – public works

However, of the greatest significance was the direct spending by the state on a range of investment projects. In June 1933 the Law to Reduce Unemployment was renewed and expanded (from a scheme which had originally been started by Papen in 1932) and the RAD (*Reichsarbeitsdienst*, Reich Labour Service) was expanded to employ 19–25 year olds. For a long time most historians assumed that rearmament was the main focus of investment, but the figures for public expenditure show that this was initially spread among rearmament, construction and transportation. So the investment in the first three years was directed towards work creation schemes such as:

• reforestation
• land reclamation
• motorisation – the policy of developing the vehicle industry and the building of improved roads, e.g. the autobahns (motorways)
• building – especially the expansion of the housing sector and public buildings.

The cumulative effect of these policies was to triple public investment between 1933 and 1936 and to increase government expenditure by nearly 70 per cent over the same period. By early 1936 the economic recovery was well advanced and then emphasis began to turn even more towards rearmament.

Table 8.1: Public investment and expenditure by billion *Reichsmarks* (RM)

	1928	1932	1933	1934	1935	1936
Total public investment	6.6	2.2	2.5	4.6	6.4	8.1
Total government expenditure	11.7	8.6	9.4	12.8	13.9	15.8

Table 8.2: Public expenditure by category by billion *Reichsmarks* (RM)

	1928	1932	1933	1934	1935	1936
Construction	2.7	0.9	1.7	3.5	4.9	5.4
Rearmament	0.7	0.7	1.8	3.0	5.4	10.2
Transportation	2.6	0.8	1.3	1.8	2.1	2.4

Table 8.3: Unemployment and production in Germany 1928–36

	1928	1929	1930	1931	1932	1933	1934	1935	1936
Unemployment (millions)	1.4	1.8	3.1	4.5	5.6	4.8	2.7	2.2	1.6
Industrial production (1928 = 100)	100	100	87	70	58	66	83	96	107

As a result of these strategies, there was a dramatic growth in jobs. From the registered peak of 5.6 million unemployed in 1932, the official figure of 1936 showed that it had declined to 1.6 million. For those many Germans who had been desperately out of work, it seemed as if the Nazi economic policy was to be welcomed. Even in other democratic countries scarred by mass unemployment, observers abroad admired Germany's achievement of job creation.

Yet, even in 1936, the government public deficit certainly did not run out of control, since Schacht maintained taxes at a relatively high level and encouraged private savings in state savings banks. Of course, it must be remembered that all this took place as the world economy began to recover and Schacht was aided by the natural upturn in the business cycle after its low-point in winter 1932. Nevertheless, it is difficult to believe that such a marked turnaround in investment and employment could have been achieved without Nazi economic policy.

The balance of payments problem

Germany made an impressive economic recovery between 1933 and 1936, but two underlying worries remained:

- the fear that a rapid increase in demand would rekindle inflation
- the fear that a rapid increase in demand would lead to the emergence of a **balance of trade** deficit.

In fact, the problem of inflation never actually materialised – partly because there was a lack of demand in the economy, but also because the regime established strict controls over prices and wages. This had been helped by the abolition of the trade unions in May 1933 (see pages 146–7). On the other hand, what was to be a recurring balance of payments problem emerged for the first time in the summer of 1934. This was a consequence of Germany's importing more raw materials while failing to increase its exports. Its gold and foreign currency reserves were also low.

Key question
Why was Germany's balance of trade problem so significant?

Balance of trade Difference in value between exports and imports. If the value of the imports is above that of the exports, the balance of the payments has a deficit that is often said to be 'in the red'.

Key term

Unemployed men (with shovels) enrol for work on one of the autobahns in September 1933.

The balance of payments problem was not merely an economic issue, for it carried with it large-scale political implications. If Germany was so short of foreign currency, which sector of the economy was to have priority in spending the money? The early Economics Minister, Schmitt, wanted to try to reduce unemployment further by manufacturing more consumer goods for public consumption, e.g. textiles. However, powerful voices in the armed forces and big business were already demanding more resources for major programmes, e.g. rearmament.

Hitler could not ignore such pressure – especially as this economic problem coincided with the political dilemma over the SA. Consequently, Schmitt's policy was rejected and he was removed, thereby allowing Schacht to combine the offices of Minister of Economics and President of the *Reichsbank*.

Schacht's 'New Plan'

By the law of 3 July, Schacht was given dictatorial powers over the economy, which he then used to introduce the 'New Plan' of September 1934. This provided for a comprehensive control by the government of all aspects of trade, tariffs, capital and currency exchange in an attempt to prevent excessive imports. From that time the government decided which imports were to be allowed or disapproved. For example, imports of raw cotton and wool were substantially cut, whereas metals were permitted in order to satisfy the demands of heavy industry.

The economic priorities were set by a series of measures:

- *Bilateral trade treaties*
  Schacht tried to promote trade and save foreign exchange by signing bilateral trade treaties, especially with the countries of south-east Europe, e.g. Romania and Yugoslavia. These often took the form of straightforward barter agreements (thus avoiding the necessity of formal currency exchange). In this way Germany began to exert a powerful economic influence over the Balkans long before it obtained military and political control.

- *The* Reichsmark *currency*
  Germany agreed to purchase raw materials from all countries it traded with on the condition that *Reichsmarks* could only be used to buy back German goods (at one time it is estimated that the German *Reichsmark* had 237 different values depending on the country and the circumstances).

- *Mefo bills*
  Mefo were special government money bills (like a credit note) designed by Schacht. They were issued by the *Reichsbank* and guaranteed by the government as payment for goods, and were then held for up to five years earning 4 per cent interest per annum. The main purpose of Mefo bills was that they successfully disguised government spending.

Schacht was never a member of the Nazi Party, but he was drawn into the Nazi movement and the regime. His proven economic

Key dates

Appointment of Schacht as Minister of Economics: July 1934

New Plan introduced: September 1934

Key question
How did Schacht try to resolve the balance of payments problem?

Profile: Hjalmar Schacht 1877–1970

1877		– Born in North Schleswig, Germany
1899		– Graduated in political economy
1916		– Appointed as Director of the National Bank
1923	November	– Appointed as Reich currency commissioner to set up the new currency, *Rentenmark*
	December	– Appointed President of the *Reichsbank*
1930	March	– Resigned in protest at the Young Plan
1931		– Became increasingly sympathetic to Nazism. Agreed to raise money for the Nazi Party through his contacts in banking and industry, e.g. Gustav and Alfred Krupp
1932	November	– Played a leading role in organising the letter from the petition of German industrialists who pressed Hindenburg to support Hitler's appointment
1933	March	– Reappointed as President of the *Reichsbank*
1934	July	– Appointed as Minister of Economics
	September	– Drew up and oversaw the New Plan
1937	November	– Resigned as Minister of Economics
1939	January	– Resigned as President of the *Reichsbank* in protest at Nazi economic policy
1939–43		– Remained in the government as Minister without Portfolio, but became increasingly at odds with the Nazi regime
1944–5		– In contact with the anti-Nazi resistance and arrested after the 20 July Bomb Plot. Held in Ravensbrück concentration camp until the end of war
1945–6		– Charged at the Nuremberg War Crimes Trials, but acquitted
1950–63		– Private financial consultant to the government of many countries
1970	June	– Died in Munich

Schacht was undoubtedly an economic genius. He built his reputation on the way he stabilised the German economy by the creation of the new currency, the *Rentenmark*, in 1923. He served as President of the *Reichsbank* to all the Weimar governments 1923–30, but he was a strong nationalist and eventually resigned over the Young Plan.

Schacht was increasingly taken in by Hitler's political programme. From 1930, his influence went through three clear stages.

- In 1930–3 he played an essential role in encouraging big business to finance the rise of the Nazis and he backed Hitler's appointment as chancellor.
- In the years 1933–6 Schacht was in effect economic dictator of Germany and it was he who shaped Germany's economic recovery by deficit financing and the New Plan of 1934.
- However, he fundamentally disagreed with the emphasis on rearmament in the Four-Year Plan and after 1936 his influence was gradually eclipsed.

Adolf Hitler opens the first stretch of the autobahn between Frankfurt am Main and Darmstadt on 19 May 1935. The first autobahn was not initiated by the Nazis, but was prompted by the mayor of Cologne, Adenauer; the stretch from Cologne to Bonn was opened in 1932. Nevertheless, 3000 km of motorway roads were developed before the onset of the war. They served as an economic stimulus, but were also used politically as a propagandist tool. Their military value has been doubted.

skills earned him respect both in and outside the Party and it was he who laid the foundations for economic recovery. By mid-1936:

- unemployment had fallen to 1.5 million
- industrial production had increased by 60 per cent since 1933
- GNP had grown over the same period by 40 per cent.

However, such successes disguised fundamental structural weaknesses that came to a head in the second half of 1936 over the future direction of the German economy.

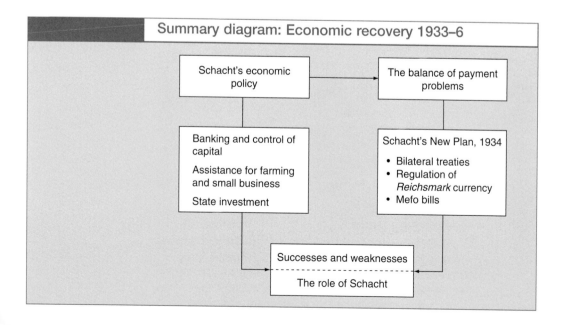

Summary diagram: Economic recovery 1933–6

Schacht's economic policy → The balance of payment problems

Banking and control of capital

Assistance for farming and small business

State investment

Schacht's New Plan, 1934
- Bilateral treaties
- Regulation of *Reichsmark* currency
- Mefo bills

Successes and weaknesses

The role of Schacht

3 | Implementation of the Four-Year Plan 1936

In many respects, as Schacht himself was only too aware, he had merely hidden the balance of payments problem by a series of clever financial tricks. And, despite his apparent sympathy for deficit financing, Schacht believed that a combination of a budget deficit and a balance of payments deficit could not be maintained indefinitely. In early 1936 it became clear to him that, as the demands for rearmament and consumption of goods increased, the German balance of payments would go deeply into the red. He therefore suggested a reduction in arms expenditure in order to increase the production of industrial goods that at least could be exported so as to earn foreign exchange. Such a solution had its supporters, especially among industries geared to exporting, e.g. electrics, tools. However, it was unacceptable to the armed forces and to the Nazi leadership. By the mid-1930s, then, this debate was popularly summed up by the question: should the economy concentrate on producing '**Guns or Butter?**'

Key question
What was the main purpose of the Four-Year Plan?

Key term

Guns or Butter?
A phrase used to highlight the controversial economic choice between rearmament and consumer goods.

Guns or Butter? A cartoon published by the German magazine *Simplicissimus* in 1933. Critics of the new Nazi regime felt that it was more interested in rearmament than encouraging trade and peace.

The aims and objectives of the Plan

Most significantly, Hitler himself expressed his position in a secret memorandum in August 1936. This has been seen as one of the most important documents of Nazi history, as it provides a clear insight into Hitler's war aims and the development of the Nazi economy. He concluded by writing:

> There has been time enough in four years to find out what we cannot do. Now we have to carry out what we can do. I thus set the following tasks.
>
> (i) The German armed forces must be operational within four years
> (ii) The German economy must be fit for war within four years.

Key date

Four-Year Plan established under Göring: October 1936

The politico-economic crisis of 1936 was resolved by the introduction of the Four-Year Plan under the control of Hermann Göring who, in October of that year, was appointed 'Plenipotentiary of the Four-Year Plan'. Its aims were clearly to expand rearmament and autarky to make Germany as self-sufficient as possible in food and industrial production. In order to achieve this, the Plan highlighted a number of objectives:

- To regulate imports and exports, so as to prioritise strategic sectors, e.g. chemicals and metals at the expense of agricultural imports.
- To control the key sectors of the labour force, so as to prevent price inflation, e.g. the creation of a Reich Price Commissioner and increased work direction by DAF (see page 182).
- To increase the production of raw materials, so as to reduce the financial cost of importing vital goods, e.g. steel, iron and aluminium.
- To develop *ersatz* (substitute) products, e.g. oil (from coal), artificial rubber (buna).
- To increase agricultural production, so as to avoid imported foodstuffs, e.g. grants for fertilisers and machinery.

Key question

Why was the creation of the Four-Year Plan so significant?

The effects of the Four-Year Plan

The decision to implement the Four-Year Plan marked an important turning point in the Nazi regime. Nazi control over the German economy became much tighter, as Schacht described in his own book written in 1949:

> ... On December 17th 1936, Göring informed a meeting of big industrialists that it was no longer a question of producing economically, but simply of producing. And as far as getting hold of foreign exchange was concerned it was quite immaterial whether the provisions of the law were complied with or not ... Göring's policy of recklessly exploiting Germany's economic substance necessarily brought me into more and more acute conflict with him, and for his part he exploited his powers, with Hitler and the Party behind him, to counter my activity as Minister of Economics to an ever-increasing extent.

Profile: Hermann Göring 1893–1946

1893		– Born in Bavaria, the son of the governor of German Southwest Africa
1914–18		– Served in the First World War and became a pilot officer of the Richthofen Squadron
1922		– Dropped out of university and joined the Party as an SA commander
1923	November	– Took part in the Munich *putsch* and was seriously injured
1928	May	– Elected to the *Reichstag*
1933	January	– Appointed to the cabinet of Hitler's government as Minister without Portfolio
	February	– Exploited the *Reichstag* fire to discredit the communists
	March	– Organised the terror to impose the dictatorship and to uphold co-ordination
1934	June	– Helped to organise the Night of the Long Knives
1935		– Commander-in-Chief of the new *Luftwaffe* (airforce)
1936	October	– Appointed Plenipotentiary of the Four-Year Plan by Hitler
1939		– Named as Hitler's successor, and at the height of his power and influence
1940–1		– After the failures of the *Luftwaffe* to win the Battle of Britain, his influence declined
1941–5		– He retained most of his offices, but he was increasingly isolated within the Nazi leadership
1946		– Committed suicide two hours before he was due to be executed at the Nuremberg trials

Göring played a crucial role in the rise of Nazism and during the consolidation of its power 1933–40. He came from a well-to-do family and with this status and the contacts provided by his aristocratic first wife, he was able to give Nazism a more respectable image in high society.

Göring's approach was uncompromising and brutal. During 1933–4 he organised the infiltration of the German police with the SA and SS – and willingly used violence and murder in the terror to secure Nazi power. He was deeply involved in the *Reichstag* fire (see page 143) and the Night of the Long Knives (see pages 151–3).

At first, he was popular because of his witty and charming conversation, but he became increasingly resented for his ambition and greed – he was given a whole host of titles and posts. From 1936 he became in effect economic dictator, though after the failures of the *Luftwaffe* to win the Battle of Britain, his influence sharply declined.

Key date

Resignation of Schacht as Minister of Economics: November 1937

Schacht had no real respect for Göring, who had no economic expertise and deliberately and increasingly ignored Schacht's advice. Schacht recognised that his influence was on the wane and eventually in November 1937 he resigned. He was replaced by the weak Walther Funk, although from this time Göring himself became the real economic dictator.

The success of the Plan was mixed over the years (see Table 8.4). On the one hand, production of a number of key materials, such as aluminium and explosives, had expanded greatly, or at least at a reasonable rate. On the other hand, it fell a long way short of the targets in the essential commodities of rubber and oil, while arms production never reached the levels desired by the armed forces and Hitler. All in all, the Four-Year Plan had succeeded in the sense that Germany's reliance on imports had not increased. However, this still meant that when war did break out Germany was dependent on foreign supplies for one-third of its raw materials.

Germany found itself at war in September 1939 really because of diplomatic miscalculation. Its economy was still a long way from being fully mobilised, but it was certainly on more of a war footing than Britain or France. The question now was whether Germany could complete the economic mobilisation and thereby bring about military victory.

Table 8.4: The Four-Year Plan, launched in 1936

Commodity (in thousands of tons)	Four-Year Plan target	Actual output 1936	Actual output 1938	Actual output 1942
Oil	13,830	1,790	2,340	6,260
Aluminium	273	98	166	260
Rubber (buna)	120	0.7	5	96
Explosives	223	18	45	300
Steel	24,000	19,216	22,656	20,480
Hard coal	213,000	158,400	186,186	166,059

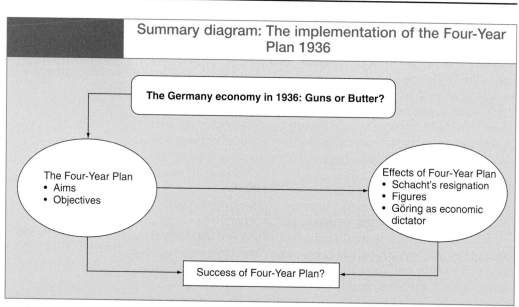

Summary diagram: The implementation of the Four-Year Plan 1936

The Germany economy in 1936: Guns or Butter?

The Four-Year Plan
• Aims
• Objectives

Effects of Four-Year Plan
• Schacht's resignation
• Figures
• Göring as economic dictator

Success of Four-Year Plan?

4 | The Nazi Economy at War 1939–45

The string of military successes achieved by the German armed forces with their use of *Blitzkrieg* strategy up to December 1941 won Hitler and the regime valuable popular support. Moreover, it gave the impression of an economy that had not been over-strained by the demands of war. Such a view, however attractive, does not actually square with either Nazi intentions or the economic statistics.

The expansion of the Nazi economy

First, Hitler himself was determined to avoid the problems faced by Germany in the First World War and to fight the coming war with an economy thoroughly prepared for a major and perhaps extended conflict. To this end, a series of war economy decrees was issued by Hitler in December 1939 outlining vast programmes for every possible aspect of war production, e.g. submarines and aircraft. These plans suggest that the Nazis went well beyond the demands of *Blitzkrieg* and a limited war.

Secondly, in real and percentage terms, German military expenditure doubled between 1939 and 1941, as shown by Table 8.5. (However, the figures have important implications, as Britain trebled expenditure in the same categories.)

Key question
How did the German economy expand?

Blitzkrieg
Literally 'lightning war'. It was the name of the military strategy developed to avoid static war. It was based on the use of dive-bombers, paratroopers and motorised infantry.

Key term

Table 8.5: Military expenditure of Germany and Britain

Year	Germany (RM billions)			Britain (£ billions)		
	GNP	Military expenditure	Military expenditure as a % of GNP	GNP	Military expenditure	Military expenditure as a % of GNP
1937	93	11.7	13	4.6	0.3	7
1938	105	17.2	17	4.8	0.4	8
1939	130	30.0	23	5.0	1.1	22
1940	141	53.0	38	6.0	3.2	53
1941	152	71.0	47	6.8	4.1	60

Thirdly, food rationing in certain items was introduced from the very start of the war and the German labour force was rapidly mobilised for war so that, by the summer of 1941, 55 per cent of the workforce was involved in war-related projects – a figure which then only crept up to a high-point of 61 per cent by 1944. In this light it is hardly surprising that the first two years of war also witnessed a 20 per cent decline in civilian consumption.

Hitler's War Economy decrees: December 1939

Key date

The limitations of economic mobilisation

However, despite the intent of wholesale mobilisation the actual results, in terms of armaments production, remained disappointingly low. Admittedly, there was a marked increase in the number of submarines, but amazingly, Germany's airforce had only increased from 8290 aircraft in 1939 to 10,780 in 1941 while in Britain over the same period the number of aircraft had trebled to 20,100. Likewise, Hitler was astonished to learn when

Key question
To what extent did the Nazis fail to mobilise the economy during the war?

drawing up plans for the invasion of the USSR that the Germans' armoured strength totalled only 3500 tanks, which was just 800 more than for the invasion of the West.

It seems that despite the Nazi image of German order and purposefulness, the actual mobilisation of the German economy was marred by inefficiency and poor co-ordination. The pressures resulting from the premature outbreak of war created problems, since many of the major projects were not due to be ready until 1942–3. So, at first, there was undoubtedly confusion between the short-term needs and long-term plans of the Nazi leadership.

Nevertheless, this should not have been an impossible barrier if only a clear and authoritative central control had been established over the economy. Instead, a host of different agencies all continued to function in their own way and often in a fashion which put them at odds with each other. So, although there was a Ministry of Armaments, it existed alongside three other interested governmental ministries, those of Economics, Finance and Labour. In addition, there was political infighting between the leading Nazi figures – for example, the *Gauleiters* tried to control their local areas at the expense of the plans of the state and the Party (see page 237) – and also considerable financial corruption.

There were a number of groups responsible for armaments: the Office of the Four-Year Plan, the SS bodies and the different branches of the armed forces, **Wehrmacht**, *Luftwaffe* and navy. The armed forces, in particular, were determined to have their way over the development of munitions with the very best specifications possible and as a result the drive for quality was pursued at the expense of quantity. The consequence of all this was that after two years of war, and with the armed forces advancing into the USSR, Germany's economic mobilisation for total war had not achieved the expected levels of armaments production.

Total war 1941–5

By the end of 1941, Germany was at war with Britain, the USSR and the USA and yet its armaments production remained inferior to that of Britain. Preparations for a new approach had begun in the autumn of 1941 and Hitler himself had issued a 'Rationalisation Decree' in December of that year.

However, it was the appointment of Albert Speer as Minister of Armaments in February 1942 that marked the real turning point. Speer had previously been the *Führer*'s personal architect and he enjoyed excellent relations with Hitler. He now used the *Führer*'s authority to cut through the mass of interests and to implement his programme of 'industrial self-responsibility' to provide mass production. The controls and constraints previously placed upon business, in order to fit in with Nazi wishes, were relaxed. In their place a Central Planning Board was established in April 1942, which was in turn supported by a number of committees, each representing one vital sector of the economy. This gave the industrialists a considerable degree of freedom, while ensuring that Speer as the director of Central Planning was able to maintain overall control of the war economy. Speer also encouraged industrialists and engineers to join his ministerial team. At the same time, wherever possible, he excluded military personnel from the production process.

Speer was what would now be called a 'technocrat'. He simply co-ordinated and rationalised the process of war production and more effectively exploited the potential of Germany's resources and labour force. Speer was able to exert influence because of his friendship with Hitler and he used his personal skills to charm or blackmail other authorities. In his way, he took a whole range of other personal initiatives to improve production, such as:

- employing more women in the arms factories
- making effective use of concentration camp prisoners as workers
- preventing skilled workers being lost to military conscription.

Key dates

Rationalisation Decree issued by Hitler: December 1941

Appointment of Albert Speer as Minister of Armaments: February 1942

Profile: Albert Speer 1905–81

1905		– Born in Mannheim
1924–8		– Trained as an architect at Karlsruhe, Munich and Berlin
1931	January	– Joined the Nazi Party
1934		– Became Hitler's personal architect
1942		– Minister of Armaments
1946	October	– Sentenced to 20 years as a result of the Nuremberg trials
1966		– Released from Spandau prison
1969		– Publication of his books, *Inside the Third Reich* and *Spandau: The Secret Diaries*
1981		– Died in London on a visit

Speer remains as an interesting, and significant, figure on several counts:

- He was a talented and able architect who was commissioned for the design of the German pavilion at the Paris Exhibition in 1937, the Reich Chancellery in Berlin and the Party Palace in Nuremberg. His close friendship with Hitler and their common interest in architecture allowed him to exert increasing political influence.
- He quickly proved himself a skilful manager of the war economy, resulting in a fundamental increase in armaments production, 1942–4.
- Despite his friendship with Hitler, he clashed with leading Nazis, particularly Himmler.
- He always claimed after the war that he opposed forced labour in the occupied countries, yet his opponents maintained that this policy had more to do with efficiency than morality, and even claimed that he was aware of the treatment of the Jews.

The successes and limitations of Speer's economic rationalisation

In a famous speech in February 1943, after the German army surrender at Stalingrad, Joseph Goebbels invited the crowd to support 'total war'. However, the transformation of the Nazi economy really pre-dated Goebbels's propagandist appeal to 'total war' and was down to the work of Speer. As a result of Speer's first six months in power:

- ammunition production increased by 97 per cent
- tank production rose by 25 per cent
- total arms production increased by 59 per cent.

By the second half of 1944, when German war production peaked, it can be noted that there had been more than a three-fold increase since early 1942.

Despite Speer's economic successes, Germany probably had the capacity to produce even more and could have achieved a level of output close to that of the USSR or the USA. He was not always able to counter the power of the Party *Gauleiters* at a local level and the SS remained a law unto themselves, especially in the conquered lands. Indeed, although the occupied territories of the Third Reich were well and truly plundered, they were not exploited with real economic efficiency. Above all, though, from 1943 Speer could not reverse the detrimental effects of Anglo-American bombing.

After the war, 'blanket bombing' by the Allies was condemned by some on moral grounds and its effectiveness denied; indeed, critics pointed to Speer's production figures as proof that the strategy had failed to break the German war economy. However, it is probably more accurate to say that the effects of bombing

Table 8.6: Number of German, British, US and Soviet tanks produced 1940–5

	Germany	Britain	USA	USSR
1940	1,600	1,400	300	2,800
1941	3,800	4,800	4,100	6,400
1942	6,300	8,600	25,000	24,700
1943	12,100	7,500	29,500	24,000
1944	19,000	4,600	17,600	29,000
1945	3,900	N/A	12,000	15,400

Table 8.7: Number of German, British, US and Soviet aircraft produced 1940–5

	Germany	Britain	USA	USSR
1940	10,200	15,000	6,100	7,000
1941	11,000	20,100	19,400	12,500
1942	14,200	23,600	47,800	26,000
1943	25,200	26,200	85,900	37,000
1944	39,600	26,500	96,300	40,000
1945	N/A	12,100	46,000	35,000

prevented Germany from increasing its levels of arms production even further. The results of Allied bombing caused industrial destruction and breakdown in communications. Also, Germany was forced to divert available resources towards the construction of anti-aircraft installations and underground industrial sites. Because of this Germany was unable to achieve a total war economy. As it was, German arms production peaked in August 1944 at a level well below its full potential.

In the end, the Nazi economy had proved incapable of rising to the demands of total war and the cost of that failure was all too clearly to be seen in the ruins and economic collapse of 1945. (See also Chapter 12.)

Peak of German munitions production: August 1944

Key date

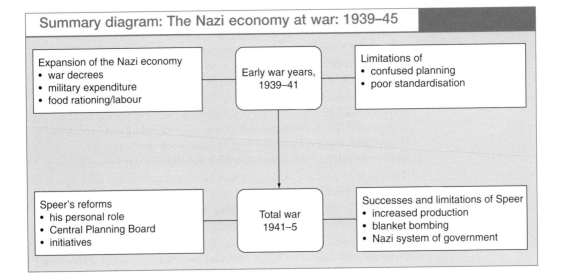

Summary diagram: The Nazi economy at war: 1939–45

Expansion of the Nazi economy
- war decrees
- military expenditure
- food rationing/labour

Early war years, 1939–41

Limitations of
- confused planning
- poor standardisation

Speer's reforms
- his personal role
- Central Planning Board
- initiatives

Total war 1941–5

Successes and limitations of Speer
- increased production
- blanket bombing
- Nazi system of government

Study Guide: AS Question

In the style of OCR A

To what extent was German economic recovery to 1939 due to the Four-Year Plan? (50 marks)

Exam tips

The question asks you to assess the relative importance of causal factors. That means you must establish a clear rank order of importance between the relevant factors. One cause is given in the question (Four-Year Plan) and you must weigh up the importance of the plan, even if you are going to reject it in favour of a cause of recovery that you believe to have been more important.

Why was the 1936 Plan significant in helping economic recovery? It led to increased production of key materials, such as aluminium and explosives. It kept the level of imports under control. Why might its significance be overrated? Increases in production were limited (oil was especially weak) and only one sector reached the Plan's target output. Dependence on imports may have grown, but no significant cut was achieved, so balance of payments problems remained serious. Germany was not self-sufficient in food and industrial production. What might have had a greater influence on economic recovery? You should assess the contributions of state help to farming and state investment in public works. What contribution did they make to reducing unemployment? Finally, in reaching your decision, you might question how far an economic recovery was achieved (the 'guns vs butter' debate) and how far any recovery was due more to international recovery from the Depression.

9 Nazi Society

POINTS TO CONSIDER

The purpose of this chapter is to consider Nazi social aims and policies and their effects on the Third Reich. However, this chapter will introduce the concept of *Volksgemeinschaft*, which is essential to an understanding of German society in the period. It will examine the following themes of German social history and should help you to answer the historical question of whether *Volksgemeinschaft* fundamentally changed German society during the Third Reich:

- Nazi views on society: *Volksgemeinschaft*
- Social groups
- Education and youth
- Religion
- Women and the family
- Culture
- Outsiders
- The Nazi social revolution

The major issue of anti-Semitism will be covered in Chapter 10, The Racial State.

Key dates

1933	May	The burning of the books
		Creation of German Labour Front
	July	Concordat signed with the Papacy
1934		Reich Ministry of Education created: control of education was taken away from *Länder*
		Creation of the Confessional Church
1937	March	Papal encyclical, *Mit Brennender Sorge*, issued
1941	August	Bishop Galen's sermon against euthanasia
1944	November	Execution of 12 Edelweiss Pirates in Cologne

Key question
What was the purpose of the Nazis in creating the *Volksgemeinschaft*?

1 | The Nazi *Volksgemeinschaft*

When Nazi ideology developed in the 1920s it was based on three key elements: racism, nationalism and authoritarianism (for details see pages 92–5 in Chapter 5). However, Hitler always claimed that National Socialism was more than just a political ideology. It was a movement that aimed to transform German society. It rejected the values of communism, liberalism and Christianity and in their place upheld the concept of *Volksgemeinschaft*.

Volksgemeinschaft was probably the vaguest element of Nazi ideology and it is therefore difficult to define precisely. Indeed, historians are divided between those who see it as a 'pseudo-ideology' built on image alone, and those who see it as a more concrete movement with genuine support.

The essential purpose of the *Volksgemeinschaft* was to overcome the old German divisions of class, religion and politics and to bring about a new collective national identity by encouraging people to work together. This new social mentality aimed to bring together the disparate elements and to create a German society built on the Nazi ideas of race and struggle.

Very closely associated with Nazi racism was the aim of *Volksgemeinschaft* to get people working together for the benefit of the nation by promoting traditional German values. The ideal German image was that of the classic peasant working on the soil in the rural community; this was exemplified in the concept of 'Blood and Soil' (*Blut und Boden*) (see pages 184–7) and the upholding of traditional roles by the two sexes.

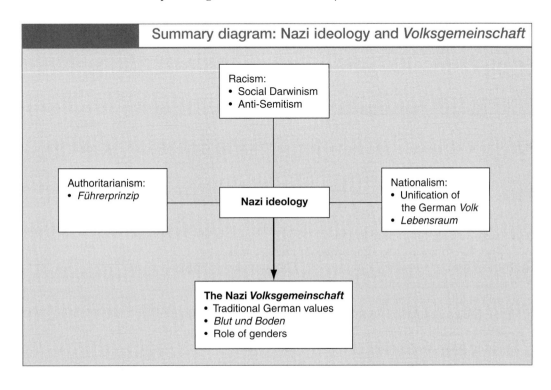

Summary diagram: Nazi ideology and *Volksgemeinschaft*

Racism:
• Social Darwinism
• Anti-Semitism

Authoritarianism:
• *Führerprinzip*

Nazi ideology

Nationalism:
• Unification of the German *Volk*
• *Lebensraum*

The Nazi *Volksgemeinschaft*
• Traditional German values
• *Blut und Boden*
• Role of genders

2 | Social Groups

The revival of the economy (see pages 164–9) in conjunction with Hitler's diplomatic successes contributed greatly to the German people's acceptance, or at least tolerance, of the regime. In the pre-war years it really did seem to many Germans as if the Nazis had pulled their country out of the economic quagmire. However, in material terms the effects varied considerably from one class to another.

Key question
Did the workers benefit under the Third Reich?

Industrial workers

The working class was by far the largest social group in German society (see Table 9.1). The Nazi regime definitely could not assume that the workers could be won over to the promised ideas of the *Volksgemeinschaft*. Under Weimar, many workers had belonged to independent trade unions and politically they had generally voted for the left-wing parties – the Social Democrats and Communists.

At first, the Nazi regime simply wanted to establish its authority and so it closed down all the established trade unions (see pages 146–7). As a result, workers completely lost the right of industrial bargaining. Consequently management and the government controlled pay increases and were able to limit workers' freedom of movement.

Table 9.1: German society

	Working class	Middle classes			Peasants	Others
		White-collar workers	Self-employed	Government officials/ employees		
German society as a whole in 1933 (%)	46.3	12.4	9.6	4.8	20.7	6.2

In the place of the unions, from May 1933, the only available option to workers was to join the German Labour Front (DAF, *Deutsche Arbeitsfront*). Led by Robert Ley, DAF became the largest Nazi organisation in the Third Reich with a membership that increased from five million in 1933 to 22 million in 1939. It became responsible for virtually all areas of work such as:

Key date
Creation of German Labour Front: May 1933

- setting working hours and wages
- dealing harshly with any sign of disobedience, strikes or absenteeism
- running training schemes for apprenticeships
- setting stable rents for housing
- supervising working conditions through the DAF subsection called the Beauty of Labour (SdA, *Schönheit der Arbeit*). The SdA aimed to provide cleaning, meals, exercise, etc.
- organising recreational facilities through the Strength through Joy (KdF, *Kraft durch Freude*). It provided very real opportunities

to millions of workers: cultural visits, sports facilities and holiday travel – although such benefits were only available to the loyal workers.

However, assessing the material effects of the Nazi regime on the workers is a highly complicated issue mainly because there are so many variables, such as age, occupation and geographical location. The obvious and most significant benefit for industrial workers was the creation of employment. For the many millions who had suffered from the distress of mass unemployment, the creation of jobs was accepted gratefully (see pages 164–6).

A Nazi propaganda poster advertising the benefits of saving for 'Your own KdF car'. Workers enthusiastically paid millions of marks to the scheme but the Volkswagen was never actually produced until after the war.

Profile: Robert Ley 1890–1945

1890	– Born in the Rhineland, the son of a farmer
1914	– Graduated with a degree in chemistry
1914–17	– First World War pilot
1920–8	– Worked with the major chemicals company IG Farben, but sacked for drunkenness
1924	– Joined the NSDAP
1930	– Elected to the *Reichstag*
1933–45	– Leader of the German Labour Front. Used the money to fund KdF (the Volkswagen scheme, see pages 182–3) and the élite training schools, *Ordensburgen* (see page 191)
1939–45	– Lost influence to Todt and Speer
1945	– Captured by US forces, but committed suicide before trial

Ley enjoyed a very significant power-base as the leader of DAF, which was the largest Nazi organisation in the Third Reich. However, he personally failed to develop the institution to its political potential and simply exploited the position for his own self-advancement. He became an alcoholic and although he retained his position, he lost the support of other leading Nazis.

Indeed, by the late 1930s Germany had achieved full employment and there was a growing shortage of workers.

Yet, to put that major benefit into context, it is important to bear in mind a number of key factors:

- Average workers' **real wages** only rose above 1929 levels in 1938. Also, workers were forced to pay extensive contributions for DAF and insurance/tax.
- The generalised picture disguises the fact that the biggest gains were clearly made by the workers associated with the boom in the rearmament industries, whereas those in consumer goods struggled to maintain their real incomes.
- Working hours increased over time. The average working week was officially increased from 43 hours in 1933 to 47 hours in 1939 – and as military demands grew, there was pressure on many workers to do more overtime.

So, there is considerable evidence to suggest there was workers' discontent even before 1939. Once the war set in, pressures increased further – especially from 1942 when bombing began to hit German industrial urban sectors. By 1944 the working week had grown to 60 hours.

Peasants and small farmers

The farming community had been attracted to the Nazi cause by the promise of financial aid, as they had suffered from a series of economic problems from the mid-1920s. Moreover, peasants felt

> **Key term**
>
> **Real wages**
> The actual purchasing power of income taking into account inflation/deflation and also the effect of deductions, e.g. taxes.

> **Key question**
> Did the peasantry and small farmers benefit under the Third Reich?

Profile: Richard Darré 1895–1953

1895		– Born in Buenos Aires, Argentina, of German and Swedish parents
1914–18		– Served in the First World War and reached the rank of lieutenant
1920–5		– Studied at Halle and gained a doctorate in agriculture specialising in animal breeding
1928–30		– Publication of three books on Nazi views of race; the most significant was *The Peasantry as the Life-source of the Nordic Race*
1930	June	– Created a Nazi agrarian political organisation
	July	– Joined the Nazi Party
1933	May 28	– Appointed Reich Peasant Leader
	June 29	– Appointed Minister of Agriculture and Food
	September	– Responsible for introducing the Reich Entitled Law and the Reich Food Estate (see pages 164 and 186–7)
1938	September	– Made leader of the Central Office for Race and Settlement (RuSHA)
1940		– Delivered his infamous speech outlining the fate of the British people in his plans for race and settlement
1942		– Forced to resign from all his positions
1945		– Arrested and held by Allied forces
1949		– Sentenced to seven years in prison for confiscating Jewish and Polish property
1953		– Died in Munich

Darré was more intellectual than many Nazi leaders. He was well travelled, fluent in four languages and eventually was awarded a doctoral degree for his studies. In 1930 he was drawn into the NSDAP and played an important role in the rise of the Nazis by creating an agrarian political organisation. He effectively exploited the rural unrest winning electoral support in the countryside.

There were two elements to Darré's thinking:

- to restore the role and values of the countryside and to reverse the drive towards urbanisation by promoting the concept of 'Blood and Soil'
- to support the expansionist policy of *Lebensraum* and to create a German racial aristocracy based on selective breeding.

Initially, his agricultural reforms were well received by the Nazi regime and certainly helped to enable many farmers to recover in the mid-1930s. In particular, his ideas were supported by Himmler and they worked closely together in the RuSHA. The extent of Darré's racism is shown in his speech of 1940:

As soon as we beat England we shall make an end of you Englishmen once and for all. Able-bodied men and women between the ages of 16 and 45 will be exported as slaves to the Continent. The old and weak will be exterminated.

All men remaining in Britain as slaves will be sterilised; a million or two of the young women of the Nordic type will be segregated in a number of stud farms where, with the assistance of picked German sires, during a period of 10 or 12 years, they will produce annually a series of Nordic infants to be brought up in every way as Germans.

However, Darré increasingly fell out with the leadership. His idealistic vision of a rural utopia was at odds with the economic demands of war production and in 1942 he was forced to resign by Hitler.

increasingly that they were losing out to the growing urban society of industrial Germany. Yet, it seemed from Nazi ideology of 'Blood and Soil' promoted by Richard Darré (see profile on page 185) that there was a real sympathy for the role of the peasants in society. It portrayed the peasantry as racially the purest element of the *Volk*, the providers of Germany's food and as the symbol of traditional German values.

The Nazi regime certainly took initiatives on agriculture:

- A substantial number of farm debts and mortgages were written off and small farmers were given low interest rates and a range of tax allowances.
- The government maintained extensive tariffs to reduce imports.
- The introduction of the Reich Entailed Farm Law of 1933 gave security of tenure to the occupiers of medium-sized farms between 7.5 and 125 hectares and forbade the division of farms.
- The Reich Food Estate, established in 1933, supervised every aspect of agricultural production and distribution – especially food prices and working wages (although its bureaucratic meddling became the focus of much resentment, when, for example, it stipulated that each hen had to lay 65 eggs per year).

The economic realities meant that in practice the impact of Nazi agricultural policy was rather mixed. At first, all farmers benefited from an increase in prices between 1933 and 1936 and so farmers' incomes did improve markedly – though they only recovered to 1928 levels in 1938. However, it seems that by 1936–7 any benefits were giving way to a growing peasant disillusionment. This was for several reasons:

- Although the regime succeeded in increasing agricultural production by 20 per cent from 1928 to 1938, there continued to be a significant drift of workers to the towns where wages were higher. German agriculture just did not have the economic power to compete with other sectors of the economy. As a result, 3 per cent of the German population drifted from the countryside to the town.

- Of course, the positive aspects of the Reich Food Estate were accepted, but the regulation became increasingly resented.
- The Reich Entailed Farm Law also caused resentment and family discontent. In trying to solve one problem by passing on farms to just one child, farmers faced the very real dilemma of not being able to provide a future for their remaining children.

With the onset of the war in 1939 the peasantry's pressures developed in all sorts of ways. Men were increasingly conscripted to the military fronts – so the problem of the shortage of agricultural labour was exacerbated. This resulted in the transportation to Germany of cheap forced labour of peasants from eastern Europe, e.g. Poles and Czechs. This also conflicted with Nazi thinking since the labourers were not even viewed as racially acceptable.

Landowners

Key question
Did the landowners lose out?

The landed classes had been initially suspicious of the idea of radical social change. They resented the political interference of the Party, but above all they feared the Nazis would redistribute the large landed estates. However, they soon learned to live quite comfortably with the Nazi regime and in the years before 1939 their economic interests were not really threatened. Indeed, German victories in the early years of the war offered the chance of acquiring more cheap land.

The real blow for the landowners actually came in 1945 when the occupation of eastern Germany by the USSR resulted in the nationalisation of land. The traditional social and economic supremacy of the German landowners was broken.

Mittelstand

Key question
Did the *Mittelstand* benefit under the Third Reich?

Another social class that expected to benefit from the Nazi regime was the *Mittelstand*. The problems confronting the *Mittelstand* were in many ways comparable to the problems faced by the peasantry. It had suffered from the decline in commerce in Germany since the First World War and it found it difficult to compete with the increasing power of big business and trade unions.

Research has shown that in the elections 1930–3 the *Mittelstand* had voted for Nazism in greater proportion than the rest of German society and the Nazi regime was keen to take sympathetic measures to maintain that support:

- The government used the money available from the confiscation of Jewish businesses to offer low interest rate loans.
- It introduced the Law to Protect Retail Trade (1933) against large department stores, of which many were Jewish. This

banned the opening of new department stores and taxed the existing ones.
• It imposed a host of new trading regulations to protect small craftsmen.

However, despite the Nazis' attempt to implement their electoral promises before 1933 and the economic recovery, the position of the *Mittelstand* continued the decline that had started with Germany's industrialisation. The costs of small businesses meant that they could not compete with the lower costs of the large department stores. Moreover the problem was made worse because of the Nazi preference for big business, whose support was required for rearmament.

In 1933, 20 per cent of the owners of small businesses were under 30 years old and 14 per cent over 60. By 1939 the corresponding figures were 10 per cent under 30 and 19 per cent over 60, which highlighted the ageing trend of the *Mittelstand*. And in the years 1936–9 it is reckoned that the number of traditional skilled craftsmen declined by 10 per cent. The truth is that the *Mittelstand* found itself being significantly squeezed out.

Big business

The influence of big business remained very significant and generally it benefited from the Nazis' economic programme. So despite the increasing range of government controls, the financial gains were impressive. The value of German industry steadily increased, as shown by the following:

Key question
Why did big business benefit?

• The share price index increased from 41 points in 1932 to 106 in 1940, while annual dividends to investors grew from an average 2.83 per cent to 6.6 per cent over the same period.
• The improvement in salaries of management from an average 3700RM in 1934 to 5420RM in 1938 also reflected the economic growth.

Moreover, from 1939 the onset of the war provided enormous opportunities for taking over foreign property, land and companies. For example, Oskar Schindler (1908–74), a German businessman, set up business in Krakow in 1939 and drew much of his workforce from the Jewish labour camp. After initially exploiting these workers he eventually saved thousands from extermination.

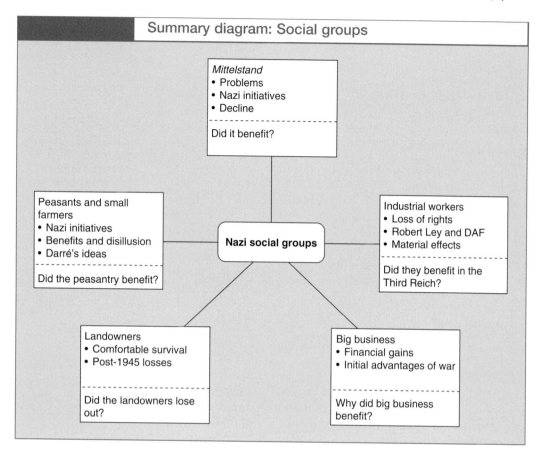

Summary diagram: Social groups

Mittelstand
- Problems
- Nazi initiatives
- Decline

Did it benefit?

Nazi social groups

Peasants and small farmers
- Nazi initiatives
- Benefits and disillusion
- Darré's ideas

Did the peasantry benefit?

Industrial workers
- Loss of rights
- Robert Ley and DAF
- Material effects

Did they benefit in the Third Reich?

Landowners
- Comfortable survival
- Post-1945 losses

Did the landowners lose out?

Big business
- Financial gains
- Initial advantages of war

Why did big business benefit?

Key question
What were the aims of Nazi education?

3 | Education and Youth

In Nazi Germany, education became merely a tool for the consolidation of the Nazi system. Hitler expressed his views chillingly in 1933:

> When an opponent declares, 'I will not come over to your side', I calmly say, 'Your child belongs to us already … What are you? You will pass on. Your descendants, however, now stand in the new camp. In a short time they will know nothing else but this new community.'

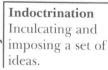

Indoctrination
Inculcating and imposing a set of ideas.

Education in the Third Reich was therefore intended to **indoctrinate** its youth so completely in the principles and ethos of National Socialism that the long-term survival of the 'New Order' would never be brought into question. A National Socialist Teachers' League official wrote pompously in 1937:

> German youth must no longer – as in the Liberal era in the cause of so-called objectivity – be confronted with the choice of whether it wishes to grow up in a spirit of materialism or idealism, of racism or internationalism, of religion or godlessness, but it must be consciously shaped according to the principles which are

recognised as correct and which have shown themselves to be correct: according to the principles of the ideology of National Socialism.

This was to be achieved not only through the traditional structure of the educational system, but also by the development of various Nazi youth movements.

Schools

The actual organisation of the state educational system was not fundamentally altered, although by a law of 1934 control was taken from the regional states and centralised under the Reich Ministry of Education, Culture and Science led by Reich Minister Bernhard Rust. The Ministry was then able to adapt the existing system to suit Nazi purposes.

First, the teaching profession itself was 'reconditioned'. Politically unreliable individuals were removed and Jewish teachers were banned, and many women were encouraged to conform to Nazi values by returning to the home (see pages 202–7). Special training courses were arranged for those teachers who remained unconvinced by the new requirements. In addition, the National Socialist Teachers' League (NSLB, *Nationalsozialistische Lehrerbund*) was established and its influence and interference continued to grow. By 1937, it included 97 per cent of all teachers and two-thirds of the profession had been on special month-long courses on Nazi ideology and the changes to the curriculum.

Secondly, the curricula and syllabuses were adapted. To fit in with the Nazi Aryan ideal, a much greater emphasis was placed on physical education, so that 15 per cent of school time was given over to it, and games teachers assumed an increased status and importance in the school hierarchy. On the academic front, Religious Studies were dropped to downgrade the importance of Christianity, whereas German, Biology and History became the focus of special attention:

- German language and literature were studied to create 'a consciousness of being German', and to inculcate a martial and nationalistic spirit. Among the list of suggested reading for 14-year-old pupils was a book entitled *The Battle of Tannenberg*, which included the following extract: 'A Russian soldier tried to bar the infiltrator's way, but Otto's bayonet slid gratingly between the Russian's ribs, so that he collapsed groaning. There it lay before him, simple and distinguished, his dream's desire, the Iron Cross.'
- Biology became the means by which to deliver Nazi racial theory: ethnic classification, **population policy** and racial genetics were all integrated into the syllabus.
- History, not surprisingly, was also given a special place in the Nazi curriculum, so that the glories of German nationalism could be emphasised.

Key question
How did German schools change under the Nazis?

Reich Ministry of Education created – control of education was taken away from *Länder*: 1934

Key date

Population policy
In 1933–45 the Nazi government aimed to increase the birth rate.

Key term

One final innovation was the creation of various types of élite schools. They were intended to prepare the best of Germany's youth for future political leadership, were modelled on the principles of the Hitler Youth, and focused on physical training, paramilitary activities and political education. The 21 *Napolas* (National Political Educational Institutions) and the 10 Adolf Hitler Schools were both for boys of secondary school age, and the three *Ordensburgen* for boys of college age.

Hitler Youth

Key question
How did the Hitler Youth try to indoctrinate Germany's young people?

The responsibility for developing a new outlook lay with the youth movements. There was already a long and well-established tradition of youth organisation in Germany before 1933, but at that time the Hitler Youth (HJ, *Hitler Jugend*) represented only 1 per cent of the total.

The term 'Hitler Youth' in fact embraced a range of youth groups under the control of its leader Baldur von Schirach and in the next six years the structure and membership of the HJ grew remarkably – although this was partly because parents were pressurised to enrol the children and by 1939 membership became compulsory.

Profile: Baldur von Schirach 1907–74

1907	– Born in Berlin, the son of an aristocratic German father and an American mother
1924	– Joined the NSDAP as a student of art history at Munich
1928	– Leader of National Socialist German Students' League
1933–9	– Youth Leader of the German Reich
1939–40	– Joined the German army and won the Iron Cross
1940–5	– *Gauleiter* of Vienna
1945	– Arrested by the Allies
1946–66	– Sentenced to 20 years' imprisonment at the Nuremberg War Crimes Trials
1967	– Publication of his book, *I Believed in Hitler*
1974	– Lived privately in West Germany until his death

Schirach's only real significant role was as 'Youth Leader of the German Reich', which gave him the responsibility to supervise all the youth organisations, 1933–9. He became obsessed with Hitler from the mid-1920s – he even wrote poetry to the *Führer*! He was not greatly respected by other leading Nazis, partly because of his effeminate nature. However, his loyalty and charm allowed him to remain influential with Hitler and he was appointed *Gauleiter* of Vienna.

Schirach denied responsibility for war crimes, but the Nuremberg Trials found him guilty of having deported the Jews from Austria.

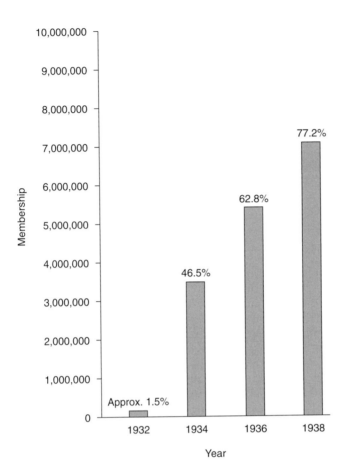

Figure 9.1: Hitler Youth movements. The percentages indicate the percentage of total youth population aged 10–18 years who were members.

Table 9.2: Youth groups

Boys 10–14 years old	German Young People (DJ, *Deutsche Jungvolk*)
Boys 14–18 years old	Hitler Youth (HJ, *Hitler Jugend*)
Girls 10–14 years old	League of Young Girls (JM, *Jungmädel*)
Girls 14–18 years old	League of German Girls (BDM, *Bund Deutscher Mädel*)

In all four groups shown in Table 9.2 there was a great stress on political indoctrination, emphasising the life and achievements of the *Führer*, German patriotism, athletics and camping. In addition, the sexes were moulded for their future roles in Nazi society. Boys engaged in endless physical and military-type activities, e.g. target shooting, and girls were prepared for their domestic and maternal tasks, e.g. cooking.

'Youth serves the *Führer*. Every ten year old into the Hitler Youth.' The Nazi propaganda poster cleverly plays on the combined images of the young boy and Hitler sharing a common vision.
It was produced in 1940, by which time war had started and membership was compulsory.

Jugend dient dem Führer

ALLE ZEHNJÄHRIGEN IN DIE HJ.

Key question
Did Nazi education succeed?

Successes and failures

It is difficult to assess the success of any educational system. It depends on the criteria chosen and the 'evidence' is open to conflicting interpretations. Therefore, conclusions must be tentative.

The teaching profession certainly felt its status to be under threat, despite its initial sympathy for the regime. Thirty-two per cent were members of the Party in 1936 – a figure markedly higher than the figure of 17 per cent of the Reich Civil Service as a whole. The anti-academic ethos and the crude indoctrination alienated many, while the Party's backing of the HJ and its activities caused much resentment. Not surprisingly, standards in traditional academic subjects had fallen by the early years of the war. This was particularly the case in the various élite schools, where physical development predominated. By 1938 recruitment of teachers had declined and there were 8000 vacancies – and only 2500 were coming out of the teacher training colleges. In higher education, the number of students had halved even before the onset of the war. The overall effect of these changes was described in 1937 in a report from the teachers' organisation in Bavaria:

> Many pupils believe that they can simply drift through for eight years and secure their school leaving certificate with minimal intellectual performance. The schools receive no support whatsoever from the Hitler Youth units; on the contrary, it is those pupils who are in positions of leadership there who often display unmannerly behaviour and laziness at school. School discipline has declined to an alarming extent.

The impact of the HJ seems to have been very mixed. In some respects the emphasis on teamwork and extracurricular activities was to be commended – especially when compared to the limited provision available in many European countries. So, the provision for sports, camping and music genuinely excited many youngsters – and for those from poorer backgrounds, the HJ really offered opportunities. However, the organisation suffered from its over-rapid expansion and the leadership was inadequate. When the war started it became even more difficult to run the movement effectively and, as a result, the increasing Nazi emphasis on military drill and discipline was certainly resented by many adolescents. This point was made by a BDM leader in her memoirs:

> Apart from its beginnings during the 'years of struggle', the Hitler Youth was not a youth movement at all: it became more and more the 'state youth organisation', that is to say, it became more and more institutionalised, and finally became the instrument used by the National Socialist regime to run its ideological training of young people and the war work for certain age groups.

Moreover, much recent research suggests that sizeable pockets of the adolescent population had not been won over by 1939 and that, during the war, alienation and dissent increased quite markedly. The regime even established a special youth section of the secret police and a youth concentration camp was set up at Neuwied.

A number of youth groups developed deliberately exhibiting codes of behaviour at odds with the expected social values of Nazism. 'Swing Youth' was one such craze among mainly middle-class youngsters who took up the music and imagery associated with the dance-bands of Britain and the USA. The **Edelweiss Piraten** was a general name given to a host of working-class youths who formed gangs, such as the 'Roving Dudes' and 'Navajos'. Their members had been alienated by the military emphasis and discipline of the Hitler Youth. They met up and organised their own hikes and camps which then came into conflict with the official ones. In several instances, 'Pirates' became involved in more active resistance, most famously at Cologne in 1944 when 12 of them were publicly hanged because of their attacks on military targets and the assassination of a *Gestapo* officer.

Key date

Execution of 12 Edelweiss Pirates in Cologne: November 1944

Key term

Edelweiss
A white alpine flower which served as a symbol of opposition.

Kittelbach Pirates from 1937. 'Pirates' was the label chosen by dissenting German youth. In what ways could these boys be seen as challenging Nazi ideals?

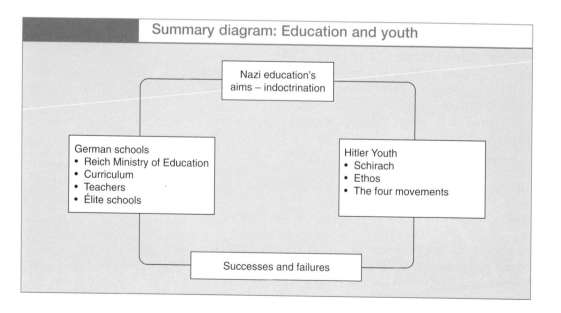

Summary diagram: Education and youth

Nazi education's aims – indoctrination

German schools
- Reich Ministry of Education
- Curriculum
- Teachers
- Élite schools

Hitler Youth
- Schirach
- Ethos
- The four movements

Successes and failures

4 | Religion

In the 1930s the majority of German people were Christian, two-thirds of whom were **Protestant** and the remaining one-third Catholic. The rise of Nazism posed fundamental political and ethical problems for the Christian Churches, while Nazism could not ignore those Churches, which were well-established and powerful institutions.

   In his rise to power Hitler avoided direct attacks on the Churches and number 24 of the Party's 25-points programme spoke in favour of 'positive Christianity' which was closely linked to racial and national views (see page 88). However, there can be little doubt that Nazism was based on a fundamentally anti-Christian philosophy. Where Nazism glorified strength, violence and war, Christianity taught love, forgiveness and neighbourly respect. Moreover, Christianity was regarded as the product of an inferior race – Jesus was a Hebrew – and therefore, it could not be reconciled with Nazi *völkisch* thought. Some leading Nazis, such as Himmler and his deputy, Heydrich, openly revealed their contempt for Christianity. Hitler himself was more cautious, although what were probably his true feelings were revealed in a private conversation in 1933:

> Neither of the denominations – Catholic or Protestant, they are both the same – has any future left … That won't stop me stamping out Christianity in Germany root and branch. One is either a Christian or a German. You can't be both.

Key question
How did the Nazis regard religion?

Key terms

Protestant
General name for the reformed Churches created in sixteenth-century Europe that split from the Roman Catholic Church. There were 28 different Protestant Churches in Germany, of which the largest was the Lutheran (the German state Church, like the Church of England).

Völkisch
Nationalist views associated with racism (especially anti-Semitism).

Profile: Alfred Rosenberg 1893–1946

1893	– Born in Russian Estonia, but of German parents
1919	– Joined the Party as one of its earlier members
1923	– Took part in the Munich Beer Hall *putsch*
1924–5	– Leader of the Party while Hitler was in prison
1930	– Elected as a member of the *Reichstag*
	– Published his book on racial theory, *The Myth of the Twentieth Century*
1941	– Minister for the Occupied Territories
1945	– Arrested by Allied forces
1946	– Executed after the Nuremberg War Trials

Rosenberg was not really an effective political leader. He was an educated and scholarly figure, but he only exerted influence with a limited number within the Party. He was portrayed as the Party's main 'ideologue' and in his lengthy book he expressed his commitment to racism, anti-Semitism and anti-Christianity. His major significance lay in his promotion of the German Faith Movement.

Key terms

Teutonic paganism
The non-Christian beliefs of the Germans in ancient history (heathens).

Cult of personality
Using the power and charisma of a political leader to dominate the nation.

The German Faith Movement

In place of Christianity, the Nazis aimed to cultivate a **teutonic paganism**, which became known as the German Faith Movement. Although a clear Nazi religious ideology was never fully outlined, the development of the German Faith Movement, promoted by the Nazi thinker Alfred Rosenberg, revolved around four main themes:

- the propagation of the 'Blood and Soil' ideology (see pages 184–7)
- the replacement of Christian ceremonies – marriage and baptism – by pagan equivalents
- the wholesale rejection of Christian ethics – closely linked to racial and nationalist views
- the **cult of** Hitler's **personality**.

However, the Nazi government knew that religion was a very delicate issue and it initially adopted a cautious conciliatory stance towards both the Churches.

Key question
Why did conciliation lead to conflict?

Conciliation and conflict 1933–5

In his very first speech as Chancellor, Hitler paid tribute to the Churches as being integral to the well-being of the nation. Members of the SA were even encouraged to attend Protestant Church services. This was done to give weight to the idea that the Nazi state could accommodate Protestantism. The 'Day of Potsdam' (see page 144) further gave the impression of a unity between the Protestant Church and the state.

Key date

Concordat signed with the Papacy: July 1933

Likewise, the Catholic Church responded sympathetically to the overtures of the Nazis. Catholic bishops, in particular, were frightened of the possibility of a repeat of the so-called *Kulturkampf* in the late nineteenth century. So, Catholic bishops were concerned to safeguard the position of the Church under the Nazis and in July 1933 a **Concordat** was signed between the Papacy and the regime (represented by Vice-Chancellor Papen who was a Catholic). In the agreement it was decided that:

Key terms

Kulturkampf
'Cultural struggle'.
Refers to the tension in the 1870s between the Catholic Church and the German state, when Bismarck was chancellor.

Concordat
An agreement between Church and state.

- the Nazis would guarantee the Catholic Church religious freedom
- the Nazis would not interfere with the Catholic Church's property and legal rights
- the Nazis would accept the Catholic Church's control over its own education
- in return, the Catholic Church would not interfere in politics and would give diplomatic recognition to the Nazi government.

In the short term the Concordat seemed to be a significant success. However, the courting of both of the Churches by the Nazis was totally insincere. They were merely being lulled into a false sense of security while the dictatorship was being established. By the end of 1933 Nazi interference in religious affairs was already causing resentment and disillusionment in both Catholic and Protestant Churches.

Profile: Pastor Martin Niemöller 1892–1984

1892 – Born in Lippstadt
1914–18 – U-boat commander and won the Iron Cross
1920–4 – Studied theology and ordained as a Protestant pastor in Berlin
1934 – Co-founder of the Confessional Church
1937 – A critical sermon resulted in his arrest
1937–45 – Held in the concentration camps of Sachsenhausen and Dachau
1946 – President of the Protestant Church in Hessen
1946–84 – A strong supporter of the World Peace Movement
1984 – Died in Wiesbaden, Germany

In the 1920s Niemöller was a nationalist, anti-communist and against the Weimar Republic – he even sympathised with Hitler in the rise of Nazism. However, during 1933 his doubts emerged because of Nazism's anti-Semitism and its attempt to control the Churches. Therefore, he played a crucial role in the formation of the Confessional Church in 1934 and after a highly critical sermon he was imprisoned from 1937 to 1945. Although his actions in the Third Reich were limited, his words have resonated through the years:

When the Nazis came for the Communists
I stayed quiet:
I was not a Communist.

When they came for the Social Democrats
I stayed quiet:
I was not a Social Democrat.

When they came for the Trade Unionists
I stayed quiet:
I was not a Trade Unionist.

When they came for the Jews
I stayed quiet:
I was not a Jew.

Then they came for me
And there was no-one left to protest.

The Nazi regime hoped that the Protestant Churches would gradually be 'co-ordinated' through the influence of the group known as the German Christians (*Deutsche Christen*). This group hoped to reconcile their Protestant ideas with Nazi nationalist and racial thinking by finding common ground. So, a new Church constitution was formulated in July 1933 with the Nazi sympathiser Ludwig Müller as the first Reich Bishop – an interesting application of the *Führerprinzip*.

Key dates

Creation of the Confessional Church: 1934

Papal encyclical, *Mit Brennender Sorge*, issued: 1937

However, such Nazi policies alienated many Protestant pastors, and there soon developed an opposition group, the Confessional Church (*Bekennende Kirche*), which upheld orthodox Protestantism and rejected Nazi distortions. Led by Pastor Niemöller, by 1934 the Confessional Church gained the support of about 7000 pastors out of 17,000. They claimed to represent the true Protestant Churches of Germany.

Key question
How did the relationship between the Churches and state change over time?

Churches and state 1935–45

By 1935 it was clear that the Nazi leadership had achieved only limited success in its control over the Churches. It was torn between a policy of total suppression, which would alienate large numbers of Germans, and a policy of limited persecution, which would allow the Churches an unacceptable degree of independence outside state control. In fact, although the ultimate objective was never in doubt, Nazi tactics degenerated into a kind of war of attrition against the Churches.

In order to destabilise the Churches, the Ministry of Church Affairs, led by Hanns Kerrl, was established. He adopted a policy of undermining both the Protestant and Catholic Churches by a series of anti-religious measures, including:

- closure of Church schools
- undermining of Catholic youth groups
- personal campaigns to discredit and harass the clergy, e.g. monasteries were accused of sexual and financial malpractices
- confiscation of Church funds
- campaign to remove crucifixes from schools
- arrest of more and more pastors and priests.

The standing of the Churches was undoubtedly weakened by this approach, but it also stimulated individual declarations of opposition from both Protestants and Catholics:

- Niemöller delivered a sermon in which he said that 'we must obey God rather than man'; he was interned in 1937 and for the next eight years he was held in various concentration camps.
- The Pope, Pius XI, eventually vehemently attacked the Nazi system in his encyclical, or public letter, of 1937 entitled *With Burning Concern* (*Mit Brennender Sorge*).

Clearly, the conflict between the Churches and the state was set to continue.

The outbreak of war initially brought about a more cautious policy, as the regime wished to avoid unnecessary tensions. However, following the easy military victories against Poland and France (1939–40), and then the invasion of atheistic Soviet Union (1941), the persecution intensified. This was the result of pressure applied by anti-Christian enthusiasts, such as Bormann and Heydrich (see page 229) and the SS hierarchy.

So, once again, monasteries were closed, Church property was attacked and Church activities were severely restricted. Even so, religion was such a politically sensitive issue that Hitler did not allow subordination of the Churches to give way to wholesale suppression within Germany. It was only in the occupied territory of Poland – the area designated as an experimental example of the 'New Order' – that events were allowed to run their full course. Here, many of the Catholic clergy were executed and churches were closed down. In the end the Nazi persecution of the Churches failed, but only because the war itself was lost.

Conclusion

The Nazis achieved only limited success in their religious policy. The German Faith Movement was a clearly a failure. Neo-paganism never achieved support on any large scale. The 1939 official census recorded only 5 per cent of the population as members, although it shows the direction that might have been taken, if the likes of Himmler had won the war.

> **Key question**
> Did Nazi religious policy succeed in its aims?

There were numerous individual Christians who made brave stands against the Nazis. This made the dictatorship wary of launching a fundamental assault on religion. As a result, German loyalty to the Christian faith in the Protestant and Catholic Churches survived in the long term despite Nazism. The historian J.R.C. Wright says: 'The Churches were severely handicapped but not destroyed. Hitler's programme needed time: he was himself destroyed before it had taken root.'

However, both the Catholic and Protestant Churches failed because of their inability to provide effective opposition to Nazism. Neither of the Christian Churches was 'co-ordinated' and therefore, both enjoyed a measure of independence. So they both could have provided the focus for active resistance. Instead, they preferred, as institutions, to adopt a pragmatic policy towards Nazism. They stood up for their own religious practices and traditions with shows of dissent, but generally they refrained from wholesale denunciations of the regime.

> **Key question**
> Did the Churches effectively oppose the Nazis?

The reasons for the Churches' reluctance to show opposition to the regime lay in their conservatism:

- They distrusted the politics of the left which seemed to threaten the existing order of society. The most extreme form of communism rejected the existence of religion itself.
- There was a nationalist sympathy for Nazism, especially after the problems of 1918–33. For many Church leaders it was too easy to believe that Hitler's 'national renewal' was simply a return to the glorious days before 1914. This was particularly true of the Lutheran Protestant Church, which had been the state Church in Prussia under Imperial Germany.
- Both Churches rightly feared the power of the Nazi state. They believed that any gestures of heroic resistance were more than likely to have bloody consequences. In such a situation, their emphasis on pastoral and spiritual comfort was perhaps the most practical and realistic policy for them.

Profile: Dietrich Bonhoeffer 1906–45

1906		– Born at Breslau, Germany
1923–31		– Studied at Tübingen, Berlin, Rome, Barcelona and New York
1931–3		– Lecturer and student pastor at Berlin University
1933–5		– Worked as a pastor on the outskirts of London
1935		– Returned to Germany and joined the Confessing Church
1935–7		– Ran a college to train pastors, but was quickly closed down
1940–3		– Banned from preaching and made contact with the active resistance movement
1943	April	– Arrested by the *Gestapo*
1943–5		– Held in various prisons and camps
1945	April	– Murdered in Flossenbürg concentration camp

From the very start Bonhoeffer was a consistent opponent of Hitler and Nazism. However, by 1940, he had moved from religious dissent to political resistance. Over the next three years he:

- helped Jews to emigrate
- was drawn into the Kreisau Circle and actively worked with the underground movement
- travelled secretly to Sweden to see an English bishop, Bell, in the hope that Britain would help the resistance (the British authorities remained very cautious).

When he was sentenced to death the SS doctor later wrote: 'in nearly 50 years as a doctor I never saw another man go to his death so possessed of the spirit of God'.

Effective Christian resistance, therefore, remained essentially the preserve of individual churchmen who put their own freedom and lives at risk in order to uphold their beliefs or to give pastoral assistance.

It has been estimated that 40 per cent of the Catholic clergy and over 50 per cent of the Protestant pastors were harassed by the Nazis. Most famous were:

Key date

Bishop Galen's sermon against euthanasia: August 1940

- Bishop Galen of Münster, whose outspoken sermon attacking Nazi euthanasia policy (see page 212) in 1941 proved so powerful that the authorities recoiled from arresting him and actually stopped the programme.
- Martin Niemöller, the founder of the Confessional Church, who languished in a concentration camp from 1937 (see page 198).
- Dietrich Bonhoeffer, whose opposition started as religious dissent but, from 1940, developed into political resistance which brought him into direct contact with elements of the conservative resistance (see above).

Such heroic examples were by no means exceptional and hundreds of priests and pastors were to die in the camps for their refusal to co-operate with the regime. Their sacrifice is therefore eloquent testimony to the limits to which people would go to defy conformity. But it also bears witness to the fact that such courageous resistance was rarely able to restrain the regime.

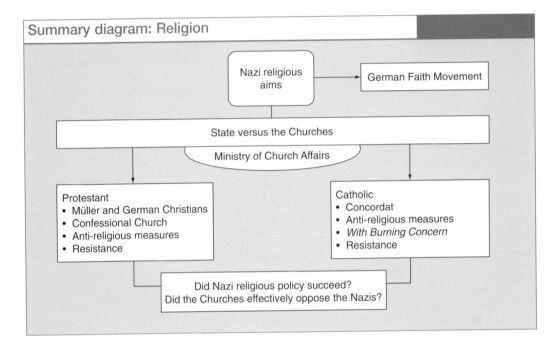

Summary diagram: Religion

Nazi religious aims → German Faith Movement

State versus the Churches

Ministry of Church Affairs

Protestant
• Müller and German Christians
• Confessional Church
• Anti-religious measures
• Resistance

Catholic
• Concordat
• Anti-religious measures
• *With Burning Concern*
• Resistance

Did Nazi religious policy succeed?
Did the Churches effectively oppose the Nazis?

5 | Women and the Family

The first quarter of the twentieth century witnessed two important social changes in German family life:

Key question
How and why was German society changed in the twentieth century?

• Germany's population growth had decelerated markedly – which is *not* to say that the actual population had declined. In 1900 there had been over two million live births per annum, whereas by 1933 the figure was below one million.
• Over the same period female employment expanded by at least a third, far outstripping the percentage increase in population.

Both of these trends had been partially brought about by long-term changes in social behaviour common to many industrialised countries. It was recognised that the use of contraception to limit family size would improve the standard of living and give the better-educated female population the opportunity to have a vocation as well as children. However, Germany's recent past history exaggerated these developments. Economic mobilisation during the First World War had driven women into the factories, while the post-war difficulties caused by the inflation had encouraged them to stay on working out of economic necessity. In addition, the war had left a surplus of 1.8 million marriageable women, as well as many wives with invalided husbands. Finally, the changing balance of the economy in the 1920s had led to an increased demand for non-manual labour and the growth of mass-production techniques requiring more unskilled workers. These factors tended to favour the employment of women, who could be paid less than men.

The Nazi view towards women

Key question
What was the ideal role of women in Nazi society?

The ideology of National Socialism was in stark contrast to the above social trends. Nazism fundamentally opposed social and economic female emancipation and had the following aims for women:

- To have more children and to take responsibility for bringing them up.
- To care for the house and their husbands.
- To stop paid employment except for very specialist vocations such as midwifery.

In the view of the Nazis, nature had ordained that the two sexes should fulfil entirely different roles, and it was simply the task of the state to maintain this distinction. What this amounted to was that 'a woman's place was to be in the home'. Or, as the Nazi slogan presented it, they were to be devoted to the three German Ks – '*Kinder, Küche, Kirche*' ('children, kitchen and Church' – see the 'Ten commandments' for choosing a spouse, below). Such dogma was upheld by the Party, even before 1933 – there was not a single female Nazi deputy in the *Reichstag*, and a Party regulation of 1921 excluded women from all senior positions within its structure.

Nazi Ten Commandments for the choice of a spouse

1. Remember that you are German!
2. If you are genetically healthy, do not stay single.
3. Keep your body pure.
4. Keep your mind and spirit pure.
5. Marry only for love.
6. As a German, choose only a spouse of similar or related blood.
7. In choosing a spouse, ask about his forebears.
8. Health is essential to physical beauty.
9. Don't look for a playmate but for a companion in marriage.
10. You should want to have as many children as possible.

Nazis' views on women tied in with their concern about the demographic trends. A growing population was viewed as a sign of national strength and status – a reflection of Germany's aspiration to the status of an international power. How could they demand nationalist expansionism in eastern Europe, if the number of Germans was in fact levelling out? It was therefore considered essential to increase the population substantially and, to this end, women were portrayed as primarily the mothers of the next generation – an image that suited Nazi anti-feminism.

Female employment

Key question
Did the Nazis reduce the number of women in employment?

Initially, attempts to reduce the number of women in work seem to have been quite successful. Between 1933 and 1936 married women were in turn debarred from jobs in medicine, law and the higher ranks of the civil service. Moreover, the number of female teachers and university students was reduced considerably – only 10 per cent of university students could be female. Such laws had a profound effect on professional middle-class women, although their actual number was small.

Nazi incentives

In other sectors of the economy a mixture of Party pressure and financial inducements was employed to cajole women out of the workplace and back into the home. From June 1933 interest-free loans of 600RM were made available to young women who withdrew from the labour market in order to get married. The effects of the Depression also worked in favour of Nazi objectives. They not only drastically reduced the number of female workers (although proportionately far less than male workers), but also enabled the government to justify its campaign for women to give up work for the benefit of unemployed men. On these grounds, **labour exchanges** and employers were advised to discriminate positively in favour of men. As a result of all this, the percentage of women in employment fell from 37 per cent to 31 per cent of the total from 1932 to 1937.

Labour exchanges
Local offices created by the state for finding employment. Many industrialised countries had labour exchanges to counter mass unemployment.

Anti-feminist
Opposing female advancement.

Key terms

Nazi women's organisations

Women were quite specifically excluded from the Nazi machinery of government. The only employment opportunities available to them were within the various Nazi women's organisations, such as the National Socialist Womanhood (NSF, *National Sozialistische Frauenschaft*) and the German Women's Enterprise (DFW, *Deutsches Frauenwerk*), led by Gertrud Scholtz-Klink. Yet, the NSF and DFW were regarded by the Party as mere tools for the propagation of the **anti-feminist** ideology by means of cultural, educational and social programmes. And so, when a campaign started in the NSF for enhanced opportunities for women within the Party, its organisers were officially discredited.

Effects

However, by 1937 Nazi ideological convictions were already threatened by the pressures of economic necessity. The introduction of conscription and the rearmament boom from the mid-1930s soon led to an increasing shortage of labour, as the Nazi economy continued to grow. The anti-feminist ideology could only be upheld if economic growth was slowed down and that, in turn, would restrict the rearmament programme. Of course, Hitler was not prepared to sanction this. Consequently, market forces inevitably began to exploit this readily available pool of labour, and the relative decline in female employment was reversed. Between 1937 and 1939 it rose from 5.7 million to 7.1 million, and the percentage of women increased from 31 per cent to 33 per cent of the total workforce (see Table 9.3) At this point the government decided to end the marriage loan scheme (see page 206) for women who withdrew from the labour market.

Table 9.3: Women in regular manual and non-manual employment

	1932	1937	1939
Millions of women	4.8	5.7	7.1
Women as a percentage of the total	37	31	33

Note: the comparative figure for 1928 was 7.4 million.

The contradictions between theory and practice of female employment were exacerbated further with the onset of war. So, although the trend of female employment continued to increase, the Nazi regime did not fully exploit the valuable resource of women as munitions workers – and the figures show that women remained underemployed right to the end of the war. This was due to:

- Germany's poor economic mobilisation. At first it was badly organised and (see pages 174–5) there was no general conscription of female labour. When in 1943 Speer did try to mobilise the economy on a total war footing by suggesting the conscription of women workers, he encountered opposition from Bormann, Sauckel (the Plenipotentiary for Labour) and indeed from Hitler himself, who was always concerned about civilian morale.
- The appeal for women to do war work was not convincing. Long hours in an arms factory made life very arduous, especially if there were the added responsibilities of maintaining a household and raising children. In addition, the Nazi government had also given all sorts of financial incentives to have more children with welfare benefits (see page 206).
- Farming responsibilities. One reason that distorts the picture of female employment was that women had traditionally played an important part in German farming. The shortage of agricultural labour had created major problems from the 1930s (see pages 186–7), but once the young men were sent away for the war it got worse. As a result many German women experienced considerable hardship meeting the continuous demands of running a farm. By 1944 it is estimated that 65 per cent of the agricultural workforce were women.

The Nazis were caught in the contradictions of their own ideology. They were motivated by military expansionism which needed to employ women effectively, so, in the final two years of the Nazi state, more and more women ended up at work. Yet, the government could not bring itself to renounce fully its anti-feminist stance. As an official in the NSF wrote, 'It has always been our chief article of faith that a woman's place is in the home – but since the whole of Germany is our home we must serve wherever we can best do so.'

Marriage and family

The Nazi state was obsessed with a desire to increase Germany's population and a series of measures was promptly introduced:

Key question
What were the effects of Nazi population policy?

- Marriage loans. The loan was worth just over half a year's earnings and a quarter of it was converted into a straight gift for each child that was born. (The scheme was introduced in June 1933, but progressively reduced from 1937.)
- Family allowances were improved dramatically, particularly for low-income families.
- Income tax was reduced in proportion to the number of children and those families with six or more did not pay any.
- Maternity benefits were improved.
- The anti-abortion law introduced under the Weimar Republic was enforced much more strictly.
- Contraceptive advice and facilities were restricted.

Inevitably, these incentives and laws were backed up by an extensive propaganda campaign, which glorified motherhood and the large family. There were also rewards: the Honour Cross of the German Mother in bronze, silver and gold, awarded for four, six and eight children, respectively. Such glorification reached its climax in the coining of the Nazi slogan 'I have donated a child to the *Führer*' (as contemporary humorists soon pointed out, this was presumably because of Hitler's personal unwillingness or inability to father children of his own).

Table 9.4: Social trends in Nazi Germany 1933–9

	Marriages per 1000 inhabitants	Divorces per 10,000 existing marriages	Births per 1000 inhabitants
1933	9.7	29.7	14.7
1936	9.1	32.6	19.0
1939	11.1	38.3	20.3

The statistics in Table 9.4 show several trends:

- From 1933 the birth rate increased significantly, reaching a peak in 1939 (although thereafter it again slowly declined).
- The divorce rate continued to increase.
- The figure of marriages was fairly consistent (apart from the blip in 1939 – probably connected to the onset of the war).

The real problem for the historian is deciding whether Nazi population policy was actually *responsible* for the demographic trends. Interpreting population statistics is difficult because it involves so many different factors – social, economic and even psychological factors. Also, it is extremely hard to assess the *relative* significance of Nazi population policy when it is set against the importance of events such as the Depression and later on the Second World War.

Lebensborn

Nazi population policy not only aimed to increase the number of children being born, but also tried to improve 'racial standards'. It led to the establishment of one of the most extraordinary features of Nazi social engineering, **Lebensborn**, set up by Himmler and the SS. Initially, the programme provided homes for unmarried mothers of the increasing number of illegitimate children who were seen as racially correct. Later, the institution also made the necessary arrangements for girls to be 'impregnated' by members of the SS in organised brothels. It is reckoned that by the end of the regime about 11,000 children were born under these circumstances.

Conclusion

Feminist historians have been highly critical of Nazi population and family policy that had reduced the status of women. One historian, Gisela Bock, in the 1980s viewed Nazi thinking on women as a kind of secondary racism in which women were the victims of a sexist–racist male regime that reduced women to the status of mere objects. Such an interpretation would, of course, have been denied by the Nazis who claimed to regard women as different rather than inferior. But some modern-day non-feminist historians have tried to explain the positive features of Nazi policy on women. Improved welfare services made life easier for women, especially in more isolated rural areas. Also, with so many husbands away during the war, women were protected from having to combine paid work with bringing up a family and running the household.

Yet, despite these different perspectives, Nazi policy objectives for women and the family could not really be squared with the social realities of twentieth-century Germany. With the changing population trend and the increasing employment of women, Nazi views on women and the family were idealistic but impractical. Consequently, Nazi policy towards women and the family was contradictory and incoherent.

Key term

Lebensborn
Literally, the 'spring' or 'fountain of life'. Founded by Himmler and overseen by the SS to promote doctrines of racial purity.

Key question
How successful was Nazi policy on women and family?

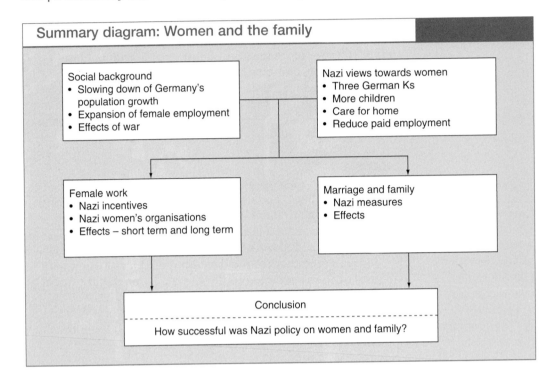

Summary diagram: Women and the family

Social background
• Slowing down of Germany's population growth
• Expansion of female employment
• Effects of war

Nazi views towards women
• Three German Ks
• More children
• Care for home
• Reduce paid employment

Female work
• Nazi incentives
• Nazi women's organisations
• Effects – short term and long term

Marriage and family
• Nazi measures
• Effects

Conclusion

How successful was Nazi policy on women and family?

6 | Culture

During the evening of 10 May 1933, in the middle of a square just off the centre of Berlin, there took place an event that soon became known as 'the burning of the books'. Thousands of volumes seized from private and public libraries were hurled into the flames by Nazi activists and university students because they were considered undesirable on account of their Jewish, socialist or pacifist tendencies. For a nation whose literary heritage was one of the greatest in Europe, it was seen by many as an act of mindless barbarism. It also rather aptly set the tone for the cultural life of Nazi Germany.

Nazi culture was no longer to be promoted merely as 'art for art's sake'. Rather, it was to serve the purpose of moulding public opinion, and, with this in mind, the Reich Chamber of Culture was supervised by the Propaganda Ministry. Germany's cultural life during the Third Reich was simply to be another means of achieving censorship and indoctrination, although Goebbels expressed it in more pompous language:

> What we are aiming for is more than a revolt. Our historic mission is to transform the very spirit itself to the extent that people and things are brought into a new relationship with one another.

Culture was therefore 'co-ordinated' by means of the Reich Chamber of Culture, established in 1933, which made provision for seven subchambers: fine arts, music, the theatre, the press, radio, literature and films. In this way, just as anyone in the media had no option but to toe the Party line (see pages 244–7),

Key question
What was the purpose of Nazi culture?

The burning of the books: 10 May 1933

Key date

Key term

Anti-modernism
Strand of opinion
that rejects, objects
to or is highly
critical of changes to
society and culture
brought about by
technological
advancement.

Key question
In what ways did the
Nazis shape German
culture?

so all those involved in cultural activities had to be accountable
for their creativity. Nazi culture was dominated by a number of
key themes reflecting the usual ideological prejudices:

- anti-Semitism
- militarism and the glorification of war
- nationalism and the supremacy of the Aryan race
- the cult of the *Führer* and the power of absolutism
- **anti-modernism** and the theme of 'Blood and Soil'
- neo-paganism and a rejection of traditional Christian values.

Major cultural themes
Music
The world of music managed to survive reasonably well in the
Nazi environment, partly because of its less obvious political
overtones. Also, Germany's rich classical tradition from the works
of Bach to Beethoven was proudly exploited by the regime.
However, Mahler and Mendelssohn, both great Jewish composers,
were banned, as were most modern musical trends. Also the new
'genres' of jazz and dance-band were respectively labelled
'Negroid' and 'decadent'.

Literature
Over 2500 of Germany's writers left their homeland during the
years 1933–45 in reaction to the new cultural atmosphere. Among
those who departed were Thomas Mann, Bertolt Brecht and
Erich Maria Remarque (see pages 78–81). Their place was taken
by a lesser literary group, who either sympathised with the regime
or accepted the limitations.

Actors, like the musicians, tended to content themselves with
productions of the classics – Schiller, Goethe (and Shakespeare) –
in the knowledge that such plays were politically acceptable and
in the best traditions of German theatre.

Visual arts
The visual arts were also effectively limited by the Nazi
constraints. Modern schools of art were held in total contempt
and Weimar's rich cultural awakening was rejected as degenerate
and symbolic of the moral and political decline of Germany
under a system of parliamentary democracy. Thus, the following
were severely censored:

- 'New functionalism' artists, like Georg Grosz and Otto Dix,
  wanted to depict ordinary people in everyday life – and by their
  art they aimed to comment on the state of society.
- The Bauhaus style started by Walter Gropius influenced all
  aspects of design. It emphasised the close relationship between
  art and technology, which is underlined by its motto 'Art and
  Technology – a new unity' (see page 79).

The modern style of art was resented by Nazism so much that in
July 1937 two contrasting art exhibitions were launched entitled
'Degenerate Art' and 'Great German Art'. The first one was

deliberately held up to be mocked and many of the pieces were destroyed; the second one glorified all the major Nazi themes of *Volksgemeinschaft* and celebrated classic styles and traditional nineteenth-century romanticism. Most admired were:

- the sculptor Arno Breker (see below)
- the architect Albert Speer, who drew up many of the great plans for rebuilding the German cities and oversaw the 1936 Berlin Olympics stadium.

Cinema

Only in the field of film can it be said that the Nazi regime made a genuine cultural contribution. Many of the major film studios were in the hands of nationalist sympathisers. However, Jewish film actors and directors such as Fritz Lang were removed – and then decided to leave Germany. Perhaps the most famous

Arno Breker, *Comrades*. Breker was sculptor-in-chief to the Third Reich. By collaborating closely with Albert Speer he undertook numerous government commissions. His statue celebrated Aryan physical perfection and the importance of comradeship.

German émigrée was Marlene Dietrich, who swiftly established a new career in Hollywood.

Goebbels recognised the importance of expanding the film industry, not only as a means of propaganda, but also as an entertainment form – this explains why, out of 1097 feature films produced between 1933 and 1945, only 96 were specifically at the request of the Propaganda Ministry. The films can be divided into three types:

- Overt propaganda, e.g. *The Eternal Jew* (*Ewige Jude*), a tasteless, racist film that portrayed the Jews like rats, and *Hitlerjunge Queux*, based on the story of a Nazi murdered by the communists.
- Pure escapism, e.g. *The Adventures of Baron von Münchhausen*, a comedy based on an old German legend which gives the baron the powers of immortality.
- Emotive nationalism, e.g. *Olympia*, Leni Riefenstahl's docu-drama of the Berlin Olympics, *Triumph of the Will*, Riefenstahl's film about the 1934 Nuremberg Rally, and *Kolberg*, an epic produced in the final year of the war, which played on the national opposition to Napoleon. These last two films are still held in high regard by film critics for their use of subtle cinematic techniques despite the clear underlying political messages.

Key question
Did the Third Reich manage to create a cultural identity of its own?

In the play *Schlageter* (1934) by Hanns Johst there is the line, 'Whenever I hear the word culture, I reach for my gun'. It is a phrase that is often, and incorrectly, attributed to Göring, but it still neatly underlines the anti-culture approach of the Nazis. Cultural life during the Third Reich was effectively silenced – it could only operate within the Nazi strait-jacket and to that extent Goebbels succeeded in censoring it. However, the regime most certainly failed in its attempts to create a new Nazi cultural identity firmly rooted in the minds of the *Volk*.

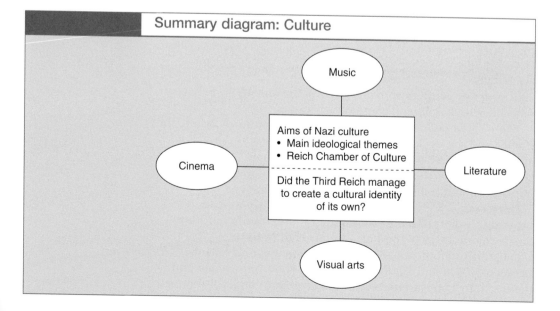

Summary diagram: Culture

Music

Aims of Nazi culture
- Main ideological themes
- Reich Chamber of Culture

Did the Third Reich manage to create a cultural identity of its own?

Cinema

Literature

Visual arts

7 | Outsiders

Key question
Who were the outsiders in the *Volksgemeinschaft*?

Despite all its claims to create a *Volksgemeinschaft*, Nazism believed that certain people were not allowed to join the Third Reich – and they were to be discriminated against and persecuted. Nazism was an all-embracing society, but only of those who conformed to their criteria – and there were certain groups who were definitely 'outsiders'.

Ideological opponents

This term could most obviously be applied to the communists, so many of whom were sent to the early concentration camps in 1933 (see pages 146–7). However, it increasingly became a term to cover anyone who did not politically accept the regime and, as the years went on, a broader range of political and ideological opponents was imprisoned or worse, e.g. Pastor Niemöller (see page 198) and General Stauffenberg (see page 251).

The 'biologically inferior'

This covered all the races that, according to the Nazis, were 'inferior' or subhuman, such as the Gypsies, Slavs and Jews (see Chapter 10).

It also included those who were mentally and physically disabled. As early as July 1933 the Nazis proclaimed 'The Law for the Prevention of Hereditarily Diseased Offspring', which allowed for the compulsory sterilisation of those with hereditary conditions – examples included schizophrenia, Huntington's chorea, hereditary blindness or deafness. Over the 12 years of the Nazi period, 350,000 people were sterilised under this law.

However, the policy went much further from 1939, when Hitler himself initiated the idea of using euthanasia for children with severe disabilities (such as Down's syndrome and cerebral palsy) by using the phrase 'mercy death'. No specific law permitted this, but patients were killed in asylums under the name of 'Operation T4'. About 70,000 were gassed in 1940–1 but, following public rumours and Catholic opposition, the operation was stopped (see page 201).

Asocials

The term was used very broadly to cover anyone whose behaviour was not viewed as acceptable.

These social outcasts included alcoholics, prostitutes, criminals, tramps and the workshy. Those asocials who were 'orderly' but avoided work were rounded up and organised into a compulsory labour force; and those who were judged as 'disorderly' were imprisoned and sometimes sterilised or experimented on.

Homosexuals were also classed as asocials. They were seen as breaking the laws of nature and undermining traditional Nazi family values. In 1936 the Reich Central Office for the Combating of Homosexuality and Abortion was established. Between 10,000 and 15,000 homosexuals were imprisoned and those sent to camps were forced to wear pink triangles (it is worth noting that lesbians were not persecuted).

Summary diagram: Outsiders

8 | Conclusion

Key question
Did Nazism's *Volksgemeinschaft* create a social revolution in the Third Reich?

In a very obvious sense, the effects of the 12 years of the Third Reich had a dramatic impact on the German people. Yet, what was the exact nature of the social changes?

Some have seen it as social **reaction** of the worst kind. This was because it reinforced the traditional class structure and strengthened the position of the establishment élites – especially the powerful interests of the military and big business – at the expense of more popular institutions, such as trade unions. Others believe that the Nazi *Volksgemeinschaft* brought about a social revolution which caused the collapse of the social élites and the traditional loyalties and values which had dominated German life since the mid-nineteenth century and that it paved the way for the emergence of a liberal, democratic West Germany. Alternatively, some historians feel that Nazism simply led to 'a revolution of destruction'; that the real changes came about through the destruction wrought by the effects of total war, economic collapse, genocide and political division. Finally, it has been suggested that very few fundamental changes in values and attitudes had any real effect in the 12 years of Nazi rule. Prevailing cultural traditions and social institutions, such as the family and the Churches, did not break down overnight.

So, in conclusion, it should be noted that:

Key term

Reaction
In this context suggesting a return to traditional established ways.

- Despite Nazi rhetorical support for the *Mittelstand* and the peasantry, both groups remained under social and economic pressure. In contrast, the traditional élites continued to dominate and property and industry stayed in private ownership. Indeed, big business prospered.
- Women were supposed to stay at home and have more children, but really their role was set by the economic demands of the situation.

'The one-pot meal.' One of the images cultivated by the Nazi leadership was the creation of the *Volksgemeinschaft* by encouraging people to eat a simple meal together.

- The Christian Churches were expected to wither away. However, the Churches survived and enjoyed the support of the vast majority of Christians, although active opposition to the regime was actually limited.
- Nazi culture was meant to establish new roots in the *Volk*, but it exerted little more than a negative, censorious role.
- It seems that the indoctrination of German youth did have some successes, especially in the pre-war years. However, even then the effects of Nazi education have been questioned on the grounds of imposing conformity without real conviction.
- If there was a 'revolutionary' core to Nazism, it is to be found in the obsessive nature and implementation of its racial policy, and that is the focus of the subject in Chapter 10.

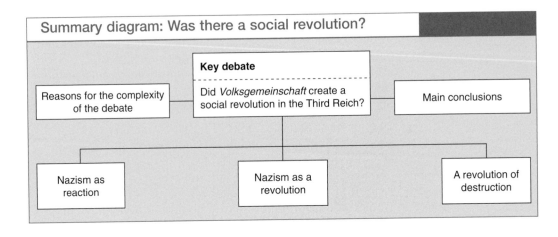

Summary diagram: Was there a social revolution?

Key debate

Did *Volksgemeinschaft* create a social revolution in the Third Reich?

Reasons for the complexity of the debate

Main conclusions

Nazism as reaction

Nazism as a revolution

A revolution of destruction

Study Guide: AS Questions

In the style of OCR A

How successful was the Nazi attempt to gain control over Germany's youth? Explain your answer.   (50 marks)

> ### Exam tips
>
> *The cross-references are intended to take you straight to the material that will help you to answer the question.*
>
> The command 'How successful … ?' requires a direct answer. You must weigh up the evidence for and against, and provide a direct answer. At first sight, it might look like the Nazis did very well: they controlled the school curriculum; two-thirds of teachers were party members; a series of youth organisations were set up for boys and girls of different age groups. Their range of activities made them very popular. In and out of the classroom, a sustained campaign to indoctrinate the next generation took place.
>
> On the other hand, Nazi Germany saw an increasing shortage of teachers. There were never enough youth movement leaders either. The Catholic Church kept control of its own schools, although the number of Church schools and youth groups (Protestant as well as Catholic) was reduced. Over 20 per cent of German children were not members of any group even at the peak of their popularity.
>
> Put those facts together and we have to question the actual ability of the Nazi state to influence Germany's youth. We know of some significant numbers who were alienated by the attempts at Nazi indoctrination; most famous are the Edelweiss Pirates and the White Rose (pages 194 and 248). Ultimately, the core question is: was it possible to achieve a fundamental revolution in attitudes in only 12 years? Control of youth was a part of the greater scheme that aimed at a social revolution. As you develop your answer, provide mini-conclusions along the way that assess the situation at the end of each section. Do not leave everything to one conclusion at the end. The examiner should be able to see how your argument is developing.

In the style of OCR A

Study the five sources on Nazi social policies and then answer **both** sub-questions. It is recommended that you spend two-thirds of your time in answering part **(b)**.

(a) Study Sources A and D.
   Compare these sources as evidence for the attitudes towards Nazi social policies. (30 marks)

(b) Study all the sources.
   Use your own knowledge to assess how far the sources support the interpretation that Nazi social policies were successfully enforced. (70 marks)

Source A

From: a SOPADE report on peasants' attitudes in Oldenburg and East Friesland, north-west Germany, in 1934. SOPADE was the SPD party leadership in exile.

The medium and better off peasants who were once enthusiastic Nazis, now completely reject the Nazis and reaffirm their old conservative traditions. Among the medium-sized farmers it is the controls on the sale of milk and eggs that are responsible. The hostility to the Nazis goes so far that they have kicked out representatives of the local party who were demanding the re-employment of dismissed workers. When the Nazis threatened to come back and bring the SA with them, the peasants replied that then there would be deaths. A peasant who was arrested after such an incident found his workmates did his work for him to show their support and solidarity.

Source B

From: the Bavarian Catholic Bishops' pastoral letter of December 1936.

Our *Führer* and Chancellor in a most impressive demonstration acknowledged the importance of the two Christian confessions to state and society, and promised them his protection. Unfortunately, men with considerable influence and power are operating in direct opposition to those promises and both confessions are being systematically attacked. Some seek to rid Germany of the Catholic Church and declare it a body foreign to our country and its people. The *Führer* can be certain that we bishops will give all moral support to his historic struggle against Bolshevism. What we do ask is that our holy Church be permitted to enjoy her God given rights and her freedom.

Source C

From: an American journalist reporting on the implementation of Nazi policies towards women in 1937.

The vigorous campaign against the employment of women has not led to their domesticity and security, but has been effective in squeezing them out of better-paid positions into sweated trades. Needless to say, this type of labour, with its miserable wages and long hours, is extremely dangerous to the health of women and degrades the family.

Source D

From: a SOPADE report written in 1938 observing a change of attitude among critics of the Nazi regime in Saxony.

Never has participation in political events been so limited as it is now. It seems to us that the indifference that has gripped large sections of the population has become the second pillar supporting the system. For these indifferent groups simply want to know nothing about what is going on around them. And that suits the Nazis fine. Only the continual collections for the Winterhelp campaign and the periodic shortages of various foodstuffs give these groups cause for slight grumbling. It is extremely rare to hear a critical word from workers who are laid off because of raw material shortages. On the other hand, we cannot speak of popular enthusiasm for National Socialism. Only the school children and the majority of those young men who have not yet done their military service are definitely enthusiastic about Hitler.

Source E

From: SS officer Greifelt reporting on the implementation of Nazi policies towards 'asocials' in January 1939.

In view of the tight situation in the labour market, national labour discipline dictated that all persons who would not conform to the working life of the nation, and who were vegetating as work-shy and asocial, making streets in our cities and countryside unsafe, had to be compulsorily registered and set to work. More than 10,000 of these asocial forces are currently undertaking a labour training cure in the concentration camps, which are admirably suited for this purpose.

Exam tips

The cross-references are intended to take you straight to the material that will help you to answer the questions.

(a) Part **(a)** requires you to examine closely the content of the two sources and to compare the way that they show a change in people's attitudes towards Nazi social policies. Source A suggests farmers changed from support to defiant opposition, whereas Source C suggests a change from active political involvement to indifference and apathy. The main focus of an effective answer is on comparing and contrasting the content and provenance of the two sources in the light of the question asked and reaching a substantiated judgement.

(b) Part **(b)** requires you to use the content and provenance of all four sources, grouping them by view, and to integrate pertinent factual knowledge into your argument to answer the question. Knowledge should be used to develop, validate or criticise the views in the sources. You should reach a balanced judgement supported by knowledge, source content and provenance.

Consider the following:

- the Nazi *Volksgemeinschaft* (the key issue in the question) (page 181)
- social groups (page 182)
- education and youth (page 189)
- religion (page 196)
- women and the family (page 202)
- outsiders (page 212).

The Racial State

POINTS TO CONSIDER

The previous chapter considered many of the social themes
covered by the concept of the *Volksgemeinschaft*, but the
essential topic of Nazi racism will be the focus of this chapter.
This topic can be broken down into three chronological
stages, but it also raises a number of broader issues:

- The origins of anti-Semitism
- Gradualism 1933–9
- War and genocide 1939–45

Key dates

1933	April 1	First official boycott of Jewish shops and professions
1935	September 15	Nuremberg Race Laws introduced
1938	November 9–10	*Kristallnacht*: anti-Jewish pogrom
1939		Creation of the Reich Central Office for Jewish Emigration
1942	January	Wannsee Conference: 'Final Solution' to exterminate the Jewish people

Key question
How was anti-Semitism in Nazi Germany rooted in the past?

Key terms

Genocide
The extermination of a whole race.

Holocaust
Term to describe mass slaughter – in this context it refers to the extermination of the Jews.

1 | The Origins of Anti-Semitism

At the very centre of Nazi social policy was the issue of race and,
specifically, anti-Semitism. Hitler's obsessive hatred of the Jews
was perhaps the most dominant and consistent theme of his
political career. The translation of such ideas into actual policy
was to lead to racial laws, government-inspired violence and the
execution of the **genocide** policy that culminated in what became
known as the **Holocaust**. For historians, such questions pose
immense problems.

Historical background

There is a long tradition of anti-Semitism in European history. It
was not the preserve of the Nazis, and it certainly has never been
just a purely German phenomenon. It was rooted in the religious

hostility of Christians towards the Jews (as being responsible for the death of Christ) that can be traced back to medieval Europe. And the reason went further than that. Jews being used as a scapegoat for society's problems was a long-established practice.

However, there emerged in Germany in the course of the nineteenth century a more clearly defined anti-Semitism based on racism and national resentment. By 1900 a number of specifically anti-Semitic *völkisch* political parties were winning seats in the *Reichstag* and, although they were comparatively few, their success shows that anti-Semitic ideas were becoming more prevalent and generally more respectable. One of the leaders of these right-wing anti-Semitic parties was the Imperial Court Chaplain, Adolf Stöcker, 1874–90. Some historians have seen this anti-Semitism as a by-product of the nationalist passions stirred up by the emergence of Imperial Germany as a world power under Kaiser Wilhelm II, 1888–1918. However, it should be remembered that a similar development had also taken place in German-speaking Austria, and there the political situation was very different.

Social factors

In reality, the emergence of political anti-Semitism was a response to intellectual developments and changing social conditions. The Jews became an easy scapegoat for the discontent and disorientation felt by many people as rapid industrialisation and urbanisation took place. And, because many of the Jews were actually immigrants from eastern Europe, they were easily identifiable because of their different traditions. Moreover, although many members of the Jewish community were impoverished, they became the focus of envy because they were viewed as privileged. In 1933, for example, although Jews comprised less than 1 per cent of the German population, they composed more than 16 per cent of lawyers, 10 per cent of doctors and 5 per cent of editors and writers.

In the late nineteenth century, anti-Semitism also began to be presented in a more intellectual vein by the application of the racial theories of Social Darwinism (see pages 92–3). According to such thinking, nations were like animals and only by struggling and fighting could they hope to survive. In this way, an image of intellectual and cultural respectability was given to those anti-Semites who portrayed the Jews as an 'inferior' or 'parasitic' race and the German race as superior:

- Heinrich von Treitschke, the leading historian, who publicly declared 'the Jews are our misfortune'.
- Richard Wagner, the musician and composer whose operas glorified German mythology and often portrayed Jewish characters as evil.
- Houston Stewart Chamberlain, an Englishman, who in his book, the *Foundations of the Nineteenth Century*, celebrated the superiority of the German *Volk*.

> **Key question**
> How did social changes affect the development of anti-Semitism?

Such thinking brings one of the leading historians of Nazi Germany, J. Noakes, to suggest that by 1914:

> In the form of a basic dislike of the Jews and of what they were felt to represent, it [anti-Semitism] had succeeded in permeating broad sections of German society from the Kaiser down to the lower middle class. Ominously, it was particularly strongly entrenched within the academic community, thereby influencing the next generation.

Key question
What were the causes of anti-Semitism in Nazi Germany?

Nazi anti-Semitism 1919–33

The emergence of right-wing racist *völkisch* nationalism was clearly apparent before 1914, but its attractions expanded in the aftermath of the First World War: the self-deception of the 'stab in the back' myth; the humiliation of the Versailles Treaty; and the political and economic weaknesses of the Weimar Republic. So, by the early 1920s, there were probably about 70 relatively small right-wing splinter parties, e.g. the Nazi Party.

In that environment Hitler was able to exploit hostility towards the Jews and turn it into a radical ideology of hatred. He was the product, not the creator, of a society that was permeated by such prejudices. Yet, it would be inaccurate to dismiss Hitler as just another anti-Semite. Hitler's hatred of Jews was obsessive and vindictive, and it shaped much of his political philosophy. Without his personal commitment to attack the Jews and without his charismatic skills as a political leader, it seems unlikely that anti-Semitism could have become such an integral part of the Nazi movement. He was able to mobilise and stir the support of the leading anti-Semitic Nazis:

- Göring (see page 172)
- Goebbels (see pages 244–5)
- Himmler (see pages 237–9)
- Streicher (see pages 89 and 223)
- Heydrich (see page 229).

It is all too easy to highlight the rhetoric of Nazi anti-Semitism as the reason for the success of the Party. Certainly, 37.3 per cent of the population may have voted for Hitler the anti-Semite in July 1932, but the vast majority of Germans were motivated by unemployment, the collapse of agricultural prices and the fear of communism. Indeed, in a 1934 survey into the reasons why people joined the Nazis, over 60 per cent did not even mention anti-Semitism.

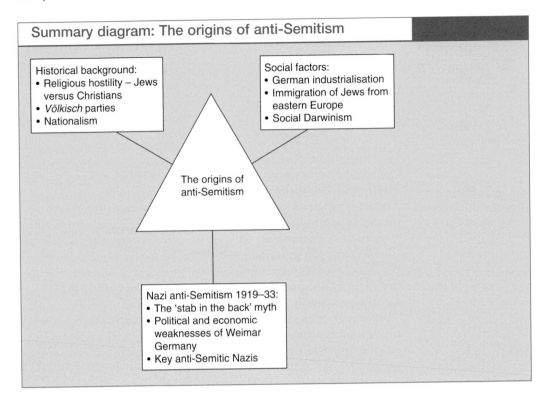

Summary diagram: The origins of anti-Semitism

Historical background:
- Religious hostility – Jews versus Christians
- *Völkisch* parties
- Nationalism

Social factors:
- German industrialisation
- Immigration of Jews from eastern Europe
- Social Darwinism

The origins of anti-Semitism

Nazi anti-Semitism 1919–33:
- The 'stab in the back' myth
- Political and economic weaknesses of Weimar Germany
- Key anti-Semitic Nazis

2 | Gradualism 1933–9

The Nazi approach to anti-Semitism was **gradualist**. The early moves against the Jews gave no suggestion of the end result. Indeed, for some Germans the discriminatory legislation was no more than the Jews deserved. For the more liberal minded, who found such action offensive, there was the practical problem of how to show opposition and to offer resistance. Once the apparatus of dictatorship was well established by the end of 1934, the futility of opposition was apparent to most people. Feelings of hopelessness were soon replaced by those of fear. To show sympathy for, or to protect the Jews, was to risk one's own freedom or one's own life. It was an unenviable dilemma.

Legal discrimination
Many radical Nazis were keen to take immediate measures against Jewish people and their businesses, but the Party's leadership was worried that it could get out of hand. And those concerns were confirmed when a one-day national boycott was organised for 1 April 1933. Jewish-owned shops, cafés and businesses were picketed by the SA, who stood outside urging people not to enter. However, the boycott was not universally accepted by the German people and it caused a lot of bad publicity abroad.

The Nazi leaders developed their anti-Semitism in a more subtle way. Once the Nazi regime had established the legal basis for its dictatorship (see pages 140–4), it was legally possible to initiate an anti-Jewish policy, most significantly by the creation of

Key question
Did Nazi anti-Semitism change over time?

Gradualism
Changing by degrees; progressing slowly.

Key term

First official boycott of Jewish shops and professions: 1 April 1933

Key date

Key date

Nuremberg Race
Laws introduced:
15 September 1935

the Nuremberg Laws in September 1935. This clearly stood in contrast to the extensive civil rights that the Jews had enjoyed in Weimar Germany. The discrimination against the Jews got worse as an ongoing range of laws was introduced (see Table 10.1). In this way all the rights of Jews were gradually removed even before the onset of the war.

Table 10.1: Major Nazi anti-Jewish laws 1933–9

Date		Law
1933	7 April	Law for the Restoration of the Professional Civil Service. Jews excluded from the government's civil service
	4 October	Law for the exclusion of Jewish journalists
1935	15 September	The Nuremberg Race Laws:
		Reich Citizenship Act. 'A citizen of the Reich is a subject who is only of German or kindred blood.' Jews lost their citizenship in Germany
		Law for the Protection of German Blood and German Honour. Marriages and extramarital relations between Jews and German citizens forbidden
1938	5 July	Decree prohibiting Jewish doctors practising medicine
	28 October	Decree to expel 17,000 Polish Jews resident in Germany
	15 November	Decree to exclude Jewish pupils from schools and universities
	3 December	Decree for the compulsory closure and sale of all Jewish businesses
1939	1 September	Decree for the introduction of curfew for Jews

Propaganda and indoctrination

Nazism also set out to cultivate the message of anti-Semitism; in effect to change people's attitudes so that they hated the Jews. Goebbels himself was a particularly committed anti-Semite and he used his skills as the Minister of Propaganda and Popular Enlightenment to indoctrinate the German people (see pages 244–5). All aspects of culture associated with the Jews were censored. Even more worrying was the full range of propaganda methods used to advance the anti-Semitic message, such as:

- posters and signs, e.g. 'Jews are not wanted here'
- newspapers, e.g. *Der Angriff*, which was founded by Goebbels himself; *Der Stürmer*, edited by the *Gauleiter* Julius Streicher, which was overtly anti-Semitic with a seedy range of articles devoted to pornography and violence
- cinema, e.g. *The Eternal Jew*; *Jud Süss*.

A particular aspect of anti-Semitic indoctrination was the emphasis placed on influencing the German youth. The message

Poster for the anti-Semitic film *The Eternal Jew*.

was obviously put across by the Hitler Youth, but all schools also conformed to new revised textbooks and teaching materials, e.g tasks and exam questions.

Terror and violence

In the early years of the regime, the SA, as the radical left wing of the Nazis, took advantage of their power at local level to use violence against Jews, e.g. damage of property, intimidation and physical attacks. However, after the Night of the Long Knives in June 1934 (see pages 151–3), anti-Semitic violence became more sporadic for two probable reasons. First, in 1936 there was a distinct decline in the anti-Semitic campaign because of the Berlin Olympics and the need to avoid international alienation.

Secondly, conservative forces still had a restraining influence. For example, Schacht had continued to express worries about the implications of anti-Semitic action for the economy (although he resigned in 1937 – see pages 171–3).

However, the events of 1938 were on a different scale. First, the union with Austria in March 1938 resulted, in the following month, in thousands of attacks on the 200,000 Jews of Vienna. Secondly, on 9–10 November 1938 there was a sudden violent **pogrom** against the Jews, which became known as the 'Night of Crystal Glass' (*Kristallnacht*) because of all the smashed glass. *Kristallnacht* started in Berlin and spread throughout Germany with dramatic effects: the destruction of numerous Jewish homes and 100 deaths, attacks on 10,000 Jewish shops and businesses, the burning down of 200 synagogues and the deportation of 20,000 to concentration camps. The excuse for this had been the assassination of Ernst von Rath, a German diplomat in Paris, by Herschel Grünspan, a Jew, on 7 November. Goebbels had hoped that the anti-Semitic actions might also win Hitler's favour, and compensate for Goebbels' disreputable affair with a Czech actress. It should be noted that much of the anti-Semitic legislation (see also page 223) came in the months after the pogrom.

Key term

Pogrom
An organised or encouraged massacre of innocent people. The term originated from the massacres of Jews in Russia.

Key dates

Kristallnacht, anti-Jewish pogrom:
9–10 November 1938

Creation of the Reich Central Office for Jewish Emigration: 1939

Forced emigration

From the start of the Nazi dictatorship a number of Jews had decided to leave Germany voluntarily. Many Jews with influence, high reputation or sufficient wealth could find the means to leave. The most popular destinations were Palestine, Britain and the USA, and among the most renowned emigrés were Albert Einstein, the scientist, and Kurt Weill, the composer.

However, from 1938 a new dimension to anti-Semitism developed – forced emigration. As a result of the events in Austria in 1938, the Central Office for Jewish Emigration was established in Vienna, overseen by Adolf Eichmann. Jewish property was confiscated to finance the emigration of poor Jews. Within six months Eichmann had forced the emigration of 45,000 and the scheme was seen as such a success that, in January 1939, Göring was prompted to create the Reich Central Office for Jewish Emigration run by Heydrich and Eichmann (see Table 10.2).

Table 10.2: The Jewish community in Germany 1933–45

	Jewish population	Emigrés per annum
1933	503,000	38,000
1939 (May)	234,000	78,000*
1945	20,000	N/A

* The cumulative figure of Jewish emigrés between 1933 and 1939 was 257,000

It is therefore estimated that the Nazi persecution led to about half of the Jewish population leaving before the war. Technically, the Jews had voluntarily emigrated but they were forced to leave behind all their belongings. Given those circumstances, the remainder decided to take their chances and stay in Germany, rather than lose their homes and all their possessions.

Conclusion

Key question
Why was the year 1938 so significant?

Despite the range of anti-Semitic measures of 1933–9, it is difficult to claim that the Nazis had pursued a planned overall policy to deal with 'the Jewish question'. In many respects the measures were at first haphazard. However, on one point it is very clear – the year 1938 marked an undoubted '**radicalisation**' of Nazi anti-Semitism. The legal laws, the violence connected with *Kristallnacht* and the forced emigration came together, suggesting that the regime had reached a pivotal year – a fact confirmed by the tone of the speech in the Reichstag by Hitler on 30 January 1939:

Radicalisation
A policy of increasing severity.

Key term

> If the international Jewish financiers in and outside Europe should succeed in plunging the nations once more into a world war, then the result will not be the Bolshevising [making communist] of the earth, and thus the victory of Jewry, but the annihilation of the Jewish race in Europe.

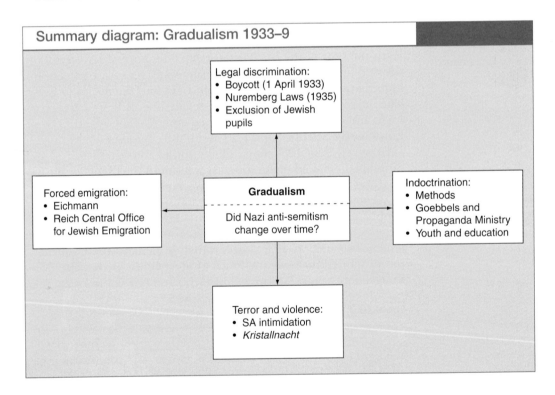

Summary diagram: Gradualism 1933–9

Legal discrimination:
- Boycott (1 April 1933)
- Nuremberg Laws (1935)
- Exclusion of Jewish pupils

Forced emigration:
- Eichmann
- Reich Central Office for Jewish Emigration

Gradualism

Did Nazi anti-semitism change over time?

Indoctrination:
- Methods
- Goebbels and Propaganda Ministry
- Youth and education

Terror and violence:
- SA intimidation
- *Kristallnacht*

3 | War and Genocide 1939–45

At the time it was inconceivable to imagine that the Holocaust was possible. Who in 1939 could have predicted the scenario of the next six years? The suggestion that millions would be systematically exterminated would have defied belief. It is an event in modern European history that even now seems almost beyond rational comprehension, although it had a terrifying logic to it. For those who lived in occupied Europe it was easier and more comfortable to dismiss the rumours as gross and macabre exaggerations, the result of wartime gossip and Allied propaganda. Yet, the unbelievable did happen and it required not only the actions of a 'criminal' minority but also the passivity of the 'innocent' majority. In Germany the moral dimension has helped to make this historical debate a particularly impassioned one.

From emigration to extermination

Germany's victory over Poland in autumn 1939 (see pages 257–8) meant that the Nazis inherited responsibility for an estimated three millions Jews. Moreover, the beginning of a general European war made emigration of Jews to independent countries more difficult. However, plans to 'resettle' so many people placed such a great strain on food supplies and the transportation system that, in the short term, the Nazi leadership in Poland were compelled to create a number of Jewish **ghettos**, e.g. Warsaw, Krakow and Lublin.

The invasion of Russia in summer 1941 marked a decisive development. From that time, it was seen as a racial war launched by the **SS _Einsatzgruppen_** that moved in behind the advancing armies. These four special 'Action Units' were responsible for rounding up local Jews and murdering them by mass shootings. During the winter of 1941–2 it is estimated that _Einsatzgruppen_ had killed 700,000 Jews in western Russia, but the bloody process clearly raised the practical implications for the Nazi leadership of finding a '**Final Solution**' to the Jewish question.

Nevertheless, there remains uncertainty and debate over when exactly it was decided to launch the genocide of the Jews (see pages 230–1). Options were probably being considered during autumn 1941, but it was only agreed as a result of the Wannsee Conference on 20 January 1942. There, in no more than a few hours, a meeting, chaired by Heydrich and organised by Eichmann, outlined the grim details of the plan to use gas to kill Europe's 11 million Jews.

In the course of 1942, a number of camps were developed into mass extermination centres in Poland, most notably Auschwitz, Sobibor and Treblinka, which were run by the Death's Head Units of the _Waffen_ SS (see pages 237–40). Most of the Polish Jews were cleared from their ghettos and then 'transported' by train in appalling conditions to their death in gas chambers. It is believed that, of the original three million Polish Jews, only 4000 survived the war. In 1943–4 Jews from all over Europe were deported to face a similar fate – so that by 1945 it is estimated that six million European Jews had been murdered.

Key date
Wannsee Conference. 'Final Solution' to exterminate the Jewish people: 20 January 1942

Key question
How did Nazi anti-Semitism degenerate into genocide?

Key terms

Ghetto
Ancient term describing the area lived in by the Jews in a city. Under Nazi occupation the Jews were separated from the rest of the community and forced to live in appalling and overcrowded conditions.

SS _Einsatzgruppen_
'Action Units'. Four of the units were launched in eastern Europe after the invasion of Russia. Responsible for rounding up local Jews and murdering them by mass shootings.

Final Solution
A euphemism used by the Nazi leadership to describe the extermination of the Jews from 1941.

Table 10.3: The Nazi extermination of the Jews 1940–5

Date		Event
1940		First deportations of Jews from some German provinces
1941	June	Action squads (*Einsatzgruppen*) of SS moved into the USSR behind the advancing armies to round up and kill Jews
1941	1 September	All Jews forced to wear the Yellow Star of David
1942	20 January	Wannsee Conference. Various government and Party agencies agreed on the 'Final Solution' to the Jewish problem
	Spring	Extermination facilities set up at Auschwitz, Sobibor and Treblinka
1943	February	Destruction of Warsaw Ghetto
1943–4		Transportation of Jews from all over German-occupied Europe to death camps began
1945	27 January	Liberation of Auschwitz by Soviet troops

Henri Pieck, *Behind Barbed Wire*. Painting drawn in Buchenwald concentration camp.

Profile: Reinhard Heydrich 1904–42

1904		– Born at Halle in Saxony, Germany
1922–8		– Joined the navy but discharged (probably for a sexual offence against a woman)
1931		– Joined the NSDAP and the SS
1932		– Appointed leader of the newly created SD (the Party's intelligence security service, see pages 238–9)
1934	June	– Worked closely with Himmler in the Night of the Long Knives. Appointed SS Lieutenant-General
1936		– Appointed Chief of Secret Police (but still under Himmler's authority)
1939	January	– Created Reich Central Office for Jewish Emigration
	September	– Appointed Head of RSHA (Reich Security Head Office), but still under Himmler's authority
1941		– Reich Protector of Bohemia and Moravia (Czech lands)
1942	January	– Chaired the Wannsee Conference meeting to exterminate the Jews
	May	– Assassinated by the Czech resistance in Prague

Heydrich was undoubtedly talented – he was not only physically the image of the perfect Aryan but also a very good sportsman and a talented musician and linguist. Yet, his skills gave way to the dominating traits of selfishness, ambition and brutality that earned him the title of 'the butcher of Prague'. He advanced extremely quickly within the SS, so at the age of 32 he was appointed Chief of Secret Police. With his abilities he was responsible for:

- developing and running the policing system of surveillance and repression
- implementing the Nazi racial policy
- chairing the notorious meeting at Wannsee Conference which agreed on the Final Solution.

Key question
Why were the Gypsies persecuted?

Gypsies

In addition to the Jews, the Gypsies (Sinti and Roma) were also subject to racial persecution and became victims of Nazi genocide. The Gypsies had been viewed as 'outsiders' throughout European history for several clear reasons:

- they were non-Christian and they had their own Romany customs and dialect
- they were non-white – because they had originated from India in the late medieval period
- their 'traveller' lifestyle with no regular employment was resented.

So, even before the Nazi dictatorship and during Weimar's liberal years, there was official hostility towards the Gypsies and, in 1929, 'The Central Office for the Fight against the Gypsies' was established.

By 1933 it is believed that the number of Gypsies in Germany was about 25,000–30,000, and they, too, were beginning to suffer from the gradualist policy of Nazi discrimination:

- Gypsies were defined exactly like the Jews as 'infallibly of alien blood' according to the Nuremberg Laws of 1935.
- Himmler issued, in 1938, a directive titled 'The Struggle against the Gypsy Plague', which ordered the registration of Gypsies in racial terms.
- Straight after the outbreak of the war, Gypsies were deported from Germany to Poland – and their movements were severely controlled in working camps. Notoriously, in January 1940, the first case of mass murder through gassing was committed by the Nazis against Gypsy children at Buchenwald.

As with the Jews, the Gypsies during the war were the focus of ever increasing repression and violence but there was no real, systematic Nazi policy of extermination until the end of 1942. In the first months of 1943 Germany's Gypsies were sent to Auschwitz camp and over 1943–4 a large proportion of Europe's Gypsy population from south-eastern Europe was exterminated, a figure between 225,000 and 500,000.

Conclusion

Key question
Why did the Holocaust happen?

The issue of the Holocaust remains one of the most fundamental controversies in history. For some historians Hitler remains the key, as he was committed to the extermination of the Jews at an early stage in his political career. It is argued that this was followed by a consistent gradualist policy, which led logically from the persecution of 1933 to the gates of Auschwitz. In the simplest form these historians suggest that the Holocaust happened because Hitler willed it. On the other hand, other historians have rejected the idea of a long-term plan for mass extermination. Instead, they have suggested that the 'Final Solution' came to be implemented as a result of the chaotic nature of government during the war. As a result, various institutions and individuals improvised a policy to deal with the military and human situation in eastern Europe by the end of 1941. Schleunes therefore describes the road to Auschwitz as a 'twisted one' and concludes, 'the Final Solution as it emerged in 1941 and 1942 was *not* the product of grand design'.

This controversy has generated a close scrutiny and analysis of the available evidence, particularly in the past 20 years. So, although the exact details are not clear, it seems fair to conclude the following points about the 'Final Solution':

- The initial arrangements for the implementation of the 'Final Solution' were haphazard and makeshift and the Nazi leadership did not have any clear programme to deal with the Jewish question until 1941.
- No written order for the killing of the Jews from Hitler has been found, although in January 1944, Himmler publicly stated that Hitler had given him 'a *Führer* order' to give priority to 'the total solution of the Jewish question' and clearly Hitler had often spoken in violent and barbaric terms about the Jews throughout his career.
- Probably around autumn 1941 it was decided by the top Nazi leadership to launch an extermination policy and this was agreed at the Wannsee Conference in January 1942 by a broad range of representatives of Nazi organisations.

In the light of these points the terrible outcome of the 'Final Solution' could be explained as a pragmatic (practical) response to the confusion and chaos of war in 1941–2, rather than the culmination of long-term ideological intent.

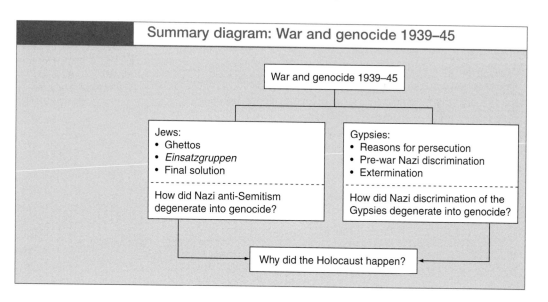

Summary diagram: War and genocide 1939–45

Study Guide: AS Question

In the style of OCR A

'Nazi racial policy was radicalised in 1938.' How far do you agree in relation to the period 1933–45? (50 marks)

Exam tips

'How far … ?' is a clear command to consider both the extent of change and whether there is an alternative date to 1938 to consider instead. That naturally gives your answer two sections to consider, but be aware that those two parts may not be totally separate: the pace and nature of development were related. Be clear what radicalisation means so that you address it properly in your answer: a major change in the scale and extent. Nazi racial policy was certainly introduced gradually from 1933, and historians are far from sure whether that means that racial policy was being worked out as they went along or whether a blueprint existed from the start and that policy initiatives were introduced slowly. The stage-by-stage approach may be shown clearly by highlighting the chronological way in which actions were taken, first in 1933, then 1935, then 1938 and then 1939 (but do not write out a long list, let alone describe each one in turn). Consider what was so special about the events of 1938 that might mark a 'radical' change in pace and/or intensity compared to, say, the Nuremberg Laws (1935). How might Hitler's speech of January 1939 about 'the annihilation of the Jewish race' show this? In this, do not forget to think about an alternative date being even more significant for radicalising racial policy. You will already have thought about 1935. The other possibility is 1941–2 and the decision to implement the 'Final Solution'. Weigh up these possibilities and reach your decision.

11 The Nazi Regime

POINTS TO CONSIDER
It is all too easy to assume that the Nazi consolidation of power in 1933–4 led to Hitler creating an all-powerful personal dictatorship. Yet, there were various other important forces in the Nazi regime and the Third Reich, as well as political resistance, particularly during the war. The main areas to consider are:

- The role of Hitler
- The apparatus of the police state
- The propaganda machine
- Resistance

Key dates

1934	June 30	Night of the Long Knives
1935		Mass arrests by *Gestapo* of socialists and communists
1936	June	Appointment of Heinrich Himmler as Chief of the German Police
1938	September	Planned *putsch* by General Beck if war resulted from Czech crisis
1939	September	Creation of RSHA
1942		Red Orchestra discovered and closed down
1942–3	Winter	Military 'turn of the tide'; German defeats at El Alamein and Stalingrad
		White Rose student group; distribution of anti-Nazi leaflets
1944	July	Stauffenberg Bomb Plot on 20 July failed to overthrow regime. Army purged

1 | The Role of Hitler

Key question
What was the role of Hitler in Nazi Germany?

In theory, Hitler's power was unlimited. Nazi Germany was a one-party state and Hitler was undisputed leader of that Party. In addition, after the death of Hindenburg in August 1934, the law concerning the head of state of the German Reich combined the posts of president and chancellor. Constitutionally, Hitler was

Ein Volk, Ein Reich, Ein Führer. Hitler at the centre of Germany. This postcard is dated 13 March 1938, the day after the Nazi take-over of Austria.

also commander-in-chief of all the armed services. (This image of Hitler was very much presented in the postcard shown above: *Ein Volk, Ein Reich, Ein Führer.* 'One people, one empire, one leader.')

'Führer power'

However, if one studies contemporary documents, such as this extract from a leading Nazi theorist, E. Huber, it is clear that Hitler's personal dictatorship was portrayed in more than purely legal terms:

> If we wish to define political power in the *völkisch Reich* correctly, we must not speak of 'state power' but of '*Führer* power'. For it is not the state as an impersonal entity that is the source of political power, but rather political power is given to the *Führer* as the executor of the nation's common will. '*Führer* power' is comprehensive and total: it unites within itself all means of creative political activity: it embraces all spheres of national life.

Huber's grandiose theoretical claims for '*Führer* power' could not mask basic practical problems. First, there was no all-embracing constitution in the Third Reich. The government and law of Nazi Germany emerged over time in a haphazard fashion. Secondly, there was (and is) no way one individual could ever be in control of all aspects of government. Thus, Hitler was still dependent on sympathetic subordinates to put policy decisions into effect. And thirdly, Hitler's own personality and attitude towards government were mixed and not conducive to strong and effective leadership.

Hitler's character

Hitler certainly appeared as the charismatic and dynamic leader. His magnetic command of an audience enabled him to play on 'mass suggestion'; he portrayed himself as the ordinary man with the vision, willpower and determination to transform the country.

However, this was an image perpetuated by the propaganda machine and, once in government, Hitler's true character revealed itself, as is shown in the memoirs of one of his retinue:

> Hitler normally appeared shortly before lunch … When Hitler stayed at Obersalzberg it was even worse. There he never left his room before 2.00 pm. He spent most afternoons taking a walk, in the evening straight after dinner, there were films … He disliked the study of documents. I have sometimes secured decisions from him without his ever asking to see the relevant files. He took the view that many things sorted themselves out on their own if one did not interfere … He let people tell him the things he wanted to hear, everything else he rejected. One still sometimes hears the view that Hitler would have done the right thing if people surrounding him had not kept him wrongly informed. Hitler refused to let himself be informed … How can one tell someone the truth who immediately gets angry when the facts do not suit him?

Hitler liked to cultivate the image of the artist and really he was quite lazy. This was accentuated further by Hitler's lifestyle: his unusual sleeping hours; his long periods of absence from Berlin when he stayed in the Bavarian Alps; his tendency to become immersed in pet projects such as architectural plans. Furthermore, as he got older he became neurotic and moody as was demonstrated in his obsession with his health and medical symptoms, both real and imagined.

Hitler was not well educated and had no experience for any role in government or administration. As cynics say, Hitler's first real job was his appointment as chancellor. He followed no real working routine, he loathed paperwork and disliked the formality of committees in which issues were discussed. He glibly believed that mere willpower was the solution to most problems.

Hitler's leadership

Key question
Was Hitler an
effective dictator?

Surprisingly, Hitler was not always very assertive when it came to making a decision. Although he was presented to the world as the all-powerful dictator he never showed any inclination to co-ordinate government. For example, the role of the cabinet declined quite markedly after 1934. In 1933 the cabinet met 72 times, but only four times in 1936 and the last official cabinet meeting was held in February 1938. Consequently, the rivalry between the various factions in the Third Reich was rife and decision-making became, more often than not, the result of the *Führer*'s whim or an informal conversation rather than rational clear-cut chains of command.

Yet, Hitler somehow still played a decisive role in the development of the Third Reich. In a telling phrase, historian Norman Rich wrote: 'The point cannot be stressed too strongly. Hitler was master in the Third Reich' and this was because:

- Hitler ran a deliberate policy of 'divide and rule'.
- Hitler took responsibility for making the 'big' decisions that shaped the direction of Nazi Germany, e.g. foreign policy.
- Despite other power bases, Hitler preserved his own authority by tolerating only key Nazis, who were personally loyal, for example Himmler.

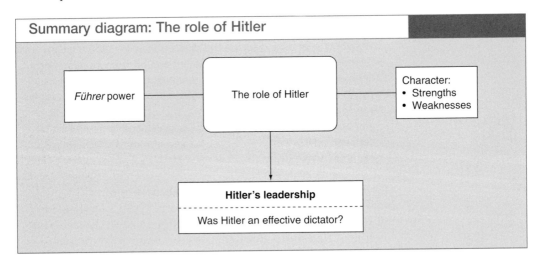

Summary diagram: The role of Hitler

Führer power — The role of Hitler — Character:
- Strengths
- Weaknesses

Hitler's leadership

Was Hitler an effective dictator?

2 | The Police State

Key question
How did the SS
emerge?

Although by July 1933 Germany had become a one-party state, in which the Nazi Party claimed sole political authority, there was really a whole array of Party and state institutions within the system of government:

- the Party with its own organisations, e.g. the Hitler Youth
- the state's institutions with its own organisations, e.g. the government ministries and the judiciary (see Figure 11.1).

However, amidst all the confusion of the state and Party structure there emerged an organisation that was to become the mainstay

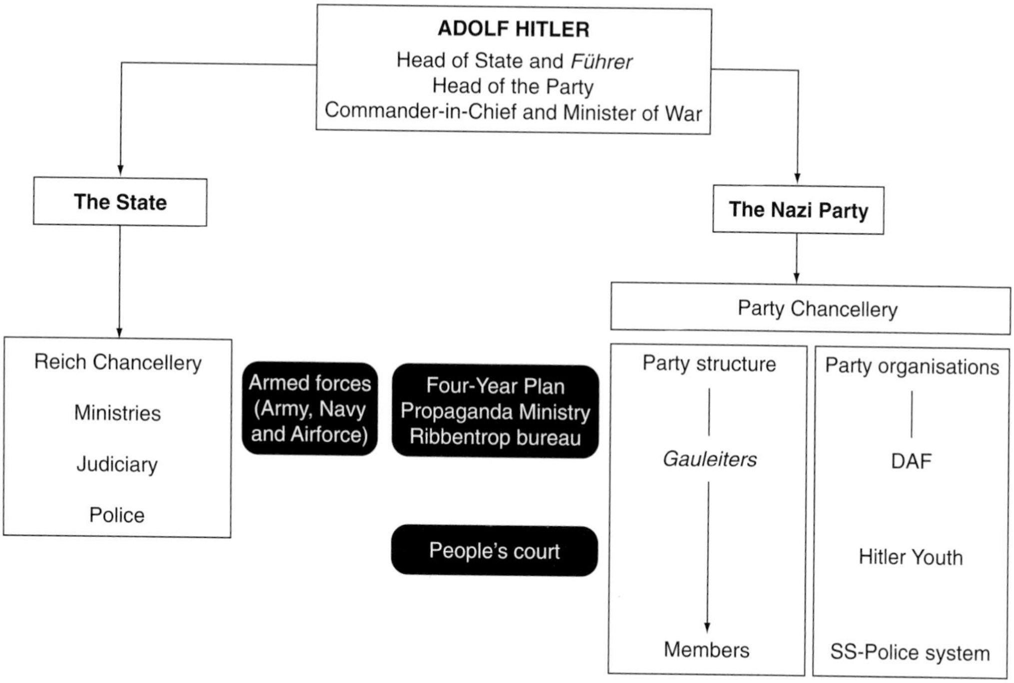

Figure 11.1: The structure of the Third Reich.

of the Third Reich – the SS. The SS developed an identity and structure of its own which kept it separate from the state and yet, through its dominance of police matters, linked it with the state.

The emergence of Himmler and the SS

The SS had been formed in 1925 as an élite bodyguard for Hitler, but it remained a relatively minor section of the SA, with only 250 members, until Himmler became its leader in 1929. By 1933 the SS numbered 52,000, and it had established a reputation for blind obedience and total commitment to the Nazi cause.

Himmler had also created in 1931 a special security service, Sicherheitsdienst (SD), to act as the Party's own internal security police. In the course of 1933–4 he assumed control of all the police in the *Länder*, including the **Gestapo** in Prussia. Thus, Hitler turned to Himmler's SS to carry out the purge of June 1934 (see page 152). The loyalty and brutal efficiency of the SS on the Night of the Long Knives had its rewards, for it now became an independent organisation within the Party. Two years later all police powers were unified under Himmler's control as '*Reichsführer* SS and Chief of all German Police', including the *Gestapo*. In 1939 all party and state police organisations involving police and security matters were amalgamated into the **RSHA**, overseen by Himmler but actually co-ordinated by his deputy, Heydrich (see Figure 11.2 on page 238).

Key terms

Gestapo
Geheime Staats Polizei: Secret State Police.

RSHA
Reich Security Office, which amalgamated all police and security organisations.

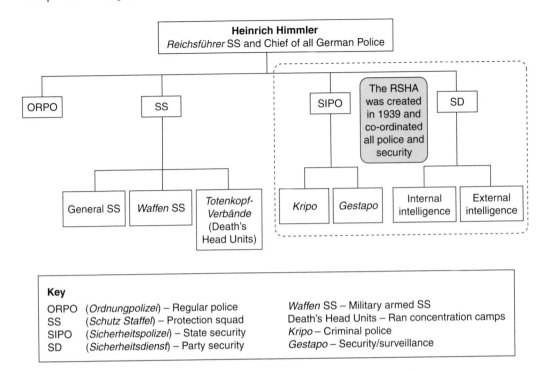

Figure 11.2: The SS-Police system in 1939.

The SS-Police system that had been created, therefore, served three main functions:

- Intelligence gathering by the SD. It was responsible for all intelligence and security and was controlled by its leader Heydrich, but still part of the SS. All its responsibilities grew as occupied lands spread.
- Policing by the *Gestapo* and the *Kripo*. The *Kripo* was responsible for the maintenance of general law and order, e.g. dealing with asocials and thieves. In 1936 the *Kripo* was linked with the *Gestapo*. The *Gestapo* was the key policing organisation for upholding the regime by using surveillance and repression. It had a reputation for brutality and it could arrest and detain anyone without trial – although its thoroughness and effectiveness have been questioned (see page 240).
- Military action by the first units of the **Waffen SS**. Up to 1938 it consisted of about 14,000 soldiers in three units – but it was racially pure, fanatically loyal and committed to Nazi ideology. From 1938 its influence grew rapidly. This was affected by the political weakening of the German army and also by the more anti-Semitic policies (see pages 225–6).

It is important to keep in perspective the extent of the position of the SS in the years 1933–9. The embryonic power of the SS had definitely been created. With the take-over of territories in 1939 the creation of the '**New Order**' really began – it was from that time that the personnel and influence of the SS expanded enormously.

Key terms

Waffen SS
Armed SS – the number of divisions grew during the war from three to 35.

New Order
Used by the Nazis to describe the economic, political and racial integration of Europe under the Third Reich.

Profile: Heinrich Himmler 1900–45

1900		– Born in Munich in Bavaria, Germany
1917–18		– Joined the cadets, but did not face action in First World War
1919–22		– Studied agriculture at the Munich Technical University
1923		– Joined the Nazi Party
1923	November	– Took part in the Munich Beer Hall *putsch*
1929		– Appointed leader of the SS
1930		– Elected as Nazi deputy of the *Reichstag*
1934	June	– Arranged the purge of the SA in the Night of Long Knives
1936		– Given responsibility as '*Reichsführer* SS and Chief of all German Police'
1939		– Created himself as the Commissar of the Strengthening of the German Nationhood
		– Formed the RSHA
1943		– Appointed Minister of Interior (replacing Frick)
1944		– Appointed as Commander-in-Chief of the Home Army
1945	May	– Arrested by British forces but committed suicide before trial

Key dates

Night of the Long Knives: 30 June 1934

Appointment of Heinrich Himmler as Chief of the German Police: June 1936

Creation of RSHA: September 1939

Himmler was in many respects a nondescript uninspiring character who before 1929 achieved little in his work or in the Party. Yet, with a reputation for an organised, obsessive, hard-working style, he became the leader of the brutally efficient SS machine which really held the Third Reich together.

When he was appointed leader of the SS he quickly converted the small group of 250 into a committed élite force of 52,000. Yet, until 1934 Himmler and the SS remained very much in the shadow of Röhm and the SA – it was his decision to take responsibility for the purge in the Night of the Long Knives that proved to be his real turning point.

From that time Himmler's political power continued to increase right until the collapse of the Third Reich. He must therefore undoubtedly take responsibility for:

- the development and control of the apparatus of terror which by surveillance and repression created the system of control
- the pursuit of his aim to create a German master-race and the development of élite institutions like *Lebensborn* and the *Ordensburgen* (see pages 207 and 191, respectively)
- the extermination of the subhuman races, such as the Jews and the Gypsies, in the concentration camps
- the exploitation of all the occupied lands for slave labour and arms production
- the development of the *Waffen* SS as an élite military force that matched the might of the German army by the end of the war.

The SS state

As *Reichsführer* SS, Himmler controlled a massive police apparatus that was answerable only to Hitler. The SS system had grown into one of the key power blocs in the Third Reich. The SS-Police system became, in effect, in the words of E. Kogon, a '**state within a state**'. It was a huge vested interest, which numbered 250,000 in 1939 and had begun to eclipse other interest groups in terms of power and influence. With the onset of war this tendency was accentuated further. As German troops gained control over more and more areas of Europe, the power of the SS was inevitably enhanced:

Key question
How powerful was the SS?

State within a state
A situation where the authority and government of the state are threatened by a rival power base.

Key term

- Security. All responsibilities of policing and intelligence expanded as occupied lands spread. The job of internal security became much greater and SS officers were granted severe powers to crush opposition.
- Military. The *Waffen* SS increased from three divisions in 1939 to 35 in 1945, which developed into a 'second army' – committed, brutal and militarily highly rated. By 1944 the SS was so powerful it rivalled the power of the German army.
- Economy. The SS became responsible for the creation of the 'New Order' in the occupied lands of eastern Europe. Such a scheme provided opportunities for plunder and power on a massive scale, which members of the SS exploited to the full. By the end of the war the SS had created a massive commercial organisation of over 150 firms, which exploited slave labour to extract raw materials and to manufacture textiles, armaments and household goods.
- Ideology and race. The racial policy of extermination and resettlement was pursued with vigour and the system of concentration camps was widely established and run by the SS Death's Head Units (see also pages 226–30). The various 'inferior' races were even used for their economic value.

The SS was not immune to the rivalries and arguments which typified Nazi Germany. Disagreements often arose, particularly with local *Gauleiters* and the governors of the occupied territories. Moreover, despite the traditional image of Nazism as an all-knowing totalitarian police state, *Gestapo* policing had clear limitations:

- It only had no more than 40,000 agents for the whole of Germany, so a large city, like Frankfurt, with about half a million people, was policed by just about 40–50 agents.
- Most of the work for the *Gestapo* was actually prompted by public informers, which were caused more often by gossip and generated enormous paperwork for limited return.
- The *Gestapo* had relatively few 'top agents', so it coped by over-relying on the work of the *Kripo*.

The oppression of Jews began early in Hitler's regime. Especially persecuted were the *Ostjuden* (Jews from eastern Europe, who had settled in Germany). Here, plainclothes *Gestapo* agents take Jews into custody.

Nevertheless, the SS state under Himmler not only preserved the Nazi regime through its brutal, repressive and often arbitrary policies of law enforcement, but gradually extended its influence. In this way it evolved over time into the key power group in the Third Reich.

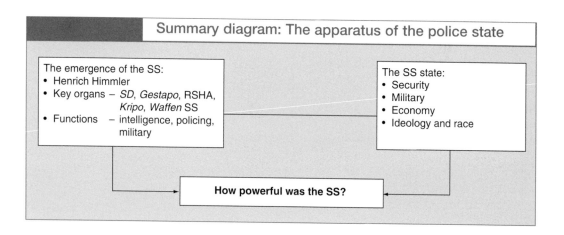

Summary diagram: The apparatus of the police state

The emergence of the SS:
- Henrich Himmler
- Key organs – *SD, Gestapo*, RSHA, *Kripo, Waffen* SS
- Functions – intelligence, policing, military

The SS state:
- Security
- Military
- Economy
- Ideology and race

How powerful was the SS?

3 | The Nazi Propaganda Machine

Key question
How did Nazi propaganda use the media?

Despite the power of the Nazi police apparatus, it would be too simple to suggest that the regime maintained itself in power simply by the use of terror and repression. From the very start both Hitler and Goebbels recognised how important propaganda could be as a vital cog in the Nazis state. As Goebbels stated at his very first press conference on 15 March 1933:

> I view the first task of the new ministry as being to establish co-ordination between the government and the whole people ... If the means achieves the end, the means is good. Whether it always satisfies stringent aesthetic criteria or not is immaterial.

As a result considerable resources were directed towards the development of the propaganda machine in order to achieve the following aims:

- to glorify the regime
- to spread the Nazi ideology and values (and by implication to censor the unacceptable)
- to win over the people and to integrate the nation's diverse elements.

Under the Nazis all means of public communication were brought under state control.

Radio

Goebbels (and Hitler) had always recognised the effectiveness of the spoken word over the written and they had already begun to use new technology during the election campaigns of 1932–3. Up until this time, German broadcasting had been organised by regional states. Once in power, Goebbels efficiently brought all broadcasting under Nazi control by the creation of the Reich Radio Company. Furthermore, he arranged the dismissal of 13 per cent of the staff on political and racial grounds, and replaced them with his own men. He told his broadcasters in March 1933:

> I am placing a major responsibility in your hands, for you have in your hands the most modern instrument in existence for influencing the masses. By this instrument you are the creators of public opinion.

Yet, control of broadcasting was of little value in terms of propaganda unless the people had the means to receive it. In 1932 less than 25 per cent of German households owned a wireless – though that was quite a high figure compared to the rest of the world. Consequently, the Nazi government made provision for the production of a cheap set, the People's Receiver (*Volksempfänger*). Radio was a new and dynamic medium and access increased markedly. By 1939, 70 per cent of German homes had a radio – the highest national figure in the world – and it became a medium of mass communication controlled completely by the regime.

'All Germany hears the *Führer* on the People's Radio.' The cheapness and popularity of the People's Radio made it easier for the Nazis to spread their propaganda.

Broadcasting was also directed at public places. The installation of loudspeakers in restaurants and cafés, factories and offices made them all into venues for collective listening. 'Radio wardens' were even appointed, whose duty it was to co-ordinate the listening process.

Press

Control of the press was not so easily achieved by Goebbels. Germany had over 4700 daily newspapers in 1933 – a result of the strong regional identities which still existed in a state that had only been unified in 1871. Moreover, the papers were all owned privately, and traditionally owed no loyalty to central government; their loyalty was to their publishing company, religion or political party.

Profile: Josef Goebbels 1897–1945

1897		– Born in the Rhineland. Disabled by a clubbed foot which affected his walking
1914–18		– Excused military service on the grounds of his disability
1917–21		– Attended the university of Heidelberg and graduated as a doctor of philosophy
1924		– Joined the Nazi Party. Originally, a supporter of the radical Nazi Gregor Strasser
1926		– Broke with Strasser and sided with Hitler
		– Hitler appointed him as *Gauleiter* of Berlin
1927		– Created the Nazi newspaper *Der Angriff*
1928		– Appointed member of the *Reichstag*
1930		– Put in charge of Party propaganda
1933	March	– Joined the cabinet and appointed Minister of Public Enlightenment and Propaganda, a post which he held until 1945
	May	– Encouraged the burning of 'un-German books'
1938		– His affair with Lida Baarova undermined his position with Hitler
	November	– Issued the orders for the anti-Semitic attacks of *Kristallnacht*
1943	February	– Called for 'total war' to rouse the nation after the defeat at Stalingrad
1945	April	– Committed suicide after poisoning his children and shooting his wife

Goebbels was a man from a humble background with many talents who became one of the few intellectuals in the Nazi leadership. However, he suffered from a strong inferiority complex over his physical limitations and he became an embittered and committed anti-Semite.

He was always a radical Nazi and, originally, a supporter of the Strassers, although he became a long-term loyal supporter of Hitler from 1926. As propaganda chief of the Party from 1930, he played a crucial role in exploiting every possible method to sell the Nazi image in the series of elections, 1930–3.

Once he became Minster of Propaganda, he developed the whole range of the regime's propaganda techniques that were frighteningly ahead of their time. Unscrupulous and amoral in his methods, he was mainly responsible for:

- using all possible methods to advance the idea of Nazi totalitarianism
- censoring all non-Nazi culture and media
- promoting all the main ideological ideas of Nazism.

He was a very highly skilled orator and he remained a central figure until the final collapse of the regime, though other leading Nazis, such as Göring and Ribbentrop, distrusted him. His rivals also exploited his many love affairs to undermine his position and he became quite isolated in the years 1938–42. But with his personal leadership and his organisational skills he played an important part in the final two years of the war in making the nation ready for total war:

- he organised help for people in the bombed cities
- he took the initiative and gave the orders to put down the July Bomb Plot (see pages 249–50)
- he maintained civilian morale against all the odds, e.g. by visiting bombed cities (unlike Hitler)
- he took the responsibility to mobilise the last efforts to resist the Allied advance.

Various measures were taken to achieve Nazi control.

- First, the Nazi publishing house, *Eher Verlag*, bought up numerous newspapers, so that by 1939 it controlled two-thirds of the German press.
- Secondly, the various news agencies were merged into one, the DNB. This was state controlled, with the result that news material was vetted even before it got to the journalists.
- Thirdly, Goebbels introduced a daily press conference at the Propaganda Ministry to provide guidance on editorial policy.
- Finally, by the so-called Editors' Law of October 1933, newspaper content was made the sole responsibility of the editor; it became his job to satisfy the requirements of the Propaganda Ministry, or face the appropriate consequences. In this way, as one historian has explained, 'There was no need for censorship because the editor's most important function was that of censor.'

To a large extent, the Nazis succeeded in muzzling the press so that even the internationally renowned *Frankfurter Zeitung* was forced to close in 1943. However, the price of that success was the evolution of a bland and sterile journalism, which undoubtedly contributed to a 10 per cent decline in newspaper circulation before 1939.

Key question
How did Nazism try to create a new social ritual?

Nazi ritual

One final aspect of the Goebbels propaganda machine was the deliberate attempt to create a new kind of social ritual. The *Heil Hitler* greeting, the Nazi salute, the **Horst Wessel** anthem and the preponderance of militaristic uniforms were all intended to strengthen the individual's identity with the regime. This was further encouraged by the establishment of a series of public festivals to commemorate historic days in the Nazi calendar (see Table 11.1).

Table 11.1: Historic days in the Nazi calendar

30 January	The seizure of power (1933)
24 February	Party Foundation Day (1925)
16 March	Heroes' Remembrance Day (War Dead)
20 April	Hitler's birthday
1 May	National Day of Labour
2nd Sunday in May	Mothering Sunday
21 June	Summer solstice
2nd Sunday of July	German culture
September	Nuremberg Party Rally
October	Harvest festival
9 November	The Munich *putsch* (1923)
Winter solstice	Pagan festival to counter Christmas

Conclusion

Although control of the press and radio was Goebbels's major objective, he gradually extended his influence so that film, music, literature and art all came under the control of the Reich (as was shown in Chapter 9, pages 208–11). However, it is very difficult for historians to assess the effectiveness of Nazi propaganda. The extent of its influence clearly has massive implications for the whole thorny issue of public opinion.

> **Key question**
> How effective was Nazi propaganda?

Historians initially assumed rather too glibly that Nazi propaganda was a major achievement because it was possible to highlight the way Goebbels exploited all the means for propaganda – photographs, Party rallies, sport, festivals. This view was underlined by Herzstein's book in the 1960s, *The War That Hitler Won*. However, more recent research from oral history of local studies has raised serious doubts about its effectiveness and tended to show that the degree of success of propaganda varied according to different purposes. Very generally it is felt that propaganda succeeded in the sense that it:

- cultivated the 'Hitler myth' of him as an all-powerful leader
- strengthened the Nazi regime after Germany's economic and political crisis, 1929–33
- appealed effectively to reinforce established family values and German nationalism.

On the other hand, propaganda failed markedly in its attempt:

- to denounce the Christian Churches
- to seduce the working classes away from their established identity through the ideal of *Volksgemeinschaft*
- to develop a distinctive Nazi culture (see pages 208–11).

Such points give backing to the view that the propaganda machine was of secondary importance compared to the power and influence of the SS-Police system in upholding the Third Reich.

Summary diagram: The Nazi propaganda machine

Aims

- glorification of regime
- spreading Nazi ideology
- integrating the nation

Radio

Press

Means

Role of Goebbels

Nazi ritual

Culture
(see Chapter 9)

Conclusion

How effective was Nazi propaganda?

---

4 | Resistance

Active resistance to the Nazi regime failed and the Third Reich only collapsed when Germany was defeated by the Allies. So those who organised activities aimed at subverting the regime – however gloriously and heroically portrayed – made enormous personal sacrifices without making any real impression on the Nazi stranglehold of power. The real question is why did they fail?

Communists

Key question
Why was active communist resistance to the Nazi state so limited?

Key dates

Mass arrests by *Gestapo* of socialists and communists: 1935

Red Orchestra cell discovered and closed down: 1942

Although the Communist Party (KPD) had a mass membership of 300,000 and polled 17 per cent of the popular vote in 1932, it felt the full force of Nazi repression from the very start (see page 143). Over half of its members were interned during the first year of Nazi rule. By 1935 the *Gestapo* had infiltrated the remains of the Party, which had tried to continue with the distribution of printed pamphlets and posters and involvement in minor acts of sabotage.

There followed a series of mass trials, although the communist underground movement was never entirely broken in spite of this onslaught. Many small communist cells continued to be formed by Wilhelm Knöckel in many of the large German cities. The most famous of the communist cells was the so-called Red Orchestra (*Rote Kapelle*), a spy network that successfully permeated the government and military through the aristocratic sympathiser Schulz-Boysen. From 1938 to 1942 it transmitted vital information back to Moscow – but all the members were eventually caught and tortured appallingly.

However, the impact of communist activities should not be overstated and German communists failed because:

- Leading activists after 1936 were also drawn away from Germany to fight for the Republicans against the Fascists in the **Spanish Civil War** in the belief that such a gesture was a more worthwhile way of resisting fascism.
- They took their orders from Moscow and yet in the 1930s Stalin purged elements of the whole communist movement.
- They were fatally compromised by the **Nazi–Soviet Pact** of 1939–41.
- Even when the USSR and Germany did end up at war with each other in June 1941 the resistance groups remained isolated.

Active communist resistance to the Nazi state was limited and in the end it really became more geared towards self-preservation, so that it was ready for the day when Nazism would be defeated and the Soviet 'liberation' could take place.

Spanish Civil War
The 1936–9 conflict between Republicans, who supported the democratic government, and the Nationalists/ Fascists (financially and militarily backed by Italy and Germany).

Key term

Students: the White Rose Group

The White Rose student resistance movement is probably the most famous of the youth groups because it went beyond mere dissent. It was led by brother and sister Hans and Sophie Scholl. *The White Rose* (the symbol of peace) was the name given to a series of leaflets printed in 1942–3 and distributed initially amongst the students of Munich University but in time to many towns in central Germany. The content of the leaflets was highly political and openly condemned the moral and spiritual values of the Nazi regime. One of the early leaflets was entitled 'Isn't every decent German today ashamed of his government?'

The group represented a brave gesture of defiance and self-sacrifice. However, from the start the group's security was weak and it was only a matter of time before the *Gestapo* closed in. In February 1943 the six leaders were arrested, tortured and swiftly executed. Sophie Scholl openly said to the court:

> What we wrote and said is in the minds of you all. You just don't say it aloud.

Key question
Did the White Rose Group achieve anything?

White Rose student group and the distribution of anti-Nazi leaflets: 1942–3

Key date

Nazi–Soviet Pact
A non-aggression pact between the USSR and Germany that opened the way for the invasion of Poland.

Key term

Conservative élites

It might seem surprising that the most influential active resistance emerged from the ranks of Germany's upper classes, who dominated the civil service and, most particularly, the officer corps. After all, these were the very same conservative nationalists who had given sympathetic backing to Nazi authoritarianism (see page 133). Yet, the army as an institution was never fully 'co-ordinated' (until the summer 1944) and therefore it enjoyed a degree of freedom from Nazi control. Moreover, with its access to arms, the army had the real capacity to resist. For these reasons the development of the active resistance of the German élites formed around the army, although once again it was to fail in its primary objective.

The opposition of the conservative élites emerged slowly. At first, most of them could give qualified support of Nazism for:

Key question
Why did Germany's 'active resistance' fail to undermine the Third Reich?

- its attacks on the left-wing movement
- its dismantling of the democratic system and the restoration of an authoritarian rule
- its hostility towards the Treaty of Versailles
- its demands for rearmament.

Most significantly, the army gave its blessing to the Night of the Long Knives which fatally linked itself with the regime (see pages 151–3). At first, then, the conservative élites did not recognise – or did not want to recognise – the true radical nature of Nazism. They unwittingly strengthened the regime to such an extent that resistance afterwards became much more difficult.

Diplomatic and military success 1938–42

Planned *putsch* by General Beck if war resulted from Czech crisis: 1938

Key date

The year 1938 marked the emergence of a real conservative resistance. Ulrich von Hassell, the ex-ambassador in Rome, and Carl Goerdeler, Mayor of Leipzig and a one-time member of Hitler's early government, both joined the Nazi opposition at this time. More significantly, Ludwig Beck, formerly Chief of the General Staff, became convinced by the summer of 1938 that Hitler's intention to invade Czechoslovakia could only lead to a continental war against Britain and France. Plans were drawn up to stage a *coup* and overtures were also made to the British Foreign Office. As it happened, the Allied **appeasement** of Hitler at Munich cut the ground from beneath the conspirators and the planned revolt was dropped while Hitler took the glory for his diplomatic gains.

Key term

Appeasement
Making concessions in order to satisfy an aggressor. In this context, it refers to the Anglo-French policy of the 1930s towards Hitler's territorial demands.

Military failings 1942–4

Effective resistance began to re-emerge in the winter months of 1942–3 with the military disasters at El Alamein and Stalingrad (see pages 257–8). The so-called Kreisau Circle was a wide-ranging group of officers, aristocrats, academics and churchmen who met at the Kreisau estate of Helmut von Moltke. The conferences discussed ideas about plans for a new Germany after Hitler and, in August 1943, a programme was drawn up. The principles of the Kreisau Circle were politically conservative and strongly influenced by Christian values. Indeed, there were pacifist elements in the group who were opposed to a *coup* against Hitler.

Nevertheless, some individual members were supporters of what became the most far-reaching act of resistance to Hitler's Germany – the Bomb Plot of 20 July 1944. A number of the civilian resistance figures made contact with dissident army officers, such as Beck and Tresckow, in order to plan the assassination of Hitler and the creation of a provisional government. In the words of Tresckow just before the attempted assassination:

> The assassination must take place, whatever the cost. Even if it should fail, the attempt to seize power in Berlin must take place. The practical consequences are immaterial. The German resistance must prove to the world and to posterity that it dares to take the decisive step.

Eventually, the lead was taken by Colonel von Stauffenberg, who came to believe that the assassination of Hitler was the only way to end the Nazi regime. He himself placed a bomb in Hitler's briefing room at his headquarters in East Prussia on 20 July 1944. Unfortunately for the conspirators, the briefcase containing the bomb was moved a few yards just a minute before it exploded. Hitler thus sustained only minor injuries. In the confused aftermath the generals in Berlin fatally hesitated, thus enabling a group of Hitler's loyal soldiers to arrest the conspirators and re-establish order. About 5000 supporters of the resistance were killed in the aftermath, including Stauffenberg, Beck, Tresckow, Rommel, Moltke and Goerdeler.

The conservative élites proved incapable of fundamentally weakening the Nazi regime and in that sense their active resistance failed. Among the reasons for this are:

- They only recognised the need to resist the regime after the crucial developments of 1934 and 1938, by which time it was too well established.
- The military oath tied the army to the Nazi regime and its leader.
- Hitler's diplomatic and military successes in 1938–42 undoubtedly blinded the élites. Even after the '**turn of the tide**' and the growing knowledge of brutal actions, the majority of army generals did not work with the resistance.
- Planning and organisation of effective action was always fraught with difficulties. Their long-term political aims lacked clarity and practical plans were inhibited by the environment of suspicion and uncertainty in a police state.

In the end the bad luck and confusion of the Bomb Plot of 20 July reflected these difficulties.

Key dates

Military 'turn of the tide'; German defeats at El Alamein and Stalingrad: Winter 1942–3

Stauffenberg Bomb Plot failed to overthrow regime: 20 July 1944

Key term

Turn of the tide
Used to describe the Allied military victories in the winter of 1942–3, when the British won at El Alamein in North Africa and when the Russians forced the surrender of 300,000 German troops at Stalingrad.

A photo taken of the room after Stauffenberg's bomb exploded. Despite the destruction Hitler was only slightly injured.

Profile: Claus von Stauffenberg 1907–44

1907		– Born in Bavaria, Germany, the descendant of an aristocratic military family
1926–30		– Joined the Bavarian Cavalry Regiment and commissioned as a lieutenant
1936–8		– Joined the army's War Academy in Berlin and graduated first in his class
1939–43		– Fought in Poland, France, Russia and Africa
1942		– Witnessed atrocities in Russia. Started to associate with the resistance of the Kreisau Circle along with Tresckow
1943	January	– Promoted to lieutenant-colonel
		– Badly injured when his staff car ran into a minefield in Africa. Lost his eye, two left-hand fingers and his right forearm
1944		– After his recuperation he decided to kill Hitler and drew up the plan codenamed 'Operation Valkyrie'. Several attempts were aborted in the first half of the year
	July 20	– Detonated the bomb at Hitler's headquarters at Rastenburg, in eastern Germany. Hitler was only injured. Stauffenberg was arrested and shot in the late evening

Stauffenberg was an able and committed soldier who, like so many, initially admired Hitler. However, his strong Catholic moral outlook shaped his increasing doubts about the regime by 1941.

He remained on the fringes of the Kreisau Circle in 1942–3, but he gave the resistance a real purpose from early 1944. Stauffenberg personally took the initiative to carry out the assassination, but for his failure he paid the ultimate price – along with his brother.

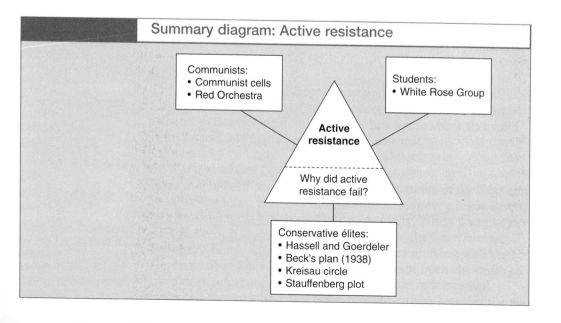

Summary diagram: Active resistance

Study Guide: AS Questions

In the style of OCR A

Assess the reasons why resistance to the Nazi regime was so ineffective. (50 marks)

Exam tips

The cross-references are intended to take you straight to the material that will help you to answer the question.

'Assess the reasons …' doesn't just mean examine each one. You must weigh them up against each other and put them in a hierarchy of importance. One place to start would be with the nature of the Nazi state. Formal opposition was very difficult: political parties and trades unions were banned. The Communist Party, perhaps the most obvious source of potential resistance, was targeted ruthlessly. In contrast, the conservatives were badly compromised and very slow to take any action. Much of the Nazi programme they liked. Indoctrination was strong (Chapter 9 and Chapter 10, pages 242–6). The Nazis controlled all official means of communication. You could build from there to consider the impact of the police state that made opposition not only very difficult but very dangerous. Which was more significant in limiting the effectiveness of opposition? To answer this properly you need to look at those who did resist. Many did, but by the very nature of the Nazi state, they had to be ultra-secret so organisation was always difficult and any kind of co-operation extremely dangerous.

Communist cells were weakened from within by events such as Stalin's purges and the Nazi–Soviet Pact. Under such circumstances, opposition groups very understandably focused on self-preservation rather than open resistance. Beck's *coup* in 1938 was thwarted by the Munich agreement. Yet there was open resistance, as the White Rose and the 1944 Bomb Plot show. Note the timing. Until 1942, the regime had success after success. That made the regime popular and opposition far more difficult. Crucially, it also meant that the Nazi regime was very established and so far more difficult to topple. With failure in Russia, however, the climate began to change.

You might end with the Kreisau Circle and the Bomb Plot, noting not so much the shared conservative background of these opponents, but the religious convictions that drove them to act. There was always opposition and resistance from elements in the Churches (Chapter 9, pages 200–2). In drawing your conclusions, was the impact of the police state the key? Equally, turn the question round and ask whether, given the difficulty of the task facing opponents, the scale and variety of resistance was actually impressive.

In the style of OCR A

Study the four sources on the impact of war on Germany and then answer both sub-questions. It is recommended that you spend two-thirds of your time in answering part **(b)**.

(a) Study Sources A and B.

Compare these sources as evidence for people's reactions to the July Bomb Plot. (30 marks)

(b) Study all the sources.

Use your own knowledge to assess how far the sources support the interpretation that the impact of war increased active opposition towards Hitler within Germany. (70 marks)

Source A

An extract from Anne Frank's diary, 21 July 1944.

I'm finally getting optimistic. Now, at last, things are going well! Great news! An assassination attempt has been made on Hitler's life, and for once not by Jewish communists or British capitalists, but by a German general. The Führer owes his life to 'divine providence': he escaped, unfortunately, with only a few minor burns and scratches. A number of officers and generals who were nearby were killed or wounded. The head of the conspiracy has been shot. This is the best proof we've had so far that many officers and generals are fed up with the war and would like to see Hitler sink into a bottomless pit.

Source B

From: SD (Internal Security Police) reports.

(a) 8 July 1943:

The telling of vulgar jokes detrimental to the state, even about the *Führer* himself, has increased considerably since Stalingrad. In conversations in cafés, factories and other meeting places people tell each other the 'latest' political jokes and in many cases make no distinction between those with a harmless content and those which are clearly in opposition to the state.

(b) 3 March 1945:

Enemy propaganda activities do all that remains to finish off the fighting spirit of the troops and the endurance of the people. The individual feels deserted and betrayed. He cries out for an unvarnished explanation from the German leadership. The politically-conscious in the Party and amongst the people still believe firmly in the historic change promised by the *Führer* but the weaker elements are growing restless and beginning to doubt. The eternal, favourable colouring of reports and parade-ground displays have darkened the perception of the *Führer* and cut him off from the people.

Source C

Melita Maschmann, formerly a member of the League of German Maidens, recalls her feelings at the time of the July Bomb Plot in 1944.

On July 20th, I left the office for home. As usual, the first thing I did was switch on the radio. The first sentence swept my feet from under me. An attempt had been made on Hitler's life. I cried out loud and felt sick; although the second sentence did give the reassuring news that, as if by a miracle, the *Führer* was almost unharmed. A friend who lived next door arrived. I think we were both in tears. To us Hitler's death would have meant the complete breakdown of our world. The perpetrators of such a deed could only be criminals or madmen.

Source D

Albert Speer, former Minister of Armaments and War Production recalls some conversations in the final stages of the war.

In Westphalia, in March 1945, I stood unrecognised in a farmyard talking to farmers. To my surprise, the faith in Hitler which had been hammered into their minds all these last years was still strong. Hitler could never lose the war, they declared. 'The *Führer* is still holding something in reserve that he'll play at the last moment. Then the turning point will come. It's only a trap, his letting the enemy come so far into our country.' Even among members of the government I still encountered this naïve faith in deliberately withheld secret weapons that at the last moment would annihilate an enemy recklessly advancing into the country.

Exam tips

The cross-references are intended to take you straight to the material that will help you to answer the questions.

(a) Part **(a)** requires you to examine closely the content of the two sources and compare the way they show people's reactions to the July Bomb Plot during the war. Source A suggests some people reacted positively, whereas Source B suggests there is loyalty and support for Hitler and condemnation of his opponents. The main focus of an effective answer is on comparing and contrasting the content and provenance of the two sources in the light of the question and reaching a substantiated judgement.

(b) Part **(b)** requires you to use the content and provenance of all four sources, grouping them by view, and to integrate pertinent factual knowledge into your argument to answer the question. Knowledge should be used to develop, validate or criticise the views in the sources. You should reach a balanced judgement supported by knowledge, source content and provenance.

Consider the following:

- the 'turn of the tide' (the key issue in the question) (page 250)
- the Nazi propaganda machine (page 242)
- Hitler Youth, resistance and the White Rose (pages 191 and 248)
- Albert Speer (page 176)
- Germany in 1945 (page 259).

12

From Occupation to Division: The Creation of Two Germanies

POINTS TO CONSIDER

There is a lot of detail in this chapter and you must be very careful not to get too lost in the military and diplomatic history. Some of the aspects refer back to the chapters on Nazism and many are related closely to the creation and development of the two Germanies (see Chapters 13 and 14). The following main themes need to be considered:

- Germany's defeat
- The role of the Allies
- The four Ds: de-Nazification, demilitarisation, democratisation, decentralisation
- The impact of the Allied occupation: the Soviet Zone and the Western Zones
- The creation of two Germanies: East and West Germany

Key dates

1945	February 4–11	Yalta conference of Roosevelt, Stalin and Churchill
	May 7–8	Surrender of German forces to Allies
	July 17–Aug 2	Potsdam conference of Truman, Stalin and Churchill (later Attlee)
1945	November 20	Nuremberg trials began
1946	April 21–22	Formation of SED by merging East German SPD and KPD
1947	January 1	Formation of Bizone between USA and Britain
	June 5	George Marshall announced the Marshall Plan or ERP
1948	June 18	Currency reform in Western Zones
	June 24	Berlin blockade started
1949	January 25–28	First SED Party Conference. Supremacy of SED in Soviet Zone
	May 12	Berlin blockade ended
	May 23	Foundation of BRD in West Germany (German Federal Republic)
	October 7	Foundation of DDR in East Germany (German Democratic Republic)

1 | Defeat and Surrender

Key date

Surrender of German forces to Allies: 7–8 May 1945

By May 1945 Germany lay in ruins. Nazi foreign policy had reached its destructive conclusion. Its ambitions had been extensive:

- To establish a 'greater Germany', which went well beyond Germany's 1914 frontiers.
- To destroy Bolshevik Russia.
- To create a new order based on the concept of Aryan racial supremacy.

The means to these ends had involved the acceptance of violence and bloodshed on a massive scale.

Key question
Why did Germany lose the war?

Germany's defeat
Military factors
On a superficial level Hitler's final failure in his ambitions could be explained by his strategic bungling. Hitler had always believed (along with most generals going back to Imperial Germany) that a war on two fronts should be avoided. To this end he needed an alliance with Britain and/or France – or at least their neutrality – so that he could be free to launch an unrestrained attack in the east. Consequently, when Germany failed to secure either British neutrality or a British surrender in 1940–1 before attacking the USSR, the foundations for defeat were laid.

Germany had become engaged in a conflict for which it was not fully prepared. As has been seen in Chapter 8 (see pages 171–5), at the start of the war Germany did not exploit fully its available resources and manpower. The alliance with Mussolini's Italy was also of little gain. Indeed, Italian military weakness in the Balkans and North Africa proved costly, since it diverted German forces away from the main European fronts. Yet, Hitler was driven on ideologically to launch an attack on the USSR with another *Blitzkrieg*.

The failure to defeat the Soviet Union before the onset of winter in 1941, combined with the entry of the USA into the war, now tipped the balance. Britain was still free to act as a launch-pad for a western front and also, in the meantime, could strike into the heart of Germany by means of aerial bombing. The USSR could maintain the eastern front by relying on its geographical size and sacrificing its huge manpower.

Economic factors
- Although the Four-Year Plan of 1936 was meant to make Germany 'fit for war within four years', the German economy was not really ready for a long war in 1939. Its capacity was only strong enough to sustain a couple of short campaigns (see pages 174–5).
- Anglo-American bombing. German industry peaked in the production of weapons in summer 1944, yet the German armed forces could not fully benefit from this because of the detrimental effect of Allied air raids.

- From the outset Germany was short of labour. Millions of workers were required to keep up the industrial and agricultural production, and the gaps were only partially filled by forced labourers and an increase in female employment.
- Germany was deeply in debt. The reserves in gold and foreign currencies were almost completely used up by 1939 and the Nazi state had run up a debt of roughly 42 billion *Reichsmark*.
- The US economy was just too powerful. In 1944 Germany's fuel supply compared to the supply of the Western Allies was 1:3. The USA sent massive support to the Allies, especially to the USSR which received 13,000 tanks and 15,000 planes.
- Soviet resources. The Soviet economy had undergone a ruthless industrialisation programme in the 1930s by Stalin and despite its limitations, Russia had vast resources of raw materials, for example of oil and manpower.

After the war Stalin is reputed to have explained the Allied victory in the simple words, 'Britain gave the time; the USA gave the money; and the USSR gave the blood'. It is a telling quote, but it does not reveal the full extent of economic and strategic factors which led to Germany's military defeat.

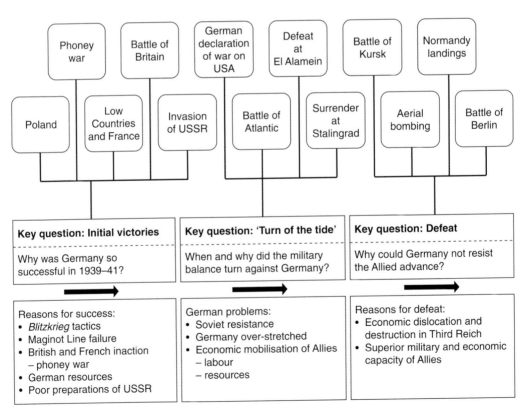

Figure 12.1: Germany's war 1939–45.

Key question
Was it a '**zero hour**' in 1945?

Key terms

Zero hour
Stunde Null. A term used in German society to describe Germany's collapse in the months after 1945.

Occupying Powers
The four Allies, the USA, the USSR, Britain and France.

Germany in 1945

In the weeks before the capital fell to the Soviets a typical Berliner's joke began to circulate: 'Enjoy the war while you can! The peace is going to be terrible.'

It is no exaggeration to say that the German state had ceased to exist by May 1945. A number of Nazi leaders had committed suicide, including Hitler and Goebbels, while others had fled or been captured and arrested. As a result, the central government had broken down in the final week of April. In its place, Germany, and the city of Berlin, had both been divided by the Allies into four zones; and each one of the **Occupying Powers** had their own military commander giving orders and guidelines for the local economy and administration (see page 263).

But, in the short term, the most telling problem facing Germany in that spring was the extent of the social and economic crisis.

Population displacement

At the end of the war it is estimated that one in two Germans was on the move. These people consisted of:

- Roughly 12 million German refugees fleeing from the east after the changes of the frontiers (see page 265).
- Ten million of the so-called 'displaced persons' who had done forced labour or had been prisoners in the various Nazi camps.
- Families torn apart by the war, who were looking for each other.

The ruins of Berlin in May 1945.

- Over 11 million German soldiers who had been taken as prisoners of war. Of these, 7.7 million in camps in the west were soon released, whereas the 3.3 million in the USSR were kept in captivity until the 1950s, and one-third of them did not survive.

All these people posed a serious problem to the Occupying Powers because of the lack of food.

Urban destruction

Major German cities, especially Cologne, Hamburg and Berlin, had been reduced to rubble because of Anglo-American bombing and Soviet artillery fire. Twenty per cent of housing had been completely destroyed, and a further 30 per cent badly damaged, which led many to accept temporary accommodation or to escape to the countryside.

Food and fuel shortages

Food was the immediate problem, and it was soon to be exacerbated by the onset of winter at the end of 1945. Compared to the average recommended calorie consumption of 2000 per person per day, actual consumption sank to 950–1150 during this period.

Economic dislocation

Surprisingly, the economy had not completely broken down, but it was very badly dislocated. Industrial capacity had obviously declined dramatically, but the extent of its destruction was exaggerated at the time. Moreover, the infrastructure of bridges and railways and the utilities, like gas and water, had broken down during the end of the war. Also, the state had massive debts, so Germany was once again facing the problem of rising inflation causing a major **black market** for the supply of food and other goods.

> **Black market**
> Illegal trading in goods or currency.
>
> *Key term*

Not surprisingly, many Germans after the war saw the destruction and dislocation as *Stunde Null*, the zero hour. However, in a way this term for 1945 is misleading, as there were major continuities in Germany:

- an efficient civil service
- long-standing local government authorities
- a well-established banking system (despite the currency problems)
- its industrial base and productive capacity.

Despite the immense social pressures, especially on the women of Germany, the fundamentals of the social fabric were not completely broken. There was no social breakdown, and the Allies restored law and order quite quickly; the entrepreneurial middle class still aspired; Christianity had survived Nazism, and the Churches were once again free to practise their faiths (although the situation in the Soviet Zone was later to prove more difficult). All these points are related to the key question of whether the Germany which emerged from 1945 was truly 'new', or largely rooted in its past.

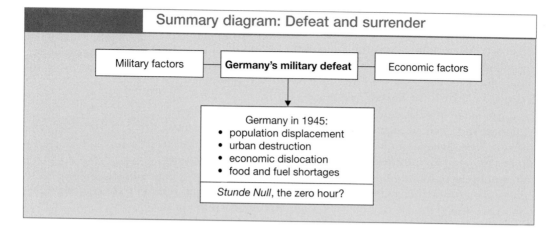

2 | Allied Plans for Post-war Germany

Early war conferences

Key question
What were the early aims of the 'Grand Alliance'?

The **Grand Alliance** of the USSR, the USA and Britain was forged out of the pressures of their military situation in the latter half of 1941. Neither the USA nor the USSR had even joined the war voluntarily, both had been attacked without warning. Therefore, the 'Big Three' of Stalin, Roosevelt and Churchill were brought together initially by the simple necessity of the military survival of their nations.

Key term

Grand Alliance
A term initially used by Churchill to describe the alliance of Britain, the USA and the USSR, 1941–5.

The Atlantic Charter

Even before the USA entered the war officially Winston Churchill and Franklin D. Roosevelt had agreed on the so-called 'Atlantic Charter' in 1941. Its aim was not only to annihilate the tyranny of the Nazis, but also to establish a new, peaceful world order along the guidelines of political freedom and self-determination for all peoples, and a liberal world market. Above all, they demanded there were to be no compromises with Hitler.

Casablanca

In January 1943 in Casablanca Roosevelt and Churchill agreed that they demanded the 'unconditional surrender' of Germany. Stalin was not present and he was upset to hear that the Western Allies would not be strong enough to invade France until 1944.

Teheran

From 28 November to 1 December 1943 the first summit of the 'Big Three' took place in Teheran. The main aim of the meeting was clearly to map out the military strategy for the final phase of the war. Yet, it also revealed the first differences in some lengthy and tough discussions about the territorial changes in Europe after Hitler. It became clear that agreements on those questions would not be easily found, and self-interest and mutual mistrust stood in the way of compromise.

At the heart of the discussions lay the issue of the borders between Poland and Germany. The USSR wanted to keep her territorial gains from the Nazi–Soviet Pact of 1939 (see page 248). The Western Allies, to keep Stalin on board, largely agreed to his demands. More difficult was the issue of the extent of compensating Poland with German territories in the west. A line along the two German rivers Oder and Neisse was finally taken as a provisional basis for further negotiations at the next meetings.

At this stage, the Allies, especially the Americans, wanted to eliminate the German threat once and for all. Several different plans for the division of Germany into smaller states were drawn up by Churchill and Roosevelt and discussed at Teheran, but no agreements were found and they were given to a special commission for further negotiation. The most notorious plan was one drawn up by the US Secretary of State Henry Morgenthau in 1944. It suggested not only to divide up Germany, but also to turn it into a backward, purely agrarian territory, demolishing all existing industry. The plan was acknowledged and seriously considered, but later was to be overtaken by practical realities.

Yalta conference, February 1945

Between the time of the meetings at Teheran and Yalta the military circumstances of the war changed, which fundamentally affected the relationship between the Allies. First, it became clear that the power of Churchill and Britain was in decline and the other two superpowers could increasingly shape events by themselves. Secondly, although victory over Germany was just a question of time, the Soviet Red Army had advanced steadily into Germany, whereas the Western Allies had struggled to make their expected rapid progress and they did not reach the Rhine until February. Thirdly, the Soviet 'liberation' of states in eastern Europe was not viewed favourably by many and it was to become the focus of discussions.

For the second big summit at Yalta from 4 to 11 February 1945, the two Western leaders accepted Stalin's invitation to the Crimean peninsula. Stalin wanted to impress his partners at Yalta with Soviet hospitality to put them in a favourable mood, but clearly contrasting aims and objectives were held.

Stalin

Stalin had already officially established a Soviet-backed provisional communist government in Lublin in Poland the month before. His obsession with security questions was growing. More and more he saw a belt of satellite states in the west that were closely bound to the Soviet Union in friendly co-operation as essential. Consequently, he aimed at securing his military and political position in eastern Europe with as little confrontation with his allies as possible.

Churchill

Churchill's mistrust of Stalin had grown over the months and would grow further. He wanted to limit Stalin's influence over the territories occupied by the Soviet army, fearing the spread of communism in those states. In this context he also became wary

Key question
What were the emerging problems of the Anti-Hitler coalition?

Key date

Yalta conference of Roosevelt, Stalin and Churchill: 4–11 February 1945

of taking too much land from Germany to give to Poland. He accepted that Germany must cede land to Poland, but worried that too much was being given.

Roosevelt

Roosevelt, who was very ill and died two months later, was driven by his idealism and keen to introduce democracy into eastern Europe. However, he trusted Stalin and was prepared to make concessions to his need for security in exchange for Russian co-operation in the fight against Japan and in his favourite 'One World' project. This envisaged a world organisation to negotiate future international conflicts and keep the world peace: the future United Nations.

The Yalta agreement

Therefore, although on the surface it seemed that the Yalta agreement was an acceptable compromise for all partners, it left important decisions postponed or open to interpretation. With a mixture of naïveté and the will to avoid too much confrontation at that stage, the Western Allies relied on terms like 'democratic' or 'free elections' without specifying their meaning, to their own cost. The Big Three agreed that:

- The 'Declaration on Liberated Europe' would allow the liberated peoples of Europe to be set up as democratic and self-governing countries.
- The USSR would join the United Nations and join the war against Japan.
- The Soviet Union would keep most of the eastern Polish territory it demanded and parts of north-east Prussia, while Poland would receive German territory in return on its western border. Although the exact frontier of the Polish–German border was again postponed for a final peace conference, it was agreed that Poland would be compensated with territory taken from Germany (see Figure 12.2, page 265).
- Germany was tentatively divided up into four occupational zones. The administration of each zone would lie in the hands of the respective Occupying Powers: the USA, USSR, Britain and France, whereas decisions concerning the whole of Germany would be taken by the four High Commanders in the **Allied Control Council** (ACC) unanimously. Similarly, the capital, Berlin, would be divided into four zones to be ruled by the ACC. The will for co-operation was stressed, while at the same time crucial decisions on the new political organisation and size of Germany were postponed.
- The Allies would set up a commission to look into reparations.

Looking at the results closely one could say Stalin should have felt satisfied with the effects of his hospitality! Yalta was intended only to be an initial understanding before a peace settlement, and yet Stalin was in an increasingly powerful negotiating position.

Key term

Allied Control Council
The name given to the military occupation governing body of the four Allied Occupation Zones.

Potsdam conference, July 1945

A couple of months after the meeting at Yalta, Germany capitulated and yet the relationship between the Soviet Union and the Western Allies deteriorated markedly. The increasing disagreements between the Allies over the future of Germany and Europe bedevilled the first few months of peace.

Truman

Roosevelt had died on 12 April leaving his inexperienced successor, Truman, with an unfinished war and an unclear situation as to Europe's future. Truman was at first prepared to continue with American policies along the lines mapped out by Roosevelt, but he was distinctly less trustful towards Stalin because of their contrasting views of democracy. These were highlighted by the Red Army's occupation of eastern Europe, which was unsympathetic to democratic ideals. In addition, the president was waiting for his scientists to bring him news of some new weapon tests in the desert of New Mexico, which might change his whole standing in Potsdam and the Pacific (see page 266).

Churchill

Churchill was even less optimistic and increasingly antagonistic to Stalin. He judged Stalin's promises for democratic elections in the east European states as a deceptive manoeuvre and urged the Americans to prevent the further spread of Soviet influence in Europe and in particular in Germany. However, Britain's position as a world power was already beginning to wane, and its status was demeaned further by the defeat of the war leader Churchill at the general election in the middle of the summit. He was replaced by the less well-known Labour leaders, Prime Minister Attlee and Foreign Minister Bevin.

Stalin

Stalin's interests at Potsdam were above all the questions of reparations and of security. The USSR had lost at least 20 million people and the country's industry and infrastructure in the west had been badly damaged. In the first year after the war compared with the year before the war agrarian production was reduced by 40 per cent and steel production by 50 per cent. Stalin needed the reparations to rebuild his country and for economical reasons he was against a division of Germany now. He wanted to have access to the industrial areas along the Rhine and Ruhr.

The Potsdam agreement

From 17 July to 2 August the three powers met in the noble residence of Cecilienhof at Potsdam, near Berlin, and at the end there was just a Protocol of Proceedings (a diplomatic statement) and not a peace settlement. The main points of agreement were:

- **The four Ds.** The principles of the treatment of the occupied Germany were built on the four Ds of: de-Nazification, demilitarisation, decentralisation and democratisation. Yet, as

Key question
Why was there no peace settlement for Germany in 1945?

Key date

Potsdam conference of Truman, Stalin and Churchill (later Attlee): 17 July–2 August 1945

Key term

The four Ds
De-Nazification, to eliminate Nazi influence; *demilitarisation*, to destroy German armed forces; *democratisation*, to re-establish democratic institutions and values in Germany; and *decentralisation*, to break down the centralised Nazi political structure and restore local/regional government.

at Yalta, it proved to be difficult to define these terms more precisely and this soon led to a range of interpretations.

- Zones of occupation in Germany. As provisionally agreed at Yalta, each occupational power was to administer its zone independently. However, at the same time, it was assumed that the Allies would soon negotiate a final settlement for the whole of Germany. In the meantime Germany was to be treated as an economic unity and all issues concerning the country were to be decided by all the four powers unanimously.

- The German–Polish border. This was an issue of great disagreement when Stalin demanded that it be confirmed further west at the line of the rivers Oder and Neisse. Churchill had no sympathy and refused to accept this, pointing out that the question of the borders could only be settled at a final comprehensive peace conference. The Americans agreed and this question was also postponed. However, in practice the Polish administration of those lands and the 'peaceful re-settlement' (expulsion) of millions of Germans tacitly were accepted by the Western Allies. The shift of Poland to the west became quickly a *fait accompli* and there was no chance of renegotiating those new realities with Stalin without risking a direct confrontation. The Oder–Neisse line was to become an issue of great grievance with many Germans.

- Reparations. The USSR demanded reparations of $20 billion, a sum which in the eyes of the Western Allies was so exorbitant that it would make it impossible for the German economy to support its population. (Although interestingly the Americans

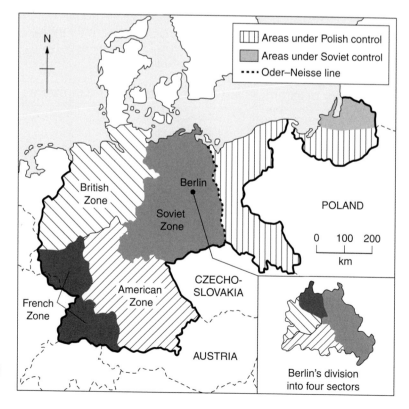

Figure 12.2: How Germany was divided by the Allies.

had estimated that Soviet damages amounted to $35.7 billion.) In the end an agreement was reached by which each power was to take reparations from its own Occupying Zone. In addition, the USSR was to receive a quarter of the reparations from the Western Zones partially in exchanges for the supply of raw materials and agricultural goods.

Allied differences over Germany had crystallised in the 12 months leading up to Potsdam in July 1945. The estrangement of the Allies had set in and it is telling that Potsdam was just a protocol, *not* a peace treaty. Indeed, Potsdam left more questions open about Germany and Europe than answered. For example:

- Within which borders should the German state be defined?
- Was Germany to stay as one state after the time of the occupation?
- Was there to be a central government at some stage again, or had the Allies already accepted a division into spheres of influence that would become permanent?

The formula of the Potsdam protocol therefore reflected the grim realities of power politics. Germany had imploded, but the vacuum was quickly filled with the international rivalry of the superpowers over the issues of:

- Ideology: communism versus democracy and capitalism.
- Military/security: the power of the Red Army in land forces versus the American development of the **atomic bomb**.
- Economy: American desire to maintain its world trade role versus the Soviet aim to recover from the enormous economic losses of the war.

As a result, from 1945 to 1949, when it came to the development of a post-Nazi Germany, all relevant critical decisions were really subject to the context of the emerging Cold War.

Key term

Atomic bomb Western scientists developed the technology to make atomic/nuclear weapons as part of the Manhattan Project 1942–5. The first bomb was tested in New Mexico in July 1945 and the next two were dropped on Hiroshima and Nagasaki in Japan in August 1945.

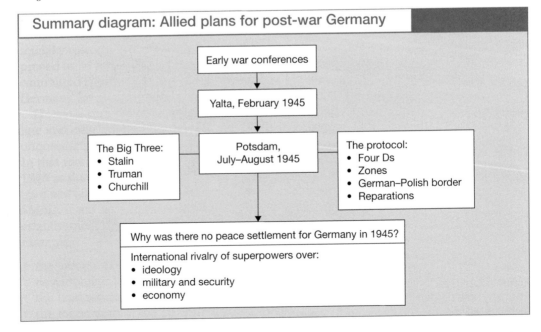

Summary diagram: Allied plans for post-war Germany

Early war conferences

Yalta, February 1945

The Big Three:
- Stalin
- Truman
- Churchill

Potsdam, July–August 1945

The protocol:
- Four Ds
- Zones
- German–Polish border
- Reparations

Why was there no peace settlement for Germany in 1945?

International rivalry of superpowers over:
- ideology
- military and security
- economy

3 | The Allies and the Nazi Legacy

Key question
Were the Nuremberg trials more like a 'show trial'?

The Nuremberg trials

When concentration camps such as Auschwitz were opened at the end of the war, the pictures of horror that were broadcast to the world shocked and outraged the public. Yet, the motivation of the victors when they set up an International Military Tribunal at Nuremberg was punishment of the Nazi leaders, rather than revenge. This military tribunal was a completely new concept and there were no real existing international laws. This has caused a lot of controversy on the validity and justification of these trials with legal and historical experts to this day (although over the years the precedent has been used for other cases, e.g. Milosevic at The Hague).

The court, made up of judges from the four Allies, was to conduct individual trials of the Nazis on four counts:

- war crimes
- crimes against peace
- crimes against humanity, for example the mass murder of Jews
- conspiring to commit the crimes in the first three counts.

Key date
Nuremberg trials began: 20 November 1945

The trials that started on 20 November 1945 indicted 22 of the leading members of the Nazi regime and also six organisations: the Nazi Party, the *Gestapo*, the SS, the SA, the SD, and the leadership of the German army. (Hitler, Himmler and Goebbels had all committed suicide before the trials.)

The prosecution lawyers of the four Allies presented 2360 documents and questioned 240 witnesses for the prosecution. The sessions stretched over 218 days. The necessity to translate all the procedures into the different languages represented only one of the many difficulties of the trials. It became clear that it would be impossible to conduct such trials against the mass of the party members somehow involved in crimes.

All in all, 12 leaders were sentenced to death, of whom 10 were actually executed. Three life sentences and four sentences of up to 20 years' imprisonment were passed on the rest. Only three people were acquitted: von Papen, Schacht and Fritzsche. The NSDAP with all its organisations was condemned as criminal and forbidden. (The fate of many Nazis can be found by referring to this book's index and the profiles in the text.)

In the following years similar trials were conducted against leading lawyers, doctors and industrialists at Nuremberg. Thousands of trials were to follow after those infamous cases and hundreds of death sentences were indeed passed. Yet, it should also be remembered that many Nazis responsible for war crimes were not brought to trial and were still able to hide their past, and even able to carry on pursuing their careers.

From their start the Nuremberg trials were controversial. On the one hand, some have claimed that the trials did not go far enough, but on the other hand many critics have seen the process as 'show trials' or 'kangaroo courts' on two counts:

The Nuremberg trials 1945–6.

- That the evidence produced was questionable to prove the legal guilt of particular individuals in a court.
- That the victors' justice applied two different sets of morals, as the Allies refused to be judged by the same international standards of justice with respect to allied war actions, for example, the use of the atomic bomb by the Americans, the behaviour of the Soviet troops in Poland and Germany, and the British mass bombing of Dresden.

Nevertheless, despite all the difficulties, the trials succeeded in revealing the cruelties of the Nazi leaders and bringing them to a kind of justice. Even in Germany, the principle of the trials was mostly acknowledged and accepted. Rather, it was the broader process of de-Nazification and re-education which caused upset within Germany.

De-Nazification

One of the foremost aims agreed on at the meeting at Potsdam was to erase Nazism in Germany and re-educate the population towards democracy. Yet, in specific terms of how to implement this aim there were practical problems:

- The Nazi Party was declared illegal in Germany and the vast majority of the 6.5 million members in 1945 threw away their membership cards in the hope of distancing themselves from the regime. Even if former Nazis could be identified, would they really become genuine democrats? And if so, how would they build an effective democracy?

Key question
How successful was de-Nazification?

- The Allies were left with a predicament when they took over the administration in their zones. Germany had been destroyed and the Allies needed German experts, such as engineers, to overcome the most urgent problems.
- This led to another major point. How could the Allies find experts who could be trusted and who had not been involved in Nazism? That was almost impossible because of the confusion between the German state and the Nazi Party (see page 237). The so-called 'educated middle classes' had been essential for the regime and obviously non-loyal elements had largely been purged from the state in the 1930s. Therefore, the original American plan to turn all Nazis out of their offices was bound to lead to chaos.

In the very first few weeks of the existence of British and American Zones, thousands of Germans were forced to visit the opened concentration camps in their neighbourhoods to confront the horrible truth they had tolerated for so long, and make them face up to their guilt. The reality may have been recognised by many Germans, but there was also resentment by many at the way the Allies seemed to be blaming the German population collectively.

Then, from the summer of 1945 the Allies embarked on screening more sternly for Nazis. All ex-members of the NSDAP were banned from all leading positions in private and public service, and thousands of officials and suspects were automatically arrested and held in internment camps. By late 1946 nearly a quarter of a million Germans were being held. However, it was clear early on that the directives were contradictory or applied differently within the zones. Nearly half of the internees had been in the American Zone: much higher than in the British and Soviet ones.

In an attempt to formalise the situation, the Western Allies, prompted by the US military governor, General Lucius Clay, decided that all German adult citizens should fill in a detailed questionnaire comprising 131 questions (although this was *not* applied by the Soviet authorities). This resulted in their categorisation into five groups:

I. Major offenders.
II. Offenders incriminated.
III. Less incriminated offenders.
IV. Fellow-travellers – sympathisers.
V. Exonerated persons.

The people who were categorised in the first three classes had to appear in front of a court for further interrogation and a possible punishment.

It soon became clear that the process of de-Nazification varied markedly between the Western Allies (see also Tables 12.1 and 12.2 on the following page).

Table 12.1: Percentage distribution of de-Nazified persons by categories in the three Western Zones of occupation

Zone	I & II	III	IV	V	Not pursued
		Categories			
US	2.5	11.2	51.1	1.9	33.3
British		1.3	10.9	58.4	29.3
French	0.1	2.5	44.7	0.5	52.2

Table 12.2: Nazi criminals before military courts

Zone	No. sentenced	Death penalty
US	1517	324
British	1085	240
French	2107	104

US Zone

The Americans had an almost missionary zeal. So, although they did not really want to destroy the capitalist structure, they felt it was necessary to purge German society of the Nazi evil. For example, all of those who were party members before 1937 were dismissed. As a result it was the Americans who judged the most sternly:

- 13.7 per cent were put into categories I, II or III
- 51.1 per cent of the people surveyed were put in category IV
- only 1.9 per cent were put in category V.

British Zone

The British took a more pragmatic approach than the Americans to the whole procedure. They tended to work on a case-by-case basis and the questionnaire was not so zealously pursued:

- only 1.3 per cent of all screened Germans in their Zone were actually in some way punished
- only 10.9 per cent were put in category IV
- and 58.4 per cent exonerated by category V.

They soon allowed ex-party members to return into their positions in the free market and as a result, British military officials often permitted ex-Nazis to assume leadership roles in their Zone, something which US policies prohibited. Also, students forbidden to enrol in universities in the US Zone because of Nazi connections were allowed to enrol in universities in the British Zone.

French Zone

The French Zone was relatively small and French manpower was limited. Also, de-Nazification was a relatively low priority compared with French concerns about defence and security. In the French Zone 2.6 per cent were punished.

Soviet Zone

The Soviets took a very different approach to the problem of de-Nazification. They believed that it was the capitalist system which was responsible for the development of Nazism, so accordingly the most efficient means to prevent the danger of another fascist state developing on German soil was to develop new social and economic conditions. Therefore, the Soviet approach was relatively sharp and decisive, and there was no 'Nazi hunt' (the US questionnaire system was not applied). As a result, by early 1948:

- a number of 'war criminals' had been executed (the figure is not exactly clear) and leading Nazi functionaries had been imprisoned and punished
- Nazi property had been confiscated and all the estates had been redistributed by the Soviet authorities (see page 281)
- 450,000 ex-Nazi Party members had been dismissed from office, including teachers, lawyers, etc.

Yet, the Soviets needed experienced and skilled Germans, especially engineers and doctors, so many were later reappointed. So, perhaps not surprisingly, de-Nazification served more as a pragmatic tool for the Soviets to get rid of opposition to the new form of society, rather than as a serious attempt to bring all the Nazi criminals to justice.

Conclusion

De-Nazification by all of the Allies did not succeed as planned. They had certainly secured the destruction of the Nazi state, yet in the end for various reasons the purge was limited and the change of values was cursory.

Justice

The process was undermined by too many examples of injustice. Too many of the small fry were caught and punished, whereas the big fish got away. For example, Germans could produce testimonies of their innocence from character references that became known as '*Persilscheine*', named after a well-known washing powder. These documents were in great demand by many Germans and were increasingly traded on the black market or signed in exchange for all kinds of favours among the population. So there were many loop-holes, even for hard-line Nazis, while among those Nazis who were imprisoned, many were given amnesties from 1951.

The size of the task

The task created by the Allies grew out of hand and they simply did not have the staff to pursue it. As can be seen, the problems in Germany were immense from the start, and the questionnaire system then created enormous amounts of paperwork. Ironically, the massive task of evaluating all those questionnaires and passing judgements was increasingly passed to local German authorities.

The street name Adolf Hitler-Strasse is removed by Germans overseen by an American soldier.

Differences between the zones

It became clear very soon that the zones were at odds and the different approaches between the Allies undermined their initial aim. This problem was not just a practical one, it also reflected the domestic political interests of the Allies.

German attitudes

German opposition to de-Nazification increased because of the introduction of questionnaires and the inconsistencies of the whole process. In addition, Germans were increasingly concerned with the reconstruction for the future (rather than looking at the past).

Cold War

In 1947–8 the Allies' interests moved away from de-Nazification and towards the Cold War. The Western Allies became more concerned about 'containing' Soviet influence by creating a bulwark from a strong Western Germany.

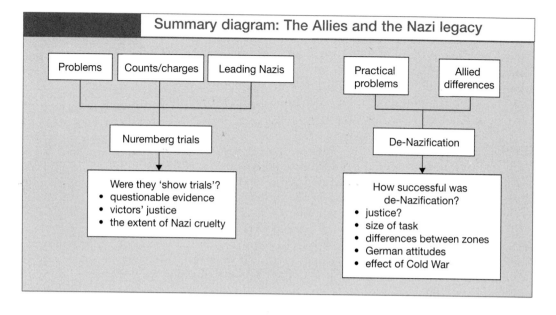

Summary diagram: The Allies and the Nazi legacy

4 | Democratisation and Decentralisation

At Potsdam the Allies had outlined the principles of the treatment of the occupied Germany built on the four Ds of de-Nazification, demilitarisation, decentralisation and democratisation (see page 264). De-Nazification had been applied with mixed success, whereas demilitarisation was thoroughly applied at first: no armed forces were permitted and the manufacture of all arms was banned (the issue of remilitarisation in the 1950s can be looked at on page 331). The two principles of decentralisation and democratisation 'as rapidly as is consistent with military security' were, therefore, at the heart of what kind of Germany would emerge.

Decentralisation

Key question
Did the Allies really try to decentralise?

On one issue the Allies did agree: namely that Prussia was seen as the symbol of militarism, nationalism and power politics and it could not remain a political unit. Admittedly, some of it became part of Poland (see map on page 265), but it was dissolved for good with the aim of decentralisation by restructuring the regional area. However, the Allies had very different views of the process of political decentralisation.

Soviet Zone

Certainly, the Soviet Zone had accepted the principle and had created by the end of 1945 five *Länder* as regional states. Yet, the five *Länder* proved to be of less political importance than first thought. The Soviets distrusted the idea of a genuine federal structure and also established at the same time a range of centralised authorities responsible for transport, housing and so on. Therefore, the regional authorities were controlled and directed by the communists, and in 1952 they were dissolved.

US Zone

The Americans were the strongest supporters of German decentralisation: a result of their own federal government system. Under the influence of the military governor, General Lucius Clay, the foundations of the administrative structure for three *Länder* had been established in his zone and as early as May 1946 the first free federal state elections were held.

British Zone

At first, the British doubted the ability of the Germans' capability to build up a genuine democracy and were very wary of giving political freedom and powers to them. They preferred to keep close control over their Zone through their own centralised administration, and so, although they took in German experts, it was within clear limitations. Nevertheless, it seems that the financial costs of the occupation pushed the British towards encouraging decentralisation and in May 1947 free elections for federal state parliaments were held.

French Zone

Because of its own security and financial interests, France continued to remain the strongest supporter of the lasting dismemberment of Germany. Consequently, it blocked any attempt of the other two Western powers in the Allied Control Council for a more co-ordinated, centralised administration of Germany. The French Zone was therefore held under tight rule and economically cut off from the others. France even stubbornly resisted the re-establishing of democratic parties and it was not until March 1947 that *Länder* elections were permitted in its Zone.

Conclusion

The Allies believed that decentralisation would be achieved by restructuring the German regions, to reflect some of its old historical territories (see also the federal structure in Weimar Germany, page 22). Yet, for the first two years the process was implemented in different ways at different paces by all four of the Occupying Powers. By 1947 a clear contrast lay between the Soviet Zone with its centralised authorities and the three Western Zones, which had established the nine newly created federal *Länder*, albeit still under strict Allied control (see also the map on page 299).

The re-emergence of German political life

Alongside the issue of decentralisation was the necessary one of democratisation. If Nazism was to be wholly extinguished the Allies wanted it to be replaced with genuine democratic political parties. Yet, it did not take long for political party life to be revived. As early as 10 June 1945 the Soviets permitted the re-establishment of non-fascist, democratic parties and the formation of free unions. Within the next few months the Western Allies also agreed to 'license' the formation of democratic parties, mainly because the Allies wanted to control political

Key question
How did democratisation affect German politics in the Western Zones?

developments in their zones. As a result, by the end of 1945 the essence of party politics had been re-established by the creation of four major parties: the SPD, the CDU, the LDPD and the KPD.

The Social Democrats (SPD)

It was not difficult for the SPD to re-establish itself, as it enjoyed a large and traditionally loyal mass electorate of workers and it was simply able to revive and rebuild the old organisational structures that pre-dated 1933. Its first national party leader was Dr Kurt Schumacher and his main problem in 1945–6 was to fight off the demands from left-wing members of the party to merge with the communists to create one united socialist party. This he was able to prevent in the Western Zones, but not in the Soviet Zone, where the SED was created (see pages 278–9).

The post-war SPD has been described as a 'moralistic' party, although its programme was shaped very much by its history and by a rather dated outlook:

- It wanted to improve living conditions for the working class, but very much within the context of parliamentary democracy.
- It was in theory an anti-capitalist party and regarded itself as Marxist. It was committed to working for a socialist economy by transferring natural resources and key industries to the state.
- It remained deeply opposed to the communists and refused any political compromise, which reflected their bitter hostility from the Weimar years.
- It viewed positively the possibility of a neutral socialist Germany located between the capitalist economies of the West and the Soviet dictatorship of the East.

Christian Democrats (CDU)

At first, it seemed difficult for the conservative forces to re-emerge as a viable political influence because of their regional and religious differences. However, in the creation of the CDU on 16 December 1945, its founders astutely recognised the need for a unified Christian conservative party, although its various organisations were only officially merged into a national party in 1950.

Thus, this new party had only partly played on its traditional roots in the pre-Hitler era. It appealed to

- Catholics, from the old ZP (Centre Party) like its first national leader Konrad Adenauer, with their geographical base in the Rhineland and the south
- Protestants, from the DVP and DNVP, with their strength in the north.

In that way, in the use of the word 'union', the CDU effectively expressed its desire to unite all Christian Democrats, Protestant and Catholic alike, and address the broadly conservative middle classes. In Bavaria an independent sister party to the CDU was launched, the CSU (Christian Social Union), which was more conservative and focused predominantly on Bavarian interests.

An astute French journalist described the establishment of the CDU as: 'socialist and radical in Berlin, clerical and conservative in Cologne, capitalist and reactionary in Hamburg and counter-revolutionary and separatist in Munich'. However, the CDU had more to offer than its appeal to political unity, as it was strongly built on Christian social ideas and the Christian trade union movement. So, its Ahlen programme of 1947 adopted radical social policies, which demanded the public ownership of key industries and a greater influence for the workers' unions in political decisions.

Liberal parties (LDPD and FDP)

At first, the liberal parties had tried to establish one German Liberal Democratic Party (LDPD) across the zones. But the leader of the party in the east, Wilhelm Külz, had to concede so much to the primacy of the SED (see pages 278–9) that the membership from the Western Zones established the FDP (Free Democratic Party) in 1948. It stressed the right of private property and upheld the advantages of a free market in its programme. The new party was initially led by Theodor Heuss, who later became the first president of West Germany.

Table 12.3: The major parties licensed by the Allies by the end of 1945

Party	Major leaders	Background and aims
KPD German Communist Party	Walter Ulbricht (see pages 346–7) Wilhelm Pieck	Banned under the Nazis and had only survived underground. Resurrected by Moscow exiles in spring 1945 and enjoyed substantial grassroots support. Aimed to unify the working classes from the whole of Germany under its leadership. They led the way in the merger of the SPD and the KPD in the Soviet Zone by creating the SED in 1946
SPD Social Democratic Party of Germany	Kurt Schumacher, national party leader (see pages 309–10) Otto Grotewohl, party leader in the Soviet Zone	Once licensed, it was easy for the SPD to re-establish itself, as it enjoyed a large and traditionally loyal mass electorate from the workers. Its programme was shaped very much by its history and by a rather dated outlook. In theory, it was still an anti-capitalist party and regarded itself as Marxist working for a socialist economy. Yet, the vast majority were deeply opposed to the communists and refused any political compromise
CDU Christian Democratic Union	Konrad Adenauer, leader of the party in the British Zone (see pages 305–6) Jakob Kaiser, co-founder and leader of party in Soviet Zone	A new party, which grew out of the old ZP, DVP and DNVP from the Weimar years. It portrayed itself as a Christian conservative party aiming to unify Germany's regional and religious differences
LDPD Liberal Democratic Party of Germany	Wilhelm Külz, leader of the party in Soviet Zone Theodor Heuss, based in the French Zone	The liberal parties had been weak and divided in the Weimar years. In 1945 the LDPD was established across the zones, but differences soon emerged and in 1948 Heuss created the Free Democratic Party (FDP)

The Communists (KPD)

The KPD still enjoyed quite substantial grassroots support and its aim was to unify the working classes of the whole of Germany under its leadership. The Communists enjoyed the full political backing of the Soviets in their zone and they played a crucial role in the merger of the KPD and SPD to create the SED (see pages 278–9). In the Western Zones, it really had only a limited chance to gain real political power once it came to be seen as a tool of the Soviets. In the first elections of 1949 it gained about 5 per cent of the vote.

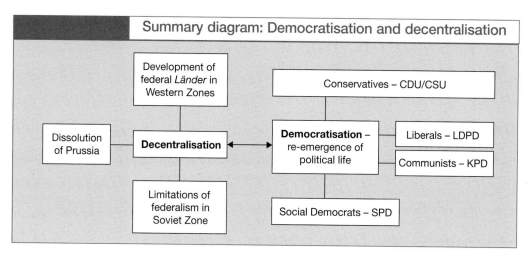

Summary diagram: Democratisation and decentralisation

5 | Allied Occupation: The Soviet Zone

Key question
What were the aims of the 'Ulbricht group' in 1945–6?

Even before the Red Army had launched the Battle for Berlin, the Soviets had started to plan the reorganisation of their zone. And as early as the end of April 1945 they flew in a small group of exiled German Communists under the leadership of Walter Ulbricht, who had worked for Comintern (see profile on pages 346–7).

The new political powers in eastern Germany

Ulbricht and his supporters had been trained by the Soviets as advisors for the Red Army. They had already developed detailed plans to gain political power in Germany in order to achieve social and economic changes. So, the Soviet Military Administration, **SMAD**, which was established in the Soviet Zone, was initially prepared to follow their advice to win over the co-operation of the German population. The 'Ulbricht group's' aims were:

- to destroy the remnants of Nazism
- to create a unified working-class party under the leadership of the KPD
- to occupy the key power positions in local administration, such as the chief of police

Key term

SMAD
The Soviet Military Administration in Germany. The name given to the Soviet authorities that supervised the occupation in the Soviet Zone. It was renamed the Soviet High Commission in October 1949.

- to arrange for the appointment of respected non-communist representatives, such as mayors (although their deputies were communists and in this way the communists managed to build a democratic appearance while at the same time keeping everything under their firm control).

Somewhat surprisingly, SMAD did allow the re-establishment of non-fascist, democratic parties and the formation of free unions and this led to the re-creation of the KPD, SPD, CDU and LDPD within a month in the Soviet Zone (see Table 12.3 on page 276). Yet, what looked like the rebirth of German democracy soon turned out to be a sham. Under Stalin's personal pressure the four parties were forced to create a united front called the 'Block of Anti-Fascist Parties' (*Antifas*). The parties technically had their organisational independence, but in fact their co-operation was forced over all important decisions because of harassment by the SMAD with its single-minded support of Ulbricht and the KPD.

The creation of the SED

It was soon clear that the communists were not winning sufficient popularity to secure a mass political base. The elections in Austria and Hungary were catastrophic for the communists there, while in the Soviet Zone the membership of the democratic parties was increasing, mainly because the KPD was seen as blindly serving Soviet interests. As a result, in the winter of 1945–6, Soviet pressure increased to bring about a political merger of the KPD and its rival, the SPD.

From the start, the issue of the merger was highly controversial within the SPD. The leader of the SPD in the Western Zones, Kurt Schumacher, was a committed anti-communist and warned strongly against the plan. Moreover, many of the grassroots of the SPD in the Soviet Zone were wary and wanted a genuine conference of the whole party. Finally, the pressure which the SMAD put on the SPD – in the main by threats, arrests and censorship – had its success. At a conference on 22 April 1946 the SPD from the Soviet Zone, led by Otto Grotewohl, and the KPD merged to create the new Socialist Unified Party, the **SED**. Ballots on this issue for the members of the SPD had been forbidden before by the SMAD in their zone – and the one held in the Western Sector of Berlin had shown that 72 per cent of the SPD members there rejected the idea.

The establishment of the SED was undoubtedly a crucial development. This meant that:

- the SED enjoyed the backing of SMAD and it was hoped by SMAD that the communists were on the path to political success
- the SPD had lost its long-established status as the strongest political party across the whole of Germany
- it put up a new hurdle for the chances of future political co-operation in the Eastern and Western Zones.

Key question
How did the SED become the dominant political party in the Soviet Zone and why was the merger of the SPD and KPD so significant?

Key date
Formation of SED by merging East German SPD and KPD: 21–22 April 1946

Key term
SED
Sozialistische Einheitspartei. Socialist Unity Party of Germany. The new party created in April 1946 by the merger of the KPD and SPD in the Soviet Zone.

However, despite all the pressure put on other parties, the SED still could not gain an overall majority of votes in the state elections in October 1946.

Table 12.4: Regional elections in the Soviet Zone, October 1946, percentage of vote

SED	CDU	LDPD	Peasants' League
47.5	27.3	21.6	3.5

Key term

Eastern bloc
A label given to the countries controlled by the USSR in eastern Europe from 1945: Poland, Czechoslovakia, Hungary, Romania, Bulgaria, Albania and the DDR.

Key date

First SED Party Conference. Supremacy of SED in the Soviet Zone: 25–28 January 1949

The new SED party with its compromise programme had therefore failed to convince with its claim to offer 'a special independent German path to socialism'. Moreover, the development of the Cold War and the rising tensions between the Soviet Union and most communist parties in the '**Eastern bloc**' resulted in Moscow taking a much harder stance on the issue of loyal party discipline. Over the next few years the SED was regularly purged and forced to conform to Soviet policies. This process culminated at the SED party conference of January 1949, which adopted a party structure after the model of the CPSU in the USSR, proclaiming 'a party of a new type' committed to 'democratic centralism'. In the words of Berghahn: 'The Soviet Zone of Occupation had effectively become a copy of the Stalinist dictatorship' (see page 345).

'Junkerland in Bauernhand.' The lands of the Junkers in the hands of the peasants.

Economic and social changes

In 1945 the Soviet Zone of occupied Germany had several advantages and disadvantages. On the one hand:

Key question
What were the economic and social aims of the Soviets in their zone?

- the territory benefited from large areas of agricultural land, although of mixed quality
- it had areas of well-developed light industry, such as textiles, chemicals and optics, in Saxony and Thuringia
- it was less war-damaged than the Western Zones, with the main exceptions of Dresden and Berlin.

On the other hand:

- it lacked raw materials compared to the Ruhr area in the British Zone; its only natural resource were potash and brown coal, which was of much lower energy value
- it had lost important provinces to Poland: Silesia, an industrial area with coal and iron reserves, the important port of Danzig and the agricultural land of Prussia
- it was suffering from a major influx of refugees from the east and starvation was even worse than in the Western Zones
- the transportation infrastructure had been seriously dislocated; railways had been destroyed and roads from east to west Germany were blocked by border checkpoints
- it had no effective currency.

These features were to be exacerbated by the two major aims of Soviet economic and social policies: the pursuit of reparations in order to rebuild the USSR, and the application of a socialist economic policy in order to transform the socio-economic structures. Also, because in the eyes of the Soviets the Nazi state had been rooted in a capitalist society, it was seen as quite justified to destroy old Nazi capitalist power structures.

Despite the difficult conditions in the Soviet Zone, the Soviets significantly dismantled much of the industry. By 1946 1400 industrial plants from the zone were sent to Russia, with the result that by 1948 the overall industrial capacity had fallen by 26 per cent. The scale and impact of dismantling had its human side, and many skilled workers and scientists were sent to the USSR to work. In addition, 213 firms were brought directly under Soviet financial control. As these companies produced over 30 per cent of the zone's industrial output, this represented a major loss for the economy of the zone and it also weakened all efforts at rebuilding the zone.

Key question
What were the effects of Soviet socio-economic policies?

However, Soviet economic policy was not just about compensation, it was at the heart of the Soviet socialists' aim to restructure Germany and the following decisions were therefore taken quickly and with significant consequences.

State control of banking

Privately owned banks were dispossessed and replaced by state control as early as June 1945. Twenty-five Soviet joint stock companies (**SAGs**) were created in the next year from 200 firms.

SAGs
Sowjetische Aktiengesellschaft. Soviet joint stock companies. Set up in January 1946.

Key term

Key terms

VEB
Volkeigener Betrieb.
People-owned
companies.

Collectivisation
The policy of
creating larger and
more efficient
agricultural units
controlled by the
state. It was
initiated by Stalin
in the USSR in the
1930s.

DWK
*Deutsche
Wirtschaftkommission.*
German Economic
Commission.
Created in 1947 to
administer the
economy of the
Soviet Zone. It was
very much in
response to the
creation of the
German Economic
Council in the
Bizone.

Nationalisation of industry and commerce

From 1946 the process of nationalisation was pushed through, so
that by 1948 only 39 per cent of industry and commerce
remained in private hands. The rest was in the ownership of the
SAGs companies and the state-run companies, the **VEB** (people-
owned companies) which took over many 'abandoned companies',
whose owners had fled to the west or were forced to leave.

Land reform

From 1945 to 1947 far-reaching land redistribution was carried
out. More than 7000 estates of the *Junkers* were dispossessed
(those with more than 100 hectares, equivalent to 250 acres).
Altogether two-thirds of the land was redistributed to small
private smallholders, refugees and expellees, and they generally
saw the process very positively. However, the results in terms of
efficiency and production were disappointing, and by the early
1950s it was decided to implement **collectivisation**.

The pace and thoroughness of the reforms in the Soviet Zone
show very clearly that in the years immediately after 1945 the
Soviets had the will and the means to push through 'socialist'
changes in the zone. The directives of the SMAD and the SED
had made strong efforts to nationalise all means of production
and to change the social structures of the society in the Eastern
Zone. Moreover, the creation of its own German Economic
Commission, **DWK**, in June 1947 suggested that the Soviet Zone
had laid the basis for a planned state economy. These changes
raised serious questions for the Western Allies, which are
considered in the next section.

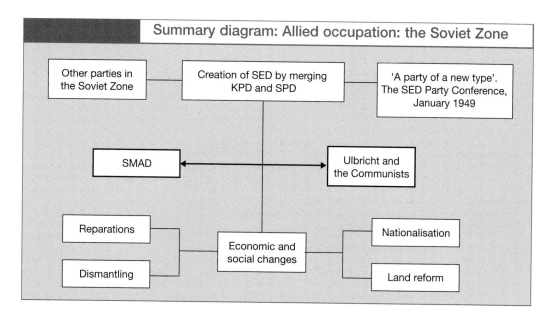

Summary diagram: Allied occupation: the Soviet Zone

6 | Allied Occupation: The Western Zones

The section on pages 259–60 identifies the extent of the problems faced in Germany in 1945, and it soon became clear that there were no quick solutions. Indeed, the practical problems were exacerbated by several harsh winters, especially the one of 1946–7. Yet, as has been seen, the Soviets had already set their own agenda, and so the immediate problem for the Western Allies was to make sure that the German population could survive the next winter and restart economic life to sustain the millions of needy as well.

Basic problems and basic solutions

The Western Allies were also confronted by having to cope with the nature of the structure of the system of occupied zones:

Key question
Did the Western Allies cope with the problems in Germany after the war?

- As each zone was administered individually, each occupying power had to take care of food, shelter, heating, medical services, etc. This proved particularly difficult in the north and west of Germany under the British. As the most heavily industrialised areas, they had the densest population, and many of the worst damaged cities.
- The French also sought to extract as much as they could from Germany and the Saar was again controlled (see page 328).
- The Soviets continued to demand the payment of the additional reparations out of the Western Zones as laid down in Potsdam.

So increasingly the British and Americans resorted to 'crisis management' in 1945–6 as the extent of Germany's problems emerged.

Housing
Many families had to live in old bunkers or ruined houses without any sanitation or heating. And those people with undamaged houses had to take in refugees or bombed-out families, so that each one often had no more than one room at its disposal. To partially alleviate the housing problem, the British put up provisional shelters, 'Nissen-huts', which actually became more permanent accommodation, lasting some years.

Fuel
House heating and industrial energy was a major problem, as coal production had collapsed disastrously by mid-1945. The Western Allies were so concerned about the implications of the short supply that they made massive efforts together with German authorities to get the mines moving again. Although the real industrial recovery only came with the 1950s, the three-fold increase in the figures of coal production by early 1946 was crucial and prevented the fuel crisis getting even worse.

Food

The Germans had been used to food rationing ever since the beginning of the war but the rations fell dramatically from 1945, even though the Allies had tried to control the scarce resources. As a result, the level of malnourishment, along with the cold, led to illnesses like typhus, diphtheria and whooping cough, which took its toll on many Germans during the first two winters. It is no exaggeration to say that by 1947 Germany faced real famine. Every available patch of land was turned into a vegetable garden and in the Anglo-American Zone the authorities were sometimes forced into distributing a maximum of between 700 and 1200 calories per day for an average adult. Private aid initiatives also started across the world. In the USA and Canada CARE (Cooperative for American Remittances to Europe) organised initiatives sending food and clothes, which were given to the German Red Cross, the Churches and other social organisations. Also significantly, these parcels became one of the first symbols of a newly growing bond between the Germans in the Western Zones and their occupying powers.

Conclusion

It is difficult to escape the conclusion that the extent of the problems the Allies in Germany had to face was grossly

Life in the centre of Berlin in 1946.

underestimated. However, whereas the British and American authorities were initially moved by revenge and punishment, they soon came to recognise the reality of starvation and social dislocation. The early directive of non-fraternisation gradually gave way to pragmatic co-operation and indeed, elements of trust began to grow on both sides. They worked very hard and actually coped remarkably well, which is not to say that millions of Germans did not still suffer from many traumatic experiences in those early years. It soon became clear that the Allies needed to confront the more fundamental problems beyond human relief, and solutions had political implications.

Economic revival

German political life had revived in 1945 in the Western Zones, but the process of decentralisation and democratisation had been cautious and in slow stages (see page 273). Moreover, political developments had been controlled very much by the Western Allies. As early as 1946 it became increasingly clear for the British and Americans that the fundamental economic problems in Germany could be managed much better if the Occupying Powers co-operated much more closely. This was for several reasons:

- The extent of the humanitarian crisis was getting worse because of the influx of the millions of expellees and refugees.
- It made no real sense to dismantle the industry of the continent's strongest economy when Europe needed every bit of help to reconstruct.
- Britain, in particular, was so desperately indebted from the war that the government was increasingly keen to offset the financial costs of maintaining the old enemy.
- There was increasing concern about the perceived threat of the Soviets, who had started to rebuild the economy in their zone along socialist lines, which did not conform to the concepts of a 'free market economy'.

These political concerns were reinforced by Churchill's '**iron curtain**' speech in March 1946 at Fulton in the USA.

The **Bizone**

In the course of the year a series of talks among the Allies tried to determine a basis for economic co-operation. In reality they underlined the emerging differences between Britain and USA, on the one hand, and the USSR and France on the other. Indeed, in May 1946 General Clay even stopped the deliveries of industrial goods from the American Zone to the Soviet Zone, as the Soviets had failed to fulfil their part of the Potsdam agreement to send agricultural goods, which were needed in the industrial areas in the west. Moreover, two months later the Americans even suggested a merger with any of the zones – an offer accepted by the British, but rejected by the French and the Soviets. The frustration of the Americans came to a head in a speech in Stuttgart on the 6 September by the US Secretary of State, James Byrnes, which signalled a change in his country's

Key terms

Iron curtain
A term used by Churchill in 1946 to describe the border between Soviet-controlled countries and the West.

Bizone
The name given to the two zones of Britain and the USA which were merged into a unified economic zone in January 1947.

Key question
Why was the Bizone created?

Key date
Formation of Bizone by USA and Britain: 1 January 1947

policies on Germany. In effect, the speech was a cautiously worded offer to the Germans of co-operation and protection in rebuilding their state, as a member of the free democratic world rather than the old official American stance of control and punishment of the Germans.

The change in direction was strongly supported by the British and so, on 1 January 1947, the British and the Americans agreed to merge their two zones into a unified economic one, the Bizone. This was supposedly not intended to be a political union, yet during 1947 when Inter-Allied conferences had more disagreements the two Occupying Powers of the Bizone very soon permitted the passing of increased authority to the Germans. All this laid the basis for a sort of German administrative government, which has led the historian Eschenburg to describe the Bizone as 'the germ cell of the **BRD**'. Most significantly the Bizone created the German Economic Council, which had the power to pass laws on a range of economic matters such as taxation.

The Marshall Plan

From 1945 to 1946 the USA had pumped an immense amount of goods, raw materials and money into Europe, and by 1947 there were still real anxieties that the European market was continuing to decline. The US government was therefore very concerned that this would destabilise many European countries making them politically more susceptible to communist influence. Also it increasingly realised that it was impossible to bring about a lasting economic recovery in Europe without Germany, and Germany was seen as economically and politically vital.

Nevertheless, developments within Germany must be put very much in the context of the growing Cold War, and in 1947 several international events exerted significant influence:

- The revival of the **Greek Civil War** which highlighted the issue of the spread of communism.
- The declaration of the '**Truman doctrine**' on 12 March 1947 when the President proclaimed that it was the mission of the United States to help all free nations threatened by what he saw as communist aggression and to contain the spread of that ideology.
- The offer on 5 June 1947 from the new Secretary of State, George Marshall, to seek Congress's agreement to provide enough money (in the form of grants) to stabilise and strengthen a European free market. This became known as the European Recovery Programme (ERP, or **Marshall Plan**).

The Marshall Plan aimed to achieve a comprehensive economic recovery for Europe. It was therefore offered to all European states, including the four German zones, the USSR and its satellites. Although Stalin predictably forbade his satellites and the Soviet Zone from taking up the offer, the Western Zones welcomed it as a political necessity (this included the French

Key terms

BRD
Bundesrepublik Deutschland. The Federal Republic of Germany (FRG) was formed on 23 May 1949.

Greek Civil War
A conflict between communists and monarchists, which was backed by British troops until their withdrawal in February 1947.

Key question
What were the aims and effects of the Marshall Plan?

Truman doctrine
In March 1947 President Truman explained his decision to help the anti-communist forces in Greece. Truman's doctrine was to contain communism by sending money and equipment to any country.

Marshall Plan
Also known as the European Recovery Programme (ERP). It aimed to provide enough money (in the form of grants) to stabilise and strengthen Europe.

Zone, although the Trizone was not legally formed until April 1949).

The Western Zones welcomed it, and the integration of the three zones into the ERP run by the OEEC (Organisation for European Economic Co-operation) took important decisions away from the Occupying Powers. This marked another step in widening the gap between the east and the west of the country.

Economically, by 1951 out of the $12.7 billion of the Marshall Plan, Germany was given $1.5 billion. These investments, together with the currency reform in the Western Zones, were to prove to be the spark for economic recovery, and the returns went back into the Western German economy accelerating the growth further (see also pages 312–16).

Currency reform: the creation of the Deutsche Mark

It was becoming increasingly clear that it was only possible to sustain hopes of economic revival by reforming the currency. The German currency, the *Reichsmark*, had been severely distorted by Nazi policies and the effects of the war, and so in the years after 1945 the currency was not the base for economic stability, because:

- The financing of the war had created inflation and there was far too much money in circulation for the few goods that were available.
- The inflation was hidden by the state-regulated economy of the Nazis, which continued as the Allies tried to control prices, wages, production and rations.
- The real value loss of the German *Reichsmark* had led to a thriving black market based on barter, which was reckoned to amount to nearly one-half of economic activity in the Western Zones.

These financial problems were seen as a main barrier to production and trade, and the quickest and most efficient solution was to introduce a new hard currency in which the Germans and their trading partners could trust again.

The introduction of a new currency had not only economic implications, but also profound political ones: it would be opposed by the Soviets, for instance, which would fundamentally divide Germany. Nevertheless, despite the reservations, the German Economic Council decided to go ahead, very much backed by the Americans. Indeed, the new banknotes and coins were produced in the USA and sent to the *Bank Deutscher Länder* (later the *Bundesbank*) under the strictest secrecy in order to avoid financial disturbance and to confront the Soviets as much as possible with a *fait accompli*.

The terms of the new Deutsche Mark (DM) were introduced on 20 June 1948 to all three of the Western Zones and to the western sectors of the city of Berlin. They gave every German DM60 at a rate of one-to-one for the old currency; they also revalued wages, pensions, rents and property at exactly the same level, while savings in banks were exchanged at the rate of 100 *Reichsmarks*

George Marshall announced ERP (Marshall Plan): 5 June 1947

Key date

Key question
Was the currency reform a total success?

into DM6.50 Deutsche Mark (DM4.2 = \$1 in 1949). At the same time the markets in the Western Zones were largely freed from state regulations by a law passed in the German Economic Council, so prices were set by supply and demand.

On one level the implementation was a really painful cut, which was in effect a major devaluation. Small savers, as in 1923, lost out once again, whereas industrialists, share-owners and landowners were protected. Nevertheless, the new currency had a liberating aspect because:

- The black market collapsed almost immediately and goods returned to the market quite legally again.
- Hard work was encouraged and workers' absenteeism plummeted.
- It stimulated business to increase production and selling.
- It complemented the Marshall Plan and resurrected trade.

Economically, the currency reform was an undoubted success. It seemed almost immediately to liberate the economy, and the German people could almost see the effects in the streets. An American banker wrote: 'The spirit of the country changed overnight. The grey, hungry, dead-looking figures wandering about the streets in their everlasting search for food came to life.' In statistical terms, it is estimated that by the end of 1948 the index of industrial production had increased so much that there were inflationary pressures. Moreover, the political effects of the creation of the Deutsche Mark were profound indeed. The Soviets were taken completely by surprise and it prompted a major international crisis in Berlin.

Key date

Currency reform in Western Zones:
18 June 1948

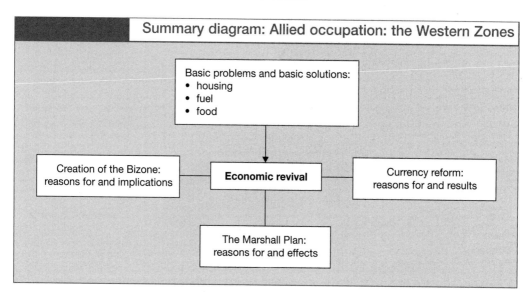

Summary diagram: Allied occupation: the Western Zones

Basic problems and basic solutions:
- housing
- fuel
- food

Creation of the Bizone:
reasons for and implications

Economic revival

Currency reform:
reasons for and results

The Marshall Plan:
reasons for and effects

7 | The Division of Germany

The Berlin crisis

In the short term, the decision of the Western Allies to push through the currency reform was the direct cause of the Berlin crisis in 1948–9. For the Soviets this measure was seen as a deliberate attempt by the Western Allies to undermine the Soviet Zone and contrary to the unanimity of the Allied Control Council. Therefore, immediate plans were made for introducing their own new currency for the whole of the Soviet Zone (including the western sectors of Berlin) known as the *Ostmark*. A more serious response to this Western action was the decision of the Soviet authorities to block all access by road, rail and canal to West Berlin from 24 June, as well as water, power and food supplies from the Soviet Zone. West Berlin had become a sort of isolated island in the Soviet Zone.

The Soviets hoped by this blockade to pressurise the Western Allies into giving up their plans of the new currency and, moreover, to make the three powers surrender the western sectors of Berlin to them. However, the vast majority of West Berliners wanted to stay part of the Western Zones, while the Western Allies were determined not to lose control of their sectors. Therefore, the Berlin crisis really became the first major flashpoint of the Cold War, like a great battle of brinkmanship without starting the

Key question
What was the Soviet purpose of the Berlin blockade and what were its effects?

Key date
Berlin blockade started: 24 June 1948

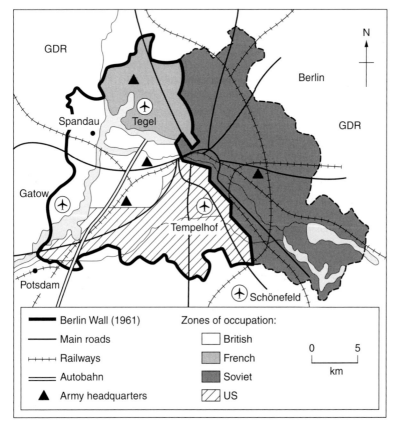

Figure 12.3: Berlin 1945–61. Like Germany itself, its old capital Berlin had been divided into four sectors by the Allied Powers in 1945 (see page 265) and they agreed to co-ordinate the administration for Berlin and rule it together. However, each sector was placed under the control of one power. As Berlin was in the east of Germany, the Western Allies could only reach it by passing through the Soviet Zone and access was only possible to West Berlin by four roads, two railways and three air-corridors.

Key to map:
- ▬▬ Berlin Wall (1961)
- ——— Main roads
- ┼┼┼ Railways
- ═══ Autobahn
- ▲ Army headquarters

Zones of occupation:
- ☐ British
- ☐ French
- ■ Soviet
- ▨ US

0 — 5 km

Third World War. Using the blockade Stalin wanted to recover his influence over the whole of Berlin and to regain the political initiative over Germany. The Americans simply did not want to lose their presence in the city.

In their desperation, the population of West Berlin found a strong advocate in General Clay, the supreme commander of the American Zone, who started to organise an airlift which flew through the air-corridors across the Soviet Zone to bring basic supplies into West Berlin. This was quite legal by the Potsdam agreement and in effect it meant that the supplies could only be stopped by the Soviets shooting down the British and American planes.

The Berlin airlift, as it became known, was essentially a logistical operation, which arranged for:

- 279,000 flights, one every minute at its peak
- providing 2.3 million tons of food and supplies providing 7000 tons of goods daily to West Berlin
- supplying 1.5 million tons of coal.

Key date

Berlin blockade ended: 12 May 1949

After 11 months it was ended on 12 May 1949 when the Soviets realised it was useless to carry on with the blockade. There was a human cost, as 76 aircrew lost their lives in 24 plane crashes, but the '*Rosinenbomber*' (raisin bombers), as the people affectionately

Berliners wave to an American plane as it approaches Tempelhof airfield for a landing on 5 May 1949.

called them, had allowed West Berlin to survive the winter. The commitment of the Western Allies was crucial for the morale of West Berliners, who gratefully joked: 'Better to be occupied by the Americans than liberated by the Soviets.' Even more significantly, the Berlin airlift reinforced the growing integration between the Germans in the Western Zones with the Western Occupied powers. Yet, the Berlin crisis had only been solved in the short term: there remained an ongoing problem (see pages 378–82).

Two Germanies

The consequences of the dramatic months in the Berlin crisis were really the opposite of what the Soviets had hoped for. They lost a lot of credit with the German population, while the blockade had brought the Western Allies and the majority of Germans together as friends rather than enemies. Berlin itself, therefore, was officially divided with West and East sectors creating their own mayors and administrations, while the whole of Germany itself was politically split (until 1990) by the creation of two new states: the BRD (*Bundesrepublik Deutschland*) the Federal Republic of Germany, on 23 May 1949; and the DDR (*Deutsche Demokratische Republik*), the German Democratic Republic, on 7 October 1949.

However, the Berlin crisis was really just the occasion, *not* the fundamental cause of creating two Germanies in 1949. Indeed, from 1945 it seems that the chances of establishing a united Germany were unlikely. That is not to say of course that the political division cemented by 1949 had been inevitable, but the unfolding of events between 1945 and 1949 increasingly narrowed the chances of politically uniting Germany.

In particular, it is clear from the earlier pages that several crucial economic decisions had really created the *basis* for separated political entities. So on the one hand the Western Allies decided to:

- stop paying reparations to the USSR in response to Soviet failure to fulfil their obligations, May 1946 (see page 284)
- create Bizonia, January 1947 (see pages 284–5)
- introduce the Marshall Plan, June 1947 (see pages 285–6)
- create the Deutsche Mark, June 1948 (see pages 286–7).

And on the other hand the Soviets decided in their zone to:

- nationalise industry and land reform, 1945–6 (see pages 280–1)
- establish a German Economic Conference, June 1947 (see page 281)
- create the *Ostmark* currency, June 1948 (see page 288).

The economic division of Germany was becoming ever more apparent by 1947 and when the Cold War exacerbated the atmosphere, the development of political institutions was driven further forward, particularly by the Americans and British. Interestingly, there are documents in the British Foreign Office dated from as early as autumn 1946 that show that Bevin recognised fully the implications of zonal fusion, and knew that if

Key question
Was the Berlin crisis the cause for creating two Germanies in 1949?

Key dates

Foundation of BRD in West Germany (German Federal Republic): 23 May 1949

Foundation of DDR in East Germany (German Democratic Republic): 7 October 1949

the Soviets refused to join, the Bizone would represent 'a measure which implied a clear division between Eastern and Western Germany'.

The creation of the BRD

Political partition was obviously accelerating by the end of 1947, so when a Foreign Ministers Council failed at London in November–December 1947, the Americans and the British were quite satisfied by early 1948 to start establishing a democratic West German state with a democratic constitution amalgamating the French Zone. As a result, even a few days *before* the currency reform and the start of the Berlin crisis, a London Six Power Conference of the Western Allies and the Benelux states (Belgium, Netherlands and Luxembourg) on 20 April–6 June 1948 had agreed on the outlines of a new federal state in West Germany and handed the terms over to the Länder of West Germany in Frankfurt (the Frankfurt Documents). The Parliamentary Council of 65 delegates therefore provided the legal framework for the new state and was officially called the *Grundgesetz* ('basic law'). It was ratified in May 1949 by the three Occupying Powers and the *Länder* parliaments from West Germany. On 23 May 1949 it became law. The new capital was to be Bonn, a small provincial town on the Rhine, a symbolic contrast to the old imperial Berlin.

The creation of the DDR

Although the Soviets pushed through the fundamental economic reforms in terms of land and property ownership as early as 1945, it is probably fair to say in the words of Fulbrook that the foundation of the DDR arose 'in response to, and lagging behind, developments in the West'.

Indeed, while the authorities in the Western Zones were carrying on their plans to establish a West German state during the 'Berlin crisis', the Soviets and the SED leadership were unwilling to go as far as creating an East German state. So, a new constitution was only drawn up at the end of May 1949 *after* the creation of the BRD; and it was only *after* the BRD elections and the formation of the first government under Adenauer that the

Table 12.5: Summary of the divided Germany

	West Germany	*East Germany*
German title	BRD, *Bundesrepublik Deutschland*	DDR, *Deutsche Demokratische Republik*
English title	FRG, Federal Republic of Germany	GDR, German Democratic Republic
Capital	Bonn	Berlin (East)
Date of creation	23 May 1949	7 October 1949
First leaders	Chancellor: Konrad Adenauer 1949–63 President: Theodor Heuss 1949–59	President: Wilhelm Pieck 1949–60 Prime minister: Otto Grotewohl 1949–60 SED party leader: Walter Ulbricht 1946–71
Status	Parliamentary democratic federal republic	In effect, one-party communist republic

SED created a provisional government and announced the creation of the DDR on the territory of the Soviet Zone on 7 October 1949. The president of the new state was the communist Wilhelm Pieck and the prime minister was Otto Grotewohl, the ex-leader of the SPD from the Soviet Zone. Two states had finally come into existence.

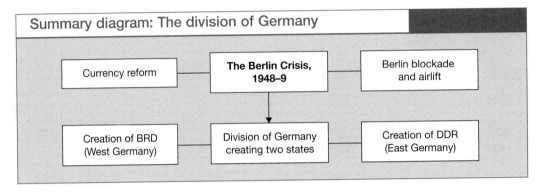

Summary diagram: The division of Germany

8 | Conclusions: The Creation of Two Germanies

The division of Germany in the years 1945–9 had not really been envisaged at all and yet it showed itself to be one of the most significant developments in twentieth century history:

- It brought an end to the German national state created back in 1871 and not re-created until the reunification of 1990.
- It became the initial focus of the Cold War, which was to last for 40 years.
- It resulted in the joint control of central Europe by the USA and the USSR.

Nazi Germany
At first, it should not be forgotten that Nazi Germany was responsible for initiating and waging the brutal war of 1939–45. For many Germans, it might have been very difficult to accept the division of their country and all too easy for them to pass the blame for it on to the Allied Powers from 1945. Yet, if Germany had not pursued its policy of military expansionism, it would not have resulted in the collapse of German forces and Allied forces winning control in central Europe in May 1945.

Key question
Who was responsible for the division of Germany?

The 'Big Three' Allied leaders
The Grand Alliance had emerged out of extraordinary wartime circumstances; initially each power had two objectives: national defence and the defeat of Nazi Germany. The conferences of Yalta and Potsdam made many plans for Germany; however, there was no fixed decision for permanently settling the 'German problem'. As a result, this gave plenty of scope for different ideologically based interpretations and for each of the Allies to put most emphasis on their own economic and political interests.

The superpowers

As Germany came to be seen as the 'battleground' of the Cold War, historians have argued over the relative responsibility of the two superpowers for the division of Germany.

Stalin and the Soviets

It might seem that the Soviets were simply motivated by the desire to create a major security buffer. Yet, to a large extent Russia's defence concerns were satisfied by the belt of satellites, for example, Poland and Czechoslovakia. Therefore, although they wanted to exploit all the economic potential of Germany, it is not really conclusive that the Soviets were at first set on the establishment of an East German state. Indeed, Stalin probably held out on the hope of the Allies agreeing on a united neutral Germany which would leave him with the chance to exert influence.

Truman and US 'containment'

It is now clearer that the US position on Germany changed very significantly from summer 1945 to early 1947. First, US perceptions (rightly or wrongly) of Soviet policies had become more hostile, and secondly, the grim reality of the European economy was motivating the USA to reconstruct the Western

'The Ballast.' A cartoon by Kurt Poltiniak from 1949. It shows Federal Chancellor Adenauer and Federal President Heuss, influenced by the USA, throwing overboard the common interests of the whole of Germany in order to make the balloon (West Germany) rise. The caricaturist, taking up the line of the DDR-propaganda, implies that the GDR cares more for the unity of Germany than the BRD.

Zones. Therefore, 1947 was a crucial year, as the president outlined the Truman Doctrine and the Marshall Plan. This meant that from that time the USA was committing itself to its global foreign policy of 'containment', which had serious implications for the zones in Germany, namely that:

- The USA would aid the reconstruction of the West German economy (on the basis of capitalism) to enable it to become self-sufficient once again.
- The USA would actively defend Western Germany with its troops from any threat of Soviet expansionism going beyond the emerging iron curtain.
- In that way the American position had made the chance of restoring German unity very unlikely.

Zonal disagreements

From the very start the four Allied Occupying Powers were in a way 'victims' of their misperceptions and, as tensions increased, this made co-operation more difficult.

Surprisingly, it was the French who at first blocked co-operation in the ACC to prevent any chance of a unifying Germany because of their historical worries of German recovery. Because the ACC depended on unanimous decisions, effective policy-making for the whole of Germany was very difficult. Also, the early differences over reparations were crucial. The Soviets saw reparations as reasonable recompense for the cost of the war. They dismantled German industrial equipment and transferred much of it to Russia; they also received extra money from the Western Zones. Yet, increasingly, the Western Allies found it difficult to bear financially the draining effects of the Occupation while at the same time footing the bill for Soviet reparations.

Therefore, by the end of 1946, in an attempt to avoid the growing chaos, the military governors of the Western Allies started to act in the interests of their own governments and the German people under their control within their zones. This was most obviously demonstrated by the creation of the Bizone.

Post-war German politicians

Finally, developments from 1945 to 1949 might give the impression that Germans were impotent in the face of the other forces. Yet, it should not be forgotten that German political leaders were quite prepared to work with the Allied Powers who shared their mutual political and economic objectives, at the expense of German unity. Thus, Ulbricht and the SED leadership could only really envisage a united Germany under a communist model. In the Western Zones, the CDU leaders Adenauer and Erhard became increasingly committed to a partial German state which was capitalist and pro-Western.

If the German political forces had really been committed to German unity they might have achieved a way forward. Instead, the famous conference of representatives of all German *Länder* in Munich in May 1947 to discuss Germany's problems failed even to find a common agenda. Contemporaries, among them General Clay, saw this as a missed chance, perhaps the last one for the Germans to act in their own interests. And significantly, when the German Economic Council began to work on the plans for currency reform by autumn 1947 it really marked 'the funeral of German unity' (Graml).

Conclusion

Before Hitler's war of 1939 the division of Germany was totally unthinkable, so primary responsibility for that division lay with those Germans who supported an amoral and unjustified war. Once defeated, the capacity of Germans to control events was lost and it meant that the Allies could exert their influence over future developments. Yet, the emerging ideological gulf between the Western Allies and the Soviets (even before the end of the war) meant that Germany was split right in the middle. All attempts at co-operation gave way to growing confrontation, and so the Occupying Powers were increasingly set on stabilising and securing their respective zones of influence. Nevertheless, in the changing international climate of the Cold War, it was the Americans and British by 1947 who were taking the initiative to create a western German state. Moreover, even if the German people still had hope for a united Germany after the war, it seems that the German political leaders were in fact moving towards co-operation with their respective Allies. Therefore, the eventual division of Germany reinforces the words of O'Dochartaigh: 'Ultimately, both chose to settle for half a cake baked to their own recipe. The respective recipes had been supplied by the Occupying Powers.'

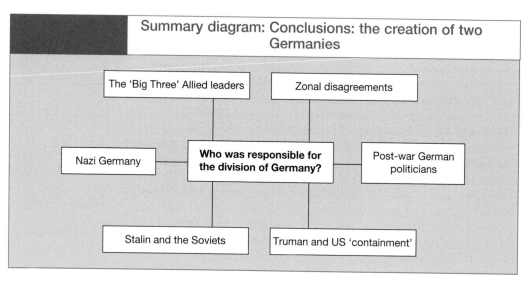

Summary diagram: Conclusions: the creation of two Germanies

Study Guide: AS Question

In the style of OCR A

'Currency reform was the Western Allies' greatest success in the non-Soviet Western Zones in Germany from 1945 to 1949.' How far do you agree with this view? (50 marks)

> ### Exam tips
>
> *The cross-references are intended to take you straight to the material that will help you to answer the question.*
>
> The question asks you to assess the relative importance of a series of elements outside the Soviet Zone and the Soviet Union's activities, and decide which was the greater/greatest success. That means you must establish a clear rank order of importance between them. One success is given in the question and you must examine the significance of currency reform seriously, even if you are going to reject it in favour of another that you believe to have been more important. In essence, you will be assessing how successful the Allies were in fulfilling the tasks set at Potsdam.
>
> The creation of the Deutsche Mark opened up the German economy, brought inflation under control, brought political as well as economic stability to the shattered country, and raised national morale. Economic revival was essential if post-war Germany was to stand on its feet. Finally, given emerging Cold War realities, it made possible a Western-orientated, democratic Germany. What might challenge that? The restoration of democratic politics is one contender. That could include de-Nazification as that was central to any democratic revival, but you might think the erasing of Nazism was a success of fundamental importance in its own right. Whether treated as separate successes or not, the development of a healthy democratic life was essential in the ever-worsening Cold War climate and made possible zonal fusion into Bizonia, then Trizonia and, finally, the *Bundesrepublik*. Another would be the massive investment in Germany that came from the Marshall Plan which guaranteed long-term US backing, even though much of the money came in after 1949 (see also Chapter 13, pages 314–18). Germany needed massive economic as well as political support. Only the injection of US dollars year-on-year could guarantee viability. Your job is to weigh up the alternatives and justify your choice with clear argument and good evidence.

13 West Germany 1949–63

POINTS TO CONSIDER

The purpose of this chapter is to consider how successfully the new democratic state in West Germany, the BRD, developed in its early years.

The challenges were immense for West Germany, yet it made much progress because of its political leadership and the commitment of the people. The main themes are:

- The creation of the new constitution
- Political stabilisation, and the political supremacy of Adenauer and the CDU/CSU
- The 'economic miracle'
- West German society
- Foreign relations and BRD's integration into the West
- Adenauer's fall from power and the significance of his era

Key dates

1949	May 23	Basic Law came into force; BRD set up
	Sept 15	Konrad Adenauer elected chancellor following first *Bundestag* election
	November	Petersberg Agreement
1951	April	Creation of ECSC
1952	August 21	Death of Schumacher
		Equalisation of Burdens Law
1952	May	EDC treaty agreed (but rejected in 1954 by French parliament)
1954	October	Paris treaties signed and later approved
1955	May	BRD became a sovereign state
		BRD joined NATO
	Nov 12	Basic Law amended by the *Bundestag* to create the *Bundeswehr* (federal army)
1957	March	Treaty of Rome signed creating the EEC
	Sept 15	Adenauer re-elected for his third term with a CDU/CSU overall majority
1959	November	Godesberg programme of SPD confirmed
1961	August 13	Berlin Wall started
1962	Oct–Nov	*Spiegel* affair
1963	October 15	Resignation of Adenauer

1 | The Bonn Republic

The new constitution

At the London Six Power Conference in 1948 (see page 291) it was decided to draft a new constitution for a West German state and this was quickly initiated, with two caveats:

- First, the new constitution was to remain under the strict control of the Western Occupying Powers. This was to be expressed in the Military Occupation Statute.
- Secondly, the new constitution was to be drawn up by a parliamentary council of 65 delegates from the *Länder*, not by a constituent assembly elected by all of the people (as it had been in January 1919).

Clearly, the fathers of the new constitution were very much aware of the failure of the Weimar state, the rise of the Nazis and the threat of communist totalitarianism they saw in the East. It was the highest aim of these people to create a stable and strong democracy that could not be overthrown. In their eyes the Weimar state had enabled Hitler to come to power and then undermine democracy while seemingly staying within the legal constitutional framework. Accordingly, the new framework was meant in many respects to be made safer and to fend off future threats from the right or left. And yet, when the BRD was founded in May 1949, the new constitution was still recognised as a provisional arrangement called the '**Basic Law**' (*Grundgesetz*). This was because the preamble spoke to all Germans and it was meant to be capable of making change until all parts of Germany were reunited again. It should not be forgotten that the BRD claimed to be the only legal successor of the Weimar Republic and the 'Basic Law' was seen to be fundamentally built upon Weimar (see pages 21–5). Therefore, both were federal, parliamentary, democratic and republican, but with several significant differences to Weimar.

Rights

At the very start the new constitution placed special emphasis on human and civil rights. They were seen as even standing above constitutional laws, which were 'unalienable' (a term also used in the US constitution). Yet, in Weimar those rights had been listed within the constitutional framework and could be suspended or abolished by a two-thirds majority in parliament.

The head of state (*Bundespräsident*)

The **federal president's** powers were dramatically diminished to mainly representative functions and his or her term in office was reduced from seven to five years – only re-electable for one further term. He or she was chosen by a special assembly made up of the all the members of the ***Bundestag***, and an equal number of members elected by the *Länder* parliaments. In contrast, in Weimar, the people had elected the president who came to be seen as a 'substitute Kaiser' with far-reaching political

Key question
Did the fathers of the BRD Constitution learn from the Weimar Constitution?

Key date

Basic Law came into force; BRD set up: 23 May 1949

Key terms

Basic Law
Grundgesetz. Technically, the document approved in May 1949 was *not* a constitution, as it was not permanent because the founding fathers wanted to have the flexibility for the reunification of the whole of Germany. Thus, all the terms had the features of a constitution but it was called the Basic Law.

Federal president
Bundespräsident. The head of state.

Bundestag
The 'federal assembly' or 'lower house' of the BRD German parliament. It claimed to be the successor of the *Reichstag*.

Figure 13.1: West Germany was created as the BRD in May 1949. It was a democratic parliamentary republic, but with strong federal autonomy. The 11 federal states (*Länder*) elected their own provincial assemblies, which sent representatives to the *Bundesrat*.

- Capital: Bonn
- Currency: Deutsche Mark
- Flag: a horizontal tricolour of black, red and gold
- Population: 47.5 million (1951)

powers (see page 24) such as influence over the appointment of the chancellor and the use of Article 48 to make law by decree. These presidential powers had been misused and discredited the parliamentary democracy.

(see page 24)

Parliament

The new constitution created was like Weimar with a two-tiered parliamentary structure made up of the *Bundestag* (the federal parliament) and the **Bundesrat** (the federal council). However, because the president's role could only be ceremonial, the chancellor (*Kanzler*) had a clear line of authority, as he had to be elected by and solely responsible to the *Bundestag*. Moreover, unlike Weimar, where a *simple* vote of no confidence had regularly brought down a government and destabilised the political system,

Key term

Bundesrat
The 'federal council' or upper house of the German parliament. Its members were appointed by members of the *Länder* governments.

in the new constitution the *Bundestag* could only bring down the chancellor and his government by a so-called, '*constructive* vote of no confidence'. This meant that the opposition not only required a majority supporting the vote of no confidence, but also had to be able to offer a stable positive majority for a new alternative government.

Electoral system

The new constitution upheld the **pluralism** of political parties as a necessity for a stable, functioning democracy. The constitution therefore prevented another abolition of them as had happened in Weimar. Also, the option for using direct votes on laws and other important issues (plebiscites or referenda) was not allowed by the new democracy. This was because the Third Reich had used such methods to manipulate the people.

Moreover, the election system was changed too. Weimar had been based on straightforward proportional representation (see page 23), which had led to many small parties in parliament, making it more difficult to form a coalition government. So, although the concept of proportional representation was maintained by the new constitution, it introduced the additional member system or mixed member proportional representation. This allowed for representatives for half the seats in the *Bundestag* to be elected by a majority vote in their constituencies and the other half from party lists, through proportional representation.

Additionally, in 1953 a 5 per cent hurdle was introduced for elections. By this any party that won less than 5 per cent of the national vote was barred from parliament. In these ways the electoral system was geared to favour the larger parties at the expense of the smaller ones, in the hope of establishing more stable coalitions.

Supreme court

Although Weimar had created the idea of a supreme court, its judiciary had not been wholly sympathetic to democracy (see page 25). The new constitution went much further to protect its values. A new agency was created with the right to investigate and prevent any anti-democratic activities from left or right in the BRD. Together with the BRD's new **constitution court** this was intended to fend off possible threats to democracy.

Therefore, in the 1950s various parties and organisations were deemed as threatening to the democracy, and forbidden:

- The right-wing Socialist Reich Party (SRP) in 1951.
- In 1950 11 communist organisations, most notably the Free German Youth.
- The League of German Youth (an extreme right-wing group) in 1953.
- Most controversially, the Communist Party, which gained 2.2 per cent in the 1953 elections but no representatives, was banned after a long legal case in 1956.

Key terms

Pluralism
The idea that *democratic* parties are an essential part of the constitution and cannot be abolished (Article 20). In the second paragraph of this article it says that if a party acts or aims against the constitution and is anti-democratic it can be forbidden.

Constitution court
Bundesverfassungsgericht. The main task is to review judicial cases. Therefore it can declare acts as unconstitutional.

Table 13.1: The Weimar and West Germany constitutions compared

	Weimar constitution	Basic Law of the BRD
Rights	• Suspendable by constitutional legislation	• Unalienable and standing above the constitution
Head of state	*Reichspräsident* • extensive powers: to dissolve the *Reichstag*, to appoint and dismiss the government, to pass emergency decrees without parliamentary consent • direct election by the people for seven years: re-election always possible	*Bundespräsident* • mainly ceremonial functions • very limited powers in the case of emergencies • elected by parliament and special representatives for five years: only one re-election possible
Parliament	*Reichstag* • able to bring down the chancellor's government by a simple vote of no confidence • main legislative power (in normal times) *Reichsrat* • only able to delay bills passed in the *Reichstag*	*Bundestag* • approved the chancellor • able to take control of the government through the 'constructive vote of no confidence' • participated in the election of the head of state and federal court judges *Bundesrat* • participated in legislation in assenting acts • participated in the election of the federal court judges
Government	National government (*Reichsregierung*) • weak position: chancellor and ministers dependent on the president and the *Reichstag* • chancellor quite easily removed from office by a simple vote of no confidence by the *Reichstag* or dismissed by the president	Federal government (*Bundesregierung*) • strong position: chancellor solely responsible to the *Bundestag* • chancellor only removed from office by a 'constructive vote of no confidence' in the *Bundestag* (to guarantee stability/continuity)
Electoral system	• right of political parties not fixed in the constitution • plebiscites and referenda allowed • pure proportional representation system in *Reichstag* (leading to many parties in the *Reichstag* and making it more difficult to form a government)	• party pluralism defined in the constitution as essential to democracy • plebiscites and referenda not allowed • mixed member proportional representation with a 5% hurdle in *Bundestag* elections (leading to fewer parties in the *Bundestag* and more stability)

Key question
Did the new constitution help to stabilise the development of democracy in the BRD?

In many respects the Basic Law successfully laid the basis for the BRD to create a stable democracy in the 1950s. Of course, it is easy to say that the Germans 'learnt' from the mistakes of Weimar, but it should be remembered that the political and socio-economic environment was much more favourable in the 1950s. First, West Germany experienced real economic growth and secondly, it overcame its diplomatic isolation and soon found major friends and allies. These factors allowed the BRD to evolve more easily than Weimar in the 1920s.

A few critics on the political extremes have pointed to aspects of the constitution, which suggested that the BRD was not so genuinely democratic; for example, the 5 per cent rule, and the banning of left- and right-wing extremists. Nevertheless, despite everything, the foundations of the new constitution and its cautious flexibility did create an effective democracy and the BRD could survive its pains of birth. Particularly, its federal structure and constitutional court allowed the democracy to mature in the long term, most significantly in the way it effectively embraced the eastern *Länder* in the political reunification of 1990.

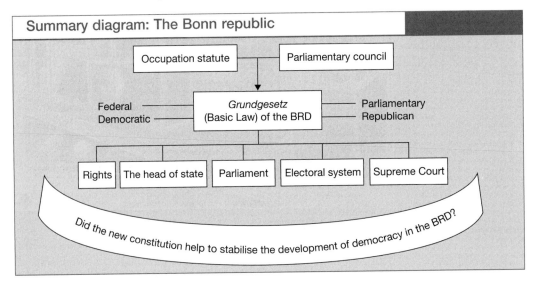

Summary diagram: The Bonn republic

2 | Party Politics

Key question
How did Adenauer create the first BRD government?

At first sight it was quite an achievement to draw up the new constitution and to make arrangements for the BRD's first *Bundestag* election within four years of 1945. Furthermore, it can be seen in Table 13.2 that the votes of the three major parties were a strong endorsement of the democratic process, which showed the German people's general acceptance of the new state:

Table 13.2: Results of 1945 *Bundestag* election

	Percentage of vote	No. of seats
CDU/CSU	31.0	139
SPD	29.2	131
FDP	11.9	52
Communist	5.7	22
Others	22.2	65

However, the election results did not so easily provide the basis for creating an effective government. The fourth largest party was the Communist Party, which polled 5.7 per cent. Perhaps more significantly, the remaining 22.2 per cent of the vote for the first

Bundestag was won by a diverse range of regional and splinter groups. All in all 11 parties and two independent members got into parliament, some with distinctly right-wing leanings. In 1949 six of the parties reached less than 5 per cent of the votes, but still won seats before the hurdle was introduced in 1953.

Although the left wing of the CDU was sympathetic to the idea of creating a great coalition with the SPD, Adenauer, the leader of the CDU, was determined to form a small coalition with the FDP and one of the smaller parties. This was because of the significant differences between the CDU and SPD over economic policy and foreign policy, over which Adenauer did not really want to compromise (see pages 303–5 and 308).

In this way Adenauer was able to put together a coalition made up of 208 out of 402 seats, not a really comfortable majority, but one with a strong common working basis. On 15 September 1949 Adenauer was elected chancellor of the first government with a majority of just one: including his own vote! Theodor Heuss, the leader of the FDP, was invited to become the first president of the BRD.

Key date

Konrad Adenauer elected chancellor following first *Bundestag* election: 15 September 1949

Adenauer and the CDU 1949–63

With hindsight it is all too easy to assume that the story of the 'Adenauer era' was bound to unfold. Yet, many contemporaries had limited faith in Adenauer's government to survive. It was felt that the difficulties in creating the government could lead to disagreements within the coalition and the withdrawal of partners. Also, the new government faced a range of problems:

- Economic. Despite the liberating effects of currency reform, the fledgling economy still faced difficulties and in 1949–50 it suffered a recession. Unemployment rose to two million, about 13 per cent, and yet prices continued to rise.
- Social. The need to build millions of houses to make up for the bombing and to accommodate the millions of refugees from eastern Germany.
- Political. The BRD was still under the control of the the the 'Occupation Statute' and did not have sovereignty. Only the Allies could approve many aspects of government, such as trade and internal security.

However, from this delicate political power-base Adenauer and his party were to dominate and stabilise the BRD until the mid-1960s. He personally was to win four *Bundestag* elections and his leadership was to shape post-war Germany, as can be seen from Table 13.3.

Key question
What was Adenauer's vision for the CDU?

Adenauer's aim

Adenauer identified himself as a supporter of Western liberal democracy and Catholic conservatism; very much in contrast to the atheism and planned economy of the socialist movement. In political terms, therefore, the coalition of the CDU and CSU proved itself successful in uniting a broad majority of conservative Christian middle-class voters.

Table 13.3: *Bundestag elections*

Date	August 1949	March 1953	September 1957	September 1961
Electorate (millions)	24.5	28.5	31.1	32.8
Turnout (%)	78.5	85.8	87.8	87.7
CDU/CSU Percentage (seats)	31.0 (139)	45.2 (243)	50.2 (270)	45.3 (242)
SPD Percentage (seats)	29.2 (131)	28.8 (151)	31.8 (169)	36.2 (190)
FDP Percentage (seats)	11.9 (52)	9.5 (48)	7.7 (41)	12.8 (67)
KPD Percentage (seats)	5.7 (15)	2.2 (0)	–	–
Others Percentage (seats)	22.2 (65)	14.3 (44)	10.3 (17)	5.7 (0)

Adenauer's aims in the 1950s were shaped by four major issues:

1. Western integration. Like the majority of the West Germans Adenauer mistrusted and feared the Soviets and consequently he looked for protection from the West. He wanted to gain the trust of the Western Powers in order to revise the restrictions of the Occupational Statute as quickly as possible and to become a reliable ally and strong economic partner.

2. The 'German question'. On the 'German question' Adenauer believed that the reunification of the BRD and the DDR had to be on the terms of maintaining a Western capitalist-orientated state. He publicly assured the people that reunification was close to his heart, but he was determined not to make any concessions to communism and he saw other priorities first. He believed that if the BRD could achieve a Western partnership not only would it secure the state against communism, it would also attract East Germans to join West Germany by their own decision. In a way, this 'magnet theory' was a success, as nearly three million refugees left East Germany for the West before the closing of the frontiers with the building of the Berlin Wall in 1961.

3. Economic policy. The economic history of Germany, 1914–45 was traumatic. So Adenauer and his finance minister, Ludwig Erhard, were determined to create economic stability for the new state in the wake of depression, war and the spread of communism. Certainly, the onset of the **Korean War**, 1950–3, spurred the German economy out of recession and into boom. This boom was also shaped by the economic reforms initiated by Erhard's 'social market' policy. This aimed to create a free market, but one limited with social regulations by the state. This 'economic miracle' sustained years of major growth until the recession of 1966–7, and provided the economic context

Korean War
The first armed confrontation of the Cold War in 1950–3. The BRD was not in a position to give military support, but the war did act as a major boom to the production of German goods.

Key term

Profile: Konrad Adenauer 1876–1967

1876		– Born in Cologne of a Catholic lawyer
1894–1901		– Studied law at Freiburg, Munich and Bonn
1904		– Married Emma Weyer and later had three children
1905		– Joined the ZP (Catholic Centre Party), see page 275
1917		– Elected mayor of Cologne
1933		– Refused to receive Hitler during a campaign visit to Cologne and removed from office by the Nazis
1944		– Arrested after the '20 July bomb plot' and held in a camp
1945	May	– Restored as Mayor of Cologne by the Americans, but soon removed from office by the British in October
	December	– Co-founder of the CDU and became its party chairman for the British Zone
1948		– Elected president of the Parliamentary Council, which drew up the political foundations for the BRD
1949	August	– Elected as a representative in the German *Bundestag*
	September	– Chosen by the *Bundestag* as Germany's first federal chancellor
	November	– Petersberg Agreement
1951–5		– Served additionally as foreign minister
1953		– Re-elected as chancellor
1954		– Paris treaties signed
1955	May 5	– BRD became a sovereign state
	May 9	– BRD joined NATO
	November 12	– Basic Law amended to create *Bundeswehr*
1957	March	– Treaty of Rome signed creating the EEC
	September	– Re-elected as chancellor: CDU/CSU won overall majority
1961		– Re-elected as chancellor
1962		– The Spiegel affair
1963		– Resigned as chancellor at the age of 87 (although he still remained the head of the CDU until 1966 and a *Bundestag* representative until his death)
1967		– Died at his villa in Rhöndorf near Bonn and was granted a state funeral

Adenauer's political framework was shaped by his strong Catholicism and he joined the original ZP in Imperial Germany. His moral integrity was proved by his refusal to co-operate with the Nazis, despite suffering persecution. Although in 1949 he was already 73 years old, he then won four elections for his party, the CDU, and stayed in his position of power for 14 years. The 'old man' became the political father and most influential leader for the emerging young democracy of West Germany.

He was a strong-willed character and a strong anti-communist, which reflected his determination to follow what he saw as the only possible course for West Germany: namely, to gain the trust of the Occupying Powers and to lead the country into a strong alliance with the West. By the mid-1950s that trend had been established. Moreover, his single-minded pro-Western course and his refusal to believe in the possibility of a reunited neutral and free Germany during the Cold War brought him criticism from the opposition for being a 'Chancellor of the Allies' sacrificing Germany's national interests. He was unimpressed by this and at the same time blocked all possibilities for negotiations with the East on their terms.

Together with Erhard, minister of finance, he instigated the success story of the 'economic miracle' and led West Germany into the EEC. Yet, in his final years in office this obstinate attitude and his rigid style of government brought him increasing criticism even within his own party. Unable to read the signs of change in national and international politics and not wanting to let go of his power he was finally forced to resign in 1963.

Adenauer may have outstayed his time in office, yet at his death in 1967 his state funeral was attended by every international key figure. It was under his leadership that the country recovered from the Nazi dictatorship, built Europe's strongest economy, and gained a leading role in Europe.

for so many features of the development of the BRD (see pages 312–18).

4. Social aspects. Adenauer recognised the need for the CDU/CSU to give more than economic growth. Above all, it needed to provide a social dimension that would overcome the privations of the poor and refugees by new social legislation, industrial peace and a quick growth in living standards. In that way, it was hoped to create a degree of social consensus that would put the privations of the German people behind them and counter the threat of communism.

CDU political domination

In the second election of 1953 the CDU/CSU increased their share of the vote to 45.2 per cent, which, because of the complicated distribution of the seats in parliament, gave the CDU/CSU an absolute majority of one seat (although Adenauer maintained the coalition with the FDP).

Key question
How did Adenauer and the CDU politically stabilise Germany in the 1950s?

CDU election poster of 1957. It simply appeals to the electorate by offering 'no experiments'. How do you think this simple poster was meant to appeal? Was it successful in the election?

In 1957 the successful election campaign with the leading slogan 'no experiments' enabled Adenauer and the CDU/CSU to reach their high point, which underlined his success and the growing political stability since 1949:

- Adenauer and the CDU/CSU had gained an absolute majority of 50.2 per cent of the votes and the FDP did not join the government.
- Significantly, democratic participation had improved markedly. In the first *Bundestag* election in 1949 78.5 per cent of the electorate had gone to the polls, but by 1957 the issues raised in the election campaigns were generally met with interest, which was to grow even further in the next two elections until it reached 87.8 per cent.
- Also, the small rather extremist splinter groups and parties in the first parliament, which seemed a possible danger to the new democracy, quickly disappeared; not only because the 5 per cent hurdle was introduced in 1953, but also because the big parties proved to have a highly integrating force and gave a new home to many voters on the extreme right and left.

Perhaps unsurprisingly, the success of the CDU is intimately connected with the role of Adenauer and indeed, the years 1949–3 have been called the 'Adenauer era'. In view of Germany's immediate past the political domination of Adenauer and the

Key date

Adenauer re-elected for his third term with a CDU/CSU overall majority:
15 September 1957

CDU could have revoked old fears within the state and abroad. But the leadership of Adenauer proved to be very positive, not only in the eyes of most West Germans, but in those of the Western powers too. Under the liberal-conservative governments in the 1950s the economy was stabilised, a balanced social security system established, the participation of the unions in industry enhanced and regulated, and the early political and economic restrictions and control of the new state through the Western Allies revised and turned into close co-operation and partnership.

His early successes in the first half of the 1950s confirmed to Adenauer's supporters that he had made the right decisions economically and politically by opting for a clear way West and rejecting temptations from the communists for a quick reunification process under the restricted conditions demanded by the Soviets. Even his opponents in the end had to admit grudgingly that their criticism and alternative ideas might have been misguided and impracticable in the context of the Cold War at the end of the 1950s.

The role of the SPD

When the SPD was reconstituted in the Western Zones in 1945 it saw itself first and foremost as the heir to the old social democratic values and the ideas of the Second Reich and the Weimar Republic. And in the 'Heidelberg Programme of 1925' the SPD outlined that it considered itself to be primarily a workers' party with its roots in the Marxist ideology. In the light of the awful experiences of the Nazi state the vast majority of the Party were therefore committed to strong demands for:

Key question
What were the aims of the SPD in the 1950s?

- nationalisation of the financial sector, such as banks and insurance companies
- nationalisation of key industries, such as coal, steel and electricity and the railways
- the redistribution of large private property, as had happened in the Soviet Zone.

Therefore, the SPD saw Erhard's economic plan as liberal capitalism, albeit with the term of the 'social market', which was not in the interest of the majority of the people and a threat to the new democracy. Indeed, the promises of Adenauer and Erhard to make a quick increase in living standards and a rise in social security for everyone were denounced by Schumacher as unachievable. Not surprisingly, the two different economic concepts became the key issues in the first election campaign and turned more bitter when Schumacher himself in the *Bundestag* declared that the 'CDU's promises were just a bag of lies'.

With regard to the 'German question' after 1945, the SPD saw itself as the only party which could serve the true interests of the whole of Germany. In 1946 the SPD in the Western Zones had rejected a merger with the KPD as the latter was seen as an instrument of Stalin's interests which would harm the

Profile: Kurt Schumacher 1895–1952

1895		– Born in Kulm, West Prussia (now Poland)
1914	August	– Joined the German army as a volunteer
	December	– Seriously wounded which resulted in his arm being amputated
1915–19		– Studied law and politics at Berlin University
1918		– Joined the SPD
1920		– Appointed editor of the party newspaper in Swabia, south-west Germany
1930		– Elected as an SPD representative of the *Reichstag*
1933–45		– Arrested by Nazis and held in various concentration camps
1945		– Immediately got to work with building up the SPD again
1946	Jan–April	– Rejected the plan to merger the KPD and the SPD (which resulted in the creation of the SED in the Soviet Zone)
	May	– Elected chairman of the SPD in the Western Zones
1948	September	– Suffered a thrombosis resulting in the amputation of a leg
1948–9		– In negotiations over the constitution, the Western Allies accepted Schumacher's proposal for it to be 'as centralised as necessary and as federal as possible'
1949	August	– SPD defeated in the first *Bundestag* election
	September	– Applied for the post of federal president, but was defeated by Heuss
1949–52		– Led the opposition in the Bundestag against Adenauer and the CDU, but his style became more antagonistic; and he even opposed the development of the ECSC
1952		– Died unexpectedly in Bonn

When Kurt Schumacher re-entered the political scene of West Germany in 1945 he was a man broken in his body, although not in his spirit and his commitment to socialism. This son of a tradesman, he was a highly intelligent student who gained a doctorate in law, but lost an arm fighting in the First World War and later a leg as a consequence of the torture he had suffered at the hand of the Nazis. He then used his astute mind and his charismatic rhetorical skills to restore the SPD and to turn himself into the leader of the Party in the Western Zones.

In the next seven years with his energy and conviction he came to be seen as one of the founding fathers of West Germany:

- he became the SPD party chairman in 1946 and committed it to the nationalisation of key industries and banking and more democratic participation in industry
- he vehemently opposed the communists (whom he partly blamed for the rise of Hitler) and he strongly opposed the merger of the SPD and the KPD into the SED in 1946 in the Soviet Zone
- he campaigned for a reunified, largely demilitarised and neutral Germany.

Yet, the SPD defeat in the first *Bundestag* election was a real blow for him and he largely failed with his aim of a priority for Germany's reunification in contrast to Adenauer's Western orientation. Therefore, in his final few years he became increasingly embittered and disappointed with his political achievements; his hostility to Adenauer was vehement at times, and Germany's improving stability and the Cold War were undermining Schumacher's stance. His early death in 1952 was a heavy loss to the SPD.

development of a democratic, unified Germany. So unification – albeit on their terms – was a major principle of the SPD.

For similar reasons, but from a very different perspective, the SPD was hostile to Adenauer's policy with the West (see the Petersberg Agreement on page 328). In a heated debate about this issue Schumacher mocked Adenauer as a 'chancellor of the Allies', a serious affront for which he was suspended from parliament for 20 days! So the SPD viewed Adenauer's rapprochement with the Western powers as a sell-out which ruined the chances of negotiating with the Soviets to agree on a reunified, largely demilitarised, and politically neutral Germany.

Schumacher's unexpected death in 1952 saw the loss of a dynamic, charismatic party leader who was replaced by Erich Ollenhauer, a rather colourless character. However, in a way the political tone had been set in the years immediately after 1945 and so the SPD's limitations in the 1950s were really more of substance than character. As a result, the Party failed to engage the sympathies of more than one-third of the electorate, whereas the vision of Adenauer's CDU stirred more and more West Germans, and it became stronger and stronger. Therefore, throughout the decade 'the SPD itself was somewhat in disarray' (Fulbrook) and its limitations are clear:

Key question
When and why did the SPD change its political outlook?

- The economic recovery led to a steep fall in unemployment and although pay rises were initially still very moderate people felt that progress and a spreading optimism put the opposition in a more and more difficult position.
- The open confrontation of the Cold War and the specific crises over the Berlin blockade and the Korean War exacerbated the mistrust and fear of communism. Many people sympathised with Adenauer who figured that a largely defenceless West Germany had a high risk of falling prey to Soviet influence.

Key dates

Death of
Schumacher:
21 August 1952

Godesberg
programme of SPD
confirmed: November
1959

- The SPD had opposed German rearmament and Adenauer's western integration and yet the people increasingly had got used to the realities of a divided Germany. Indeed, protection by the Western allies and integration with the West became increasingly attractive.

The victory of Adenauer in 1957 was the SPD's third defeat in a row and it seemed that the Party was destined to stay in political opposition. Yet, at an extraordinary Party conference at Bad Godesberg in 1959 the SPD rejected the traditional Marxist line with its demands for nationalisation and a neutral Germany and resolved on a change of direction. In its place, the SPD adopted a more liberal economic course while aiming to overcome the social inequities of an increasingly affluent society. Moreover, it acknowledged the Western integration and remilitarisation as necessities, thereby signalling its will to work with the political realities of the time in order to prove that it could take on government responsibilities.

Therefore from 1959, in electoral terms the SPD had opened itself to a much broader electorate that could embrace the middle classes. In that way the SPD was set to portray itself as a mass movement, a *Volkspartei*, rather than a class-based workers' party.

SPD poster for the 1949 election with the campaign slogan: 'With the SPD for a free, social and united Germany.'

This strategy was rewarded, albeit slowly, so it took more than another 10 years for the SPD to increase its support and overtake the CDU/CSU in votes. It was not until 1969 that Willy Brandt became the first SPD chancellor since 1930.

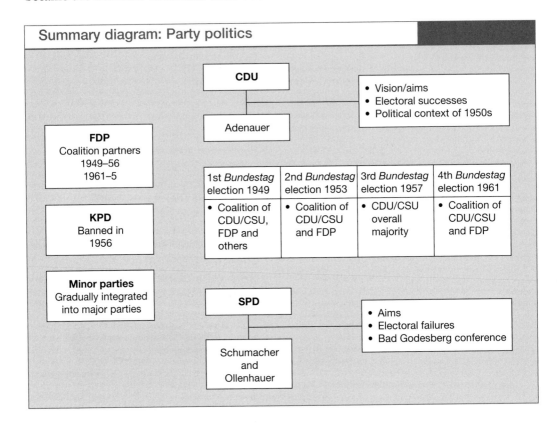

Summary diagram: Party politics

CDU
- Vision/aims
- Electoral successes
- Political context of 1950s

Adenauer

FDP
Coalition partners
1949–56
1961–5

1st *Bundestag* election 1949	2nd *Bundestag* election 1953	3rd *Bundestag* election 1957	4th *Bundestag* election 1961
• Coalition of CDU/CSU, FDP and others	• Coalition of CDU/CSU and FDP	• CDU/CSU overall majority	• Coalition of CDU/CSU and FDP

KPD
Banned in
1956

Minor parties
Gradually integrated
into major parties

SPD
- Aims
- Electoral failures
- Bad Godesberg conference

Schumacher
and
Ollenhauer

3 | The 'Economic Miracle'

The 'social market economy'

Although the CDU had drawn up the so-called Ahlen Programme in 1947 (see page 276), the Party quickly drew back from its tentative ideas of nationalisation and instead came to uphold a new form of economic liberalism. This idea was named the 'social economy' and it was principally put into practice by one man, the minister of trade and industry, Ludwig Erhard, 1949–63. He became the symbol of the 'economic miracle' in the 1950s (see his profile).

The thinking behind the concept of the 'social market' had evolved among his colleagues at Nuremberg Business School even during the Nazi years. However, it was only as the Director of the German Economic Council of the Bizone from 1948 that he began to put his principles into effect. Therefore, he played a crucial role with the Western Allies in preparing the currency reform and in ending state regulations. This opened the market for industrial and consumer goods and stimulated their production (see page 286–7).

Key question
What is the 'social market economy'?

Profile: Ludwig Erhard 1897–1977

1897		– Born in Fürth, Bavaria
1913–16		– Commercial apprentice
1916–18		– Served in the First World War and was badly wounded
1919–25		– Studied economics and sociology at Frankfurt University
1928–42		– Joined the staff of a Business School at Nuremberg and became its director
1942		– The Nazis removed him from this position, when he refused to join the Party. He spent the last few years of the war as a consultant to business enterprises
1944		– Wrote his study, *War Finances and Debt Consolidation*
1945–48		– Attended various posts as an economic consultant in the Western Zones
1948	March	– Appointed Director of Economic Council of the Bizone
	June	– Oversaw the currency reform and the creation of the Deutsche Mark, and largely freed the market from state regulations so prices were set by supply and demand
1949	July	– The CDU adopted Erhard's policy of a social market economy
1949	September	– Joined the CDU and elected as a member in the first *Bundestag* election
1949–63		– Minister of economics in all four of Adenauer's governments
1957		– Publication of his own book, *Prosperity for All*
1959		– Presidency fiasco: Adenauer highlighted his doubts about Erhard as successor
1963		– Elected by the *Bundestag* as chancellor following resignation of Adenauer
1965		– Re-elected and his coalition won with increased majority
1966		– Resigned as chancellor following withdrawal of FDP from the coalition, but stayed as a member of *Bundestag* until his death
1977		– Died

Erhard was not a born politician: he refused to join any Nazi organisations. Instead, he developed his economic expertise by academic study and with practical business experience concentrating on teaching and working out his theories on market mechanisms along the lines of liberal market policies.

His apolitical background and economic ideas stood him well with the Western Allies, especially the Americans, and he was able to present well-argued plans for rebuilding the ruined German economy. When he was made Director of Economics for the Bizone his role proved to be vital by:

- implementing the currency reform in the Western Zones
- lifting most restrictions on control prices in the market
- reducing taxation.

The immediate effects of Erhard's reforms on the German economy were dramatic and quickly recognised. He expressed his concept of the social market economy, which has been described as a 'free economy with a social conscience' and in 1949 he joined Adenauer's CDU. He then joined the government and served as minister of economics continuously from 1949 to 1963; in effect, he oversaw the Germany economy and in that time it developed into an economic giant.

By 1957 Erhard became vice-chancellor and his popularity rivalled that of Adenauer. The public saw him as the 'crown prince' and felt he should succeed Adenauer, which soured their relationship. Adenauer saw Erhard as too weak and not politically refined enough for the highest post. Nevertheless, although he became chancellor in 1963, Adenauer's instincts seemed to have had some basis and after only three years in office Erhard stepped down in 1966 when the country faced recession.

Erhard remained a member of the *Bundestag* and when he died in 1977 at the age of 80 he was celebrated by his countrymen as 'the father of the economic miracle'.

Erhard believed that the aim of the 'social market economy' lay in rising consumption and economic growth. However, he did not support the theory of classical liberal economists who opposed state intervention. Instead, the 'social market economy' was attempting to construct a 'third way' between unrestrained capitalism and an over-regulated socialist economy. Its aim was to combine political and economic freedom with social justice and security. While private property should be protected, and enterprise and investment supported with as many financial incentives as possible, a strong state should also be able to intervene in the free market in order to defend the common interests of the individual.

The economic record: from recession to boom 1948–66

Key question
How strong was the West German economy up to 1966?

Erhard's implementation of the social market economy in 1948–9 did not immediately bring about economic take off. Admittedly, the currency reform and the abolition of price controls liberated the economy, which made more consumer goods available. But the steep rise of prices was not matched by the rate of wage increases, which caused hardship for the poorer elements in society. In addition the shortages of many resources, especially coal, which were required for rebuilding industry, led to a sharp increase in imports and a serious balance of payments deficit. So, 1949–50 were the years of the 'foundation crisis', when the German economy actually faced recession because there was not enough demand to sustain growth and a lack of foreign currency for investment. With unemployment as high as 13.5 per cent and with prices still rising (the cost of petrol went up by 50 per cent!) Erhard was under pressure from many quarters by 1950 to change his economic policy by a return to state controls. Yet, although it was not recognised at the time, the worst was over by 1951, as the economic stimulus of the Korean War had begun to kick in and exports, especially to the USA, rose steeply.

By 1952 the success of the economic recovery could not be denied from the statistics:

- Economic growth was high and carried on for nearly 15 years until the first recession in 1966–7. Nowadays, in Britain an annual growth rate of 2.5–3 per cent is deemed very pleasing, yet the BRD had rates of 12 per cent and 10 per cent and the *average growth rate per year was 8 per cent* (see Table 13.4).
- From 1950 to 1955 the GNP almost doubled, and by 1960 it nearly increased another 50 per cent. By the middle of the 1950s more coal was being mined in the BRD than in the whole of Germany in 1936. Most significantly, production went hand in hand with the massive growth of motorisation: bicycles, motor scooters and cars. This was symbolised by the dream of the man in the street with the VW, *Volkswagen*, or 'Beetle'.
- From its worrying deficit in 1950, the balance of trade quickly turned positive from 1952 because of Germany's rapid growth of exports. By 1954 the BRD had already become the third biggest trading power behind Britain and the USA again, especially for tools, machines, cars, electronic and chemical products. It proudly sold its products with the label 'Made in Germany' that stood for good quality at reasonable prices. (The DM price was at first quite undervalued.)
- The economic expansion was reflected in the creation of jobs and the decline of unemployment. Unemployment went down to just one million (4.2 per cent) by 1955 and within a few years West Germany enjoyed a period of full employment which did not really end until the early 1970s. More telling was the fact that the creation of jobs even managed to satisfy the influx of another three million people who arrived from the DDR before 1961. By the early 1960s the shortage of workers had led to the recruitment and immigration of foreign labour from Italy and Turkey.
- The one economic sector which enjoyed mixed fortunes was agriculture. It, of course, had faced problems since the 1920s (see pages 102 and 184). Although farmers continued to receive heavy subsidies the structure of the economy was changing, and as a consequence the proportion of the workforce employed in farming was nearly halved – from

23 per cent to 13 per cent – in the 10 years of the 1950s. Nevertheless, the rationalisation by more mechanisation still brought about a substantial increase in production – nearly 25 per cent over the same years.

Table 13.4: Real growth of the West German economy

Year	1951	1953	1955	1957	1959	1961	1963	1965
Growth (%)	10.4	8.2	12.0	5.7	7.3	5.4	3.4	5.6

Table 13.5: West German industrial production

Year	1950	1955	1960	1965
Index of industrial production (100 = 1961)	36.5	64.4	90.7	118.3
Change on previous year (%)	–	15.5	11.8	5.4

Table 13.6: Unemployment in West Germany

Year	1950	1955	1960	1965
No. of unemployed (millions)	1.87	1.07	0.27	0.15
Working population unemployed (%)	8.1	4.2	1.0	0.5

Table 13.7: Exports and imports in West Germany

Year	1950	1955	1960	1965
Exports (DM millions)	8,363	25,717	47,900	71,700
Imports (DM millions)	11,373	24,461	42,700	70,400

The 'economic miracle'

At the time Erhard himself did not like the use of the term 'economic miracle'. And, as the historian Overy acknowledged, Germany's recovery was not really a miracle 'in the sense that [it] defied explanation'.

In the long term the BRD inherited several advantages. It had access to extensive resources, such as coal and iron from the Ruhr region, and the country's population was well educated with a high level of technical skills. Moreover, in the medium term the Marshall Plan provided the economic context for recovery. The generous terms of this programme enabled the BRD to get off to a good start by building new factories and equipping them with modern machinery. By 1951 Germany was given $1.5 billion out of the $12.7 billion of the Marshall Plan. This was therefore a stimulus to the German economy and an important boost of political morale to the emerging state. Nevertheless, over time historians have considered its impact from a broader perspective. First, the amount of money should not be exaggerated, and it should be noted that Britain received twice as much as Germany. Secondly, Erhard's financial reforms (including the 'currency reform') are now generally seen as by far the most significant

Key question
Why did the BRD become an 'economic giant'?

A caricature of Erhard drawn in 1959. What impression does the cartoonist try to convey by the drawing?

factor. As Singleton writes: 'In other words, it is policy that principally matters, rather than the amount of aid a country gets.'

The long boom from 1951 to 1966 can also be explained by several additional key factors which evolved in the 1950s.

World trade

Ever since the First World War, world trade had been seriously hampered by the effects of the wars and the economic depression. Yet, after 1945 the USA used its influence to reduce tariffs globally. The Korean War then led to a real growth in world trade in the early 1950s. Initially the aid from the Marshall Plan was only meant to last three years, but the creation of the OEEC helped to open up the European markets and speeded up the reintegration of German trade into the world market. In western Europe specifically, German exports received another boost by the creation of the **ECSC** in 1951 and more significantly by the foundation of the **EEC**.

Refugees

At first the number of refugees was seen as an imposing problem, but as industry began to grow again they became an advantage. The continued influx of refugees from the DDR provided a continuous supply of qualified, disciplined and highly motivated employees on the labour market who were easily satisfied with moderate incomes.

Industrial peace

The government was keen to establish more peaceful industrial relations by creating a sense of responsibility and ownership in the trade unions. The idea of co-determination between

Key terms

ECSC
The European Coal and Steel Community, created in 1951.

EEC
The European Economic Community. The Treaty of Rome, signed in March 1957, created a customs union of six countries: BRD, France, Italy and Benelux (Belgium, the Netherlands and Luxembourg).

employers and employees was shaped by two crucial laws: the Co-determination Law of 1951 and the Works' Constitution Law of 1952 (see in more details on page 320 in social change section). The number of strikes in West Germany fell dramatically and the country enjoyed real industrial peace for 20 years; both sides reaped the benefits.

Consumption demand

Demand expanded enormously for capital and consumer goods. Six million houses were built up to 1961, initiated by state investment for social housing. This was the motor of economic recovery. Incentives like special subsidised savings programmes to buy your own property pushed up private demand. As confidence recovered, the demand for consumer goods, such as cars, televisions, refrigerators and vacuum cleaners, began to show all the signs of increasing prosperity (see also page 323).

Financial stability

In contrast to the financial problems of the years 1914–48, West German banking afterwards came to be a symbol of financial correctness. Initially, the *Bank Deutscher Länder* was created in 1948 by the Western Allies (see pages 286–7) to establish the Deutsche Mark, but in 1957 it was restructured and officially became the federal bank, the *Bundesbank*. In this capacity the *Bundesbank* was the central bank, but it operated independently from the government. It watched over the stability of the currency by controlling the money circulation, and raising interest rates in order to prevent an overheating of the market and inflation.

Government expenditure

Although in 1952 the BRD signed an agreement in London to pay debts from the Marshall Plan credits and the Dawes Plan, it did not have to pay reparations and its defence costs were at first limited. (It was only allowed to form an army in 1955.) Therefore, its government expenditure was more limited than other countries, like Britain for example, and Erhard was more able to be generous with social spending, which enhanced the stability of the young democracy (in comparison with Weimar).

Summary

There is little doubt that the economic record of the BRD in its early years stands out. Moreover, the years of growth, 1951–66, laid the long-term foundations that enabled the BRD to mature into an economic giant. However, although Erhard's own book, *Prosperity for All* (1957), was obviously written with pride at his economic success, critics have pointed that the country became somewhat obsessed with financial success. In that way, the economic miracle was achieved at the expense of other factors, which are focused on in the section on social history on pages 319–27.

Summary diagram: The 'economic miracle'

Erhard's background	The 'social market economy'	Theory and aims

Economic growth GNP	**The economic record: from recession to boom 1949–66**	Balance of trade Employment Agriculture

Marshall Aid World trade	The 'economic miracle' Why did the BRD become an 'economic giant'?	Financial stability Government expenditure

Refugees	Industrial peace	Consumption

4 | West German Society

Social policies

The success of Erhard's social market economy put West Germany on an upward course. The gross national product (GNP) grew in the 1950s at a yearly average of 8 per cent and by 1956 full employment was almost achieved, despite the continuous influx of emigrants from the DDR. The flourishing economy enabled the government to realise its promises to build up the welfare state and to integrate more effectively all social groups into society.

Social redress

The 'economic miracle' can disguise the fact that many millions of the West German population were still in a dire situation in the aftermath of the war. Therefore, one of the first pieces of legislation in 1950 provided relief for 4.5 million people: refugees, prisoners of war and the disabled.

Very importantly for the social peace in the newly established state was the passing of the 'Equalisation of Burdens Law' of 1952. This introduced a property levy on capital and real estate that had not been affected by the war to give something to those people who had suffered heavy losses. Through this legislation over DM143 billion were gradually redistributed in the next three decades. Although this did not fundamentally change the old social and economic structures of society, like a real redistribution of the property as demanded by the SPD would have done, it eased social tensions.

Also, the 131 Law of 1951 restored the employment and pension rights of civil servants. This was financially very expensive and quite controversial. However, it did reconcile millions of middle-class public employees to the emerging new

Key question
What steps were taken by the German government to guarantee social peace after the war?

Key date

Equalisation of Burdens Law: 1952

state. It regulated the pensions and in many cases reintegrated ex-civil servants and military into the new state administration to help its quick rebuilding. In this way quite a few Nazi sympathisers (for example, the secretary of state and Adenauer's right-hand man, Globke) who had been dismissed by the Allies at the end of the war were generously re-employed in their old positions. Although this was later a highly disputed move it served its purpose in fostering the reintegration of a relevant group of people with the new democratic state.

Integration of the trade unions

Trade unions had begun to be recognised during the occupation, although ironically bearing in mind Britain's poor post-war industrial relations history, many of the BRD developments originated in the British Zone. As a result, in the years from 1949, a new understanding emerged between labour, employers and government.

First, old internal conflicts were overcome when the trade union system was simplified in 1949 by the creation of 16 workers' unions based on industry sector. Moreover, they were affiliated to one umbrella organisation, the **German Federation of Trade Unions** and did not see themselves as party organisations. They co-ordinated their activities in the individual companies instead of counteracting each other. All this made them much stronger in their negotiations with the government and the employers' associations.

Secondly, although the workers' unions and the SPD had wanted a complete restructuring of the economy and society, through, for example, a redistribution of property, nationalisation of key industries and a planned economy, Adenauer's government recognised the importance of achieving industrial peace. He therefore mollified the unions by introducing the **Co-determination** Law of 1951, which gave workers representatives on managerial boards in the coal, iron and steel industries.

Thirdly, the principle of co-determination was extended by the Works' Constitution Law of 1952, which created a works council for all employees of companies with more than 500 workers.

In the most obvious way these initiatives were very successful, as West Germany had very few strikes compared to Britain and France and the industrial peace coincided with much improved conditions for the union members. Yet, most significantly, the 1950s witnessed the development of a new approach from German trade unions which, to a large extent, agreed to abstain from party politics, despite their partisanship for the SPD. They overcame their initial doubts about the economic policies of Erhard and eventually warmed towards capitalism in its free social market. And in the end they started to act as critical partners rather than antagonists to the employers.

German Federation of Trade Unions *Deutscher Gerwerkschaftsbund.* Similarly, the civil service and unions of other professional sectors organised themselves in two large umbrella organisations (*Deutscher Beamtenbund* and *Deutsche Angestellten-Gewerkschaft*).

Co-determination *Mitbestimmung.* The practice in which employees have a role in management of a company.

Key terms

The welfare state

The SPD had campaigned for a completely new tax-based system aimed at thoroughly reforming the welfare state. However, the essence of the insurance system initiated by Bismarck and developed by Weimar was kept as the model by the government in the 1950s. In that way, the system of social security was reinstituted, but expanded for:

- Unemployment benefit: based on the 1927 legislation until 1969 (see page 61).
- Accident insurance.
- Sickness insurance: much improved by a law of 1957 which increased sick pay.
- Pensions: one of the most important achievements after the war was the reform of the pension insurance system in 1957. It raised a person's pension to 60 per cent of final-year earnings (Britain's was 29 per cent).
- Public assistance: for desperate cases (see above, for example, for the relief for refugees).
- Family welfare: families were particularly supported by a whole range of measures: tax-based child allowances and from 1954 by the introduction of child benefit, for example, on page 319.

Of course, house building played an important part in restoring the economy, but the emphasis clearly had a social dimension. Right from the start throughout the 1950s the state supported and subsidised the public and private building sector in order to alleviate the shortage of housing and create affordable accommodation, especially for families. From 1949 to 1961 six million new flats were built, and significantly half of the new accommodation was social housing or council homes.

Further reforms were to be introduced in the 1960s, yet the policies and laws of the BRD government had laid the basis for a highly advanced welfare state. It compared very well in this field with other Western industrialised societies.

Table **13.8**: West German's social welfare budget 1950–70

Year	Budget (DM millions)	Percentage of GNP
1950	16.8	17.1
1960	62.8	20.7
1970	174.7	25.7

Key question
Why was the German education system not improved after the war?

Education

From 1945 the Allies had aimed to reshape fundamentally the German educational system as Nazi influence in that area had had such a devastating effect. Therefore, they wanted educational reforms to make Germany a democratic society. In the Soviet Zone educational reform was introduced fundamentally and quickly (see page 368). Yet, it never really happened in the British and US Zones. The Western Allies could not agree on a common educational policy. The US strongly pushed for an American-style comprehensive school system, whereas the British were less directive and more pragmatic by simply issuing guidelines. Moreover, German regional authorities resisted Allied proposals.

As a result, when responsibility for education passed on to the *Länder* in 1949, it meant that the traditional school system was not fundamentally changed, and the majority of Germans generally welcomed that. Most obviously, they still maintained the primary school and the selective system between grammar and vocational schools. German universities were retained as 'ivory towers': a preserve for the intellectual élite.

All in all school teaching had a makeshift image and practical problems prevailed because there was:

- a lack of school buildings
- a shortage of appropriate teaching material (as most school books had been prepared by the Nazis)
- many large classes (as a high proportion of qualified teachers had been killed in the war or removed as Nazis).

Too many new teachers were not properly qualified, and certainly had no in-service training for the changes and demands of the new West Germany. Educational authorities resorted to the curriculum and the teaching methods of the Weimar years.

Therefore, in the early 1950s there was no clear consensus on how to proceed with educational developments. The changes that were made were limited, for instance: the abolition of fees (1958) and the Düsseldorf Agreement (1955) that covered the number of examination subjects length of studies, holidays, the beginning of school years, A-level examination standards and so on. This led to some describing it derogatively as *Schulchaos* (school chaos).

The limitations of the BRD educational system in the 1950s can probably be put down to:

- the economic prosperity disguising the nature of Germany's educational weaknesses
- the conservative atmosphere of the BRD which tended to look back beyond the Nazi era to the Weimar years
- the anti-communist suspicions of West Germans who had no desire to mimic the reforms of the DDR
- most importantly, the inability of the *Länder* to overcome their differences for a more national educational policy.

However, eventually, in 1959 an overall draft of the commission from the *Länder* for a new modern school system (*Rahmenplan*) triggered fierce discussions in politics and public. This marked a beginning for the expansion and changes of the educational system from the mid-1960s and eventually the age of student revolt.

Women

The experiences and pressures of women during the war and in the post-war occupation played an essential role in the survival and stability of German society. Women significantly outnumbered men because of the war and were able to take on new roles out of necessity that had been denied previously.

Key question
Were German women emancipated?

On one level, the legal one, it is clear that women's status was advanced in the 1950s by the BRD. Article 3 of the 1949 Basic Law gave women equal rights and superseded any old rules with legal judgments. And the Law of Equality of the Sexes of 1957 went a further step towards female emancipation, which gave wives the right to take up work even without the permission of their husbands and enabled them to keep control of their property after marriage.

In addition, in economic terms women were helped in a period of full employment, as the competition of the female workforce was seen not as a problem but as a welcomed addition. Particularly, the expanding service and administration sector offered new career chances to women, whose numbers especially in the civil service grew. And the great growth of new household gadgets gradually made the chores at home more manageable, thus making it easier for young women to combine work and family.

However, these developments cannot disguise the fact that the prevailing ethos of the 1950s and early 1960s was conservative, even patriarchal – a view which was very much promoted by the Catholic Church. The distinction was statistically clear:

- Working women in many cases could not expect equal pay for equal work.
- The average woman's wage was still about 40 per cent less than the average man's.
- In higher education the number of female students had only risen from 19 per cent in 1950 to 30 per cent in 1968.

Moreover, despite the improvements in the system, social welfare was more geared to preserving the family rather than equality. The typical female role reflected by the married women of the three Ks (see page 202) prevailed widely until the mid-1960s and Kolinsky writes: 'the expectations that a woman should marry, raise a family and build her life around the private sphere remained in force'. Real emancipation was still a long way off.

Social change
A consumers' society?

Key question
How far was West German society changed in the 20 years after the war?

Although the economy began to boom in the early 1950s, the income of industrial and office workers grew slowly at first and most people lived very modestly. Remembering the war and the recent years of privation, people saved every penny and were prepared to work hard and long hours. Therefore, up to 1955 it should be remembered that:

- 20 per cent of the households still had little more than the mere subsistence level
- over half of the population had no more than a one-bedroom flat to live in
- only 11 per cent owned a fridge
- the average weekly working hours were 49 and over a third of the population had never been on a holiday in their life.

However, in the second half of the 1950s there was a marked rise in living standards for 'the man in the street' as unions became more self-confident in their demands for higher pay rises. The working week was reduced to 45 hours in the introduction of the five-day working week, and in 1965 it was reduced again to 40 hours, and with increasingly longer holidays.

So by 1962 in households:

- 63 per cent owned a fridge
- 42 per cent owned a television
- 38 per cent owned a car
- 36 per cent owned a washing machine.

And very significantly, the number of privately owned houses increased steeply thanks to special tax relief programmes.

Therefore, with the rising living standards of the 1950s the general mood of optimism and satisfaction prevailed. Social envy was not a major issue as many believed in progress and felt that they would soon have their share of the economic miracle, too. People who could afford it were not ashamed to show off their new wealth. However, by the mid-1960s this new prosperity was at last starting to show the signs of a rather complacent and smug consumerist society. It was these signs which laid the basis for the more critical and revolutionary decade.

A poster produced by the German trade unions, DGB: 'On Saturdays, daddy belongs to me.'

A travel advertisement of the 1950s showing the growth in holidays. In what ways does the advert appeal to the German people?

'Home sweet home'?

In the early years of the BRD most people were simply happy for their newfound stability, though this was soon followed by an urge to make good of the 'lost years' of chaos, hunger and destruction. The longing for private happiness and normality helped to form a society that concentrated on material achievements and family life. As a consequence, the great majority of the West German population was fed up with the ideology and militarism of the Nazi years and enjoyed the freedom of individual choice again.

In a way the popular suspicion of politics and ideology also led to the emergence of a '**without me**' (*ohne mich*) mentality. This became most clear in the controversy about the remilitarisation of the BRD, which many people did not want. In the end, however, the trust in Adenauer's alliance with the West was stronger than the scepticism and fear. Despite all criticism he remained the reliable father figure most West Germans were prepared to trust. The slogan of the CDU election campaign in 1957, 'no experiments – vote Adenauer', put it in a nutshell.

Changed lifestyles

In many ways the influence of Germany's traditional culture and class divisions gradually declined. The modern mass media, especially the cinema and by the late 1950s the first TVs, began

---

Key term

Without me
Ohne mich. A phrase used to describe the tendency of many West Germans in the 1950s to put politics to one side. This mentality saw politics in terms of work, home and family, with little interest in international and military issues.

to spread new ideas and cultural values, particularly because many West Germans had got to know about the American way of life first through the occupying troops.

The first signs of globalisation in the form of American mass culture began to influence the young people who were soon attracted by the definitive features of jeans, rock n' roll, chewing gum and Coca Cola especially. This influence was noticeable and regarded with a lot of scepticism by the older generations, as it was often coupled with protest. In 1956–8 there were a number of teenage riots by 'teddy boys' who were against the old-fashioned family values and the strict working ethos of their parents.

A modern industrial society?

With a booming economy and developed technology West Germany in the 1950s turned into a modern industrial society undergoing all kinds of changes. Its population grew markedly from 47.5 million in 1951 to 58.6 million in 1965 (although the population growth was to decelerate markedly from the mid-1960s).

But even more telling was the shift in the structure of the labour force. Social mobility grew as more and more people moved from the countryside to the cities. This trend was in spite of real efforts by the government to improve the situation of the farmers through subsidies and a new pension system. So, the number of people working in the agrarian sector declined drastically. The old-fashioned, hard and rather limited lifestyle and low income in the countryside lost its attraction for many young people.

Table 13.9: Number in millions employed by each economic sector in the BRD

Year	1955	1970
Industry	10.2	12.4
Agriculture	4.3	2.3
Mining	0.6	0.5
Transport/commerce/banking	5.7	7.6

The lure of jobs in urban Germany was not to be found in the older heavy industries such as coal mining. Rather, the search for employment was to be found in the light, electronics and service industries. Most marked was the massive expansion of transportation which saw the growth of the number of cars from two million in 1950 to 12.1 million in 1965 along with the systematic expansion of the road network.

West German society presented contradictory images. On the one hand nearly all Germans were much better off and more secure and yet, the new wealth exacerbated financial inequalities and the disparity in the distribution of wealth and income remained to a large extent in 1960. Therefore 1.7 per cent of all households still owned 35 per cent of private wealth, whereas in contrast 33.7 per cent of households owned a mere 17 per cent of private wealth. And 0.1 per cent of the population held 13 per cent of all private assets.

However, on the other hand the modernising elements support the fact that West Germany was not so much a class-based society; in contrast to Britain. The influence and status of the Prussian *Junkers* had gone. The Ruhr barons who had dominated heavy industry from Germany's industrialisation were in decline. So there was a kind of levelling effect within West German society, particularly in psychological terms. Ideological gaps got smaller as the new materialism forged a bond of new common values. Workers gradually adopted the lifestyle and values of the middle classes. That is not to say that it was a classless society but 'West Germans appeared rather homogenously middle class' (Fulbrook).

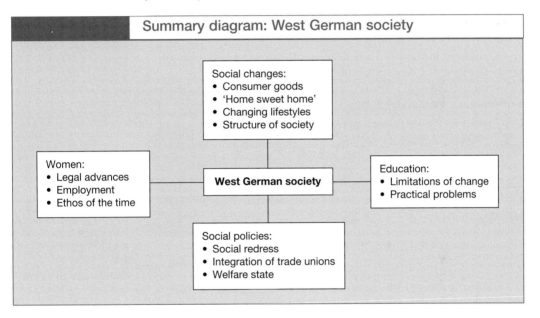

Summary diagram: West German society

West German society

Social changes:
- Consumer goods
- 'Home sweet home'
- Changing lifestyles
- Structure of society

Women:
- Legal advances
- Employment
- Ethos of the time

Education:
- Limitations of change
- Practical problems

Social policies:
- Social redress
- Integration of trade unions
- Welfare state

5 | Foreign Relations

Adenauer's foreign policy aims

Key question
What were Adenauer's foreign policy aims in the international context?

The new West Germany was born out of the Cold War at a time of tensions and fears between the East and the West. By 1949 the Soviets had developed the atomic bomb and in 1950 the outbreak of the Korean War seemed to confirm all the fears of 'the free Western world' about communist aggression. Divided Germany was therefore at the frontline of the Cold War and Adenauer was very much aware that maintaining the peace and freedom of the BRD was vital. Moreover, the BRD in the early 1950s remained politically impotent. The country was under the control of the Allied High Commission and it did not enjoy real sovereignty, as the Western Allies had the ultimate authority. (The BRD was not even allowed to have a foreign office, which is why Adenauer himself acted as chancellor and foreign minister.)

In this situation Adenauer's foreign policy was geared to establish sovereignty for the new state and to exploit the economic, political and military strength of the free Western world by fully integrating the BRD. His aims and visions therefore went far beyond his own state. His aim was a united west Europe led and protected by the superpower USA. To reach this ideal, Adenauer saw that it was essential for the BRD to put to one side national interests and create a close network of political, economic and military multinational institutions. In Adenauer's plan the BRD was to play an active and vital part in this process: stability, reliability and close co-operation were to be the principles with which he hoped to win the trust of partners in the West.

Most significantly Adenauer had a strong antipathy to communism. He mistrusted the Soviets and felt that only a policy of strength could really deter communist aggression. He was, therefore, opposed to attempts at reunifying Germany if it left the BRD neutralised, as it would be left largely defenceless and prey to communist influence. In his eyes reunification could only be considered under Western conditions. As Carr writes of Adenauer: 'Above all a realist cast in the mould of Bismarck and Stresemann, Adenauer supposed that the temporary division of Germany was likely to be of long duration and that West Germany's only hope of recovery lay in full co-operation with the Western Powers.'

Eyes to the West: economic integration

Of course, the major hurdle overcoming Adenauer's aims was winning the trust of western European states, especially that of France. Indeed, the new state was also constrained by significant economic conditions, as well as the political ones, such as:

Key question
In what ways was the BRD economically integrated into western Europe by 1963?

- The Occupation Statute of April 1949, which gave the Occupying Powers the right to supervise the country's trade.
- The International Ruhr Authority, which gave the right to France, Belgium, the Netherlands and Luxembourg to control the distribution of the area's resources, especially coal and steel.
- The status of the Saar, a mainly German-speaking area, but very rich in coal, which since 1947 had been virtually a puppet state controlled by France by means of a customs union (see pages 28 and 331).

Adenauer therefore reckoned that economic co-operation was the best way to establish the basis of political trust.

The Petersberg Agreement

As early as the autumn of 1949 the BRD government agreed to sign the Petersberg Agreement with the Allied High Commission. Primarily, the purpose of this agreement was simply to allow the BRD to join the International Ruhr Authority. Indeed, Schumacher attacked Adenauer viciously as a 'chancellor of the Allies'. However, the Chancellor actually gained a lot from this co-operation:

Petersberg Agreement: November 1949

Key date

- the dismantling of industry by the Allies was radically limited
- the BRD gained the right to establish diplomatic relationships with other states
- the BRD was allowed to join the European Council in 1950.

The European Coal and Steel Community (ECSC)

The shoots of the seeds sown by the Petersberg Agreement soon began to emerge. The mistrust of some French began to give way to the insight that co-operation could bring economic advantages, as well as security. Therefore, in 1950 the French foreign minister, Robert Schuman, suggested a supranational organisation to oversee German and French steel and coal production. His own initiative became known as the Schuman Plan and led to the foundation of the ECSC in 1951 by its six members: the BRD, France, Italy and the Benelux states. The members agreed on a common policy for prices, subsidies and investment, and most significantly, it lifted restrictions on imports and exports of coal and steel between member states.

The establishment of the ECSC supplanted the old International Ruhr Authority, which allowed the BRD to be treated as an equal partner in that area (see also Stresemann's fulfilment policy on pages 72–7). Perhaps most significantly in the long term, the nature of the agreement laid the basis for Franco-German understanding after generations of hostility.

The European Economic Community (EEC)

The ECSC was an immediate success and production of coal and steel within the community increased by 44 per cent from 1952 to 1957. Not surprisingly, the six members began to take Western integration further and extensive negotiations culminated in the Treaty of Rome, which was signed in March 1957. This in effect created the EEC as a customs union within 'the six' which set out to harmonise measures of trade and prices in areas, such as agriculture and fisheries. By 1964 85 per cent of West German agricultural produce lay within the EEC terms and its success led to 'lay the foundations of an ever closer union among the peoples of Europe' with its plans to:

- co-ordinate transportation systems
- develop general economic policies
- remove measures restricting free competition
- assure the mobility of labour and capital.

The EEC was colloquially known as the 'Common Market'. It proved to be a turning-point for Europe and also even more so for the BRD. Erhard himself saw the creation of this major European institution as a development comparable to the establishment of the customs union that led to German unification in 1871. As the BRD was the largest member of the EEC, Adenauer recognised that working within the union provided the chance for the BRD to exert political and economic influence.

Key dates

Creation of ECSC: April 1951

Treaty of Rome signed creating the EEC: March 1957

Other economic agencies

In addition, West Germany readily joined a broad range of organisations to improve international economic co-operation and co-ordination:

- General Agreement on Tariffs and Trade (GATT). Formed in 1948 with the main objective of reducing barriers to international trade. BRD joined it in 1951.
- Organisation for European Economic Co-operation (OEEC). Created in 1948 to administer the Marshall Plan and to continue work on a joint recovery programme by economic co-operation. The Bizone was one of the original founding members.
- International Monetary Fund (IMF). Created in 1945 to stabilise exchange rates and supervise the world's international payment system to prevent financial imbalance. BRD joined in 1952.

Yet, all these points were not just economically important; they all played an important part in the rehabilitation of Germany in the international community.

Eyes to the West: military and political integration

Economic co-operation was only one factor that helped Adenauer to speed up the acceptance of West Germany as a valued and trusted partner. The outbreak of the Chinese revolution (1949) and the Korean War (1950) heightened the fear of communism and led to a change in attitudes between US and west European politicians. The USA particularly urged Europeans to make a greater effort to contribute to their own defence, especially the BRD. However, the idea of German rearmament was still regarded very warily among its neighbours, especially France. So, understandably, the early plans of French prime minister, Pleven, were to create a **European Defence Community** (EDC) that was

Key question
How successful was Adenauer's policy of integration with the West?

European Defence Community
A plan proposed by France's prime minister, Pleven, to form a pan-European defence force. The plan was signed in May 1952 by the BRD, France, Italy and the Benelux states, but not initially ratified by the French parliament.

Key term

'Gruenther: for a start 24 divisions are enough for a warm-up shooting practice', 1956. As a new NATO member West Germany supported the Western defence alliance; from the point of view of the caricaturist it provided above all 'human material'. Gruenther, a US general, was the supreme commander of NATO in Europe. In 1956 in agreement with the *Bundestag*, the legal prerequisites were established for the creation of the new West German army (*Bundeswehr*) under defence minister Theodor Blank.

Key terms

Bundeswehr
The name given to the German army created in the BRD by the Paris treaties. It was ratified by the *Bundestag* in 1955 and came into effect in the following year. It introduced conscription for all men aged over 18 years.

NATO
The Berlin blockade resulted in the emergence of a Western military alliance, NATO, the North Atlantic Treaty Organisation. NATO was formed in 1949 and included USA, Canada, Britain, France and seven other countries. The BRD was invited to join in 1955.

Key dates

EDC treaty agreed (but rejected in 1954 by French parliament): May 1952

Paris treaties signed and later approved: October 1954

BRD became a sovereign state: May 1955

BRD joined NATO: May 1955

Basic Law amended by the *Bundestag* to create the *Bundeswehr* (federal army): 12 November 1955

very much under French leadership and with a strictly limited German contingent.

Adenauer himself, therefore, quickly agreed to make the BRD a member of the EDC while at the same time making this German contribution dependent on the return of sovereignty for West Germany and the end of the Occupation Statute. Yet, the agreement signed in 1952 creating the EDC caused some intense political opposition. In Germany, although the treaty was ratified by the *Bundestag*, there was serious resistance to German rearmament. This came not only from within the SPD, but also from elements within the CDU; a leading government ex-minister, Gustav Heinemann, left the CDU Party.

At first, the proposal was defeated by the French parliament and to overcome French doubts Adenauer went straight back to the negotiating table. Within a few months new terms were signed in the Paris Treaties of October 1954 to settle openly all the major political and economic disputes between Germany and France. This time they were signed by their respective parliaments, which agreed on a number of areas considered below.

German sovereignty
The Occupational Statute was ended and the BRD became a fully sovereign state in May 1955. The Western Powers kept their rights and responsibilities over West Berlin, the stationing of their troops in West Germany to guarantee its security was assured, and the question remained of German reunification and a future peace settlement.

West European Union
The EDC plan was put to one side and instead the West European Union (WEU) of France, Britain and the Benelux states was expanded to include West Germany and Italy. This was a defensive pact, which allowed the BRD to create its own national armed forces, the ***Bundeswehr*** (whereas the EDC had originally suggested a European army which would have caused problems).

NATO
The military alliance called the North Atlantic Treaty Organisation (**NATO**) had been formed in 1949. The BRD was allowed to become a full member in 1955 (although it abstained from atomic, biological and chemical weapons).

The future of the Saar
Adenauer agreed to accept the autonomous status of the Saar and its close economic connection with France. However, it was agreed to give the population of the Saar a plebiscite. When it was held, a 68 per cent majority rejected the terms for the Saar; instead two-thirds of the Saar parliament pushed for unifying with West Germany. Five years previously this could have been the cause of a major political conflict. Yet, Franco-German relations had improved so much that as a result of negotiations between the two

capitals it was agreed to accept the return of the Saar to West Germany in 1957 as the eleventh *Land*.

Summary

By the mid-1950s the BRD was thoroughly integrated into the West, although Adenauer's triumph was not undisputed at home. The ratification of the Paris treaties was harshly attacked by the political opposition and by elements of the population because of the revival of remilitarisation, which seemed to take away the last chance of reunification. Also, this kind of criticism was fuelled by the line of the Soviet Union, as Stalin had tried to obstruct the process of integration by offering new negotiations for the reunification of Germany on seemingly generous terms in 1952 (see below on page 333). When Adenauer and the Western Allies rejected the offer fairly promptly, it confirmed the views of the opposition that he had sacrificed the national interest of reunification to Western integration.

Nevertheless, just 10 years after the trauma of 1945 the position of the BRD had been transformed. Adenauer's achievement is particularly striking in comparison with Weimar Germany after 1918 and Carr has written: 'Seldom in history has a defeated power recovered so quickly. The BRD had become a fully integrated part of a Western military defence system and its freedom was guaranteed: it had gained back its political sovereignty; it was being accepted on an equal level with the other West European states'.

In office the confirmation of his policies was achieved by Adenauer's greatest personal triumph in 1963, the year of his resignation, when he signed with the French president, Charles de Gaulle, the French–German treaty. This secured the basis for a lasting friendship and political co-operation between the two old national enemies. His unambiguous devotion to Western integration paid off in this respect – and even set the direction of BRD foreign policy until 1989.

Relations with the DDR and the USSR

Because of Adenauer's firm commitment to the West and his own mistrust of the USSR it is quite clear that relations between the BRD and the East were difficult and strained. The BRD claimed to be the only rightful heir to the Weimar Republic and it saw itself as the only legal representative of the German nation. This obviously implied that the DDR was not even accepted as a state:

Key question
Did Adenauer miss the chance to reunify Germany in the 1950s?

- In the official language of the BRD East Germany was referred to as simply the 'Soviet occupation zone'.
- There were no official international diplomatic relations between the BRD and the DDR.
- When the DDR signed a peace treaty with Poland in 1950 and accepted the Oder–Neisse frontier, this was not recognised by the BRD.
- People generally spoke of it in derogative language as *'drüben'* (over there) or *'Ostzone'* (the east zone).

Adenauer clearly wanted to negotiate on the 'German question' only from a position of strength. His strategy, known as the 'magnet theory', was based on the assumptions of developing an economically and politically strong BRD within the West to contrast with the failings of the communist system. It was believed therefore that the peoples of east Europe, including the DDR, would be attracted to support liberal democracy and to join the West, which of course would facilitate the reunification of Germany. Indeed, the fact that there were three million refugees from the DDR flooding into the BRD during the 1950s served to confirm that theory (see page 366).

The 'Stalin notes'

The question of German reunification has become the focus of much controversy during events in March 1952, when the USSR sent a seemingly tempting offer to the Western Allies (at the same time as negotiations about the EDC Treaty, see page 330). These proposals have become known as the 'Stalin notes' and suggested a negotiated settlement to the German question on the following terms:

- The signing of a final peace treaty for a united Germany with free democratic elections.
- The establishment of a united Germany with the Oder–Neisse line as the eastern border.
- The removal of all foreign troops from Germany. It was not allowed to join any military alliance and had to stay neutral.
- The creation of a defensive army for the new state.

Stalin's offer was rejected by the Western Allies, especially by the USA, as they were keen for the success of the EDC negotiations (see page 330). It seems that Adenauer himself viewed the offer as a dangerous one, as it would make Germany a weak neutral state prey to communist power. So almost certainly he used all his influence to make certain that the offer did not make any more progress. The Soviet offer was renewed again on several occasions in the years 1954–5 after Stalin's death. Yet, Adenauer himself did not budge from his position and at Geneva in 1955 there was no breakthrough from the Western Powers.

The negotiations with the USSR over the 'German question' between 1952 and 1955 have been the focus of much controversy over the years. Adenauer was blamed by his opponents for not seriously pursuing the negotiations and therefore missing a very real chance to bring about German unification. In contrast, his supporters have seen Stalin's offer as simply a bluff to prevent remilitarisation and to block Western interests before restoring communist influence over Germany.

The opening of the Soviet archives after 1990 now seems to have shed some light on the matter. It suggests that the very first note from Stalin was more than likely a tempting offer motivated by an attempt to prevent the BRD from being absorbed into the Western military alliance. Once it had been rejected by the West, though, the later Soviet offers were more motivated by propaganda aimed at presenting the right image. With regard to Adenauer's responsibility, it is recognised that his foreign policy aims for Germany were rooted in the integration of the West, and so his position coincided with those of the USA and Britain. Adenauer abhorred the idea of a weak, neutral state that could fall under communist influence, and he saw this offer not only as disadvantageous but also as dangerous, and therefore used all his influence to make sure it would be rejected.

Hallstein doctrine

By the summer of 1955, the relationship between the BRD and the East was at last clearer. Adenauer did visit Moscow in the September and he was at least prepared to establish diplomatic relations with the USSR in exchange for 10,000 prisoners of war and 20,000 civilians still held in Russia since 1945.

However, the two sides were strongly entrenched by that time. On the one hand the USSR had recently launched its 'two-state theory', which claimed that there were two sovereign German states, both representing the German nation. (This was directly in contrast to the claim of the BRD to be the only rightful representative of German interests.) Moreover, around the same time the USSR officially changed its policies over Germany by giving the DDR full sovereignty and by integrating the DDR into the **Warsaw Pact**.

On the other hand, on his return from Moscow Adenauer stated that his own government would refuse to have diplomatic relations with any state that officially recognised the DDR (with the exception of the USSR). This became known as the Hallstein doctrine, named after the state secretary in the foreign office who was a close advisor of Adenauer. For 10 years it was generally successful. In that time, it effectively discouraged many countries from recognising the DDR by the offer of extensive economic aid to countries in the developing world and only two countries – Yugoslavia (1957) and Cuba (1963) – were to break relations.

Therefore, there was no real chance 'lost' to reunite Germany in the years 1952–5 or after. The competing forces were irreconcilable and so, although Stalin's death did lead to a gentle thaw in the Cold War, the talks on German reunification drove them further apart in the later years. As a result, relations between the two Germanies stayed very frosty. Indeed, the integration of the two Germanies into the different blocs had not clarified one vital issue, namely the ongoing clash of interests over Berlin. That was to come to a head in the Berlin crisis, 1958–61, and led to the construction of the Berlin Wall (see page 378).

Warsaw Pact
The USSR viewed NATO as an offensive alliance and Soviet concern was highlighted when BRD was rearmed and brought into NATO. So, on 14 May 1955, the Warsaw Pact was created, which included the USSR and the countries of central and eastern Europe under Soviet regimes.

Key term

Summary diagram: Foreign relations

```
        International context ─────── Adenauer's aims
              │           │                   │
    ┌─────────┘           │                   └──────────┐
    ▼                     ▼                              ▼
┌──────────────────┐ ┌──────────────────┐ ┌──────────────────┐
│ Eyes to the West:│ │ Eyes to the West:│ │ Relations with   │
│ economic         │ │ military         │ │ DDR and USSR     │
│ integration      │ │ and political    │ │                  │
│                  │ │ integration      │ │                  │
├──────────────────┤ ├──────────────────┤ ├──────────────────┤
│ In what ways was │ │ How successful   │ │ Did Adenauer miss│
│ the BRD          │ │ was Adenauer's   │ │ the chance to    │
│ economically     │ │ policy of        │ │ reunify Germany  │
│ integrated?      │ │ political        │ │ in the 1950s?    │
│                  │ │ integration?     │ │                  │
└──────────────────┘ └──────────────────┘ └──────────────────┘
    │                     │                              │
    ▼                     ▼                              ▼
┌──────────────────┐ ┌──────────────────┐ ┌──────────────────┐
│ Key developments:│ │ Key developments:│ │ Key developments:│
│ • Petersberg     │ │ EDC → Paris      │ │ • 'Stalin notes' │
│   Agreement      │ │ treaties:        │ │ • Hallstein      │
│ • ECSC           │ │ • German         │ │   doctrine       │
│ • EEC            │ │   sovereignty    │ │                  │
│ • International  │ │ • WEU            │ │                  │
│   organisations  │ │ • NATO           │ │                  │
│                  │ │ • Saar           │ │                  │
└──────────────────┘ └──────────────────┘ └──────────────────┘
```

6 | The Adenauer Era

Adenauer's fall from power

Key question
What were the long- and short-term causes of Adenauer's fall from power?

In the 1957 election with the slogan 'no experiments – vote Adenauer', the CDU/CSU had triumphantly won an absolute majority, which secured the ageing Adenauer his dominant position for a third term in office. Yet, his authority soon started to wane, partly accelerated by his own poor judgement and stubbornness in his old convictions on home and foreign affairs.

'The presidency fiasco'

In spring 1959 the first president, Heuss, was obliged to retire and the chancellor, urged by leading members of the CDU, first signalled his willingness to become a candidate for the highest office in the state. Yet, he caused quite a bit of irritation when a few weeks later he withdrew his nomination. This was mainly because he had recognised that the new office would not give him enough influence and power to guarantee the continuity of his policies, especially on his hard stance over the DDR and USSR. Moreover, Adenauer did not rate Erhard's political skills highly and he was becoming growingly concerned that the finance minister would become chancellor.

This dithering lost Adenauer a lot of public sympathy, as he was seen as damaging the image of the highest office in the state for the sake of personal interests and strategies. In addition, within the CDU, a lot of voices were disappointed, as they had assumed that nominating the 83-year-old chancellor was the ideal solution giving him a chance to leave at the pinnacle of his political career. Instead, Adenauer seemed to have lost his clear-sighted political instinct and intuition, and misjudged the psychological long-term consequences of this affair, which delayed his departure for four years.

'The TV dispute'

Adenauer's reputation was also seriously hit by a long-lasting legal conflict during 1958–61. He had set up a national TV company, Deutschland-Fernsehen-GmbH, which in effect was to be controlled by the federal government. Of course, he recognised the potential political value of such an organisation, but the SPD claimed that the company was a threat to German federalism and to the freedom of the media. In the end in February 1961 the company was declared 'unconstitutional' by the constitutional court and it was dissolved. Adenauer had overstretched his competence and his political opponents had used the dispute to raise the spectre of undermining federalism and of the government aiming at more central control.

The 1961 election and the new coalition

Despite the above problems faced by Adenauer and the CDU, and the threat posed by the revived SPD, the polls suggested that they could win the 1961 election. The economy was still going well, and many Germans remained cautious of supporting the youthful SPD leader, Brandt, compared to the experienced Adenauer.

However, when the DDR put up the Berlin Wall during the election campaign, Adenauer significantly misjudged the situation. Most West Germans were appalled by the events in Berlin, but instead of hurrying to the scene of the emerging concrete wall along the border, he carried on campaigning and did not visit Berlin until a week later. Moreover, although his response was reserved, he continued to attack Brandt, who was the mayor of West Berlin and won much public sympathy, in contrast to Adenauer.

In the end, the CDU/CSU won the election again with a vote of 45.3 per cent. Yet, without an absolute majority, they were obliged to enter into negotiations with the FDP, who had considerably increased their vote to 12.8 per cent. Also very significantly, the FDP had publicly opposed a fourth period in office for Adenauer. Therefore, after difficult negotiations they agreed to join a coalition government under Adenauer's leadership on the condition that he agreed to step down before the end of the four-year period. It was a humiliating condition and it was a question of time before the old chancellor stepped down, although the government crisis of 1962 brought things to a head rather more quickly.

Der Spiegel affair

Der Spiegel ('The Mirror'), a rather left-wing political weekly magazine, had long criticised Franz-Joseph Strauss, the leader of the CSU, since his appointment as minister of defence in 1956. It had attacked him for various dubious financial dealings, but its main focus was his political stance on foreign relations. Strauss

Key dates

Berlin Wall started: 13 August 1961

Spiegel affair: October–November 1962

was a 'hawk', who believed strongly in the concept of 'a massive deterrence' to fight against the threat of communism; and it seemed that he was in favour of a pre-emptive nuclear strike by NATO in case of danger.

Then, on 10 October 1962 (the same month as the **Cuban missile crisis**), *Der Spiegel* published an article with information about NATO military manoeuvres in the event of an attack by the Warsaw Pact and came to the conclusion that the Strauss strategy was dangerous and at odds with the country's security. Soon all hell broke loose. The offices of the magazine in Hamburg and Bonn were searched and closed down; Augstein, the publisher, himself, and some journalists were arrested; and Ahlers, the writer of the article, who was in Spain on holiday, was seized by Spanish authorities and sent back to Germany. In the end the defendants were charged with public treason and corruption on the grounds of publishing highly secret information. Obviously, the whole affair revolved around the freedom of the press, and Strauss was harangued widely for endorsing methods reminiscent of the Nazis. Yet, at first Adenauer publicly defended Strauss and amazingly resorted to attacking Augstein in the *Bundestag* by suggesting that the country was on the 'abyss of treason'.

This triggered a government crisis. Five FDP members left the cabinet demanding the resignation of Strauss. Adenauer only managed to rescue the coalition in the end by sacking Strauss and by his own promise to step down in the next year. Moreover, Adenauer was never really prepared to accept any personal responsibility or blame over *Der Spiegel* affair even when the government's charges were kicked out by the court. The scandal showed him at his worst as lacking political judgement and showing arrogance. He was too seriously politically wounded.

Foreign relations

Although internal factors and Adenauer's advancing age eventually brought about the end of Adenauer's political career, it should also be noted that his rather inflexible policy towards the 'Eastern bloc' contributed in the end to his isolation and political problems.

Despite the opposition of the SPD Adenauer's foreign policy had generally enjoyed great success in the early half of the 1950s. Yet, in the latter half the international context was changing and he showed no sympathy to the new environment. For example, he remained unashamedly committed to:

- the non-recognition of the DDR
- the Hallstein doctrine
- Strauss's leadership as defence minister.

Moreover, Adenauer's suspicions about the intentions of the USA and Britain over the Berlin crisis, 1958–61, contributed to problems within the government coalition. Adenauer's stance was opposed by the coalition partner FDP and a strong pro-American fraction within the CDU led by Erhard, which became known as the 'Atlanticists'. They made Adenauer's position within the Party

Cuban missile crisis
The most serious flashpoint in the Cold War between the superpowers in October 1962. The dispute was over the installation of nuclear missiles by the USSR on Cuba, a short distance from the US mainland.

and the government more difficult in his last few years, pushing for him to be replaced by Erhard as chancellor.

Resignation

Adenauer's days were now numbered. In the elections in West Berlin and Rheinland-Pfalz in early 1963 the CDU lost a lot of votes and the voices within the Party for a great coalition with the SPD started to grow. In April Adenauer had to accept the nomination of Erhard as his successor. In October 1963, aged 87 years, he resigned as promised from his office. However, he kept his seat in parliament and position as leader of the CDU, from which he only resigned a year before his death in 1966. Like other great leaders in his final years he could not accept the change of times and found it very difficult to withdraw from power.

Key date
Resignation of Adenauer: 15 October 1963

'Chancellor democracy'

Even during his time in office Adenauer's style of government and leadership was labelled 'chancellor democracy', a term which is interpreted in positive or negative terms, depending on your political standing. Yet, Adenauer had a very strong personality and he was self-confident enough to ignore it.

Key question
How was Adenauer able to secure such a powerful position for himself?

Although already 73 years old when he became chancellor for the first time, he was still a very agile, far-sighted and, much more importantly, politically very experienced man. His long years as the mayor of Cologne in the Weimar Republic had taught him everything he needed to know about democratic processes and the need to lobby support. As a committed Catholic, he had disapproved of the political ideologies of communism and Nazism and had kept his moral and political integrity throughout. He was not easily impressed by 'opinion polls' or by 'expert comments'. Instead, his rather practical, sober approach to politics and a good instinct for the feasible helped him to integrate different interest groups in government and in parliament.

However, his style of government was not only framed by his personality, but also by the circumstances of the time:

- As the first chancellor of a new state with no exact precedents he felt entitled to generously interpret his decision-making for the strengthening of the new democracy (*Richtlinienkompetenz*). He himself called this 'an extensive interpretation of the Basic Law'.
- In the years up to 1955, when the BRD's sovereignty was still restricted, his personal role in the negotiations with the Western Allies made his position particularly significant – even dominating. Under the Occupation Statute he combined the role of chancellor and foreign minister and oversaw foreign and defence policies.
- Another advantage that strengthened his position was the amount of freedom he had in the choice of his personnel in the formative early years. He left the economics to Erhard, but

otherwise he looked for a group of loyal people around him. Quite notoriously, he also appointed quite a large number of Nazi sympathisers to support his policies, for example Hans Globke, the state secretary in the chancellery, was one of Adenauer's most trusted and important men.

- Clearly, success led to success. The SPD failed to provide a real political alternative until the 1960s and Adenauer's electoral victories reinforced his political status as party leader and chancellor. The decade of economic success strengthened the feeling of trust in his government and his patriarchal image fitted in nicely with the rather conservative culture.

Although Adenauer did face some serious examples of harsh criticism, the above factors show that he was virtually undisputed as leader in his first 10 years. In his final few years, as his political instinct waned, the criticism got much stronger and he was forced to make concessions, especially to the coalition partners. Yet, despite the fact that Adenauer's chancellor democracy raised some comments again about his leadership style, he always stayed within his constitutional limits and acted strictly on the majorities in parliament. Finally, it is telling that his successors were not to rule so long and so effectively. In that way the term 'chancellor democracy' did not become institutionalised and really can only be applied to Adenauer's years in office.

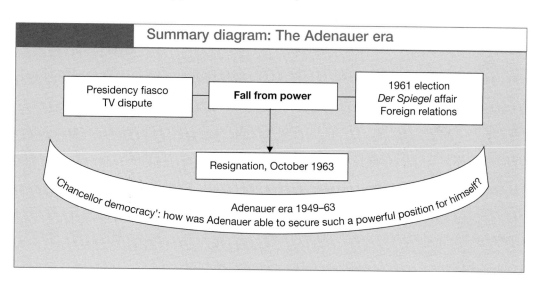

Summary diagram: The Adenauer era

Study Guide: AS Questions

In the style of OCR A

How successful was Adenauer's foreign policy? (50 marks)

Exam tips

If you are to judge the chancellor's success in foreign relations, you must identify his aims because they give you the baselines against which to take your measurements. You might divide his aims into two periods: 1949–55 when West Germany was still under the control of the Western Powers and 1955–63 when the BRD was a truly sovereign state. In the first phase, he did not just work towards achieving full independence, but worked for an economically strong and politically free West in which the new Germany would take a full role. Germany had to be accepted again as a reputable state in the community of free nations. Above all, French political trust and economic co-operation had to be won – no mean feat after generations of hostility. The creation of the ECSC was a major pillar of that strategy. Adenauer was criticised at home for always giving too much, for being the 'chancellor of the Allies'. Was that fair? Were his acceptance of the Saar's autonomy and rejection of possible reunion in 1952 betrayals of German interests? Was his support from the abortive EDC a step too far? From May 1955, the BRD's joining of NATO was vital. So too was founder membership of the EEC. The recovery of the Saar was of great symbolic significance, but far more important was the French–German Treaty of 1963 that not only 'proved' Germany's full acceptance into the community of nations, but marked the triumph of his quest to build a stable and close relationship with France.

Looking west from Bonn, you might sum him up as the architect of a spectacular recovery. What if, however, you look east? Was he the chancellor who betrayed Germany's true interests by accepting partition, denying the DDR and rejecting both the Oder–Neisse border with Poland and the 'Stalin notes' for reunification, and then pushing the Hallstein doctrine? In assessing this other side to Adenauer's foreign policy, your job is to decide whether his 'magnet theory' was right and whether he should have negotiated with Stalin (note the timing of the offer, coinciding with the EDC plan). Did Adenauer's absolute commitment to integration into the Western system mean that relations would always be poor with the DDR and the USSR? Or, was he too inflexible, especially during the post-Stalin era when East–West relations were improving? The contrast between his policies to the East and to the West gives you clear choices when you assess his success in 1949–55, in 1955–63 and overall.

In the style of OCR A

Study the five sources on Germany's economy from 1947 to 1963 and then answer **both** sub-questions. It is recommended that you spend two-thirds of your time in answering part **(b)**.

(a) Study Sources C and D.

Compare these sources as evidence for German views of the European Coal and Steel Community (ECSC). (30 marks)

(b) Study all the sources.

Use your own knowledge to assess how far the sources support the interpretation that Germany benefited more than it lost from Western European economic initiatives between 1945 and 1963. (70 marks)

Source A

The Committee for European Economic Cooperation (CEEC) meeting in Paris in August 1947, draws up a document devoted to the economic reconstruction of Germany and to the country's place in a democratic Europe.

Germany's economy is closely linked with those of other European countries. The Western Zones are in a special position because Germany must pay reparations to assist the recovery of countries victimised by her during the war. Security demands careful control of the rate and nature of Germany's economic recovery. The German economy must be fitted into the European economy to contribute to a general improvement in the standard of living. Increased production and export of Ruhr coal is essential for European recovery, so machinery, raw materials, food and other supplies must be provided for this. Other Western European countries cannot prosper while the economy of the Western Zones is paralysed. Germany will require help.

Source B

In June 1948, the Soviet authorities announce a raft of measures seeking to block the supply of provisions to the Western Zones of Berlin in reaction to the monetary reform introduced in Germany by the Western Allies.

In order to protect the interests of the population and economy of the Soviet Zone and prevent disorganisation of currency circulation, the Soviet Military Administration has been obliged to carry out the following measures in view of the separate currency reform in the Western Occupation Zones in Germany: passenger train traffic, automobile and horse traffic between the Soviet Occupation Zone in Germany and the Western Zones will cease; persons may no longer proceed on foot from the Western Zones to the Soviet Occupation Zone in Germany.

Source C

In 1952, Walter Hallstein, Junior Minister in the Foreign Ministry of the BRD, publishes an article in the French magazine Notre Europe *on the repercussions of the Schuman Plan in Germany.*

Germany's reconstruction and economic reform have been crippled, and her coal and steel industries subjected to the laws imposed by the occupying powers. The Schuman Plan will end all that. From now on, German industry will be subject to the same law as the French and Belgian industries. The principle of equal rights is basic to the new European Coal and Steel Community, offering us a unique opportunity to share in the common expansion of Europe's economy. The free and democratic community of nations created can no longer revert to their former narrow views and nationalistic opposition. We cannot make history if we hesitate.

Source D

One month before the common market for coal and iron ore came into force on 10 February 1953, the West German newspaper Die Freiheit *considers the harm it might cause to the West German economy.* Die Freiheit *was a long-running and well-known anarchist journal, known for advocacy of violence that might inspire people to revolution.*

Captains of industry know precisely the exact consequences of the ECSC. There will be a rise in coal prices, causing spiralling inflation and a higher wage-price gap with all its consequences. Electricity and gas companies will have to pass on the price increases! This will affect consumers, the goods industry as a whole and, more importantly, local transport. Given Germany's bad past experiences, the Schuman Plan has obvious dangers for the nation's social security. The end of the German coal sales agency will undermine miners' Christmas bonuses. The men with the toughest working conditions will come off worst.

Source E

On 1 March 1957, commenting on the imminent signing of the Treaties establishing the EEC and Euratom on 25 March in Rome, the German daily newspaper Süddeutsche Zeitung *considers the impact of the provisions governing the Common Market on the West German economy in the context of world trade.*
Süddeutsche Zeitung *was a southern, Bavaria-based newspaper, from an area where agricultural concerns were very important.*

West Germany's economically most significant partner, France, will be given special status allowing it to introduce into the Common Market its confusing system of import and export levies, shield itself against competition from its partners and safeguard its own economic and financial power. If agriculture is left out, because German and French farmers constantly fear each other, very little freedom of movement remains. The proportion of West German imports affected is higher because, in the past year, these have shifted overseas, particularly to the dollar area. The weak currencies will cripple the strong ones.

Exam tips

The cross-references are intended to take you straight to the material that will help you to answer the questions.

(a) Part **(a)** requires you to examine closely the content of the two sources and compare the way they show German attitudes towards the European movement. Source C is supportive of the ECSC and views it as an opportunity not to be missed, whereas Source D is hostile and hints it may cause a repetition of previous social and economic problems. The main focus of an effective answer is on comparing and contrasting the content and provenance of the two sources in the light of the question asked and reaching a substatiated judgement.

(b) Part **(b)** requires you to use the content and provenance of all four sources, grouping them by view, and to integrate pertinent factual knowledge into your argument to answer the question. Knowledge should be used to develop, validate or criticise the views in the sources. You should reach a balanced judgement supported by knowledge, source content and provenance.
   Consider the following:

- the economic impact of the European movement on Germany (the key issue in the question) (pages 328–30)
- Allied occupation: the Western Zones, the Marshall Plan (pages 282–7)
- the Berlin Crisis (page 288)
- the Schuman Plan and ECSC (page 329)
- the Treaty of Rome (EEC and Euratom) (page 329)
- the 'economic miracle' of the BRD (page 316).

14 East Germany 1949–63

POINTS TO CONSIDER

The purpose of this chapter is to consider how successfully
the new communist state in East Germany, the DDR,
developed in its early years, 1949–63. The challenges were
immense for East Germany. It had made progress but it still
faced fundamental problems and it was questionable
whether it could be seen as a viable state. The main themes
are:

- The creation of the SED dictatorship
- The political survival of the regime: the workers' uprising
  of 17 June 1953 and de-Stalinisation
- The development of the communist economy
- East German society
- The creation of the Berlin Wall

Key dates

1949	January 25–28	First SED Party Conference: SED became a new-type party
	October 7	Foundation of DDR in East Germany (German Democratic Republic)
1950	February	Creation of State Security Service (*Stasi*)
	October	Elections to the first People's Chamber
1952	July	*Länder* in DDR dissolved
1953	March 5	Death of Stalin
	June 17	Uprising in DDR
1955	May 11–14	Warsaw Pact concluded with DDR as a member
	September 20	USSR recognised sovereignty of DDR
1956	February	Khrushchev's speech denounced Stalin and his methods
1958	November 27	Khrushchev's Berlin ultimatum
1960		Collectivisation of agriculture in DDR completed
1961	August 13	Creation of Berlin Wall
1963	June	Introduction of the New Economic System

1 | The Creation of the SED Dictatorship

Key question
How did the leaders of the DDR control their people?

The formation of the DDR in October 1949 was unequivocally shaped by the years of the Occupation (see Chapter 8) and particularly by:

- the influence of the KPD and the Soviets in the early months of the administration after the end of the war (see pages 277–8)
- the nationalisation of key industries and land reform (see pages 280–1)
- the collapse of Allied co-operation and the growing Cold War (see page 290)
- the declaration of the BRD (May 1949) (see page 291).

In theory, the new constitution of the DDR was a multi-party system with two parliamentary chambers, like the BRD:

- the *Volkskammer*, the highest institution in the state, with free and secret general elections on the basis of proportional representation
- the *Länderkammer* to represent the interests of the regions.

So, the constitution of the DDR claimed it to be a democratic state with its power coming from the people and with guaranteed civil rights, such as freedom of speech and the freedom of the press. It looked as if democracy should flourish.

However, in reality the DDR as directed by the Soviet Union quickly developed into a totalitarian state, which shaped its politics, economy and society on the model of the USSR. At no time did the leaders of the new system really have the support of the majority of their people behind them, and therefore, in order to maintain their power they made use of:

- the SED and the party system
- the judiciary
- the *Stasi* – the DDR state secret service
- Soviet troops and SMAD, which was renamed as the Soviet High Commission in October 1949.

The transformation of SED and the party system

Already, before the DDR had been created, the SED, under directives from Moscow, had begun to reform itself into a so-called 'party of a new type'. The new principle introduced was that of 'democratic centralism', as practised by the CPSU, the Communist Party of the Soviet Union. This meant there were strict hierarchical structures and no room for democratic decision-making within the Party. In that way the real decision-making was made by the **Politbureau** and its secretariat, led by:

- Walter Ulbricht, the party leader, 1946–71 (general secretary or first secretary)
- Wilhelm Pieck, president of the DDR, 1949–60
- Otto Grotewohl, prime minister of the DDR, 1949–60.

Key dates

Foundation of DDR in East Germany (German Democratic Republic): 7 October 1949

First SED Party Conference: SED became a new-type party: 25–28 January 1949

Key terms

Stasi
Staatssicherheitsdienst (SSD). The state security service. The secret police of the DDR. Created in February 1950, it was modelled closely on Soviet secret intelligence.

Politbureau
The term is short for political bureau and it refers to the highest executive body of a Communist Party. It was first used by the Communist Party of the Soviet Union (CPSU), but was applied in many Eastern bloc states.

Profile: Walter Ulbricht 1893–1973

1893	–	Born in a poor working-class family in Leipzig
1908–12	–	Trained as a carpenter and joined the SPD
1915–18	–	Served in First World War, but arrested for desertion on political grounds
1919	–	Joined the KPD
1928–33	–	Elected a KPD *Reichstag* representative
1933–45	–	Fled from Germany and lived in Paris and Prague before staying in Moscow until the end of the war
1945 April	–	Returned to Germany with the Red Army as the leader of the Ulbricht Group
1945–9	–	Worked closely with SMAD in Soviet Occupation Zone
1946	–	Fully supported the formation of SED by merging the East German SPD and KPD
1949	–	On the founding of the DDR he became Deputy to Grotewohl as prime minister
1950	–	General secretary of the SED making him party leader
1953	–	Strengthened his political position in the wake of the uprising
1956	–	Survived Khrushchev's de-Stalinisation
1960	–	Chairman of the Council of State following the death of President Pieck; in effect, leader of the Party and the head of state until 1971
1961	–	Ordered the building of the Berlin Wall
1971	–	Forced to resign on health grounds and replaced by Erich Honecker
1973	–	Died following a stroke

Ulbricht never gave the impression of an imposing charismatic revolutionary. He lacked personality and deliberately kept his distance from the people; indeed, with his goatee beard and high squeaky voice he was regularly caricatured. Nevertheless, he proved to be a shrewd and intelligent political operator who was committed ruthlessly to the communist cause. He shaped East Germany for a quarter of a century.

He was a committed communist who blindly followed the party line and only survived his years in the USSR by being an unquestioning Stalinist, unlike many other German communists. In that way he was well prepared for his return to Germany in 1945 as the leader of a group of élite German Stalinists to build up a new socialist system. Therefore, in conjunction with the SMAD, it was he who efficiently managed the early stages of the establishment of the communist structures in East Germany, for example:

• the merger of the SPD and the KPD into the SED and its development into a 'party of a new type'
• the land reform and the nationalisation of industry
• the foundation of the DDR in October 1949.

As the general secretary of the central committee of the SED he became the most powerful man of the DDR and despite all the crises, he showed himself to be a great survivor. This can be put down to two things: his single-minded loyalty to the USSR and his ruthless control of the party and state apparatus supported by frequent purges and the role of the *Stasi*.

Ulbricht also oversaw the development of the DDR economy by socialist principles regardless of the costs to the population and the environment, as it is now clear. Therefore, in 1961 he was the driving force behind the building of the Berlin Wall, even though a few weeks before he famously stated: 'Nobody intends to build a wall.'

In defence of Ulbricht one might point out that under him the DDR achieved a degree of prosperity and that his totalitarian regime did not indulge in the brutality of Hitler and Stalin. Yet, he passed unloved, not even respected.

Key terms

CDUD
Christliche Demokratische Union Deutschlands. Christian Democratic Union in the DDR.

LDPD
Liberaldemokratische Partei Deutschlands. Liberal Democratic Party in the DDR.

NDPD
National-Demokratische Partei Deutschlands. National Democratic Party of Germany.

DBD
Demokratische Bauernpartei Deutschland. Democratic Farmers' Party of Germany.

FDGB
Free German Federation of Trade Unions. Formed in 1945 in the Soviet Zone to form a single trade union for all German workers.

Absolute loyalty to the USSR and the leaders of the SED was the guideline expected from all party members and it was thoroughly cleansed of unreliable and critical elements. In the first two years after the foundation of the DDR Ulbricht, with the backing of the Soviet secret police, removed over 150,000 party members (mainly ex-SPD people). Moreover, some communists, even quite high-level functionaries, who were not sympathetic to the Stalinist line were put on show trials and expelled from the Party or even imprisoned. A new Party Control Commission was established to watch over the right ideological attitude of all party members, which in effect meant it removed critics of Ulbricht. Power remained in the hands of a small circle of top-ranking functionaries.

Unlike the USSR, the DDR did allow a certain degree of party pluralism, although this was only tolerated to give the image of a democratic system. In reality, all parties and other mass organisations had to accept the SED's monopoly of power as 'the undisputed leader of the workers' movement'. So although the leading figures of the **CDUD** (Otto Nuschke) and the **LDPD** (Hermann Kastner) did join the government, they had little real influence. From the start within those parties all voices critical of the SED were eliminated by various degrees of intimidation. By 1952–3 the two parties had officially accepted the leading role of Ulbricht and the SED and the Soviet High Commission.

In addition, in 1948 the SMAD had allowed the foundation of two other officially non-communist parties, the **NDPD** and the **DBD**. As instruments of the SED they were to exert influence among the rural and conservative areas of society. Like the CDUD and the LDPD, they were to camouflage the one-party dictatorship of the SED and support government ideas in non-communist circles.

A similar role was given to the major mass organisations, like the Free German Federation of Trade Unions (**FDGB**) and the

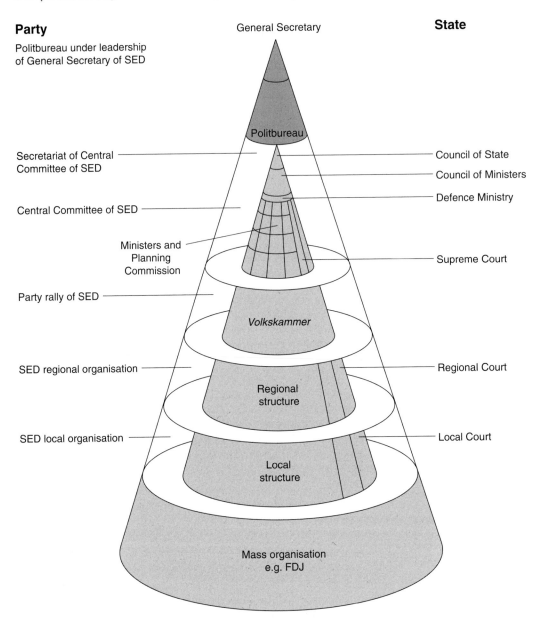

Party

Politbureau under leadership
of General Secretary of SED

General Secretary

State

Secretariat of Central
Committee of SED

Central Committee of SED

Ministers and
Planning
Commission

Party rally of SED

SED regional organisation

SED local organisation

Politbureau

Council of State

Council of Ministers

Defence Ministry

Supreme Court

Volkskammer

Regional
structure

Regional Court

Local
structure

Local Court

Mass organisation
e.g. FDJ

Figure 14.1: State and party in people's democracy.

Free German Youth (**FDJ**) (see also page 371). They were to
implement the will of the SED and to spread its political ideology
and in the early years the cult of Stalin portrayed the Soviet
leader as 'the great teacher of the German workers' movement
and the best friend of the German people'.

As a result all the parties and the mass organisations were
integrated in the 'National Front of the DDR' as a broad umbrella
organisation. Elections were held on the basis of a unified single
list of candidates presented to the *Volkskammer*. This exerted
considerable pressure on the electorate and effectively 'fixed' the
results by pressurising people to vote and massaging the figures.

FDJ
Free German Youth.
A communist-
inspired youth
group which
encouraged support
for the state.

Key term

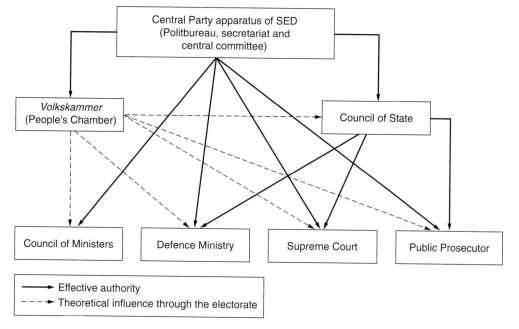

Figure 14.2: Party and state in the DDR.

Key date

> Elections to the first
> People's Chamber:
> October 1950

Not surprisingly in 1950, the election to the first People's Chamber brought a participation of 98 per cent and a 99.7 per cent approval, and the SED and its mass organisations together held an absolute majority of seats.

The judiciary

De-Nazification in the Soviet Zone was used by the communist leaders to reform the judiciary and to centralise the system. As a result, the large majority of judicial appointments were replaced on political grounds and by 1950 half of judges and 86 per cent of public prosecutors were members of the SED.

Many of those new judges were retrained on short intensive courses and many lacked good legal qualifications. Indeed, the real criteria required to become a people's judge (*Volksrichter*) were a good political reputation and a solid record as a political functionary of the communists. Contrary to the constitution, judges were not independent, but were guided and controlled by the Supreme Court and the SED's institutions.

In many ways, criminal law was adapted over the years by the communists to suppress all opposition. Accusations of 'Nazi crimes' or 'agitation against democratic institutions', or, even more vaguely, 'subversive agitation' or 'disturbance of the public and social activities' were used to control dissent. It is estimated that in 40 years about 200,000 people were prosecuted in the DDR for political reasons and the process served to intimidate and criminalise any kind of opposition.

The Politbureau also played a central role in the political trials. Show trials against higher-ranking critics of Ulbricht were staged publicly. In these cases members of the Politbureau often gave minute instructions to the court as to the proceedings and the sentence.

In addition to criminal law, the civil, labour and family law were all controlled by the DDR political authorities. Critics and their families were hindered in their career aspirations and their freedom to travel. For more severe 'crimes' against the state parents could have their children taken from them, which caused a climate of fear and insecurity reinforced by the secret police, the *Stasi*.

The secret police

The SED leaders had one more very effective means to keep down any opposition, the state security service, which the man in the street called the *Stasi*. It was founded in February 1950 and in the official propaganda the *Stasi* was called 'the sword and shield of the party'. Its stated aims were 'to fight against "saboteurs" and "capitalist agents" who were trying "by order of the American imperialists to undermine the progress of the young socialist state"'. It was closely modelled on the Soviet secret intelligence service and from the start the two organisations were closely connected.

Creation of state security service (*Stasi*): February 1950

Key date

The structure and organisation of the *Stasi* was like that of an army with military-like hierarchy, ranks and punishments. It started with only 1000 permanent members of staff, but by 1955 the number had grown to 13,000. The real expansion of the system and the extent of its surveillance can be seen by the dominating influence of Erich Mielke as the *Stasi* minister. He remained in power until 1989, by which time 91,000 people worked full-time for the *Stasi*, including its own paramilitary units. This made it far bigger than the Nazi *Gestapo*, which had overseen a much larger country.

In addition there were informal members (known as IM), citizens from all walks of life who were deemed reliable to spy on and denounce colleagues, neighbours, friends or even family. They were contacted and guided by a *Stasi* officer and for each IM a file was kept meticulously under a pseudonym and code. By the time of the fall of the regime the *Stasi* had 175,000 IMs to help spy on the population of 16.1 million people.

The *Stasi* worked under the strictest secrecy and with direct authorisation by the SED Politbureau. In reality there was no legal restraint on its aims or methods. To control and suppress the opposition the *Stasi* stopped at nothing: private letters were opened, homes bugged and searched secretly, bank statements and patients' records combed through to criminalise or ruin critics of the state. People could be arrested and questioned without charge and kept in prison under psychological torture. Over the years the *Stasi* developed into an omnipresent organisation for the surveillance and control of the whole population.

Military forces

The last line of defence for the SED dictatorship was the use of military forces:

- People's Police (*Volkspolizei, VP*, or *Vopo*). Founded in 1949 with traditional policing roles, but also with uniformed paramilitary rapid response units. It proved quite ineffective in the 1953 uprising (see page 354) and then it was closely monitored by the *Stasi*. Its most obvious function was to oversee frontier checks, especially after the erection of the Berlin Wall.
- National People's Army (*National Volksarmee, NVA*). The NVA was founded in 1956 after the creation of the *Bundeswehr* (see page 331) and the Warsaw Pact in 1955 (see page 334). Its doctrine and structure were strongly influenced by the Soviets. It was not only a traditional army, but also a means of control and described itself as 'the instrument of power of the working class'.
- SMAD was renamed as the Soviet High Commission in October 1949 and Soviet troops remained stationed in barracks throughout the DDR. Their role was to defend the USSR in the event of a NATO attack, but they also served as the last line to crush internal disturbances, most obviously during the 1953 uprising and the creation of the Berlin Wall.

Key date

Warsaw Pact concluded with DDR as a member: 11–14 May 1955

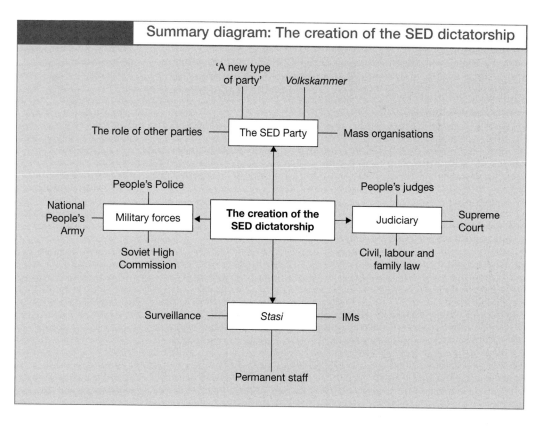

Summary diagram: The creation of the SED dictatorship

III · PARTEITAG
DER SOZIALISTISCHEN EINHEITSPARTEI DEUTSCHLANDS
BERLIN 20.- 24. JULI 1950

Poster advertising the SED party rally of July 1950. It portrays a young worker looking forward with optimism supported by the political backing of Marx, Engels, Lenin and Stalin.

2 | The Political Survival of Ulbricht's DDR

The workers' uprising of 17 June 1953

The events of 17 June 1953 grew out of the decision by Ulbricht and the SED to accelerate 'the systematic building of socialism'. In practice, this meant 'Stalinisation' with its policies of rapid industrialisation and collectivisation supported by state centralisation and control. For example:

- The *Länder* states were abolished.
- The Churches were intimidated and hampered in their activities.
- Direction of education and media was increased.
- The *Stasi* was expanded to suppress any political criticism.

Wide circles of the population were increasingly alienated from the government not only by the ruthless nature of the regime, but also by consequences of the DDR economic policies:

- For the remaining middle classes involved in private businesses and shops there was extremely high taxation, administrative harassment and political persecution. It seemed that their position was at the expense of the rapid building up of the large nationalised industrial plants (see page 361).
- The majority of farmers were still independent in the early 1950s, but they still resented the low prices paid for their agricultural produce and the state's strict directives. Above all, they also feared the ongoing threat of forcible collectivisation.
- The workers faced rising prices and food shortages, yet their wages were strictly controlled.

Therefore, the DDR presented an austere environment in the early 1950s characterised by growing popular dissatisfaction.

Key question
What were the causes of the workers' uprising?

Key dates

Uprising in DDR: 17 June 1953

Länder in DDR dissolved: July 1952

Basic foods, like bread or fresh vegetables, were still only to be obtained on food ration cards, and sometimes not at all. Consumer goods were not being produced, even though the controlled press continuously proclaimed new successes in industrial production levels. One symptom of public attitude, which could not be disguised, was the number of refugees from the DDR to BRD, especially through the 'island' of West Berlin. The number of DDR citizens who had 'voted with their feet' had increased from a figure of 75,000 in 1949 to 171,000 in 1952.

The emerging crisis was brought to a head in early 1953 by two coinciding events: one external and one internal. First, Stalin's death on 5 March resulted in the new Soviet leaders quickly recommending an easing of the strict Stalinist course for the SED. This signified an attempt to overcome the catastrophic economic situation and the bitter atmosphere in the population. Secondly, in May 1953, in an effort to meet the planned economic targets more quickly and to match the industrial development in West Germany, the DDR government proposed a 10 per cent rise in the norms (productivity and working hours). This triggered strikes in some big cities.

Yet, even when Ulbricht and Grotewohl were summoned to a special meeting with the new Soviet leadership in Moscow, the new crisis was not defused effectively. Ulbricht afterwards spoke of the 'new course' to appease the discontent, but on 13 June the DDR leadership reaffirmed that the rise in norms would *not* be withdrawn. This proved to be its major mistake.

On 16 June the building workers of the Stalinallee in East Berlin assembled for a peaceful protest march against the norms. The march was quickly joined by workers from all over East Berlin and radicalised into a general protest against the government and the party. Political demands, such as more democracy and even German reunification, dominated the

Key date

Death of Stalin: 5 March 1953

"The building site .... in connection with the East Berlin building workers. We demand:
1. Full protection for the strike speakers
2. Free speech and freedom of the press
3. The abolition of the norms
4. The revision of the whole price level for foodstuffs and consumer goods
5. Free elections for all Germany
6. The abolition of zone boundaries
7. Withdrawal of all occupation troops
8. The abolition of the militarised People's Police
9. The immediate resumption of the rebate workers return tickets
10. The release of all political prisoners
11. The repatriation of all prisoners of war
12. The abolition of the 'People's Controls' "

The manifesto of a building site in East Berlin dated June 1953.

protests. And although the government revoked the decree in the evening, it was impossible to stop the disturbances and the workers made plans for a general strike.

By noon on 17 June, it is reckoned that there were 100,000 protestors on the streets of East Berlin. Within a few hours the protests had spread like wildfire to over 500 cities, towns and communities with between a further 200,000 and 300,000 protesters (amounting to 5–7 per cent of the workforce). However, despite the broad discontent of the middle classes and the farmers, the great majority of demonstrators were industrial workers. Ulbricht and the SED Politbureau were helpless – and it seemed as if the regime could collapse.

The failing of the workers' uprising

Although the SED leadership were in a weak position and lacking direction, the hopes of East Germans for a real change were short lived. The uprising was not really put down by the DDR's forces, so its failures can be explained by the following factors.

Key question
Why did the uprising fail?

Soviet intervention

By midday Ulbricht appealed for help from the Soviets and a state of emergency was declared. This gave the Soviet commander in East Berlin the right to send Soviet tanks and troops to crush the uprising. Similar orders were given throughout the country ordering martial law. The Soviets met only feeble resistance.

'The "poison of sedition" harms the troublemaker himself.' A cartoon from 17 June 1953. The uprising against the SED regime is seen as a 'counter-revolutionary *putsch*'. It puts the main responsibility for it on the USA.

Poor organisation

The uprising was spontaneous without any effective national co-ordination or planning. Some strike committees of workers were formed, as at Magdeburg and Halle, and they did formulate statements of political and economic objectives, which were printed out on the day (see page 353). But no arrangements were made to seize power by taking control of key strategic points, such as radio stations, railway lines or roads. The demonstrators had no effective weapons to support their cause against the Soviet army.

Non-intervention by the West

The demonstrators had been naïve to expect support from the West. Although the Western Powers paid lip service to the idea of the liberation of the suppressed people in eastern Europe, none would risk direct military involvement in the highly charged atmosphere of the Cold War.

Therefore, by the evening of 17 June the Soviet forces had re-established order on behalf of Ulbricht's government, though a few strikes and protests carried on until 21 June. Estimates have varied between 20 and 50 fatalities across the country.

Key question
What were the consequences of the 17 June uprising?

The consequences of the uprising

The claim of the DDR to be a democratic workers' state had been exposed as a sham by the events, and yet amazingly in the wake of the insurrection Ulbricht's regime was strengthened. The main 'ringleaders' were identified and about 1300 people were put on trial: most received long prison sentences and two the death penalty.

Official propaganda blamed the uprising on 'Western agents' and described it as a 'fascist *putsch*' instigated and directed by the imperialistic Western powers. Yet, although the uprising of 17 June did not end Ulbricht's power, he was astute enough to recognise the inadequacies of his regime's power base, and introduced the following changes to bolster it:

The purge of the Party

Two of Ulbricht's critics, Zaisser and Herrnstadt, were expelled from the Politbureau and later in January 1954 from the Party itself. This was followed by an extensive purge within the Party at all ranks, especially many previous SPD members, who were charged with slowing the development of socialism. Altogether, it is estimated that 20,000 leading SED functionaries were removed in the months after the uprising and replaced by thousands of new 'party activists'.

The security apparatus

In the wake of the uprising military and security forces were reformed and strengthened. The *Stasi* was given the authority to suppress any opposition and the number of agents was significantly increased. It was at this time that the extensive surveillance started.

Concessions

Ulbricht did not publicly back down from the 'New Course', which might have suggested weakness and error, but the SED did decide to slow down the pace for a while to appease the frustration of the masses of the population:

- the work norms were withdrawn
- controlled prices of basic foods were lowered
- more consumer goods were introduced
- the taxes and administrative constraints of farmers and private businessmen were reduced.

Although the uprising was a major embarrassment to Ulbricht and his clique, this historic day proved to be a milestone in the evolution of the DDR. It showed that the one-party structure and the development of its mass organisations had become established and that the presence of Soviet troops could never be ignored. In that way Ulbricht had to find a way to work with the Soviet leadership, whoever was in power. As a result the DDR was politically recognised by the USSR in 1955 and joined the Warsaw Pact (see pages 334 and 351). Also, there was a slight improvement in living standards and the regime was able to take some consolation that the number of refugees declined in the five years from 1953 (see Table 14.6 on page 380). However, this new stability was threatened in 1956 by a crisis generated by the new Soviet leader, Nikita Khrushchev.

Key date

USSR recognised sovereignty of DDR: 20 September 1955

The 17 June 1953 uprising. Russian tanks and DDR police regain control of a main street in East Berlin.

'The crux of the matter.' A Western cartoon from 1956. The SED party leader Ulbricht presents a uniform of the newly created National People's Army on a clothes hanger made of a hammer and sickle. The new uniform resembles that of the old German *Wehrmacht*. The cartoonist's intention was to point to the unbroken lines of tradition to the undemocratic army of Nazi Germany and at the same time to the Soviet Union as the true 'commander-in-chief' of the National People's Army.

De-Stalinisation

Key question
How and why did Ulbricht survive de-Stalinisation?

Key date
Khrushchev's speech denounced Stalin and his methods: February 1956

Ulbricht and the SED leadership had shown themselves keen to preserve and expand the Stalinist structures of the DDR, even after the death of Stalin when the USSR had gradually started to distance itself from his thinking and policies. So, when, in his speech in February 1956, Khrushchev officially proclaimed the end of Stalinism and denounced his terrorist control methods (de-Stalinisation), it caused turmoil among SED members and in other communist parties in Europe. Official propaganda had always held up Stalin as an idol. Stalin's policies and ideology had been the founding principles of the new state and party, and had secured Ulbricht's power.

Khrushchev's declaration of de-Stalinisation generated an atmosphere of change throughout eastern Europe. Poland had riots at Posen and with Khrushchev's agreement its Communist Party appointed Gomulka to introduce moderate reform in June. In Hungary, in October, a reforming communist leader, Imre Nagy, was pushing for Hungary to withdraw from the Warsaw Pact. In the DDR this raised the hopes of a new communist intelligentsia within the SED who had been shaped by Marxism–Leninism combined with a more democratic and humane socialism. Well-known philosophers and writers, such as Ernst Bloch and Wolfgang Harich, started to criticise the system of the DDR, openly demanding a 'third way' between anti-capitalism and anti-Stalinism. Such prominent Marxist rebels clearly threatened the structure and direction of the Party shaped by Ulbricht.

The dramatic events in eastern Europe in 1956 came to a head in November when Soviet troops invaded Hungary. Over 3000 people died and Nagy was captured and executed along with 2000 others. However, three things prevented the Hungarian crisis from triggering a new uprising in the DDR:

- Ulbricht himself had learned from the 1953 uprising and party discipline had become much stricter.
- The concession of shortening the working day and the freeing of 21,000 political prisoners in October 1956 reduced discontent.
- The brutality with which the Hungarian uprising was put down damped down any rebellious tendencies.

Nevertheless, Ulbricht's personal authority was not certain. He was 'a reluctant de-Staliniser', who faced dangerous opponents within the highest ranks of the Party, particularly two of the leading men in the SED, Karl Schirdewan and Ernst Wollweber. They wanted far-reaching reform of the party's policies over the direction of the economy and the relationship between the DDR and the BRD. During 1956 their support in high positions in the Party had increased. It was even rumoured that Khrushchev had been sympathetic to the replacement of Ulbricht by Schirdewan to back his new direction.

Despite the odds, Ulbricht survived. First, the intellectual Marxist rebels were quickly removed from public life. Bloch was forced to resign his post at Leipzig and later escaped to the West. The philosopher Harich fared worse, as he was arrested and given a long prison sentence in 1957. Secondly, it seems that by the early months of 1957 Khrushchev himself had begun to have doubts about removing Ulbricht in the wake of the USSR's problems within the 'Eastern bloc'. Ulbricht's hard-line leadership at least gave a degree of stability in that vital Soviet satellite. Thirdly, Ulbricht showed great skill and ruthlessness in the internal party battle during 1957–8. He bided his time, and eventually, in February 1958 Schirdewan and Wollweber were removed from their posts in the Politbureau and the Central Committee. This prompted yet another purge within the Party of all elements sympathetic to moderate policies. 'Ulbricht successfully dealt with factionalism in the higher ranks of the SED, such that by the end of the 1950s he was in command of a well-disciplined party of committed communists' (Fulbrook).

As a postscript, the concentration of power and the rigid hierarchical organisation of the Party were confirmed when President Pieck died. Ulbricht became the chairman of the Council of State, and as he was First Secretary of the Central Committee of the SED and also a member of the Politbureau, he held all-encompassing powers. He and his supporters had managed to suppress or drive out all opposition within the Party and outside.

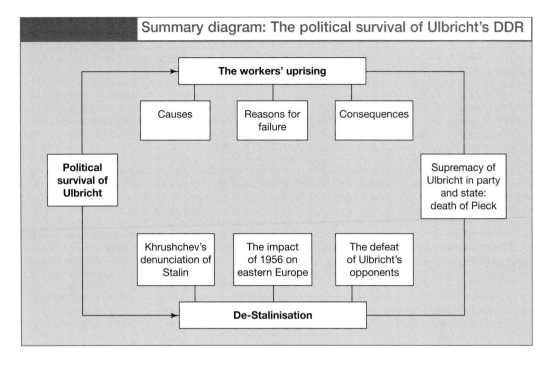

Summary diagram: The political survival of Ulbricht's DDR

3 | The DDR Economy

The economic legacy of the war and the Occupation Zone

Key question
What were the disadvantages faced by the DDR trying to rebuild its damaged economy?

It can be seen from Chapter 12 that the Soviet Zone enjoyed some economic benefits, but these were outweighed by a number of disadvantages (see page 280):

- a shortage of raw materials
- the loss of provinces to Poland
- the dislocation of population
- the limitations of industrial development.

By the time the Soviet Zone had become the DDR, the economic consequences of the years 1945–9 were dramatic:

- dismantling and reparations (see page 280)
- nationalisation (see page 280)
- land reform (see page 281).

It was no wonder that the DDR's path to economic stability and development was problematic.

The international context

Key question
In what way did the Cold War shape the economic development of the DDR?

Before the war Germany was one economic unit with close economic ties between the eastern and western parts of the country. Industry in eastern Germany had relied on resources from western Germany and it could sell its products in the larger western markets.

After 1945, and the onset of the Cold War, the economic development of the Western and Soviet Occupation Zones became increasingly separated. By 1950 this led to the evolution of two Germanies with different economic and political systems. Not surprisingly, trading links became rather complicated because of the DDR's unique position.

The DDR at first still looked to the West, even though Stalin had refused to let it join the Marshall Plan, because of its ongoing lack of hard currency. This led to a sort of bartering between the two Germanies on the basis for the 1951 Berlin Treaty, which facilitated trading. It provided the DDR with tariff-free access to the West German market and allowed it to pay in goods rather than currency. In addition, the DDR was given some interest-free overdraft privileges.

However, in September 1950 the DDR joined **Comecon** and from that time was gradually economically integrated into the Eastern bloc. The DDR could not keep up with the pace of development of modern technology in the West and its methods of production were far too expensive to compete in free markets anyway. So the possibilities of breaking into the Western markets were rather limited. Therefore, its products were geared to the demands of the USSR and the other 'Eastern bloc' countries.

Within Comecon the DDR was the second largest industrial power after the USSR and came to play a crucial economic role. Foreign trade between the DDR and its brother countries trebled between 1950 and 1955, and by 1954 three-quarters was done with the socialist bloc countries, of which 40 per cent was with the USSR alone.

Yet, although the DDR was emerging as the most economically developed country in the Eastern bloc, the advantages associated with its membership of Comecon were still limiting in other respects. From the start the DDR's industrial production was geared to the demands of the USSR, which aimed to gradually merge the national economies of the two states. Most obviously, the DDR's Seven-Year Plan in 1958 was formulated within guidelines laid down by the USSR for all countries within Comecon. In that way engineering machinery, such as agricultural tools, ships and railway wagons, were dispatched to the USSR in return for natural resources, like oil or iron ore. The USSR never really paid the real-world market prices for goods and so it was a rather unprofitable business for the DDR. Yet, until the mid-1960s the USSR and DDR continued to have a very close economic relationship until the introduction of the **New Economic System** (NES) reforms dislocated the intimacy of the two states.

Key terms

Comecon
Council for Mutual Economic Assistance. Formed in 1949 to facilitate and co-ordinate the economic policy of Soviet states in the Eastern bloc. The DDR joined in 1950.

New Economic System
Name given to the economic policy adopted by the SED in 1963. It rejected the Seven-Year Plan in favour of decentralisation in the management of the economy and even the consideration of market criteria.

Key date

Introduction of the New Economic System: June 1963

Industry

Even before the foundation of the DDR, the SED had started discussions for a centralised, planned economy with a Stalinist model in its declaration 'Planned Construction of Socialism'. And in its own words, the SED publicly announced the guideline by proclaiming: 'To learn from the Soviet Union means learning to win.'

The first Five-Year Plan, 1951–5

Key question
Was the first Five-Year Plan bungled?

A short transitional Two-Year Plan steered the DDR economy to extend nationalisation and by 1950 76 per cent of industrial production was already under the control of the VEBs and SAGs (see pages 280–1), and banking and insurance was completely directed by the state. It also directed the economy into the appropriate channels, in order to raise the low levels of industrial productivity. Therefore, the first Five-Year Plan from 1951 to 1955 had ambitious plans particularly for heavy industry: fuel and power, iron and steel, chemicals, metallurgy and building. As with Stalin's Five-Year Plans in the USSR, the aim and objectives were drawn up by a State Planning Commission, which intended to supervise every aspect of the operation.

Table 14.1: Industrial production in the DDR 1950–5

Product	1950	1955 Plan	1955 Actual
Coal	2,805	3,500	2,667
Lignite	137,050	205,000	200,612
Electricity	19,466	31,600	28,695
Iron	337	1,250	1,517
Steel	999	3,000	2,507
Sulphuric acid	245	400	483
Cement	1,412	2,600	2,971

Note: lignite was easily accessible in East Germany, but it is much dirtier than black coal. The environmental cost has been very great.

On one level the first Five-Year Plan can be seen as a great success. It was officially proclaimed as overfulfilling its many targets and overall industrial production had doubled since 1950. As the above table shows, particularly successful were production of iron, sulphuric acid and cement, whereas production of steel and lignite, although dramatically increased, fell short of their targets. So, as a result of the fierce exertions and privations suffered by the DDR population, the SED leaders managed to expand its economy. However, it is tempting to say that the imitation of the Soviet Union model proved to be a mistake, as the performance of the first Five-Year Plan still raised fundamental problems:

- Despite the lack of natural resources in the country, the SED leaders set an ambitious target to build up heavy industry, particularly coal and steel. Many new industrial enterprises created were established at inappropriate locations and were often unprofitable. The emphasis on heavy industry was achieved at the expense of consumer goods, whose production would have helped to revive the domestic market more quickly and kept the people happier. So, a more realistic alternative would have been to modernise the economic patterns by investing in more modern technologies and lighter industry.

- Centralised planning discouraged private initiatives and investment. Moreover, the planning processes were often too slow and inflexible to react to short-term necessities and problems. The system meant that production pursued quantity at the expense of quality.
- Despite the workers' legal rights and the promise of better working conditions, the productivity quotas put pressure on the workforce. Not surprisingly many workers were sceptical of the system and were tempted to go to the West.

All these points suggest that the very idea of complete central planning in a relatively advanced economy was ineffective. Moreover, ideological influences carried more weight than expertise or knowledge. The bungling happened at the core of the planning process and things could have worked out much better with less ideology and more pragmatism.

Later plans

A second Five-Year Plan was initiated in 1956 and it aimed to combine the production of capital and consumer goods. Indeed, it even put some stress on technological progress with the slogan 'Modernisation, Mechanisation and Automation'. It backed the development of nuclear energy and the first nuclear reactor in the DDR was activated in 1957.

Key question
Did the SED leadership learn from the mistakes of its economic planning in the years 1953–63?

By the late 1950s it seemed at last as if the DDR's economy and its citizens were making real advances, and in the years 1958–9 the DDR economy grew by 12 per cent per annum. Consumer goods were at last being produced and living standards improved (see pages 375–6). In 1958 the rationing cards for meat, fat and sugar disappeared. The new 'achievements of socialism' allowed for the creation of workers' recreational homes, cultural centres and polytechnics. And housing and basic goods, such as bread, milk and potatoes, were set at low prices. Even the numbers of refugees dropped substantially and it seemed as if Ulbricht's DDR had at last stabilised.

Of course, these stabilising social improvements were bought at high costs to the economy and the state could not invest this money into other needy sectors, such as the infrastructure and the modernisation of industry. Also, the DDR was desperately short of hard currency, when the fixed exchange rate between the West DM and the East German Ostmark was really artificial as it was kept at 1:1 out of pride (the reality was 4:1).

Economic planning

1949: Two-Year Plan (1949–50)
1951: Five-Year Plan (1951–5)
1956: Five-Year Plan (1956–60). Aborted in 1958
1959: Seven-Year Plan (1959–65). Aborted in 1962
1963: New Economic System (1963–8)

The fundamental problems were not confronted indeed, the SED leadership exacerbated them by a change of direction. At the Fifth Party Congress Ulbricht proudly proclaimed that the DDR aimed 'to catch up and overtake' West Germany by 1961 in per capita consumption. As a result, the second Five-Year Plan was aborted and in its place an ambitious Seven-Year Plan was outlined (1959–65) to co-ordinate DDR economic development more closely with the USSR. Its aims were:

- To increase industrial production by 188 per cent.
- To increase consumer goods production by 177 per cent.
- To extend collectivisation.

These figures were unreal. The DDR economy had expanded so quickly that the industrial growth rate declined sharply from 1960 and the number of refugees to the West climbed again up to 1000 per day in 1960–1. The results were dramatic: the building of the Berlin Wall (1961) and another change of policy in the introduction of NES (1963) providing for more decentralisation in the management of the economy and even the consideration of market criteria.

'Heavy industry – the basis of independence and well-being.' A propaganda poster from 1952 about the first Five-Year Plan. What does the poster try to convey?

Agriculture

There had been immediate dramatic changes in agriculture under the Soviet occupation (see also page 281). These meant that:

Key question
What were the consequences of the DDR government's decision to implement collectivisation?

- All owners of estates larger than 100 hectares (250 acres) were dispossessed without any compensation, regardless of their political standing. Altogether this land represented about one-third of the agricultural area of the Soviet Zone.
- The majority of the land seized was handed over in smallholdings up to seven hectares to landless farm workers and refugees from the East (nearly four million settled permanently or temporarily).
- The remains were given to local communities for cultivation to create the first early state-owned farms.

By implication the other two-thirds of agricultural land was still in the hands of small- and middle-sized farmers.

On one level, the land reforms seemed quite positive, as they reinforced the egalitarian spirit. However, by 1949 the new state faced fundamental problems in the agricultural sector. There were hardly any modern machines, fertiliser, or even sufficient seeds with which to work the land. Many of the new refugee farmers had little or no agricultural experience. Most significantly, agriculture was dominated by small landholdings, too small to survive independently, let alone make a profit. By 1948 crop and livestock yields had fallen dramatically so farmers were moving to the cities for work or to the West.

The idea of collectivisation of agriculture was a fundamental principle of developing a communist planned economy. Yet, the first Five-Year Plan had unequivocally put its emphasis on trade and industry. It had not deeply invested in agriculture and at first it was politically and economically cautious about proceeding with collectivisation.

However, by 1952 the SED leadership was so concerned about the difficulties with food supplies that it decided to start introducing voluntary collectivisation by the creation of **LPGs**, agricultural production co-operatives. The introduction of the LPG meant that collectivisation actually proceeded slowly. It attracted the small-scale farmer, who was given financial incentives to join, whereas it alienated the larger farmer, who declined to participate. By 1953, in the year of the 17 June uprising (see pages 352–6), 13 per cent of the land was *not* being farmed, which contributed to the number of refugees to the West reaching high levels.

Key term

LPGs
Landwirtschaftliche Produktionsgenossen-schaft. Agricultural Production Co-operatives. The name LPG was given to the large collectivised farms.

The political crises of the uprising and de-Stalinisation served to ease the pace of collectivisation and by 1958 two-thirds of DDR agriculture was not collectivised, leaving farming independent. However, partly because of the economic pressures, and partly because Ulbricht had secured his personal political supremacy, the SED leadership decided in 1959 to confront the issue of collectivisation for once and for all. In 1960 the second wave of collectivisation was pushed in an attempt to create a socialist

Key date

Collectivisation of agriculture in DDR completed: 1960

society on the land. This was strongly enforced, mainly by denying farmers access to collective machinery and by setting very high targets. Ideologically committed SED functionaries were sent into the villages to convince the population of the merits of collectivisation schemes. And when many did not give in, arrests and land confiscations, for not fulfilling the quotas, were used to speed up the process of collectivisation.

In the short term collectivisation was a disaster:

- Farmers voted with their feet by going to the West and, of course, refugee figures reached a peak in 1961 (see Table 14.6 on page 380).
- Food production declined markedly.
- Rationing was reintroduced in 1961.

In a political sense the DDR communist government achieved its ideological aim of collectivising agriculture. In the longer term agricultural matters did improve. By achieving economies of scale collectivisation did make agriculture more efficient. From 1963 the SED leadership started to invest substantially more money into the agricultural sector. Therefore, by the 1970s the productivity of LPGs was higher than most other east European countries. Of course, the low fixed prices for basic food meant that the LPGs had to be highly subsidised, just like many farms in the EEC, and the DDR was actually more efficient than the smaller farms in the West!

Table 14.2: Collectivisation of East German agriculture 1952–62

Year	No. of collectives	Percentage of farmed area
1952	1,906	3
1954	5,120	14
1956	6,281	23
1958	9,637	37
1960	19,261	84
1962	17,860	85

Key question
Was communism an economic disaster for the DDR?

Conclusion

The basic principles of the DDR state economy were those of nationalisation, centralisation and planning. And for such a small state its achievements stand out. By the early 1960s the DDR had by far the highest level of consumer goods production within the Eastern bloc, and the country was officially ranked tenth in economic production in the world. Yet, the 'Building up of Socialism' in the DDR did not mean a new modern beginning. To a large extent the DDR economy was a kind of 'state capitalism' adapted to the backward-looking system of the USSR. It should really have done so much better, and its limitations had fatal consequences for the DDR.

Ideological inflexibility

The key problem was that economic policies had to be drawn up under the supremacy of fixed Stalinist ideology. This made it extremely difficult for the DDR to build up a balanced economy and to sustain permanent high economic growth. Consequently, hardly any room was left for economic flexibility or individual initiatives, which caused economic mismanagement and inefficiency. Even after the start of the NES reforms there was no real preparedness to overcome the structural imbalance of the national economy.

Effect of the Cold War on world trade

The problems were heightened by the Cold War, which largely cut off the DDR economy from Western markets and forced it to produce for the demands mainly of the USSR and the Eastern bloc, with the unfortunate consequences already seen. This even developed an autarky mentality – and the production of artificial substitutes for missing natural resources was costly and inefficient.

The 'brain drain'

Probably the biggest failure made by the DDR leadership in the 1950s was that its economic policies did not effectively win over its people. The neglect of consumer industries and the enforced process of collectivisation and nationalisation proved to be catastrophic, as the citizens of the DDR continually compared their life with the 'capitalist heaven' of West Germany. So, although DDR citizens were economically better off than those in all other Eastern bloc countries, the option of moving 'next door' was just too attractive. The ongoing labour drain of refugees right up to 1961 – more often the young and able – cost the DDR economy dearly.

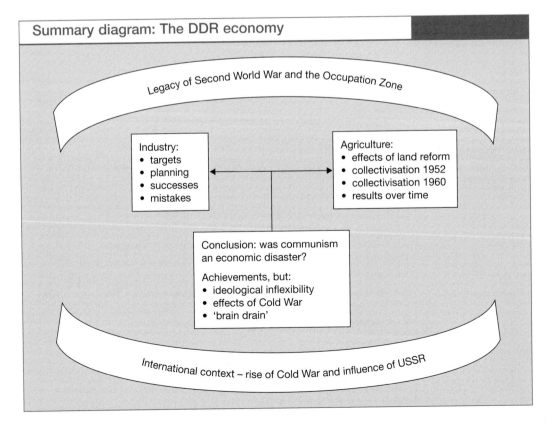

Summary diagram: The DDR economy

Legacy of Second World War and the Occupation Zone

Industry:
- targets
- planning
- successes
- mistakes

Agriculture:
- effects of land reform
- collectivisation 1952
- collectivisation 1960
- results over time

Conclusion: was communism an economic disaster?

Achievements, but:
- ideological inflexibility
- effects of Cold War
- 'brain drain'

International context – rise of Cold War and influence of USSR

4 | East German Society

Welfare

The DDR developed its own social welfare in a very different way to the BRD. Whereas the BRD was built on the principle of social insurance, the SED in a communist state increased its control over political and social institutions over welfare. Therefore, by 1956 the DDR had developed a system, which was compulsory and centrally controlled; and it provided universal flat rate benefits (although special provision was given for state employees, including the army and the police). So, although there were compulsory insurance contributions by all people, the welfare was very heavily subsidised (unlike the BRD). Therefore, its main features were:

- Health care: free for all from the state hospitals and medical centres.
- Pensions: available to all men aged 65 and women aged 60.
- Accident insurance: free for all.
- Unemployment benefit: was not provided, as some kind of work was found for all citizens.

Accommodation was a particular problem in the DDR because its two largest cities, Dresden and Berlin, had been devastated by

---

The Ten Socialist Commandments of the DDR

1. You should always stand up for the international solidarity of the working classes and workers as well as the close bonds of all socialist countries.
2. You should love your mother country and always be prepared to give all your strength and abilities for the defence of the workers and farmers.
3. You should help to stop the exploitation of one man by another.
4. You should perform good deeds for the socialist movement because socialism leads to a better life for all working people.
5. For the building up of the socialist society you should act in the spirit of mutual help and comradely co-operation, whilst respecting the community and heeding its criticism.
6. You should protect the people's property.
7. You should continuously strive to enhance your performances and to consolidate socialist working discipline.
8. You should bring up your children in the spirit of peace and socialism to become educated, highly principled human beings.
9. You should lead a clean and respectable life and respect your family.
10. You should show solidarity with the peoples fighting for their national liberation and defending their national independence.

bombing. Moreover, at first the emphasis of economic policy was on heavy industry, not on housing. It was not until the late 1950s that housing building really took off, peaking in 1959–62. However, the impressive number of new homes, reaching 100,000 built per year, should not disguise the fact that many of them were flats in the Soviet-style tower blocks and were rather dreary, functional buildings.

Education and youth
De-Nazification

Key question
How and why was education radically reformed in the DDR?

All schools were officially opened on 1 October 1945 with the stated purpose of cleansing from them all elements of racism, militarism and reaction. As a result, 80 per cent of teachers were dismissed and emergency teacher-training classes were organised. Nazi textbooks were thrown away and in their place old ones from the Weimar era were reintroduced (when available). But, not surprisingly, for the next few years, the schools in the Soviet Zone had to contend with great shortages of staff, books and materials.

School and higher education

The communist leaders of East Germany were committed from the start to overhaul the education system, unlike the approach in the Western Zones. They wanted to abolish the old school system, since it mirrored the old bourgeois social classes and values which they believed had contributed to the rise of Nazism, and in its place they wanted to build up a new socialist society. Therefore their aims were:

- To give all children equal opportunities by creating a centrally state controlled school system based on socialist ideals and not tarnished with educational privileges.
- To extend technical and practical skills, especially in the natural sciences, by schools closely linking to theory and practice to the requirements of modern industry.
- To establish a strong commitment to socialism and to ensure that future generations would serve the socialist cause.

To those ends SMAD and the emerging SED imposed dramatic changes within a few months.

The Law for the Democratisation of German Schools was put into effect in 1946, offering:

- The expansion of pre-school education (*Kindergarten*).
- The abolition of private and religious schools.
- The abolition of selective schools and the reorganisation of the system to establish co-education comprehensive schools for all children aged 6–14, *Grundschule*. This then provided the chance for the more able for further education at *Oberschule*.
- The introduction of a centralised curriculum with new textbooks.

However, despite these structural changes in the school system, the DDR in the 1950s wanted to go further and establish a real socialist ethos. It wanted to increase social mobility and egalitarianism and to satisfy the demands of the people in a workers' and peasants' state rather than satisfying the academic and professional classes. This prompted a period of great debate in political and educational circles within the DDR, but over the years 1956–65 three major laws were passed which created a system of 'polytechnic education'. As a result its main features were:

Key term

POS
Politechnische Oberschule. The acronym given to the 10-year school system for children aged from six to 16 years.

- The creation of Polytechnic Upper Schools (**POS**) based on a 10-year system for children from six to 16 years. (Pupils' education could then be extended for two more years to achieve their *Abitur*, like A-levels, for university and college.)
- Education was centralised and uniform throughout the country, so POS was the compulsory type of school for all children.
- The curriculum was amended substantially with an emphasis on sciences and technological skills, moral and ideological indoctrination, and Russian as the first foreign language.
- Compulsory practical work for one day a week from the age of 14.
- Sport and paramilitary training to raise the general fitness and performance level of the population and to achieve success in international competition (although interestingly between 1956 and 1964 the DDR competed as part of a united German team in the Olympics). For boys it was seen as a preparation for military service, which was made compulsory in 1962.

Key question
How successful was DDR educational policy?

Of course, critics of the DDR education structure focused on some of the effects of the highly centralised system. It did not encourage individual self-expression, and there was limited choice involving the parents. Moreover, a pupil's equal opportunity in the DDR was constrained, if he or she did not conform to the state's ideology. For example, pupils were obliged in their summer holidays to work some weeks on the seasonal harvest work for the socialist community. And those who did not join the youth associations (see below) or those who were actively engaged in church congregations could be discriminated against. Most famously, the regime's response to critical thinking is shown by the case of the pupils at the school of Werdau who openly protested against the voting list for the first election of *Volkskammer* (see page 291). They got prison sentences of two to 15 years!

Most obviously, the school administration could block career advancement and/or advanced training. Entry to university was dependent on a commitment to the political system. In this way the schools became an effective tool for the state to influence and control its youth, and young people learned from very early on to conform and pay at least lip service to the system.

Nevertheless, the co-ordinated education system initiated in the DDR achieved a great deal by the investment of money, time and effort into it. Indeed, as a percentage of GNP the DDR spent 7 per cent on education compared with the BRD's 5 per cent. Therefore, over the years it considerably raised educational standards and minimised social selection, which was still very strong in West Germany in those years.

The emphasis was placed on providing opportunities for students of working-class and farming backgrounds, which definitely had positive results:

- In the first years after 1945 the percentage of university students from working-class backgrounds rose from 19 per cent in 1946 to 36 per cent in 1949.
- From 1951 to 1958 the number of universities and colleges had risen from 21 to 46 and the number of students had doubled to 60,000.
- Whereas in 1951 only 16% of pupils attended school for more than eight years, by 1970 this number had grown to 85 per cent.

Moreover, the improvement was not just quantitative. The initially low standards in maths and natural sciences were gradually raised and the practical advice from the POS helped less gifted pupils, thereby reducing the percentage of drop-outs. Ironically, by the 1970s the DDR came to be a victim of its own educational success because there was a significant glut of graduates who were forced to accept jobs of a much lower standard. The primary aims of the educational policies of the SED had at least been fulfilled in the main.

Youth organisations

As well as the changes imposed by the SED on the schools system to direct its young people, it aimed to extend its influence into their private lives through the youth organisation, the FDJ, with its subdivision, the JP (see Table 14.3).

Table 14.3: East German youth organisations

Abbreviation	Title	Year formed	Age range	Membership
FDJ	Free German Youth *Freie Deutsche Jugend*	1946	14–25	Boys and girls
JP	Young Pioneers *Junge Pioniere*	1948	6–14	Boys and girls

Schoolgirls of Ossietzsky school in Berlin, 1964.

Key question
Did the FDJ really achieve its aims?

From 1957 the FDJ became the only officially acknowledged and promoted youth organisation in the DDR and it was built on the principles of 'Marxist–Leninist ideology'. It was therefore very much led and controlled by the party leaders in line with the principles of 'democratic centralism' (see page 345).

The aims of the FDJ were:

- to organise recreational activities, especially sports
- to indoctrinate the youth with a socialist education
- to fight against capitalist Western influences
- to give military and paramilitary training
- to support community projects to build up the socialist economy, for example through harvest work and basic building work.

Yet, its political status is underlined by the fact that the FDJ, like other socialist mass organisations, had a fixed number of seats in the *Volkskammer*, which helped to secure the dominating position of the SED.

The FDJ never became compulsory, but in 1950 it already had a membership of over three million people and so the percentage not belonging became increasingly small because of the fear of discrimination over jobs and university places.

Pictures of FDJ members marching and singing evoked memories of the Hitler Youth. The structure and activities were very similar to **Komsomol** in the USSR. The FDJ had solemn rituals, including an oath of allegiance to the state and an initiation rite taken at the age of 14. So young people who wanted to get on in life literally had to march in the party's step.

The FDJ did have a great deal to offer. The range of activities, sports and trips was extensive. However, its rather prude, old-

Key term

Komsomol
The Communist Union of Youth. The youth wing of the CPSU, founded in 1918.

An FDJ rally in 1964 in East Berlin. What image of the youth of the DDR is being presented in this photo?

fashioned and socially conforming approach could not prevent the growing Western influence on the DDR youth that was portrayed via the modern media of magazines, radio and later the TV (see also pages 325–6). By the early 1960s many young East Germans admired and tried to copy at least in looks the Western lifestyle expressed in jeans and rock 'n' roll. This suggests that young people learned to lead a kind of 'double life', one officially aligned with the state and one in which they privately more or less rebelled against the state expectations and official ideology through their lifestyle.

Churches

According to the DDR constitution all citizens were granted religious freedom, and it is estimated that in 1950 over 80 per cent of the population were Protestants and 10 per cent were Catholics. However, the ideology of an atheistic state claimed that religious beliefs were nothing but superstition, and assumed that religion would gradually disappear in a socialist community. The SED therefore saw the Christian Churches with their anti-communism as natural adversaries and it viewed the existing structures of the Churches with great suspicion: the Catholic Church was an international organisation; and the Protestant Churches had synods reaching across the BRD and DDR.

Key question
How well did the Churches survive in the DDR?

The Churches in the DDR were allowed to manage their own affairs to some extent, but there was a governmental Department for Ecclesiastical Affairs which laid down a strict division between the Church and the state. For example:

- Religious education was abolished at all schools and gradually the curriculum was replaced by Marxist–Leninist ideology.
- Religious matters were deliberately ignored by the media.
- No financial support was given to churches from the state (whereas in the BRD a church tax raised money to contribute to churches). So it became very difficult to maintain churches in the DDR. The cathedral in East Berlin was not restored until 1990 and some were simply blown up, for example the famous Potsdam Garrison Church (see page 144).

In the Ulbricht years, life for Christians in the DDR was difficult. Young people who did not conform to the system and remained strong Christians were pressurised by schools and universities with the threat of barring them. Careers and promotions were later blocked for Christians. The *Stasi* started to tightly control the clergy and often positioned IMs within the congregations to keep a close eye on their activities.

The most severe cases of repression came in the years 1952–3 (and have been closely linked to the months before the uprising of 17 June). Over 50 clergymen and youth leaders were arrrested and a youth Christians' organisation, the Young Congregation, was defined as anti-socialist and subversive.

Further pressure was put on East German youth by the introduction from 1955 of the *Jugendweihe*, which can only be seen as an atheist initiation ceremony with a pledge to the DDR

Poster of a *Jugendweihe* ceremony. What image of the youth of the DDR is being presented in this photo?

and socialism. Every 14 year old, regardless of denomination, was expected to make the pledge and be inducted into adulthood when they received their identity papers. Those who did not take part obviously had to face the consequences.

DDR society was increasingly de-Christianised and the DDR regime did result in a significant reduction in the number of Church members over the years. It is estimated that in the 1970s only about half of the population were professed Christians who became more marginalised as fringe groups. Nevertheless, despite living in an ideological totalitarian system, the Churches still managed to retain sufficient support for them to be the most significant niche in a 'society of niches'. In that way, the emergence of the peace movement in the 1980s and the final days of the DDR demonstrate that the Church could play an important social and even political role within the state.

The socialist woman

Key question
How emancipated were women in the early years of the DDR?

Female emancipation was seen as an essential feature of socialist ideology and a self-perpetuating consequence of the establishment of a socialist society. So, the constitution of the DDR of 1949 proudly proclaimed:

Men and women are equal before the law. All legislation and regulations that are opposed to this principle are repealed. … Women are entitled to the same wages as men for the same work.

Yet, real advantages for women were not so clear-cut in the first 20 years of the DDR because of the legacy from the war:

- There was a real dearth of working men, so it was necessary to increase the employment of female labour, although they could not compensate for the shortage of skilled workers.
- At the same time to relieve the desperate public finances in 1947 the Soviet Occupation Zone repealed the pensions of hundreds of thousands of widows. This forced women to look for jobs to support themselves.
- Many of the refugees leaving to head West were mainly younger people with families, so the population was threatened with over-ageing. The shortage of labour remained a problem before and after the building of the Berlin Wall.

Family

The propagandist image of liberating mothers from household chores to direct their labours into the work market was realised only in part. In the first 20 years of the DDR the facilities lagged quite a long way behind the demand of the situation. Maternity leave was given for six weeks after birth and there were child-care facilities, but at first they were actually limited. (And abortion was strictly limited until 1972 in the DDR.) For many mothers the reality was that they were working in unskilled jobs while also taking the responsibility of looking after the children and the household. It was not until 1966 that the Family Law offered more help and protection for families by the state and stressed the equality of men and women.

Education and career advancement

Again in terms of education the DDR aspired to offer equal opportunities between the sexes. From the start much was achieved for girls in schools, yet in the 1950s the number of female students as a percentage increased quite slowly.

Table 14.4: Percentage of female students at East German universities and higher colleges 1953–61

1953	1955	1957	1959	1961
20.4	25.7	25.5	26.9	25.4

So although the figures tended to favour the DDR over the BRD, it seems that the priority of the SED leadership was to support those students from lower social backgrounds and those with strong political beliefs at the expense of female equality. Nevertheless, as a result of a much greater drive in the 1960s and 1970s nearly half of students in higher education were women by 1980.

Also, women who graduated successfully from university generally had to put up with fewer chances for career advancement and much lower salaries in all fields. The equality between genders was not enforced by special supportive measures within the job market. So overall traditional attitudes towards gender roles in the DDR society in the 1950s and early 1960s changed only in small parts and not primarily to the advantage of women. Many women joined the workforce out of economic necessity, rather than because they were offered equal opportunities.

Active support for the emancipation of women was not really given by the SED until a critical survey in 1961 highlighted the position of women in the DDR. It was backed by the Politbureau and published as *Women – Peace and Socialism*, which revealed the limitations in the emancipation process and demanded changes. Although new laws were introduced in the 1960s, it was the continuing decline of the birth rate in the 1970s which was the most powerful stimulus for genuine and generous gains for women in the DDR. The demand for women in the workforce and an increase in the population paved the way for the so-called *Mutti-Politik* – 'mummy politics'.

Social change
Standard of living

Key question
Did East Germans become better off?

In statistical terms it is clear that the growth in the DDR economy had a limited effect on the people until the late 1950s, and more particularly from the mid-1960s when there was a marked improvement in material standards of living with the introduction of the NES.

Table 14.5: Consumer goods and the percentage of East German households owning them

	1955	1966
Cars	0.2	9
TVs	1.0	54
Washing machines	0.5	32
Fridges	0.4	31

Nevertheless, the issue of standard of living needs to be put into perspective on various levels. The DDR had definitely become more affluent compared to the citizens living in eastern Germany in 1955, 1945 and 1935. Moreover, the DDR was by far the most well-off of the Eastern bloc states. Certainly, a visitor from Poland would have been impressed with what was available in the DDR shops. Also, the state provided extensive subsidies for all citizens for basic foods, rent and public transport. So all of these were maintained at very low prices, and there was no threat of unemployment as the state guaranteed to provide full employment.

Yet, despite the increasing material benefits of life in the DDR there was no real 'feel-good factor'. Life was quite austere in the 1950s. The economy was one of scarcity with long queues in front of shops for all kinds of products, from fresh vegetables to spare parts for bicycles. And many other goods were either not available or only of poor quality. All meat and sugar stayed rationed until 1958.

And although the government established state-owned HO-shops to sell food and other dearer consumer goods beyond the rationing system, for many people the overpriced goods at the HO-shops were an unachievable luxury. For example, in 1955 the average worker earned 345 marks per month, but he or she had to pay 12 marks for one kilogram of sugar in an HO-shop and 24 marks for a kilogram of butter: those prices were almost six times as much as those available on the food ration card.

Therefore, despite the eventual material improvements in the 1960s the DDR could not escape from its status and condition. The cities of Dresden, Leipzig and Berlin had been great international commercial centres and somehow the DDR could not re-create the past. It was just too obvious that the DDR's material standard of living was inferior to the BRD, and in the end that is why East Germans voted with their feet.

A 'workers' state'?

Although the DDR was portrayed as a 'workers' state' the vast majority of historians for once have been able to agree that it was not really a paradise. Real democratic participation by workers in workers' councils or free trade unions was effectively blocked from above after the war. Instead, the SED supplanted the capitalist middle classes and quickly formed a privileged bureaucratic 'intelligentsia', which directed the workers. Therefore, the interest of this new leadership and its technocrats clashed with the interests of the workers, who were denied any real open participation. So, the trade unions in the FDGB (Free German Unions' Association) were purged several times in the first years to make certain that their organisation became a loyal instrument of the SED. In fact, the FDGB became the largest mass organisation of the SED and all of its leading positions were held by SED members. In that way, it could be said that the DDR was not so much 'a dictatorship of the proletariat', as a 'dictatorship *over* the proletariat'.

On the other hand, in terms of the DDR's social structure and living standards it is clear that the DDR was becoming much closer to a classless society than the BRD. The wealth and authority of the landed classes and big business were broken once and for all in the occupation years. Moreover, the socialist ideology and economy distinctly levelled the income and social status between the traditional working classes and the middle classes.

So, although general income levels in the DDR were well below the average of the BRD, the disparities in wealth were much more marked in the BRD. Certainly, the DDR élite looked after its own interests by acquiring financial privileges, for example, access to good cars and Western currency, but there were far fewer people earning high incomes. Also, the DDR still provided a broad window of opportunity in the sense that everyone had a realistic chance to cross the line from the ruled to the rulers. Nevertheless, it is important to remember that political and ideological conformity still depended very much on the individual to integrate into the system.

Key question
Did the DDR become a fairer society?

Key question
Were there
alternatives in DDR
society?

Conformity and dissent

Officially in the DDR there was no opposition or fundamental criticism in the 'workers' state', as the interests of the state and of its population were proclaimed to be identical. Of course, the SED leadership recognised that this was by no means the reality, so it created an all-encompassing system of control and suppression after the 1953 uprising (see pages 355–6). Obviously, as it became more dictatorial it tended to criminalise any criticism of the state.

The active and most dangerous political and cultural dissent developed by small groups of people, mainly from the 'intelligentsia' and the Churches. They were not prepared to accept the SED monopoly of power and thought and they aimed to express their criticism and to gain public attention at home and abroad. Artists and scientists enjoyed a special privileged status within the system, but as soon as they expressed criticism they met all its institutional repression. And after 1961 intellectuals, most famously Professor Robert Havemann, had to smuggle their censored texts into the West to get them published.

Yet, the system could not totally enforce conformity; political, social and cultural criticism, however marginal, could be expressed in all sorts of way. For example:

- by refusing to vote or to join the SED mass organisations
- by listening to Western radio or watching Western TV (which were difficult to jam)
- by youngsters joining the youth culture, especially the American lifestyle
- by Nazi sympathisers showing their anger by writing graffiti and slogans on walls
- by farmers resisting the establishment of collective farms.

And, of course, until 1961 people could most obviously express their dissent by emigrating to the West.

However, after 1961 it became more apparent that the development of dissent has shown that most DDR citizens increasingly lived in parallel worlds with a private and public life. They recognised that the surveillance by the *Stasi* became more imposing; and so learnt to withdraw into private refuges with their family, good friends and common interests, which was later described by writer Günter Gaus as 'a niche society'.

Summary diagram: East German society

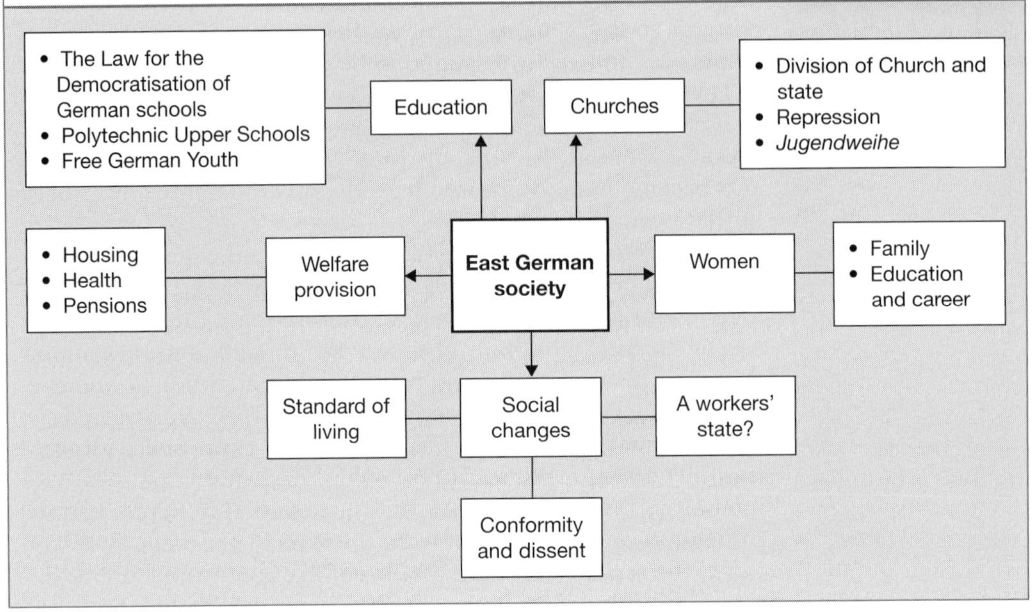
• The Law for the Democratisation of German schools
• Polytechnic Upper Schools
• Free German Youth
Education
Churches
• Division of Church and state
• Repression
• *Jugendweihe*
• Housing
• Health
• Pensions
Welfare provision
East German society
Women
• Family
• Education and career
Standard of living
Social changes
A workers' state?
Conformity and dissent

5 | The Berlin Wall

Key question
Why was the Berlin Wall built?

Berlin had remained, since 1945, in a unique status guaranteed by the agreements of the Allied Powers in 1945 and confirmed in the wake of the 'Berlin blockade' and the airlift (see pages 288–90).

The divided city

Military

The four Allied military governors of Berlin had far-reaching rights in all four sectors. Their troops were stationed in their own sectors, and their military patrols were guaranteed free movement throughout the whole city. The Western Powers still had access to their sectors via the guaranteed air-corridors and the connections via rail and motorways had been reopened after the crisis in 1949.

Political

The division of Berlin into West and East had been deepened by the foundation of the two German states. The constitutional laws of the BRD applied to West Berlin with some exceptions. It elected members to the *Bundestag*, but they were only observers and had no right to vote. Meanwhile, East Berlin was named as the capital of the DDR in 1949 and the USSR handed back its authority over the city to the DDR government (although this was not recognised by the Western Powers, which insisted that Berlin was still an occupied city under four-power control and therefore not eligible to be called the capital of the DDR).

Social

Despite the existence of the four sectors and the division between east and west, communication and transport were not restricted. The city's underground, trains and buses travelled quite freely – and people could even live in the east and work in the west (or the reverse)! Control across the borderline of the sectors was difficult to implement.

'The Berlin fuse'

Since 1949 the USSR had been very aware of the problem of West Berlin, which it was seen as an 'isle of the imperialist enemy' in the heart of a socialist state. Most obviously, it provided a major loophole for potential refugees, which posed a serious threat to the stability of the DDR.

In the late 1950s it seemed as if the DDR was stabilising and the Berlin problem was receding. The economy reached a high point of economic growth in 1958–9 (see page 362) and the number of refugees actually declined. However, the Berlin problem came to a head in 1961, as a result of three major factors.

Khrushchev's Berlin ultimatum

Key date

Khrushchev's Berlin ultimatum:
27 November 1958

The Berlin crisis, 1958–61, was sparked off by an ultimatum from the Soviet leader which demanded that the three Western Powers withdraw from the city within six months in order to create a demilitarised free city-state. The USA did not accept the ultimatum but seemed prepared to negotiate, so the Soviet ultimatum was quietly dropped. Yet, although tensions initially mellowed a little when Khrushchev visited the United States in September 1959, the superpowers' fundamental differences over the German question and the status of West Berlin did not change. Moreover, the international atmosphere was exacerbated by the **U-2 crisis** in 1960 and so Khrushchev remained determined to take a firm stand over Berlin in the interests of the USSR and the DDR.

Key term

U-2 crisis
An international flashpoint in the Cold War when a US spy plane was shot down by a Soviet missile in Russian air-space.

The DDR Seven-Year Plan

At the same time Ulbricht decided to abort the existing Five-Year Plan and launch a Seven-Year Plan to accelerate the process of nationalisation (see page 363). This set not only extraordinary targets, but also new regulations to tighten worker discipline in the factories. However, by 1960 it was clear that the DDR economy had expanded too quickly and the industrial growth rate had declined sharply.

Forced collectivisation

Also, somewhat surprisingly, Ulbricht decided, despite the political and economic pressures, to proceed in 1960 with the second wave of collectivisation (although it has been suggested that he deliberately prompted the crisis). It was enforced quite brutally, yet as a result food production declined and in 1961 rationing was reintroduced.

'No one intends to build a wall'

In the summer of 1961 the Berlin problem came to a head. Khrushchev first met the new US president, John Kennedy, in June at Vienna and it went very badly. Khrushchev threatened war unless there was a Berlin settlement. In contrast, in a public statement, Kennedy stressed that he would guarantee the status of West Berlin and free access to the city (although his careful defensive wording made it clear to the USSR that he had no intention of threatening the Soviet sphere of influence in eastern Europe, including the DDR and East Berlin).

At the same time, the DDR government faced real pressure as the figure of refugees rose sharply. In April 1961 alone 30,000 left, most via West Berlin, and it was clear that the very survival of the young state was threatened. For the first time there were rumours circulating that the DDR was going to close the border with West Berlin, although Ulbricht publicly announced on 15 June, 'No one intends to build a wall'.

Table 14.6: Number of refugees from East Germany in West Germany (in thousands)

1949	1951	1953	1955	1957	1959	1961
75.0	161.4	331.3	252.9	261.6	143.9	207.0

Nevertheless, after intensive and secret consultations with the leaders of the Warsaw Pact and with the agreement of Khrushchev, the SED leaders decided that isolating West Berlin was the only possible step for ending the danger to their state. The preparations for this step were conducted with the greatest secrecy and in the night 12–13 August 1961, the NVA and police sealed off the western sectors of Berlin with barbed wire and barricades. In the following months a 45-km long wall was erected along the border of the Soviet sector of Berlin and similar barricades were built around the whole 160-km perimeter to cut off West Berlin from the surrounding DDR territory. The 'hole' in the East German border was closed (see map on page 288).

Key date
Creation of Berlin Wall: 13 August 1961

Conclusion

The construction of the Berlin Wall in 1961 crystallised the history of post-war Germany's division. It was an act which emotionally and physically split the country's capital, ultimately reinforced Germany's political division and tangibly symbolised the iron curtain between the East and the West. It was, therefore, a turning point, confirming the geopolitical position of post-war Germany which was not fundamentally changed until November 1989 when the fall of Berlin Wall marked the collapse of communism and the forthcoming reunification of Germany in 1990.

Western Powers

The Western Powers were taken by surprise and protested sharply against the breach of the agreement of 1945, but as the wall had been built on Soviet-sector territory their occupation rights were

Key question
What was the significance of the Berlin Wall?

The Berlin Wall from the west looking to the east of the city, 1972. Note the old buildings, the concrete wall, the 20 metre no-man's land area, and the barriers.

legally limited and they did not interfere. There was one major flashpoint in October with a stand-off of US and Soviet tanks just 100 metres apart at the Checkpoint Charlie border crossing. But it became clear that no one wanted to risk an escalation over West Berlin as long as the *status quo* of power was guaranteed. In a way therefore the establishment of the wall underlined the superpowers' lines of authority established during the Cold War. In the words of Kennedy: 'It's not a nice solution, but a hell of a lot better than war'.

DDR

In their propaganda the DDR described the wall as 'the anti-fascist protection wall'. Yet, even some communists felt that it reinforced the failings of the DDR and the Soviets. Forty-two DDR citizens died in 1962 trying to escape across the divide. Nevertheless, in the political sense the wall was a success for the SED leadership, as it achieved its aim and the numbers of refugees dropped sharply. This stabilised the country, giving the DDR a 'second chance', and the 1960s proved to be a 'decade of transition' (Fulbrook). Ulbricht embarked on the NES programme in 1963 and in its wake the economic and social reforms did improve living standards.

BRD

Even the BRD could not remain unaffected by the wall. Its construction was a real shock to West Germans and a frustration to the government. Of course, Adenauer's magnet theory had been very successful and he had stubbornly insisted that he was only prepared to accept German unification on his terms, i.e. a

'Berlin and its master builders.' A Western cartoon from 1961. The cartoonist ironically portrays Ulbricht, the DDR party and state leader, in a line of tradition with famous architects who have shaped the view of the great capital city. Ulbricht is therefore held as mainly responsible for the building of the Berlin Wall.

capitalist West-orientated Germany. Yet, he himself seemed thrown by the creation of the wall – he did not even visit West Berlin until 22 August – as if events were beyond the control of the aged chancellor. It was clear that 'German unification' was no longer to play a major role in international politics, although it played a major role in the propaganda war.

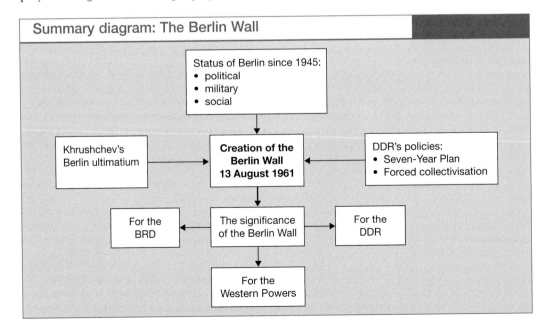

Summary diagram: The Berlin Wall

Status of Berlin since 1945:
- political
- military
- social

Khrushchev's Berlin ultimatium

Creation of the Berlin Wall 13 August 1961

DDR's policies:
- Seven-Year Plan
- Forced collectivisation

For the BRD

The significance of the Berlin Wall

For the DDR

For the Western Powers

Study Guide: AS Question

In the style of OCR A

To what extent were Adenauer's magnet theory policies responsible for the building of the Berlin Wall? (50 marks)

Exam tips

The cross-references are intended to take you straight to the material that will help you to answer the question.

The command 'To what extent …?' tells you to weigh the given causal factor against other reasons for building the wall. You must establish the various motives in a clear rank order of importance if the question is to be answered properly. Further, you must examine seriously the significance of magnet theory policy, even if you want to reject it in favour of another cause that you believe to have been more important.

At first sight magnet theory looks as if it was very significant. Aiming to defeat the DDR by drawing its population over the border to the free and prosperous BRD (see Chapter 13, pages 299–302 and 312–26), the exodus from East to West was dramatic. If that was the case, why was not the wall built much earlier to stop the mass exodus (e.g. in 1957)? The year 1961 was significant because it marked a new peak in Cold War tensions and it saw Ulbricht introduce the second Five-Year Plan, which caused major problems. Might they be better explanations of the triggers for building? The timing seems to fit. Look around. What is missing from this analysis? For one thing, there is the 'push factor' of political repression and social and economic hardship in the DDR. These might seem to provide further evidence for the magnet theory, but they are the equally important other side of the equation. The West provided the 'pull factor', but that could only operate if people in the East wanted to get away. Again, this was true year-on-year. On its own, how can that explain why the wall was built in 1961 and not, say, after the uprising of 1953? Does the start of the crisis over Berlin help? Was Khrushchev's ultimatum the trigger? If that or other Cold War problems like the U-2 incident were responsible, why did that lead to such specific action in East Berlin? You need to look within Germany and identify not just what changed the situation to make this happen, but what made it happen when it did. Decide on the immediate trigger, and then relate it to the underlying draw of the West German magnet.

Glossary

Alliance An agreement where members promise to support the other(s), if one or more of them is attacked.

Allied Control Council The name given to the military occupation governing body of the four Allied Occupation Zones.

Annexation Taking over of another country against its will.

Anschluss Usually translated as 'union'. In the years 1919–38, it referred to the paragraph in the Treaty of Versailles that outlawed any political union between Germany and Austria, although the population was wholly German.

Anti-capitalism Rejects the economic system based upon private property and profit. Early Nazi ideas laid stress upon preventing the exploitation of workers and suggesting social reforms.

Anti-feminist Opposing female advancement.

Anti-Marxism Opposition to the ideology of Karl Marx.

Anti-modernism Strand of opinion that rejects, objects to or is highly critical of changes to society and culture brought about by technological advancement.

Anti-Semitism Hatred of Jews. It became the most significant part of Nazi racist thinking. For Hitler, the 'master race' was the pure Aryan (the people of northern Europe) and the Germans represented the highest caste. The lowest race for Hitler was the Jews.

Appeasement Making concessions in order to satisfy an aggressor. In this context, it refers to the Anglo-French policy of the 1930s towards Hitler's territorial demands.

Arbitration treaty An agreement to accept the decision by a third party to settle a conflict.

Article 48 Gave the Weimar president the power in an emergency to rule by decree and to override the constitutional rights of the people.

Aryan Broadly refers to all the peoples of the Indo-European family. However, the term was more specifically defined by the Nazis as the non-Jewish people of northern Europe.

Associationism Having a strong identity or affiliation with a particular group.

Atomic bomb Western scientists developed the technology to make atomic/nuclear weapons as part of the Manhattan Project 1942–5. The first bomb was tested in New Mexico in July 1945 and the next two were dropped on Hiroshima and Nagasaki in Japan in August 1945.

Autarky The aim for self-sufficiency in the production of food and raw materials, especially when at war.

Authoritarianism A broad term meaning government by strong non-democratic leadership.

Autocracy A system where one person (usually a hereditary sovereign) has absolute rule.

Avant garde A general term suggesting new ideas and styles in art.

Balance of trade Difference in value between exports and imports. If the value of the imports is above that of the exports, the balance of the payments has a deficit that is often said to be 'in the red'.

Balanced budget A financial programme in which a government does not spend more than it raises in revenue.

Basic Law *Grundgesetz*. Technically, the document approved in May 1949 was *not* a constitution, as it was not permanent because the founding fathers wanted to have the flexibility for the reunification of the whole of Germany. Thus, all the terms had the features of a constitution but it was called the Basic Law.

Bizone The name given to the two zones of Britain and the USA which were merged into a unified economic zone in January 1947.

Black market Illegal trading in goods or currency.

Blitzkrieg Literally 'lightning war'. It was the name of the military strategy developed to avoid static war. It was based on the use of dive-bombers, paratroopers and motorised infantry.

Bolsheviks Followers of Bolshevism – Russian communism.

BRD *Bundesrepublik Deutschland*. The Federal Republic of Germany (FRG) was formed on 23 May 1949.

Buffer state The general idea of separating two rival countries by leaving a space between them. Clemenceau believed that the long-established Franco-German military aggression could be brought to an end by establishing an independent Rhineland state (though this was not implemented because Wilson saw it as against the principle of self-determination).

Bundesrat The 'federal council' or upper house of the German parliament. Its members were appointed by members of the *Länder* governments.

Bundestag The 'federal assembly' or 'lower house' of the BRD German parliament. It claimed to be the successor of the *Reichstag*.

Bundeswehr The name given to the German army created in the BRD by the Paris treaties. It was ratified by the *Bundestag* in 1955 and came into effect in the following year. It introduced conscription for all men aged over 18 years.

Cartel An arrangement between businesses to control the market by exercising a joint monopoly.

CDUD *Christliche Demokratische Union Deutschlands*. Christian Democratic Union in the DDR.

Coalition government Usually formed when a party does not have an overall majority in parliament; it then combines with more parties and shares government positions.

Co-determination *Mitbestimmung*. The practice in which employees have a role in management of a company.

Collectivisation The policy of creating larger and more efficient agricultural units controlled by the state. It was initiated by Stalin in the USSR in the 1930s.

Comecon Council for Mutual Economic Assistance. Formed in 1949 to facilitate and co-ordinate the economic policy of Soviet states in the Eastern bloc. The DDR joined in 1950.

Concordat An agreement between Church and state.

Constitution The principles and rules that govern a state. The Weimar Constitution is a good example. (Britain is often described as having an unwritten constitution. It is not drawn up in *one* document, but built on statutes, conventions and case law.)

Constitution court
Bundesverfassungsgericht. The main task is to review judicial cases. Therefore it can declare acts as unconstitutional.

Constitutional monarchy   Where the monarch has limited power within the lines of a constitution.

Cuban missile crisis   The most serious flashpoint in the Cold War between the superpowers in October 1962. The dispute was over the installation of nuclear missiles by the USSR on Cuba, a short distance from the US mainland.

Cult of personality   Using the power and charisma of a political leader to dominate the nation.

DBD   *Demokratische Bauernpartei Deutschland*. Democratic Farmers' Party of Germany.

Demilitarisation   The removal of military personnel, weaponry or forts. The Rhineland demilitarised zone was outlined by the Treaty of Versailles.

Depression   An economic downturn marked by mass unemployment, falling prices and a lack of spending. The world depression lasted from 1929 to 1933. In the USA it was called the Great Depression.

Diktat   A dictated peace. The Germans felt that the Treaty of Versailles was imposed without negotiation.

DWK   *Deutsche Wirtschaftkommission*. German Economic Commission. Created in 1947 to administer the economy of the Soviet Zone. It was very much in response to the creation of the German Economic Council in the Bizone.

Eastern bloc   A label given to the countries controlled by the USSR in eastern Europe from 1945: Poland, Czechoslovakia, Hungary, Romania, Bulgaria, Albania and the DDR.

ECSC   The European Coal and Steel Community, created in 1951.

Edelweiss   A white alpine flower which served as a symbol of opposition.

EEC   The European Economic Community. The Treaty of Rome, signed in March 1957, created a customs union of six countries: BRD, France, Italy and Benelux (Belgium, the Netherlands and Luxembourg).

Ersatzkaiser   Means 'substitute emperor'. After Marshal Hindenburg was elected president, he provided the *ersatzkaiser* figure required by the respectable right wing – he was a conservative, a nationalist and a military hero.

European Defence Community   A plan proposed by France's prime minister Pleven, to form a pan-European defence force. The plan was signed in May 1952 by the BRD, France, Italy and the Benelux states, but not initially ratified by the French parliament.

Exports   Goods sold to foreign countries.

Expressionism   An art form which suggests that the artist transforms reality to express a personal outlook.

FDGB   Free German Federation of Trade Unions. Formed in 1945 in the Soviet Zone to form a single trade union for all German workers.

FDJ   Free German Youth. A communist-inspired youth group which encouraged support for the state.

Federal president   *Bundespräsident*. The head of state.

Federal structure   Where power and responsibilities are shared between central and regional governments, for example, the USA.

Final Solution   A euphemism used by the Nazi leadership to describe the extermination of the Jews from 1941.

'First past the post' An electoral system that simply requires the winner to gain one vote more than the second placed candidate. It is also referred to as the plurality system and does not require 50 per cent plus one votes. In a national election it tends to give the most successful party disproportionately more seats than its total vote merits.

The four Ds *De-Nazification*, to eliminate Nazi influence; *demilitarisation*, to destroy German armed forces; *democratisation*, to re-establish democratic institutions and values in Germany, and *decentralisation*, to break down the centralised Nazi political structure and restore local/regional government.

Freikorps Means 'free corps' who acted as paramilitaries. They were right-wing, nationalist soldiers who were only too willing to use force to suppress communist activity.

Führer Meaning leader. Hitler was declared leader of the Nazi Party in 1921. In 1934 he became leader of the country after the death of Hindenburg.

Führerprinzip 'The leadership principle'. Hitler upheld the idea of a one-party state, built on an all-powerful leader.

Gauleiter Means 'leader of a regional area'. The Nazi Party was organised into 35 regions from 1926.

Genocide The extermination of a whole race.

German Federation of Trade Unions *Deutscher Gerwerkschaftsbund*. Similarly, the civil service and unions of other professional sectors organised themselves in two large umbrella organisations (*Deutscher Beamtenbund* and *Deutsche Angestellten-Gewerkschaft*).

Gestapo *Geheime Staats Polizei*: Secret State Police.

Ghetto Ancient term describing the area lived in by the Jews in a city. Under Nazi occupation the Jews were separated from the rest of the community and forced to live in appalling and overcrowded conditions.

Gleichschaltung 'Bringing into line' or 'co-ordination'.

GNP Gross national product is the total value of all goods and services in a nation's economy (including income derived from assets abroad).

Gradualism Changing by degrees; progressing slowly.

Grand Alliance A term initially used by Churchill to describe the alliance of Britain, the USA and the USSR, 1941–5.

Great Depression The severe economic crisis of 1929–33 that was marked by mass unemployment, falling prices and a lack of spending.

Greek Civil War A conflict between communists and monarchists, which was backed by British troops until their withdrawal in February 1947.

Guns or Butter? A phrase used to highlight the controversial economic choice between rearmament and consumer goods.

Hard currency A currency that the market considers to be strong because its value does not depreciate. In the 1920s the hardest currency was the US dollar.

Holocaust Term to describe mass slaughter – in this context it refers to the extermination of the Jews.

Horst Wessel A young Nazi stormtrooper killed in a fight with communists in 1930. The song he wrote became a Nazi marching song and later virtually became an alternative national anthem.

Hyper-inflation Hyper-inflation is unusual. In Germany in 1923, it meant that prices spiralled out of control because the government increased the amount of money being printed. As a result, it displaced the whole economy.

Imperial Germany The title given to Germany from its unification in 1871 until 1918. Also referred to as the Second Reich (Empire).

Imports Goods purchased from foreign countries.

Indoctrination Inculcating and imposing a set of ideas.

Iron curtain A term used by Churchill in 1946 to describe the border between Soviet-controlled countries and the West.

Junkers The landowning aristocracy, especially those from eastern Germany.

Kaiser Emperor. The last Kaiser of Germany was Wilhelm II, 1888–1918.

Komsomol The Communist Union of Youth. The youth wing of the CPSU, founded in 1918.

Korean War The first armed confrontation of the Cold War in 1950–3. The BRD was not in a position to give military support, but the war did act as a major boom to the production of German goods.

Kulturkampf 'Cultural struggle'. Refers to the tension in the 1870s between the Catholic Church and the German state, when Bismarck was chancellor.

Labour exchanges Local offices created by the state for finding employment. Many industrialised countries had labour exchanges to counter mass unemployment.

LDPD *Liberaldemokratische Partei Deutschlands*. Liberal Democratic Party in the DDR.

League of Nations The international body initiated by President Wilson to encourage disarmament and to prevent war.

Lebensborn Literally 'spring' or 'Fountain of Life'. Founded by Himmler and overseen by the SS to promote doctrines of racial purity.

Lebensraum 'Living space'. Hitler's aim to create an empire by establishing German supremacy over the eastern lands in Europe.

LPGs *Landwirtschaftliche Produktionsgenossenschaft*. Agricultural Production Co-operatives. The name LPG was given to the large collectivised farms.

Mandates The name given by the Allies to the system created in the Peace Settlement for the supervision of all the colonies of Germany (and Turkey) by the League of Nations.

Marshall Plan Also known as the European Recovery Programme (ERP). It aimed to provide enough money (in the form of grants) to stabilise and strengthen Europe.

Marxism The political ideology of Karl Marx. His two major books, *Communist Manifesto* and *Capital*, outline his beliefs that the working classes will overthrow the industrial classes by revolution and create a classless society.

Mass suggestion A psychological term suggesting that large groups of people can be unified simply by the atmosphere of the occasion. Hitler and Goebbels used their speeches and large rallies to particularly good effect.

Mein Kampf 'My struggle'. The book written by Hitler in 1924, which expresses his political ideas.

Mittelstand Can be translated as 'the middle class', but in German society it tends to represent the lower middle classes, e.g. shopkeepers, craft workers and clerks. Traditionally independent and self-reliant but increasingly felt squeezed out between the power and influence of big business and industrial labour.

Mutual guarantee agreement   An agreement between states on a particular issue, but not an alliance.

National Opposition   A title given to various political forces that united to campaign against Weimar. It included the DNVP, the Nazis, the Pan-German League and the *Stahlhelm* – an organisation of ex-soldiers. The 'National Opposition' was forged out of the Young Plan in 1929 to oppose all reparations payments.

Nationalisation   The socialist principle that the ownership of key industries should be transferred to the state.

Nationalism   Grew from the national spirit to unify Germany in the nineteenth century. Supported a strong policy to embrace all German-speakers in eastern Europe.

NATO   The Berlin blockade resulted in the emergence of a Western military alliance, NATO, the North Atlantic Treaty Organisation. NATO was formed in 1949 and included USA, Canada, Britain, France and seven other countries. The BRD was invited to join in 1955.

Nazi–Soviet Pact   A non-aggression pact between the USSR and Germany that opened the way for the invasion of Poland.

NDPD   *National-Demokratische Partei Deutschlands*. National Democratic Party of Germany.

New Economic System   Name given to the economic policy adopted by the SED in 1963. It rejected the Seven-Year Plan in favour of decentralisation in the management of the economy and even the consideration of market criteria.

New functionalism   A form of art that developed in post-war Germany which tried to express reality with a more objective view of the world.

New Order   Used by the Nazis to describe the economic, political and racial integration of Europe under the Third Reich.

Night of the Long Knives   A crucial turning point when Hitler arranged for the SS to purge the SA leadership and murder about 200 victims, including Ernst Röhm, Gregor Strasser and Kurt von Schleicher.

November criminals   Those who signed the November Armistice and a term of abuse to vilify all those who supported the democratic republic.

Occupying Powers   The four Allies, the USA, the USSR, Britain and France.

Pan-German League   A movement founded at the end of the nineteenth century campaigning for the uniting of all Germans into one country.

Paramilitary units   Informal non-legal military squads.

Passive resistance   Refusal to work with occupying forces.

Plebiscite   A vote by the people on one specific issue – like a referendum.

Pluralism   The idea that *democratic* parties are an essential part of the constitution and cannot be abolished (Article 20). In the second paragraph of this article it says that if a party acts or aims against the constitution and is anti-democratic it can be forbidden.

Pogrom   An organised or encouraged massacre of innocent people. The term originated from the massacres of Jews in Russia.

Polarisation   The division of society into distinctly opposite views (the comparison is to the north and south poles).

Politbureau   The term is short for political bureau and it refers to the highest executive body of a Communist Party. It was first used by the Communist Party of the Soviet Union (CPSU), but was applied in many Eastern bloc states.

Population policy   In 1933–45 the Nazi government aimed to increase the birth rate.

POS   *Politechnische Oberschule*. The acronym given to the 10-year school system for children aged from six to 16 years.

Proletariat   The industrial working class who, in Marxist theory, would ultimately take power in the state.

Proportional representation   A system that allocates parliamentary seats in proportion to the total number of votes.

Protestant   General name for the reformed Churches created in sixteenth-century Europe that split from the Roman Catholic Church. There were 28 different Protestant Churches in Germany, of which the largest was the Lutheran (the German state Church, like the Church of England).

Putsch   The German word for an uprising (though often the French phrase, *coup d'état*, is used). Normally, a *putsch* means the attempt by a small group to overthrow the government.

Radicalisation   A policy of increasing severity.

Rapallo treaty   This was not an alliance, but a treaty of friendship between Germany and the USSR.

Rationalisation Decree   An intended reform of the economy to eliminate the waste of labour and materials.

Reaction   In this context suggesting a return to traditional established ways.

Reactionary   Opposing change and supporting a return to traditional ways.

Real wages   The actual purchasing power of income taking into account inflation/deflation and also the effect of deductions, e.g. taxes.

Red Threat   A 'Red' was a loose term used to describe anyone sympathetic to the left and it originated from the Bolshevik use of the red flag in Russia.

Reichstag   The German parliament. Although created in 1871, it had very limited powers. Real power lay with the Emperor.

Revolution from below   The radical elements in the Party, e.g. the SA, that wanted to direct the Nazi revolution from a more local level rather than from the leadership in Berlin.

RSHA   Reich Security Office, which amalgamated all police and security organisations.

Rule of law   Governing a country according to its laws.

SA   *Sturm Abteilung* became known in English as the Stormtroopers. They were also referred to as the Brownshirts after the colour of the uniform. They supported the radical socialist aspects of Nazism.

SAGs   *Sowjetische Aktiengesellschaft*. Soviet joint stock companies. Set up in January 1946.

Schlieffen plan   Its purpose was to avoid a two-front war by winning victory on the Western Front before dealing with the threat from Russia. It aimed to defeat France within six weeks by a massive German offensive in northern France and Belgium.

'A second revolution'   Refers to the aims of the SA, led by Ernst Röhm, which wanted social and economic reforms and the creation of a 'people's army' merging the German army and the SA. The aims of 'a second revolution' were more attractive to the 'left-wing socialist Nazis' or 'radical Nazis', who did not sympathise with the conservative forces in Germany.

SED Sozialistische Einheitspartei. Socialist Unity Party of Germany. The new party created in April 1946 by the merger of the KPD and SPD in the Soviet Zone.

Self-determination The right of people of the same nation to decide their own form of government. In effect, it is the principle of each nation ruling itself. Wilson believed that the application of self-determination was integral to the Peace Settlement and it would lead to long-term peace.

Siegfriede 'A peace through victory' – referring to Germany fighting the First World War to victory and making major land gains.

SMAD The Soviet Military Administration in Germany. The name given to the Soviet authorities that supervised the occupation in the Soviet Zone. It was renamed the Soviet High Commission in October 1949.

Social Darwinism A philosophy that portrayed the world as a 'struggle' between people, races and nations. Hitler viewed war as the highest form of 'struggle' and was deeply influenced by the theory of evolution based upon natural selection.

Socialist republic A system of government without a monarchy that aims to introduce social changes for collective benefit.

Soviet A Russian word meaning an elected council. Soviets developed during the Russian Revolution in 1917. In Germany many councils were set up in 1918, which had the support of the more radical and revolutionary left-wing working class.

Soviet republic A system of government without a monarchy that aims to introduce a communist state organised by the workers' councils and opposed to private ownership.

Spanish Civil War The 1936–9 conflict between Republicans, who supported the democratic government, and the Nationalists/Fascists (financially and militarily backed by Italy and Germany).

SS *Schutz Staffel* (protection squad); became known as the Blackshirts, named after the uniform.

SS *Einsatzgruppen* 'Action Units'. Four of the units were launched in eastern Europe after the invasion of Russia. Responsible for rounding up local Jews and murdering them by mass shootings.

'Stab in the back' myth The distorted view that the army had not really lost the First World War and that unpatriotic groups, such as socialists and Jews, had undermined it. The myth severely weakened the Weimar democracy from the start.

Stasi *Staatssicherheitsdienst* (SSD). The state security service. The secret police of the DDR. Created in February 1950, it was modelled closely on Soviet secret intelligence.

State within a state A situation where the authority and government of the state are threatened by a rival power base.

Tariffs Taxes levied by an importing nation on foreign goods coming in, and paid by the importers.

Teutonic paganism The non-Christian beliefs of the Germans in ancient history (heathens).

Toleration Acceptance of alternative political, religious and cultural views.

Total war Involves the whole population in war – economically and militarily.

Truman doctrine In March 1947 President Truman explained his decision to help the anti-communist forces in Greece. Truman's doctrine was to contain communism by sending money and equipment to any country.

Turn of the tide   Used to describe the Allied military victories in the winter of 1942–3, when the British won at El Alamein in North Africa and when the Russians forced the surrender of 300,000 German troops at Stalingrad.

25-Points programme   Hitler drew up the Party's 25-points programme in February 1920 with the Party's founder, Anton Drexler.

U-2 crisis   An international flashpoint in the Cold War when a US spy plane was shot down by a Soviet missile in Russian air-space.

Unilateral disarmament   The disarmament of one party. Wilson pushed for general (universal) disarmament after the war, but France and Britain were more suspicious. As a result only Germany had to disarm.

Unrestricted submarine warfare   Germany's policy of attacking all military and civilian shipping in order to sink supplies going to Britain.

VEB   *Volkeigener Betrieb*. People-owned companies.

Vernunftrepublikaner   'A rational republican' – used in the 1920s to define those people who really wanted Germany to have a constitutional monarchy but who, out of necessity, came to support the democratic Weimar Republic.

Volk   Often translated as 'people', although it tends to suggest a nation with the same ethnic and cultural identities and with a collective sense of belonging.

Völkisch   Nationalist views associated with racism (especially anti-Semitism).

Volksgemeinschaft   'A people's community'. Nazism stressed the development of a harmonious, socially unified and racially pure community.

***Waffen* SS**   Armed SS – the number of divisions grew during the war from three to 35.

War bonds   In order to raise more money to pay for the war, Imperial Germany encouraged people to invest into government funds in the belief they were helping to finance the war and their savings would be secure.

Warsaw Pact   The USSR viewed NATO as an offensive alliance and Soviet concern was highlighted when BRD was rearmed and brought into NATO. So, on 14 May 1955, the Warsaw Pact was created, which included the USSR and the countries of central and eastern Europe under Soviet regimes.

Wehrmacht   The German army.

Weimar Republic   Took its name from the first meeting of the National Constituent Assembly in Weimar. The Assembly had moved there because there were still many disturbances in Berlin. Weimar was chosen because it was a town with a great historical and cultural tradition.

Weltpolitik   'World policy' – the imperial policy of Kaiser Wilhem II to make Germany a great power by overseas expansion.

White-collar workers   Workers not involved in manual labour.

White Terror   The 'Whites' were seen as the opponents (in contrast to the Reds). The 'White Terror' refers to the suppression of the soviet republic in Bavaria in March 1919.

Without me   *Ohne mich*. A phrase used to describe the tendency of many West Germans in the 1950s to put politics to one side. This mentality saw politics in terms of work, home and family, with little interest in international and military issues.

Zero hour   *Stunde Null*. A term used in German society to describe Germany's collapse in the months after 1945.

Index